Presented to:

On this day:

From:

Spokane
Our Early History

Spokane
Our Early History
Under All Is The Land

Tony and Suzanne Bamonte

Published for the
Spokane Association of Realtors® Centennial

Tornado Creek Publications
Spokane, Washington 2011

© 2011 Tornado Creek Publications
All rights reserved, including the rights to translate or reproduce
this work or parts thereof in any form or by media, without
prior written permission from the author or publisher

First edition published 2011
by Tornado Creek Publications

Printed by Sheridan Books, Inc.
Chelsea, Michigan

ISBN: 978-0-9821529-3-5
Library of Congress Control Number: 2011935717

Front cover photo:
The Aubrey White family on their front porch. *(Courtesy Charlie Willis)*

Tony and Suzanne Bamonte
P.O. Box 8625
Spokane, Washington 99203
(509) 838-7114, Fax (509) 455-6798
www.tornadocreekpublications.com

Table of Contents

About the Authors:.....vi

Foreword:.....vii

Preface:.....ix

Acknowledgements:.....x

Chapter One:
Early Land Acquisitions and the Birth of Spokane Falls.....1

Chapter Two:
Railroad Boom Town (1878-1889).....25

Chapter Three:
Fire Could Not Destroy This Town (1889-1899).....95

Chapter Four:
Setting the Stage for the Formation of the
Spokane Association of Realtors (1900-1911).....119

Chapter Five:
Spokane's Parks Were the Key to Developing Neighborhoods.....165

Chapter Six:
Building Spokane, Some of the Common House Styles in Spokane.....197

Chapter Seven:
Homes of Some of Spokane's Wealthy, Famous or Infamous.....209

Chapter Eight:
Designing Spokane: The Architects' Contributions.....237

Chapter Nine:
How Real Estate Was Sold:
Ads From the Early Real Estate Companies.....267

Chapter Ten:
Spokane Association of Realtors, 1911 to 2011: An Answer to a Calling.....285

Appendix: Historic Downtown Buildings:.....297

Bibliography:.....301

Index:.....302

About the Authors

Tony Bamonte and Suzanne Schaeffer Bamonte love their native Inland Northwest and its history. Tony wrote his first book in 1987. It was about Metaline Falls, Washington, the town in which they both were raised. This ignited a new passion, and that book was followed by one on the history of the sheriffs of Pend Oreille County, based on his Master's Thesis. Following their marriage in 1994, Tony and Suzanne began writing and publishing together. They started their own publishing company, Tornado Creek Publications, which quickly become a full-time pursuit. Collectively, they have written and/or published about two dozen books on various aspects of Spokane and Inland Northwest history. For nearly 13 years, they were also the editors and publishers of the *Pacific Northwesterner*, the Spokane Corral of Westerners' semiannual history journal.

Tony was born in Wallace, Idaho, in 1942 and grew up in Metaline Falls. After serving as a Spokane city police officer for eight years, he was elected and served as Pend Oreille County sheriff from 1978 until 1991. He has a Master's Degree in Organizational Leadership from Gonzaga University and a Bachelor's Degree in Sociology from Whitworth College. He served in Vietnam as a helicopter door-gunner, and was also a logger, miner, construction worker, and for over 12 years, a licensed Washington State Realtor.

Suzanne was born in Ione, Washington, in 1948 and also raised in Metaline Falls. She graduated from Central Washington University, with a Bachelor's Degree in Accounting, subsequently becoming a Certified Public Accountant. For 25 years prior to their marriage, Suzanne was a resident of Seattle, where, after several years in public accounting, she worked as a company controller in the private sector.

Foreword

"Under all is the land." What a great concept that is! Spokane's history is defined by the land under our feet and the people who discovered and nurtured it. When I think about the beautiful place where we live, I have to admire the effort it took to turn this area into the vibrant community that it is. This book is all about "what it took."

As we worked on the concept of a historical book about Spokane, it grew and evolved from a story about a real estate organization, to a documented history of the development and refinement of this wonderful area. As residents, we enjoy the benefits of the hard work of the "City Fathers." As Realtors, we make our living from this land and the people who buy and sell it. The authors care very deeply about the details of how Spokane "came to be," and created the historic book you now hold.

Tony Bamonte came to my attention many years ago when I read a book about him as a law officer. His determined, focused efforts to solve a 54-year-old murder captured my imagination. I first meet with him, and his wife Suzanne, the project's co-author, in May of 2010. We discussed my idea of a publication that the leadership of the Spokane Realtors could provide as a legacy of our centennial celebration. The concept was a bit hazy in my mind, but the Bamontes picked up quickly that I wanted to "make a difference." With the concepts of Rob Higgins, the Bamontes, and myself, we arrived at a comprehensive history that is powerfully written and well documented.

"Near Nature, Near Perfect" is the Spokane motto at the time of this publication. This book is a near perfect resource for you if there is any question you have about Spokane's early history. You may enjoy reading it as if it were a novel. In addition, it is a great research source. It has photo after photo of the people and places that have made Spokane "near perfect." It has anecdotes that tell the real stories of founders, developers, and other important personalities that shaped this wonderful place we call home. Maybe most importantly, it corrects many items of misinformation and misunderstandings that have persisted until now.

I know you will be proud to own this book for yourself and to offer it as a gift to others you know and respect. I am very proud to have been a part of its creation and production.

Our vision for the centennial celebration of the Spokane Association of Realtors was to "make a difference." This book has certainly achieved that and is a legacy from us to you. We are convinced that this book will "make a difference" for you.

Joe Mann
2011 president, Spokane Association of Realtors®

Preface

In the mid-1990s, we began studying Spokane's history and gathering resource materials with the goal of someday writing a comprehensive history book about Spokane. At the time, according to people who owned or worked in the various local bookstores, there was a great void of history books about Spokane and the Inland Northwest. We began poring over old newspapers in many of the region's libraries and museums, beginning with the first newspapers published in the area in the 1870s. We also began accumulating every possible publication regarding local history. We quickly learned the importance of relying on original documentation. Despite inherent shortcomings in newspapers, especially concerning exact details of an event, we came to appreciate how invaluable they are in establishing that an event did happen in one form or another and the exact date. They also offer first-person accounts that may not be available elsewhere, and the language provides a flavor of the era. We frequently employ the use of quotes, and attempt to carefully reprint them exactly as they were written, including questionable or incorrect punctuation.

We love to share our passion for the region's rich history. As such, we endeavor to make it interesting to the reader by including important events, interesting people (both the heros and the rascals), and amusing or informative anecdotes. We also know that everyone enjoys the old photographs, so always include as many as possible to help tell a story.

During the course of our years of research efforts toward the ultimate goal of a comprehensive history book on Spokane, we have already written a number of books and articles covering various aspects of the city's history. Among them are *Manito Park: A Reflection of Spokane's Past*; *Spokane's Legendary Davenport Hotel*; *Miss Spokane: Elegant Ambassadors and Their City*; and *Life Behind the Badge: The Spokane Police Department's Founding Years, 1881-1903*. Each project contributed to our knowledge base. Although we had made a fairly decent start, especially during the last few years, of beginning to write the Spokane history book, we began to face a stark reality. Especially in light of ongoing commitments to other book projects, we jokingly calculated that we would be 92 and 98 years of age before we reached our goal. Consequently, we had all but scrapped the idea of a Spokane history book when we were contacted in 2010 by Joe Mann, the incoming president of the Spokane Association of Realtors.

As Joe explained in the Foreword, he and Rob Higgins, the executive vice-president of the Spokane Association of Realtors, wanted to commemorate the Association's upcoming centennial with something that "would make a difference." They knew they wanted a book, but the concept and content was not yet clear. The four of us began to brainstorm and concluded that a book just covering the Association's history would not have widespread appeal. The idea then arose that perhaps the writing we had already done, but not yet published, about Spokane's history could be incorporated into this project. Because real estate transactions and developments were a considerable and inherent component of Spokane's early history, it fit naturally into a book sponsored by the Realtors Associations. The ideas began to flow fast and furiously, and we quickly realized it would be impossible to include them all. Consequently, we had to narrow the scope somewhat and, as they say, the rest is history.

Tony and Suzanne Bamonte

Acknowledgements

Like the adage "it takes a village to raise a child," in our experience it takes a village to write, edit, and publish a book. Whenever we begin to acknowledge those who have helped us through a project, invariably two people are always front and center: **Laura Arksey** and **Doris Woodward**. We are always overwhelmed by their selfless service in helping to preserve the history of the Inland Northwest, not just on our projects but through their countless other contributions. Both are knowledgeable about Spokane history and are accomplished published authors, editors, indexers, and proofreaders. Once again, we wish to publicly acknowledge their assistance with heartfelt gratitude.

We also extend our deep appreciation to **Joe Mann** and **Rob Higgins**, without whom this book would not exist. They were great to work with and encouraged us every step of the way. We also wish to acknowledge the following people (in alphabetical order) for their assistance in various capacities, such as advising, researching, editing, and proofreading: **Tanna Belitz, Marianne Guenther Bornhoft, Nancy Compau (Spokane Public Library Northwest Room, retired historian), Karen Curran, Jane Davey (The MAC), Angie DeArth, Tim Hattenburg, Rachel Hicks, Simone Kincaid, Chuck King, Rose Krause (The MAC), Joyce Mann, Tom McArthur, Gina McKenzie, Jayne Singleton (Spokane Valley Heritage Museum), and Holly Chase Williams.** We also appreciate the photo contributors (who have been acknowledged within the body of the photo captions).

Having had the goal of writing a Spokane history book for well over a decade and a half, and working toward that end, we obviously have interviewed numerous people, many of whom contributed resource material. Many others have also given us books, photo collections, scrapbooks, and other historical materials. After all these years, the number of contributors are simply too numerous to name – but no less appreciated. However, in terms of donating books and material, we would be remiss in not mentioning a few of those people because of their extraordinary generosity: **Nancy and Parker Compau** and **Ray and Gloria Betts**. A special acknowledgement is also extended to the **Spokane Public Library Northwest Room**. We have heavily relied on their resources over the years, and used many of their photographs, which they freely supplied.

Photo Credits

Photos from the collection at the Northwest Museum of Arts & Culture/
Eastern Washington State Historical Society, Spokane, Washington, are noted as **MAC**

Photos from the collection at the Northwest Room of the main branch of the
Spokane Public Library are noted as **SPLNWR**

Photos from *Spokane and the Inland Empire* by N. W. Durham
(S. J. Clarke Publishing Co., 1912) are credited by the book title

Other credits are as noted in the photo captions.

One

Early Land Acquisitions and the Birth of Spokane Falls

Oldest known photo of Spokane Falls, circa 1878. *(Jerome Peltier collection)*

For thousands of years before the Euro-Americans ventured into the Inland Northwest, members of the Spokane Tribe lived quietly along the banks of the Spokane River and freely roamed their aboriginal territory covering some three million acres. The site where the powerful falls cascaded through a beautiful gorge, now known as the Spokane Falls, was a part of the Upper Spokanes' native homeland. (They were one of three primary bands of Spokane Indians; the other two bands inhabited the upper and lower regions of the Spokane River.) The river was central to the native peoples' existence. During fishing season, tribes came from throughout the Inland Northwest, and the banks along the river became lined with racks of drying salmon. It was an important time to renew old friendships, dance to lively drum beats, and engage in spirited competition, such as stick games or horse racing. But this way of life began to change when the Northern Pacific Railway started construction of its transcontinental line in 1870, drawing attention to the unsettled West and the boundless opportunities it presented.

From the beginning of European settlement in America, private land ownership has been the principal basis of wealth. The government assumed ownership and sold land for private set-

Indian homes in Peaceful Valley in 1884. *(Courtesy SPLNWR)*

tlement and development. This transfer of ownership was a constitutionally protected element, which was implicitly accepted and upheld by the Supreme Court in early court cases. Because the white man's concept of private land ownership was foreign to the native peoples, it created conflicts and problems very early on.

Acquiring land from the newly formed United States government

After the Treaty of Paris was signed in 1783 and ratified in 1784 to end the Revolutionary War and grant the United States its independence from the British Crown, the newly formed government needed a way to raise revenue. The Articles of Confederation did not grant Congress the right to tax the inhabitants of the United States directly. However, because it did have the power to dispose of land owned by the federal government, Congress began to enact legislation that provided for the sales or grants of land in the largely unmapped territory west of the original states. Numerous land acts were to follow, that encouraged private land ownership, filled the government's coffers, and began to establish the government's land policies (including the basis for the Public Land Survey System). Some of these acts were also much broader in their scope; they defined new territories, which included establishing Indian territories (typically lands not coveted for white settlement, some of which were later set aside as Indian reservations).

Settlement began to move steadily west, and while the United States was sharing occupancy of the great Oregon Country of the Pacific coastal region, encouraging settlement there became significantly important. The countries vying for ultimate ownership could gain a decided advantage by populating the region with their own citizens. The United States was the victor in this quest, and in 1846, it acquired the Oregon Country by treaty with Great Britain. Two years later, it officially formed the Oregon Territory. The United States had already purchased the Lousiana Territory in 1803 and would acquire the Mexican Cession (the southwestern portion of the United States) in 1848. Nearly the entire western portion of the North American continent south of the Canadian border and north of the Mexican border was now ready for U.S. settlement on a grand scale.

To promote agricultural development, the early land acts of the late 1700s were designed to distribute large parcels (640-acre sections) to private citizens. But as economic ebbs and flows challenged the ability of individuals to make such large purchases, new acts were passed that offered more affordable and flexible options. In addition, with the abundance of land "out West," the government had to devise ways to stimulate migration to the West Coast. Congress systematically began to enact legislation that reduced the minimum parcel size, as well as the per-acre cost.

Even with the enticement of cheap and abundant land, it was more than just burdensome to reach the West Coast. Stories abound recounting the herculean efforts required to cross the Oregon Trail, and the hardships, heartbreak, and tragedies that often accompanied these efforts. Consequently, the government began to encourage the construction of railroads to transport large numbers of settlers and goods across the country. During President Lincoln's first term in office, the Pacific Railway Act was passed to help fund the construction to connect the network of rail lines on the East Coast with the largely unsettled West Coast. (For more information about the Pacific Railway Acts, see sidebar, page 4.) Completion of the first transcontinental railroad, a highly celebrated event, occurred in 1869. Construction of the much-anticipated Northern Pacific Railway, which had been chartered in 1864, was expected to follow on its heels. However, numerous unexpected obstacles prevented its completion until 1883.

With anticipation of the arrival of the Northern Pacific Railway, settlement began to take place along the proposed route. This settlement often occurred with a certain degree of speculation as to where that route might ultimately be built. Shortly after Washington Territory was created in 1853, surveying parties, under the direction and guidance of the territory's first governor, Isaac I. Stevens, began scouring the Pacific Northwest for the most economical and geographically logical route through this rugged, mountainous region. The process of fine-tuning that route and completing the necessary surveys continued on through the late 1870s.

Before the Northern Pacific Railroad reached the area, settlers in the Inland Northwest acquired

The cover of a brochure published in 1881 by Robert V. M. Schawl.

land primarily through the Homestead Act of 1862, the Mining Act of 1872 (and the amended acts that followed), and the Timber and Stone Act of 1878. Due to the delay in surveys out west, the Land Act of 1820 may not have been used frequently, but it was the most significant act in terms of the founding of Spokane, as it was the act under which James Nettle Glover, the "father of Spokane," gained title to the original town site. As the Northern Pacific Railroad claimed its land-grant properties along its intended route, as designed by the Pacific Railway Act, it sold excess land to finance construction of its line. Many of the original settlers of Spokane Falls, as it was named until "Falls" was dropped in 1891, purchased their land from the Northern Pacific. (See the related sidebars for more detailed information about the pertinent land and railway acts.)

The Pacific Railway Acts

Note: *Railroads and Clearcuts: Legacy of Congress's 1864 Northern Pacific Railroad Land Grant* by Derrick Jensen and George Coffman with John Osburn, M.D. (Inland Empire Public Lands Council, Spokane, Wash., 1995) is a very informative and well-documented book about the 1864 act and was an important source for this narrative.

Following the discovery of gold in California in the 1840s, there was a succession of bills being introduced in Congress to promote construction of a transcontinental railroad, financed primarily by means of land grants. Those attempts were unsuccessful until Abraham Lincoln was elected president. During his tenure, Lincoln granted more land to railroads than any other president. The railroads ultimately became the recipients of the largest land giveaway to a special-interest group in the history of our nation.

By 1860, Abraham Lincoln was the most prominent and active attorney/lobbyist for the railroad industry. During his presidential campaign, railroad officials worked diligently to get him elected. Lincoln spent over $100,000 on his campaign, twice as much as opponent Stephen Douglas, much of which had come from the railroads. They also offered discount rates to anyone who wished to attend the Republican National Convention in Chicago. As the Republican Party's presidential nominee, Lincoln pledged his wholehearted support in favor of a major land guarantee to the railroads. It was largely through the railroads' efforts that Lincoln was elected, and they were handsomely rewarded because of them.

In 1862, President Lincoln approved and signed the first Pacific Railway Act. This act funded the first transcontinental line, the Union Pacific-Central Pacific, through land grants and the issuance of government bonds. The Union Pacific received more than eleven million acres and the Central Pacific eight million.

With amendments every year over the next four years, the Pacific Railway Act evolved into a series of acts. The one passed in 1864 was the most significant addition to the railway acts.

The following passage from *Railroads and Clearcuts* offers a brief summation of this act:

> In 1864 President Lincoln signed into law the largest of the railroad land grants, the Northern Pacific Railroad Land Grant. This law conditionally granted public lands for the purpose of building and maintaining a railroad from Lake Superior to the Pacific Ocean. The law gave public lands for a railroad right-of-way upon which to lay the tracks and 40 million acres (an area slightly smaller than Washington state) to raise capital needed to build and maintain the railroad. The land was granted in alternating square miles, which created a "checkerboard" pattern of ownership that is still visible on maps of many Pacific Northwest forest. The checkerboard pattern was intended to guarantee that railroad access would increase the value of that part of the checkerboard not granted to the railroad.

The manner in which the land was broken up for distribution created present-day problems for management of the national forest lands. The U.S. Forest Service is unable to manage "the checkerboard" lands as ecosystems. However, sales of the excess lands to the public accomplished the intended purpose of opening them for farming, ranching, lumbering, and mining. It essentially stimulated settlement in the West, which ensured the railroad would be adequately patronized. Although this ultimately proved profitable for the Northern Pacific, the company vacillated between alternating cycles of profitability and near collapse. This, however, did not have to do with lack of subsidy but rather inefficient management, chronic overspending, and the devastating impact of economic downturns during the late 1800s. By 1917, gross receipts for the Northern Pacific Railroad's land sales amounted to over $136 million, while the costs to construct the line had not exceeded $70 million.

The 1864 act resulted in the largest land grant ever awarded a private entity. The earlier act of

1862 had also authorized issuance of government bonds, but the 1864 act did not. In exchange, the latter act increased the volume of land to be granted. (However, another law, passed by Congress in 1870, gave the Northern Pacific the right to issue bonds on the grant lands.) In *Railroads and Clearcuts* the magnitude of the amount of land granted is described as follows:

> Forty million acres equals more than 2 percent of the land mass of the 48 contiguous United States and more land than this nation's nine smallest states put together.... In essence the railroad was to be given every other square mile (section) of land in a band 40 miles wide through states (Wisconsin, Minnesota, and Oregon) and 80 miles wide through territories (North Dakota, Montana, Idaho, and Washington) from Lake Superior to the Pacific Ocean, with a branch to Portland....
>
> The Northern Pacific was not allowed to claim lands which had already been occupied by settlers [through preemption or other land-act claims]. In lieu of previously claimed lands, Northern Pacific was allowed to choose property in a strip between 40 and 50 miles from the tracks. These additional bands became commonly known as "in lieu lands" or "indemnity strips."

The government-subsidized Northern Pacific was a private corporation that included politicians, businessmen, and other influential figures of the day, such as Ulysses S. Grant and John C. Freemont. The railroad, later controlled by J. P. Morgan, and its powerful officials and investors were not the only ones to benefit from the 1864 railroad act. It also gave a great helping hand to large timber companies, such as Plum Creek, Weyerhaeuser, Potlatch, and Boise Cascade.

From the inception, the Northern Pacific Railroad, which ran through the Northwest (Spokane included), disregarded the conditions of the law that created it with chronic and serious breaches. Congress was explicitly granted oversight of the land grant in the 1864 act, but its oversight was feeble and mostly unenforced. At times, Congress exercised its role, and millions of acres of railroad grant lands were returned to public ownership. However, for the most part, the powerful railroad and timber interests operated with relatively little regulation, especially in the Pacific Northwest. This resulted in decades of irresponsible logging practices by many companies. Although Congress and President Lincoln passed the 1864 Pacific Railway Act to promote the public interest, in the end, it proved to be one of the most significant violations of the public's trust in American history.

By 1924, the violations, government giveaways, and greed had become so rampant and extreme that President Calvin Coolidge requested a Congressional investigation of the Northern Pacific land grant. The following excerpt from a letter President Coolidge received from Henry C. Wallace, Secretary of the Department of Agriculture, fairly sums up the situation:

> The defaults of the Northern Pacific were numerous and flagrant, and the supplementary benefits allowed by the Government were many and lavish, but in the absence of action by Congress the courts and the administrative departments were and are without authority to consider the resulting equities, but have been forced to act as though the company had complied with every term of the grant, both in spirit and letter.

Following its five-year investigation, Congress concluded that flagrant violations and misconduct had occurred, but little action was taken, or what slight action taken, was not enforced. Repeated attempts by Congress to bring suit against the Northern Pacific for its breaches of the land-grant law were fairly ineffective. In 1941, the Northern Pacific relinquished claims to 2.9 million acres and paid $300,000 in a partial settlement, but most major issues were still unresolved. Sadly, the blatant exploitation of the land grant, and the far-reaching resulting damage, especially in regard to effects on forestlands, remains uncorrected to this day.

What brought the Northern Pacific Railroad to the Inland Northwest

The Northern Pacific's main attraction to the Northwest was the vast amount of virgin timber, which was clearly visible to the naked eye and measurable. However, the mineral wealth proved to be the initial backbone of Spokane's economic development. Although early prospectors were at least superficially aware of the potential in what would become the Coeur d'Alene Mining District, there were no means to determine or quantify the extent of the mineral deposits. Timber companies and capitalists from the eastern states knew the government owned most of the land in the West, and they knew laws already established by Congress would make it easy for the more affluent to obtain it. The problem of transporting a workforce across the country to harvest the timber, and then carry the harvested timber to mills and markets, would be solved by the construction of the railroad. Consequently, the railroad was assured of a good customer base.

The first land acquisition at the site of present-day Spokane

With preliminary indications pointing to the Northern Pacific's route passing through the area near the Spokane Falls, a few individuals began to settle near the thunderous falls at what would become the town site of Spokane Falls. Two men, James J. Downing and Seth B. Scranton*, laid claim to 160 acres. Although James Downing's stepdaughter, known to most by her nickname "Babe," stated they each had 160 acres, one claim on the south side and one on the north side of the river, this does not appear to be correct. Two years after the initial claim was staked, James N. Glover, known as "the father of Spokane," purchased the original claim. Years later, when he was questioned about a separate 160-acre claim on the north side, he stated he had no knowledge of it – and if anyone would have had reason to know,

---

*Seth Scranton's middle initial appears variously as "R," "P," and "B." The latter is the correct according to various official documents, including his obituary, and Babe Downing (who was his first wife). The obituary listed his middle name as Bell.

it would have been James Glover. There is no documentation presently available to determine the nature of Scranton and Downing's ownership arrangement, but if it was not joint ownership but rather separate claims, the likelihood is they each had 80 acres. (The 1820 Land Act had reduced the minimum parcel size from 160 to 80 acres.) Most of Scranton and Downing's property was on the south side, but the claim was in the shape of an inverted "T," with the stem of the T spanning the Spokane River and encompassing most of the falls. The claim stretched along what became Sprague Avenue from Cedar to Bernard, with the "stem" portion extending north to Broadway. Having claimed land on both sides of the river could easily account for Babe Downing's misconception.

Seth Scranton, Spokane's first postmaster.
(Spokane and the Inland Empire)

There is very little original source material to provide a detailed biography about the original owners of the town site land, and a lot of what has been written about them over the years was passed down from verbal accounts. Consequently, there are contradictions in the details. However, more official documents have become available to help clear up some of the misinformation and add more substance to the story of these first white settlers by the Spokane Falls. Still, many questions remain unanswered and some statements cannot be proved or disproved. The following account is based largely on documented evidence or credible firsthand statements.

Where Scranton and Downing met could not be determined, but according to Scranton's friend George W. Bassett, founder of the town of Washtucna, Washington, and a former state representative, he had known the two men for several years in Montana, where they were in the stock-raising business. Scranton was found on the 1870 U.S. Federal Census in Sun River Valley, Montana (the nearest post office of which was Helena). Two other individuals in the same household under the

Land Entitlements

Numerous pieces of legislation have been enacted that led to fee title acquisition of government land. The intent of the land acts was to promote private land ownership and agrarian development. Some of the acts, however, were widely abused or exploited for commercial gain and, failing to produce the desired results, were subsequently repealed. Following is a brief summary of the acts most widely used during the settlement of the Inland Northwest.

The Land Act of 1820, also known as the Cash Entry Act: This act provided added incentive and helped make land more affordable for those who were moving west. It reduced the per-acre price to $1.25 and the minimum size claim from 160 to 80 acres. With this act, the government eliminated the purchase of public land on credit. Although good for the average American, this act was even better for wealthy investors with a lot of money to buy cheap land.

Preemption Acts: A series of acts that allowed claims to be staked by squatting on public land before they were offered for public sale. Prior to 1830, when the first of a series of temporary preemption acts was passed by Congress, squatter claims were not recognized. This act provided squatters with a path to legal ownership of their claims. The most significant of the preemption acts was the one passed in 1841, which gave squatters the right to settle on surveyed government land (later extended to unsurveyed lands) and claim up to 160 acres. After living on and making improvements to the claim for at least 14 months, by paying a minimum price established by the government (usually $1.25 an acre), the claimant could obtain title to the land before it was offered for public sale. To be a legitimate claimant, a person had to be a U.S. citizen (or had filed the formal declaration to become one) who was over 21 years of age, and either the head of a family, a widow, or a single man. This act was repealed in 1891.

The Homestead Act of 1862: This act was signed into law by President Lincoln on May 20, 1862. Under its terms, a homesteader could acquired 160 acres (320 for a married couple) for only the cost of the Land Office's fees and commissions, which amounted to about $25 for 160 acres. The basic requirements consisted of filing an entry with the District Land Office and paying the fees, living on and cultivating the homestead claim for five years, after which time, proof of claim (which required witnesses) was filed with the land office. If the conditions were met, the homesteader would receive a land patent or title from the General Land Office. This act was designed to encourage self-sustained farms and was less restrictive than the preemption acts in who could be eligible claimants. The citizenship and age requirements were the same, but any single person or head of a family who had "never borne arms against the United States Government or given aid and comfort to its enemies" was eligible, which meant single women and freed slaves could also file homestead claims. Although the act encouraged homesteading on surveyed land, it also contained a provision for homesteads on unsurveyed land. The act remained in effect until 1976 (and later in Alaska).

Pacific Railway Act of 1864: Because of its significance to western settlement, this act is covered in a previous sidebar (page 4).

The Mining Law of 1872: By obtaining a patent for $2.50-$5.00 per acre on land known to contain minerals, a claimant is granted fee simple title to both the land and the minerals.

The Timber and Stone Act of 1878: Western timberland deemed unfit for farming was sold in 160-acre blocks for $2.50 an acre. It was intended to be sold to individuals who wanted to do logging or mining on the property. Because it was widely abused by commercial enterprises, it was repealed in 1891.

Scranton name were "John" and "Martha." Because their ages, places of birth, and occupations are consistent with James Downing and his wife, Marcia, there is a high probability the enumerator erroneously listed them under Scranton when they were, in fact, the Downings. The following year, all three are found together on a Washington Territorial Census in the precinct that included the unsettled area around the Spokane Falls. According to that census, which was taken in May 1871, Scranton was 28 and Downing 42 years of age. Marcia Downing, the first white woman to set up housekeeping by the Spokane Falls, was 38. A year later, Marcia's 16-year-old daughter, Babe, joined them after graduating from school in the East. (Babe was also known as Nellie or Nettie, as indicated on some of the censuses, but according to history compiled by family descendants, her birth name was Mary J. Van Valkenburg.)

Scranton's friend G. W. Bassett was with him when he staked his claim at the falls in the spring of 1871. On February 12, 1912, a letter to the editor written by G. W. Bassett appeared in the *Spokesman-Review*. There apparently was some question at that time as to the exact date of the first white settlement at Spokane Falls. His response not only answered that question, but also provided valuable additional information about Scranton and Downing:

> ... I know of no one living who can answer that question better than myself, as I was with Seth Scranton when he stuck his first stake at the Falls, and that was in 1871.
>
> I had known Scranton and Downing for several years in Montana. Downing and myself left Helena, Montana, the fall of 1870 and went to Walla Walla to buy cattle, but prices were too high and Downing returned to Montana in mid-winter by snowshoeing it part of the way.
>
> I remained at Walla Walla until the following April and started for Montana with a bunch of horses, and when I reached Moran Prairie I found Downing and Scranton had picked claims on Moran prairie.
>
> I remained with them 10 days waiting for the snow to melt in the mountains; then it was Scranton and I visited the falls and Scranton located. I thought at the time the man was going "batty."
>
> I went on to Montana and when I returned in October to Walla Walls I called at the falls and found Downing and Scranton had nearly completed a sawmill.
>
> G. W. Bassett, Washtucna, Wash., February 10

On the censuses where Scranton and Downing were found, their occupations were generally listed as "farmer" or "raising cattle," but on the 1880 census, Scranton gave his occupation as blacksmith. One account states they came to the Spokane area because they were aware of the railroad's likely route, and they intended to be ready to sell beef to what was bound to be an influx of new settlers. In August 1899, years after leaving the area, Marcia Downing visited Spokane. In an interview with a reporter from the *Spokesman-Review*, she described her husband's plans and efforts to lay out a town site by the falls. The following excerpt from the reporter's article, printed on August 21, 1899, was quoting Marcia Downing:

> **When Town Was Laid Out**
> Mr. Downing, you know, drove the first stake in the present town site of Spokane. He hired surveyors and laid off the largest part of our quarter section in town lots and streets and avenues. But when he'd finished, he got discouraged. "What's the use, mother?" I remember his saying: "Who's ever going to want all this water power of the falls? I don't believe the railroad's coming through here, and as long as it doesn't, why, there's no good of all our town lots and our streets and avenues."
>
> I didn't quite agree with him ... But we sold all our 160 acres of land and moved out to Moran prairie, where we took up a ranch.... We staid two years on Moran prairie, then sold our ranch ...

The earliest government surveys, recorded with the Bureau of Land Management for the township and range in which Spokane is located, are dated 1874 (after the sale to Glover). Though not a government survey, Downing's survey would have established and defined the boundaries of their land claim (squatter's rights) as required for a preemption claim. Although he wasn't able to develop a town due to the lack of settlers, he and Scranton did establish the town's first commercial enterprise.

Spokane's first commercial enterprise

Several months after Scranton and Downing's arrival, a small sawmill was constructed. It was

Scranton and Downing's sawmill. At the time, most sawmills were operated by waterpower. Mills often cut with a single saw blade called a "muley," which operated in an up-and-down cutting motion. As time passed, saws became larger and more efficient, and "muleys" were replaced with circular saws. This photo was taken some time after the mill had shut down and the buildings began to deteriorate. James Glover bought this mill from Scranton and Downing in 1873 and immediately upgraded it. Seven successive sawmill companies operated at this site, though much expanded. The Phoenix mill was the longest running sawmill, in operation from 1898 to 1927. The last sawmill at this site was the Long Lake Lumber Company, 1927 to 1944, and was located at what is now Wall Street and Spokane Falls Boulevard. *(Jerome Peltier collection)*

located on the south bank of the Spokane River at the foot of Wall Street (first named Mill because of the sawmill). Seven successive sawmill companies operated on that site until the last one, Long Lake Lumber Company, closed in 1944.

The issue of who actually constructed the sawmill became the subject of some controversy. Two other men – Wilbur Fiske Bassett, a millwright, and Richard Manning Benjamin, a skilled wheelwright and blacksmith who then was widely recognized in his trade in Oregon and California – assisted in the construction, but there is conflict regarding when each was involved. According to Rowland Bond in his book *Early Birds in the Northwest* (Spokane House Enterprises, 1972), Mr. Benjamin's daughter, Caroline Abbygail (Benjamin) Costello, stated to William S. Lewis* in an interview in 1928 that the Benjamin family arrived in the spring of 1872. Bond stated:

---

*Lewis moved to Spokane with his parents in 1884 at age eight, and later authored historical books and articles about the region.

According to Mrs. Costello's interpretation of events, probably based upon second-hand reports received later from her father [she was already married and living in Oregon], the waterpower had not been put to use because the mill was not in operation. ... "He soon got his tools out and commenced to work making a waterwheel and erecting a little muley upright sawmill – not a fancy one but just a homemade mill built out of the materials on hand," she said. "It was a decided improvement over the manpower method of whipsawing lumber with one man on the platform and the other in the pit below, tediously pulling the saw back and forth to make a board."

The W. F. Bassett family is reported to have arrived in the fall of 1871. As G. W. Bassett (no known relationship) stated in the quote on the previous page, by fall the mill had nearly been completed. He made no mention of any new settlers at the falls. Although noteworthy, either he just didn't mention the Bassetts or they may have arrived after G. W. Bassett paid his visit. According to Bond, W. F. Bassett's services as a millwright may have been engaged to put the mill into operation. The Bassetts left in the spring of 1872

The Phoenix Sawmill, at Post Street and the Spokane River from 1898 to 1927. Though much larger than Scranton and Downing's sawmill, it was located at roughly the same site. *(Jerome Peltier collection)*

The Impact of the Timber Industry and the Demand for Wooden Matches on Spokane

It is widely accepted that Spokane was built from wealth produced in the mining industry, specifically in the Coeur d'Alene Mining District. However, the timber industry was also a major contributor. Affluent capitalists in both industries found Spokane a desirable place to live and raise families, and made significant marks in the development of real estate. There was a sawmill operation right in the heart of downtown Spokane for its first seven decades, and during the early half of the 20th century, the McGoldrick Lumber Company, located adjacent to Gonzaga University, was Spokane's largest employer.

Astonishing as it might seem, a driving force behind the arrival in the Northwest of two of the largest timber companies in the United States – Diamond Match and Ohio Match – was the demand for wooden matches. Until the 1930s, the majority of American households used wood stoves to heat their homes and cook their meals and burned kerosene lamps. Plus, many people smoked cigarettes, cigars or pipes. All these activities required matches. The two largest producers of wooden matches were Diamond Match Company, who took its name from the shape of the company's match head, and Ohio Match, who was known for its world-famous Ohio Blue Tip "strike-anywhere" matches.

Both companies were founded in Ohio in the late 1800s. They soon experienced the industry-wide problem of dwindling timber reserves in the eastern states. White pine was the most desirable species from which to produce matches. The choicest portion of the huge white pine trees, typically the bottom 30 feet, was used for making matches, and the remaining portion sawed into lumber. Because the largest stands of remaining white pine were in the Northwest, the Diamond Match and Ohio Match companies began to make major timberland investments and build sawmills in this area. The demand for matches declined after disposable pocket lighters became common in the late 1960s.

and settled next to a natural spring near the Four Lakes area south of Spokane. In 1975, Bassett Spring was nominated for listing on the National Register of Historic Places. (Although not the primary historical connection, in January 1872, the Bassetts' daughter Minnie Maria claimed the distinction of being the first white child born at Spokane Falls. In 1875, she drowned in Bassett Spring.) In the nomination, information about the Bassetts included the statement: "When S. B. Scranton and J. G. [sic] Downing aided by the blacksmith R. M. Benjamin decided to construct a mill on the Spokane Falls, they sent for Bassett. Bassett was undoubtedly the best millwright and carpenter available. He constructed the building and all the machinery while Benjamin did the iron work." Unfortunately, no source material is cited, but this account places Bassett and Benjamin there at the same time. To the contrary, Rowland Bond asserts, based on Mrs. Costello's account, that the Bassetts had already left the area by the time the Benjamins arrived.

Whatever the sequence, a quote in the *Walla Walla Union* on March 16, 1872, casts a bit of a shadow on Mrs. Costello's timeline. It stated:

> New Saw Mill – We learn that there has been erected during the past winter a fine new sawmill, at Spokane Falls, fifteen miles below Kendall's bridge, and is now in complete running order and prepared to furnish all kinds of lumber. This enterprise will supply a want long felt by the settlers in that vicinity. The proprietors are Messrs. J. J. Downing and S. B. Scranton.

Mrs. Costello's account has the Benjamins arriving in the spring, but the middle of March would have been quite early for Mr. Benjamin to have accomplished the task of building the waterwheel and have it in operation. And if the sawmill was not already operated by waterpower, it is doubtful the owners would claim to be able to "furnish all kinds of lumber" if they had to handsaw it all themselves. Although it may never be possible to sort out the exact timeline, enough references have been made to conclude that Bassett and Benjamin each had a hand in the construction of the sawmill. Of note, as Bond pointed out in his story about Richard Benjamin, he "was one of the first men successfully to harness the potential power of the great falls of the Spokane River."

Once in operation, Scranton and Downing's ownership of the sawmill was short-lived. Benjamin, who had arrived with cash in hand, offered to go into partnership with the two men. According to his daughter, "Benjamin had paid $500 for a one-third interest and his newly acquired partners had offered to sell him their remaining two-thirds interest for an additional $1,000." After two years at the falls, with the railroad still nowhere in sight, Scranton and Downing were becoming impatient and were anxious to move to a more settled area, but before following through on their offer, Benjamin began having second thoughts.

Again, the stories differ. From the Benjamin side, his second thoughts had to do with his concern about the character of the men he was dealing with and whether this rough area was a good place to raise his children. From the other side, it was believed that Benjamin did not have the money to complete the purchase. In her memoirs, Babe Downing made the statement: "… [James Downing] was forced back into the mill business by the failure of Benjamin to make his payments." And, according to Glover in his memoirs, when he was negotiating the purchase of Downing's claim and confronting him about the money Benjamin had already paid, Downing was alleged to have said: "Mr. Benjamin can't pay for it. He hasn't got anything to pay with, and I don't know that he would pay if he had." For whatever reason, these two men apparently were at odds with each other. Glover made mention that when it had been recommended he go check out the Spokane Falls, the person making the recommendation told him the people there "were in a wrangle and wanted to sell out."

This "wrangle" left the door open so that when James Glover arrived on May 11, 1873, and became immediately enamored with the area, he was able to negotiate a deal to purchase the little sawmill and Scranton and Downing's squatter's rights to the Spokane Falls town site land. (Today, the term "squatter" carries a derogatory connotation, but during this time, squatting on a land claim was a legal means to begin the process of ownership on public land that had not yet been surveyed. Once the survey was completed, a squatter who met the necessary criteria to prove intent of ownership, primarily occupying the site and making improvements, was given priority status to file for a deed to the property before the land was opened for sale to the general public.)

In 1917, Glover's recollections of his early days in Spokane were printed in the *Spokane Chronicle* in a series of articles, which were later published in book form. After all the fuss about who built the sawmill, in that book, *Reminiscences of James N. Glover* (Ye Galleon Press, Fairfield, Wash., 1985), Glover describes the sawmill in a most unflattering way:

> The mill was in a little shed. It worked so slowly that it really was little better tha[n] a whip saw would have been. By working industriously, it was possible to saw about 700 feet of lumber a day with it. I was unable to use any of the machinery or the big overshot wheel, 15 or 16 feet in diameter, and all I did make use of was the shed and mill frame.

Horse thieves or unjust accusations?

Before leaving the topic of this first commercial enterprise, Benjamin's concern about the character of his partners should be explained. According to Rowland Bond, his source apparently being Mr. Benjamin's daughter, a few cattle and horse rustlers, who roamed the area from Missouri to the Pacific Ocean, would visit Scranton and Downing at night to trade in stolen beef. There is enough documented evidence to support the claim that cattle and horse thieves operated quite freely in this wide open territory that had little law enforcement presence. Although the claims that Scranton and Downing were horse or cattle thieves have come to be accepted as fact, nothing substantial could be found to support or refute the claims with certainty, with one exception.

A criminal case record for horse theft against Seth B. Scranton, filed in 1873 by the Territory of Washington (the plaintiff), was found in the Washington State Digital Archives. Glover recounts how after he sealed the deal to purchase the sawmill and land, he returned to his home in Salem, Oregon, for supplies to open a small trading post and the necessary materials to upgrade the sawmill. In his absence, he left Scranton in charge of the sawmill. Needing a little more time to wrap up his affairs and, with his wife Susan, pack up their household, Glover sent his partners Jasper M. Matheny and Cyrus F. Yeaton on ahead. At the time of their arrival at Spokane Falls, newly deputized constables were combing the area in search of Scranton. Glover did not explain what was behind this search, and he was rather dismissive and demeaning in his remarks about what became of Scranton and Downing. However, if this was the criminal case for the horse theft charge, a key piece of the story was completely ignored – Scranton was found *not guilty*.

Secondary accounts, sometimes published long after the fact, repeated the theft accusations, often with even greater degrees of damnation. The most troubling accounts, especially one prepared for the Spokane Public Schools in 1960, are those that did not carefully regard the elements contained within the firsthand recitations. Glover and Benjamin were the primary sources of the assessment of these men. Although Glover was not particularly kind in his summation of them, to the point of being demeaning and dismissive, he talked about Scranton hiding out from the constables with no mention of Downing being involved in this incident. In the publication for the schools, Downing is lumped in with Scranton, indicating they were both running from the law. In short, only Scranton was involved and he was cleared of the charge. With the lack of evidence to support the claims, this may have been a rush to judgment or an unjust accusation.

More about the Scrantons and Downings

From what the authors were able to piece together through various records, neither Scranton nor Downing appears to have been a shiftless ne'er-do-well. Scranton was a Civil War veteran who fought for the Union. He had enlisted in Company

B, Minnesota 10th Infantry Regiment on February 26, 1864, and was mustered out on January 21, 1865, after being injured in battle. While in Spokane Falls, he was the town's first postmaster.

After Glover purchased Scranton and Downing's holdings, James and Marcia Downing moved to Moran Prairie, where they farmed for about two years. After selling their ranch, they purchased a herd of cattle and some horses, and moved to Grand Coulee, where Marcia was again the first white female settler. Several months later, they were uprooted as the result of an Indian scare. According to Marcia Downing, Chief Moses "issued an edict at the outbreak of the Nez Perce war that 'The White Queen of the Land' should not be hurt." After leaving that area, the Downings went briefly to Vancouver, Washington, where they sold their stock, and then moved to Walla Walla and purchased some property. They finally settled on a ranch near Dayton, Washington. James Downing died and was buried at Dayton in 1889. Marcia later remarried. She and her new husband, John R. McClure, divided their time between Pendleton, Oregon, and Walla Walla, where they each owned considerable property. No date of death could be determined for Marcia, but according to John McClure's death record of June 9, 1900, he was a widower by that time. Since Marcia had been in Spokane in August 1899, her death was either in late 1899 or early 1900.

A little of what is known about Seth Scranton after he left Spokane Falls comes from Babe Downing's memoirs. She followed Seth to California, where they were married. A handwritten document, just over nine pages in length, was signed by Mrs. E. R. Bailey, Babe's name after her second marriage around 1888. The original manuscript, written around 1909 or 1910 during her first return visit to Spokane, is secured in a vault at the Spokane Public Library. She titled it "Why Did I Sell Spokane Falls." It was written as a third-person account. Her facts, such as dates and amounts, are largely incorrect, but her impressions of Spokane Falls and glimpses of what took place in its earliest years are priceless. Excerpts that provide information about Seth Scranton and her life follow:

Only a little over a year after their settlement here Mrs. Bailey, who was more popularly known then as Babe Downing, after graduating from school in the East, started for her new home in this far off western country not the center of the network of suburban electric lines and transcontinental steam railroads that it is now, the closest she could get by rail being Kelton, Utah. Here she began a very perilous journey overland to Walla Walla where she was met by her father [although James Downing was her stepfather, she considered him "father"] completing the journey to Spokane with him. Throughout her journey she had been picturing in her imaginative mind the beauties of this new home and the glories of the new life and she longed to reach her destination. But there warmed in her young breast a passion much greater than the desire for the realization of these fancies. It was a longing to meet and clasp the hand of the man she had learned to love....

Mary J. "Babe" Bailey in 1917. She was James and Marcia Downing's daughter and first wife of Seth Scranton. *(From the Patsy Clark album, courtesy Mark Danner)*

Mrs. Bailey was the first white girl in this section of the country so her arrival was of much interest to the Indians who came from near and far to look upon this new wonder of the palefaces. But Mrs. Bailey soon adapted herself to the conditions. She spent the days roaming over the valley ... penetrated forests where nature still reigned supreme ... also started to master the native tongue, this attainment afterward serving her as a source of much pleasure and satisfaction ...

... This offer [Glover's purchase offer] was accepted, and Downing moved onto a ranch on Moran Prairie, while Scranton left for California. But the separation of the estates was not to interfere with the romance which had received so much nourishment during the joyful companionship at the falls, so late in the fall of the same year Babe Downing left for a southern clime where she entered into a life partnership with the man who had formerly been her father's business partner. They lived in California about four years when they returned to Walla Walla, but the climate of the north did not agree with Mr. Scranton who continued to become worse until he again left for California where he died.

What she neglected to mention in her account is that she (as the plaintiff) and Scranton divorced in 1887. Her marriage to E. J. Bailey took place

A float honoring James N. Glover in 1917. The banner reads: "The Father of Spokane, Sole Surviving Founder of Spokane, and The Evening Chronicle, Our Pioneer Newspaper [but note, it was not the city's first newspaper]." Seated on the front of the float are (from left) James Glover, "Babe" Downing/Scranton/Bailey (who was age 61 at the time), and James A. Perkins, founder of Colfax. "Dutch Jake" Goetz (fourth from the right with his hand on his hip) and his band are also on the float. *(From the Patsy Clark album, courtesy Mark Danner)*

shortly thereafter. Interestingly, on the 1883 and 1885 Washington Territorial censuses, Bailey is found in the same household as S. B. and M. J. (Babe) Downing.

In 1899, while living in California, Scranton married a woman by the name of Adelaide Mellis. At the time of their marriage, she had an infant daughter named Elsie, and together they had a son named Lester. Seth Scranton died on March 16, 1906, in Sacramento. He was 62.

In her memoirs, Babe lists the children from her two marriages, five of whom were residing in Spokane at the time:

> Six children had been born to their [Seth and Babe] union, the four who are still living being Frank S. Scranton of Spokane, Ada V. Sturgiss of Pendleton Oregon, Earle H. Scranton of Spokane and Vernnie L. Scranton of Pendleton.

Twenty-two years ago Mrs. Bailey was married to her present husband at Dayton, Wash. During this course of time four children have been born. They are Mrs. F. C. [Rose] Daugherty of Spokane, Mrs. Carl [Ethel] Leonard of Pendleton, Ore., Hazel R. Bailey and Bill Bailey of Spokane.

Mary J. "Babe" Downing/Scranton/Bailey died in Seattle on July 3, 1929, at age 73.

Who and what was at the Falls

Based on Mrs. Costello's account, with the Benjamins' arrival in spring 1872 with the five youngest of their ten children, the white population more than doubled. The only other people residing at the falls with the Downings, Scranton, and the Benjamins were Mr. and Mrs. L. M. Swift (some accounts refer to "A. C.," but according to Rev. Henry Cowley, who arrived in 1874, as well as local censuses, "L. M." appears to be correct).

Another man, a bachelor by the name of Walter France, was also there when Glover arrived the following year, but he was not mentioned by Mrs. Costello. She also did not mention there was a significant Indian population located there. (According to the census of 1870, the Spokane Indian population consisted of 716 people with 949 horses, 61 cattle and 49 farms. Of course, they were not all living at the falls.) This was the group of settlers who welcomed James Glover into their midst when he and his friend Jasper Matheny arrived in the spring of 1873. Having heard about the beauty and potential of the region, they had traveled from their homes in Salem, Oregon, to explore the Inland Northwest.

In Babe Downing's memoirs, she mentioned a few others who had also settled in the vicinity:

> ... At this time [when Downing and Scranton staked their land] there were but few settlers in the Spokane country, some of them who afterwards played an important part in its development being Joseph Moran situated on Moran Prairie, Batese [Baptiste] Peone of Peone Prairie, Steve Liberty near Liberty Lake and [Frederick] Post at Rathdrum.

In addition to the little band of settlers, Glover reported that, at the time of his arrival, the entire town site consisted of six board or log cabins and a small shed that housed the "muley" sawmill. (A "muley" is a single saw blade that is operated in an up-and-down cutting motion.) There was a double log cabin a little southwest of the mill, at about the end of the present Post Street Bridge. This structure had been built and occupied by Downing and Scranton, but at the time of Glover's arrival it was occupied by Mr. Benjamin and his family. About 150 yards from it was a little box house 16 feet square, occupied by the Swifts, which had been built with lumber from the sawmill. On the north side of Front (later Trent, now Spokane Falls Boulevard) between Howard and Mill (now Wall Street) was the body of a log house. It had not been roofed and had no floor. In the same block, at about the corner of Howard and Front, there was the body of another little house – also without a roof. Across Howard Street, and on the other side of Front, about where the Coeur d'Alene Hotel was later built, was another log cabin. This was the extent of the town site Glover was about to purchase.

When the white settlers began to claim land around the Spokane Falls, the area was populated by the Upper Band of the Spokane Tribe of Indians. *(Courtesy SPLNWR)*

Chapter One

The Spokane Falls, circa 1880. *(From the Patsy Clark album, courtesy Mark Danner)*

From the moment of his arrival at the Spokane Falls on May 11, 1873, Glover was irresistibly smitten with the future town site of Spokane. He fell in love with the power and beauty of the falls, with its foundation of basaltic rock. Babe Downing had a similar reaction upon her arrival, which she described as follows:

> ... In that day there was a ravine running from Cannon Hill to the river a little below the falls known as "Little Wolf Ditch." For one approaching the settlement from the southwest on the Mullan road the view of the falls and river valley was almost entirely obstructed until the opposite side of this ravine was reached. Then there flashed into view, as if by magic, a scene which for beauty and grandeur was surpassed nowhere. Here lay a broad, fertile valley completely covered with waving bunch grass and surrounded by ranges of lofty mountains whose hooded peaks towering above the fleecy clouds seemed to fade away into the serene blue of the heavens. Through the valley a river wound its snake-like course now running smoothly and now rushing with a roar over boulders and cataracts ...

Looking beyond the rocky ground that was unsuitable for agricultural development, Glover envisioned a thriving town surrounding the falls. To him, the real estate potential seemed endless. Just a short distance, in every direction, lay expanses of good agricultural land. The river provided an abundant supply of water to support a large city, and the falls could produce the necessary power to run every manner of industry. There was wild game roaming the area, and the Spokane River was plentiful with fish, about which Babe Downing made the follow comments:

> The country at this time afforded many pastimes for the early settlers. One of the most largely indulged in of these pastimes was the salmon fishing which began in the month of July at which time the red salmon coming up the river from the Columbia began to make their appearance just below the falls. The white salmon did not come up the river until later in the year in the month of October. Besides serving as a sport, it is described as a very beautiful sight to see them jumping out of the water their bright colored bodies flashing in the sunlight.

In Glover's book, *Reminiscences of James N. Glover*, he stated: "The whole situation aroused my desire of possession. I have never been able to express the force with which this country impressed my mind at the time I first saw it." But his dream would not begin to materialize for half a decade, and he would face his share of setbacks and moments of near despair before he could be assured of the little town's survival.

One final quote from Babe Downing before moving forward in time describes an interesting event that occurred during their brief sojourn at the falls:

> While they were living at this place, this region was visited by the last and most violent of the earthquakes recorded in the Northwest. It was on the night of the fourteenth of December [1872] when it came. The Downings were almost shaken from their beds and awoke terrified by the swaying of the house and the sound of various articles crashing to the floor. They rushed out-of-doors only to see large trees shaken to the ground and to find a large corral battered to the ground either by the shaking of the earth or the feet of the frightened animals it contained. On this night the region underwent its last great topographical change marked by the disappearance of many smaller streams and the appearance of new ones. It was also reported that a large point of land on Lake Okanogan [*sic*] totally disappeared from sight.

Over the years since the first settlers at Spokane Falls experienced this earthquake, other earthquakes have rattled the area, but this is a firsthand account of the first one to take place during Spokane's founding years.

Glover purchases the Spokane town site

The day after their arrival, having quickly made up his mind, Glover announced to Matheny that he intended to purchase the town site. Matheny cautioned him that perhaps he was being too hasty, but he wasted no time in approaching James Downing. Shrewd businessman that he was, he was careful not to reveal the depth of his desire to own the land, and he made it clear to Downing that, if they could agree to mutually acceptable terms, Richard Benjamin's down payment would first

Cyrus F. Yeaton
(*Spokane and the Inland Empire*)

James N. Glover, circa 1878.
(*Courtesy SPLNWR*)

have to be reimbursed. Glover stated the amount of Benjamin's down payment was $400. However, Benjamin's daughter claimed it was $500, but that he was only reimbursed $400. According to her account, that was all the cash Glover had with him, and Benjamin was willing to take a loss just to get out from under the deal.

The matter of the down payment was the beginning of the inconsistencies in the amount of money that exchanged hands in this real estate transaction, historically the most significant one to Spokane. Glover said he paid Scranton and Downing $2,000 each for their squatter's rights, Babe Downing claimed it was $10,000, and Marcia Downing stated James Downing received $500. Because no official documents regarding this transaction could be located, the amount Glover paid for the original town site remains in question. Nevertheless, he negotiated a purchase arrangement, and had Mr. Swift, who was said to be a lawyer, draw up a contract. According to Glover, the contract was "between me and Mr. and Mrs. Downing, Mr. and Mrs. Benjamin and

Mr. Scranton. Before nightfall of May 12, 1873, we had the deal closed up, and the land was mine." He then added the caveat "if the government hadn't granted it to the railroad." References by Glover on other occasions indicated there was a risk in buying the town site from Scranton and Downing because of the uncertainty of gaining title.

Although a concerted effort was made to locate the original contract between Scranton and Downing and the federal government, nothing was found. However, to be able to sell their squatter's rights to James Glover, their claim would have had to comply with the requirements of one of the land acts. In their case, because it was prior to the government survey, it would have been legitimized under the preemption acts. The Pacific Railway Act specifically precluded land from being claimed by the railroad that was already occupied by settlers through preemption, homesteading or any other legitimate means. In cases where sections of land the railroad might otherwise have claimed were already legally occupied, the railroad was granted a substitution of its choice (lieu lands).

Knowing the Northern Pacific had made a preliminary survey prior to Scranton and Downing's arrival, which passed near the Spokane Falls, Glover was fairly well assured of the railroad's intended route. However, he could rightfully have had concerns about when the Northern Pacific Railroad would be completed. The same year Glover bought the town site, construction of the railroad, which had only commenced in 1870, came to a halt due to financial failure. That impact was noticeable, and Glover did, in fact, experience his share of anxiety for a few years over whether or not people would come and put down roots in Spokane Falls. However, because the railroad had land to sell and it was competing with the U.S. government's sales of land through other land acts, it did not discourage settlement in areas that would ultimately be serviced by its line. In fact, the Northern Pacific actually founded towns along its route to create markets for its land.

Glover's assertion that he took a risk of being on railroad land was either ignorance in regard to the protection a preemption claim provided or intentional deception to make himself look good for having taken such a risk. Other statements by Glover have revealed that at times either his memory or his integrity was faulty. He was known to have claimed full credit for accomplishments that rightfully should have been shared with others. And his treatment of Susan Glover, his first wife, according to Barbara Cochran's biography of her in *Seven Frontier Women and the Founding of Spokane Falls* (Tornado Creek Publications, 2011), was less than honorable. In his book *Reminiscences,* he did not make a single mention of her. Nevertheless, having purchased the town site, Glover tenaciously clung to his vision and made enough right moves to build the town, and rightfully claim the title of "Father of Spokane."

Susan Crump Glover, first wife of James Glover, circa 1882.
(Barbara Cochran collection)

Joining forces to build a town

While at Salem, C. F. Yeaton, an acquaintance of Glover's, met with Glover and Matheny to inquire about becoming a partner in their Spokane Falls venture. Yeaton had experience in the mercantile business, which was of special interest to Glover since he intended to open a trading post. The men agreed to a three-way partnership in the purchase of Spokane Falls, and Matheny and Yeaton soon departed with the new sawmill equipment and goods for the store. According to Glover, he "hastened his preparations as rapidly as possible and followed."

Glover's new store opened around the first of November 1873 at the southwest corner of Howard and Front. Since there were so few white settlers, it was stocked with items primarily of interest to the local Indians in exchange for furs. This area was the meeting place for many of the Spokane Indians who came each fall to catch and put up enough fish to last through the winter. This activity took place at the confluence of Hangman Creek with the Spokane River. During these times, the Indians would play stick games and race their horses. Their race course followed what is now Riverside Avenue from Cedar Street to Washington Street, a distance of thirteen blocks. In spite of their carefree ways, Glover never had any problems with them paying for their purchases.

Initially, Glover and his wife, Susan, who had joined him in August, lived in a little box structure adjoining the store. Living quarters for Yeaton and his family were in the rear of the store. After Scranton's departure, Mr. Yeaton was appointed postmaster, so the post office was also located there.

The town's population fluctuated little until the end of the decade. As new settlers trickled in, others departed, including the first group of white inhabitants who became discouraged by the Northern Pacific's delay.

Two ministers were major land investors

Because of what the area had to offer, Spokane was a natural destination for land investors. Large plats were obtainable at almost giveaway prices. But for real estate investments to become profitable, an influx of people was required. Those who arrived early with the ability to wait and had the capital to invest in land development, or who were willing to spend the time and effort to develop a homestead claim, were at a decided advantage.

Following the initial procurement and staking of lands, real estate was one of Spokane's most profitable businesses, resulting in many local fortunes. Two of those fortunate ones happened to be the first ministers in Spokane – Rev. Henry Thomas Cowley and Rev. Samuel G. Havermale.

Rev. Cowley and his wife, Lucy Abigail (Peet) Cowley, moved their family to Spokane in 1874 following requests by the Spokane Indians for a Protestant mission to be established among them. When the Cowleys reached Spokane Falls with their four children (two more were born in Spokane) about the same time as the Poole family of five, they more than doubled the population.

Shortly after Cowleys' arrival, the first school district was formed, which covered the region from Spangle to Fort Colville, east from the Columbia

The Cowley family, circa 1891. Seated from left: Mrs. Lucy A. Cowley, Arthur, Henry, Agnes. Standing: Cazenovia, Frederick, Edith, and Grace. *(Courtesy SPLNWR)*

Rev. Henry T. Cowley, first white missionary to the Indians at Spokane Falls. Cowley was one who made early real estate investments that eventually turned a handsome profit. He also became the owner and publisher of the *Chronicle* (which over time operated under various versions of its name) and soon changed it from a weekly to a daily paper. *("Spokane and the Inland Empire")*

River to the Idaho line (because Spokane County did not yet exist and this region was in Stevens County, this was part of the Stevens County School District). The first school term began in January 1875 in Cowleys' cabin alongside a creek in what is now Cowley Park (west of Division between Sixth and Seventh) on a 20-acre parcel donated by Enoch Siliquowya, a sub-chief of the Spokane Indian Tribe. Cowley soon began to invest in real estate, purchasing from the Northern Pacific Railroad 140 acres that were adjacent to the 20-acre parcel.

Because there were only six white students, Cowley began teaching both whites and Indians. With his additional work among the Indians, this proved too great an undertaking, and Mrs. L. M. Swift finished the school term for the white children in their cabin a little north of Cowleys' home. The first school in Spokane integrating the white man's teachings had been established by Spokan Garry near Drumheller Springs at Euclid and Maple, but Cowley's was the first Indian school in the city run by whites. A school building was constructed near the Cowley home in 1875, and with the eager response from the Spokanes to become educated, a little village of tepees grew up around the school. (The first public school for the white children was built in 1878 on what was later determined to be Northern Pacific right-of-way. In 1881, it was moved to the middle of the block on the south side of First Avenue, across the street from where the Davenport Hotel was later built.)

In 1874, Rev. Samuel Havermale, while en route from Walla Walla to Colville, followed incorrect directions and ended up at Spokane Falls. He liked the town site and, the following spring, he moved his wife Elizabeth and two sons to the area. Havermale saw the opportunity to invest, and staked out an L-shaped, 160-acre homestead on the quarter section of land adjoining the east property line of Glover's land. They lived there until 1887 when, due to failing health, they sought a better climate in Southern California.

Samuel Havermale was the first minister to preach a sermon to the white settlers in Spokane Falls. In 1883, he and George A. Davis completed construction of Spokane's second flour mill, the Echo Roller Mills. It was located on what was then Little Island. He also served as president of the first town board of trustees, which established the Spokane City Water Works. *("Spokane and the Inland Empire")*

This perspective of Havermale Island, named for Rev. Samuel Havermale, was enlarged from an 1884 artist's sketch of Spokane Falls. The first bridge across the Spokane River at the new town connected from Howard Street on the south side and consisted of three spans, which are shown in this sketch. Havermale and Davis's Echo Roller Mill is the building on the island at the right. It was situated at the north end of the first bridge span from Howard Street. A channel of water through the island passed beneath the mill and powered its waterwheels. *(Published by J. J. Stoner, Madison Wis., 1884)*

Havermale was a Methodist minister, but he did little preaching while at the Falls, with one important exception. On November 14, 1875, he preached the first sermon delivered to a congregation of white people at Spokane Falls. The services were held in a small box house just west of Howard and Front.

His property investments at the Falls encompassed the portion of the Spokane River from Division to Mill (Wall) streets, which included the portion of the falls within those bounds, most of the island properties, and land on both sides of the river. He became quite wealthy by subsequently subdividing and selling his properties. Included in his holdings are what became the following additions: Havermale's Addition, Havermale's Second Addition, Riverfront Addition, and Keystone Addition.

In 1898, after a 12-year absence, Havermale returned to Spokane at the age of 79. He purchased a home at 807 West Chelan Avenue, where he lived out the rest of his life. He died on January 13, 1904, and was buried at Fairmount Memorial Park in Spokane.

The struggle to hang on

By 1876, with no railroad yet in sight, Yeaton and Matheny, now wearied by the isolation and struggle for survival, sold their shares to Glover. Figuring that a flour mill would encourage settlement at Spokane Falls, he put out a plea, with an offer of 40 acres of land and the lumber to build a mill, to Frederick Post, who was then living in Rathdrum, Idaho. Post moved to Spokane Falls with his wife Margaret and their five daughters, and built a home and flour mill at the site where the Washington Water Power building now stands on Post Street. The mill produced its first flour in the fall of 1877. However, Post was always drawn to the falls near the head of the Spokane River

Frederick Post built the first flour mill in Spokane. *("Spokane and the Inland Empire")*

and, while living in Spokane Falls, began developing a sawmill there. Finally, after nearly ten years, he moved to that location and founded the town of Post Falls.

The summer of 1877 was undoubtedly the most trying period for the settlers in Spokane Falls. With little or no means of support, some had given up and moved away. During this time, Glover nearly despaired of his dream to build a city by the falls. That summer, following some skirmishes between the Indians and white settlers, war broke out in eastern Oregon between a band of Nez Perce Indians and the United States government. The military pursued Chief Joseph's band northward through Idaho, which created fear and anxiety among the settlers around the Spokane region. A small band of Nez Perce had set up camp nearby and performed nightly war dances in hopes of recruiting allies from the Spokane Tribe.

The little band at the falls had never felt threatened by the local tribes, but this incident was different. Frightened settlers from the region around Spokane Falls huddled on Havermale Island in fear for their lives. To their relief, Gen. Frank Wheaton, in charge of the left wing of Gen. Oliver O. Howard's army, arrived at Spokane Falls with about 500 troops. They had been sent to insure that other Inland Northwest tribes did not join the Nez Perce against the U.S. troops. During this time, while passing through the area, Gen. William T. Sherman selected a site for a military post on Coeur d'Alene Lake near the head of the Spokane River. He ordered two companies of infantry to winter over in Spokane Falls and depart the following spring to build the new fort under Gen. Wheaton's command. (Originally called Fort Coeur d'Alene and later renamed Fort Sherman in honor of Gen. Sherman, this fort soon gave rise to the town of Coeur d'Alene.)

Although the residents at Spokane Falls dreaded the troops' departure, they were grateful for the military's presence at their most vulnerable moment – the last time they feared their survival to be threatened by the Indians. It also had to be a financial benefit for Glover. The Nez Perce War came to

This photo of the Spokane Falls was taken in 1878. The building above the falls is Frederick Post's flour mill. *(Courtesy SPLNWR)*

Lorenzo W. Rima in the foreground with the fledgling town of Spokane Falls in the background, early 1880s. *("Spokane and the Inland Empire")*

bitter resolution and, with the new military fort in the area, the climate felt safer for new settlers.

Filing for deed and platting Spokane Falls

As the decade was drawing to a close, the Northern Pacific gave out contracts for the extension of its line to Spokane Falls and, finally, the town began to assume an air of permanency. Five years had passed since Glover purchased Scranton and Downing's squatters' rights, but he had not yet filed for a deed on his land claims. Perhaps it was the uncertainty he felt from the lack of settlers and the Indian unrest, but the government had completed an official survey around the time he bought out Matheny and Yeaton, so now there was nothing standing in his way. It is not known when he applied for his land deed, but it was issued on April 5, 1878, under the Land Act of 1820 (see sidebar following page). Although the amount of acreage in his claim is generally rounded to 160 acres, the exact amount was 158.37 acres.

In 1878, Glover engaged the services of Lorenzo W. Rima, who opened Spokane's first jewelry store, to survey and plat a town site within his remaining 120 acres. According to Glover, the plat for the town of Spokane Falls was filed on February 13, 1878, at Colville, the Stevens County seat (Spokane County was not formed until the following year). However, unbeknownst to Glover at the time, Rima failed to file the plat, and Glover proceeded to sell some property within the platted town site. This created some problems with future land sales, one of which, Sengfelder vs. Hill, was settled in the Supreme Court of Washington (case 58 P. 250, dated July 19, 1899). The report for that case included the following information:

> In the spring of 1878 Glover caused a part of the lands included within his patent to be marked out on the ground into lots and blocks, and a plat to be made of the same, which plat he left with one Rymer [Rima], a surveyor, with instructions to forward it to Colville for the purpose of having it placed on record. This plat was never recorded; a fact unknown to Glover until some time afterwards, who proceeded to sell and convey certain of the lots and blocks so platted, describing them in accordance with the numbers of the unrecorded plat. In September, 1879, Glover conveyed to one A.M. Cannon and one J. J. Browne each an undivided one-fourth interest in his original land claim, reserving certain parts thereof ... After the discovery that the original plat had not been recorded, Glover, Cannon, and Browne caused the town-site to be resurveyed, and a plat there-

> ## James N. Glover's Original Deed
> **Certificate No 556 under the Land Act of 1820**
>
> The following is the exact wording on the deed:
> **The United States of America**
> **To all to whom these presents shall come, Greeting:**
>
> Whereas James N. Glover of Stevens County Washington Territory has deposited in the General Land Office of the United States a Certificate of Register of the Land Office at Walla Walla, Washington Territory, whereby it appears the full payment has been made by the said James N. Glover according to the provisions of the Act of Congress of the 24th of April 1820, entitled "An Act making further provision for the sale of Public Lands," for and the act supplemental thereto for the South half of the South West quarter, the South West quarter of the South East quarter and the North East quarter of the South West quarter of Section Eighteen in Township twenty-five, North of Range forty-three, East, in the district of lands subject to sale at Walla Walla, Washington Territory, containing one hundred and fifty-eight acres and thirty-seven hundredths of an acre. According to the Official Plat of the Survey of the said Lands, returned to the General Land Office by the Surveyor General, which said Tract has been purchased by the said James N. Glover.
>
> Now know ye, that the United States of America, in consideration of the promise, and in conformity with the several Acts of Congress in such case made and provided, have given and granted, and by these presence do give and grant unto the said James N. Glover and his heirs, the said Tract above described. To have and hold the same, together with all the rights, privileges, immunities, and appurtenances, of whatsoever nature, thereunto belonging unto the said James N. Glover and to his heirs and assigns forever; subject to any vested and accrued water rights for mining, agriculture, manufacturing, or other purpose, and rights to ditches and reservoirs used in connection with such water rights, as may be recognized and acknowledged by the local customs, laws and decision of courts, and also subject to the right of the proprietor of a vein or lode to extract and remove his ore therefrom, should the same be found to penetrate or intersect the premises hereby granted, as provided by law.
>
> In Testimony whereof, Rutherford B. Hayes, President of the United States of America, have caused these letters to be made Patent, and the Seal of the General Land Office to be hereunto affixed.
>
> Given under my hand, at the City of Washington, the fifth day of April, in the year of our Lord one thousand eight hundred and seventy-eight, and of the Independence of the United States the one hundred and second.
>
> [This was followed by the signatures of President R. B. Hayes, Secretary B. L. Lang, and Recorder of the General Land Office, S. W. Clark]

of to be made and recorded under the title of "Resurvey and Addition to Spokane Falls, Spokane County, Washington Territory," properly dedicating the streets and alleys thereon to the public use. This resurvey and addition followed very closely the original survey ...

Glover later said he had his doubts about Rima's skills as a surveyor and, for that reason, had the property resurveyed. This court case or the true reason for the resurvey was not mentioned in any of Glover's writings or recorded reminiscences. The end result, however, was the same, and the town site plat was filed before a great influx of newcomers accompanied the Northern Pacific's arrival at Spokane Falls.

The town site plat extended from Post Street east to Bernard Street, and from the Spokane River south to Sprague Avenue. Glover chose many street names for their historical significance: Sprague Avenue was in honor of Gen. John Wilson Sprague, general superintendent of the western division of the Northern Pacific Railroad; Washington Street for the first United States president and the territory; Front Avenue because it fronted the river; Stevens Street for the first governor, Isaac I. Stevens; Howard Street for Gen. O. O. Howard, who commanded the troops in the Nez Perce War; Mill (later named Wall) Street denoted the milling industry at the river; Post Street for Frederick Post; and Lincoln, Monroe, Madison, Jefferson, and Adams for former presidents. Although Glover thought Main Street (later Avenue) was going to be the main business street of the city, he missed it by one block. Glover's first name for Riverside Avenue, which did become the business center, was South Street, as that was the last street south that he had laid out when he had the town surveyed.

Glover's original patent and deed to the town site of Spokane was framed and presented to the Eastern Washington State Historical Society in 1958 and was placed on display in the Pioneer Room of the Grace Campbell Memorial Museum (now known as the Campbell House). It remains in the collection of Spokane's Northwest Museum of Arts and Culture (The MAC).

Railroad Boom Town (1878-1889)

The immeasurable importance of the Northern Pacific Railroad's transcontinental line to the Northwest was met with a corresponding degree of celebration upon its completion. This photo was taken in Spokane Falls the day after the golden spike ceremony, held on September 8, 1883, at Gold Creek, Montana, west of Helena. Completion of the long-awaited northern transcontinental railroad was the most important event of the decade and, within a few short years, transformed Spokane Falls from a little pioneer settlement to a booming metropolis. (Inset is Henry Villard, NPRR president.) *(Courtesy SPLNWR)*

Hopeful expectations about the pending route of the Northern Pacific Railroad had sustained the few weary settlers at Spokane Falls, so as construction of the line resumed in 1877 and it began inching toward Spokane Falls, news of its progress was met with eager anticipation. The good news also began to spread rapidly in other directions and attracted newcomers. In 1878, the arrival of a number of new arrivals who would make a decided difference, marked the first pivotal point in Spokane's development.

Anthony M. Cannon, who opened a store and the first bank, Bank of Spokane Falls, and John J. Browne, the first law office, arrived together in April that year. Glover sold half of his remaining town site to these two men. They also each staked 160-acre preemption claims, from which Cannon's Addition and Browne's Addition were platted and developed, the latter becoming Spokane's first upscale neighborhood. The William C. Gray family, who built the California House on the northeast corner of Front Street (later an avenue)

Looking south from the Spokane River, circa 1886. The large building in the foreground is the California House (from the back) built in 1878 at the northeast corner of Front (now Spokane Falls Boulevard) and Howard. The Western House (marked with the arrow), facing Front Street, was the first hotel of sorts in Spokane Falls. In the foreground is the first span of three bridges, which zigzagged across the island, that constituted the first bridge crossing on the Spokane River at Spokane Falls. *(MAC L86-275-2)*

William and Clara (Smiley) Gray, around the time they arrived in Spokane Falls in fall 1878 with Clara's two younger brothers, Charles Smiley, 15, and William Smiley, 11. Since Clara's mother had died five years earlier, the boys had lived with the Grays. The boys were able to assist William in the construction of the California House, which began immediately. It opened the following spring. *(MAC, L87-74 (left) and L93-66.183)*

The Windsor Hotel, circa 1888. The California House, so named because the owners had come from California, was the premier place to stay in the 1880s. But by 1887, the Grays decided they were tired of being in the hotel business, and had leased it out. Just a few months later that year, it was severely damaged by fire. Gray rebuilt it as the larger, updated Windsor Hotel. It was completely destroyed in the 1889 fire. After the fire, the Grays sold the property for $67,000 to the city as a site for a new city hall. (*Teakle Collection, courtesy SPLNWR*)

and Howard Street, Spokane's first quality hotel, arrived in the fall. The previous year, Dr. James H. Masterson had built the Western House, a two-story rugged boarding house on the south side of Front near Stevens. It had a sleeping "corral" on the second floor, which was little more than a place to lay out a bedroll or buffalo hide. There was a definite need for a place that offered a few amenities and was a suitable place for women guests. The California House became the setting for some of the most important community events and where many decisions were made by civic leaders.

Another significant contributor to Spokane's early history was Francis Cook. As the presiding officer of the 1879/80 Territorial Legislature responsible for creating Spokane County, Cook had visited the area in 1878. He decided to move there the following year to establish a newspaper, the *Spokan Times*. At the time of his arrival, there was disagreement among the 75 residents about how to spell the town's name. Cook purposely omitted the *e*, arguing it was more phonetically correct. Due to difficulties along the way, the first issue of the S*pokan Times*, dated April 24, 1879, was printed in Colfax. The first issue printed in Spokane Falls was on May 8, 1879. From 1879 to 1882, as owner and editor of the *Spokan Times*, Cook was Spokane's most ardent and vocal supporter, publicly striving to represent the best interests of the community. His efforts were essentially the first explicit promotion of the region, which was of considerable importance at that point in the town's existence.

In 1879, along with Francis Cook's new paper, the town's first organized church was started, and the year was capped by the territorial legislature passing a bill to organize Spokane County with Spokane Falls as the temporary county seat. New businesses built up around the intersection of Howard and Front. Spokane Falls was inhabited by less than 200 people as it greeted the new decade. The town consisted of about 50 houses on the south side of the river, a scattering of Indian tepees along the riverbanks and nearby hillsides, and finally a business district of sorts. Even a library association had been formed.

Spokane's First Newspaper

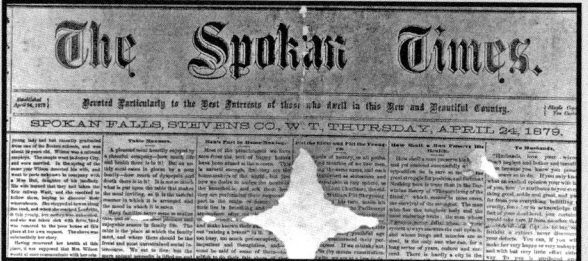

Masthead for the first issue of the *Spokan Times*.
(Courtesy Adi Song, great-granddaughter of Francis Cook)

The weekly paper consisted of four 18" by 24" pages, each containing eight two-inch columns, a common style until the early 1900s. Printed on the masthead of the *Spokan Times*, which ran from 1879 into 1882, was the statement: "*The Spokan Times* is the first newspaper printed in the great Spokan country. Its circulation promises to be very large, among a wide awake, progressive, reading people. The *Spokan Times* is published every Saturday morning by the *Times* Publishing Company at Spokan Falls, in the wonderful Spokan country." The paper's masthead typically included the caption: "Devoted Particularly to the Best Interest of those who dwell in this New and Beautiful Country." Cook unabashedly extolled the area's virtues in a regularly featured column "On Our Territory," where he included such promotions as: "There is no point in Spokan country more promising than Spokan Falls, which is beautifully situated at the wonderful falls on the Spokan River, where the Northern Pacific Railroad is already located. Business and professional men cannot locate at a point in Northeastern Washington which gives promise of greater importance in the future." As the first in Spokane to receive national telegraph wires from the Associated Press, the county commissioners declared it Spokane County's official newspaper. In July 1881, the *Times* became Spokane's first daily, which only lasted until April 29, 1882. Cook sold the paper soon thereafter. The *Independent*, as it was renamed, was discontinued before year's end.

Chapter Two

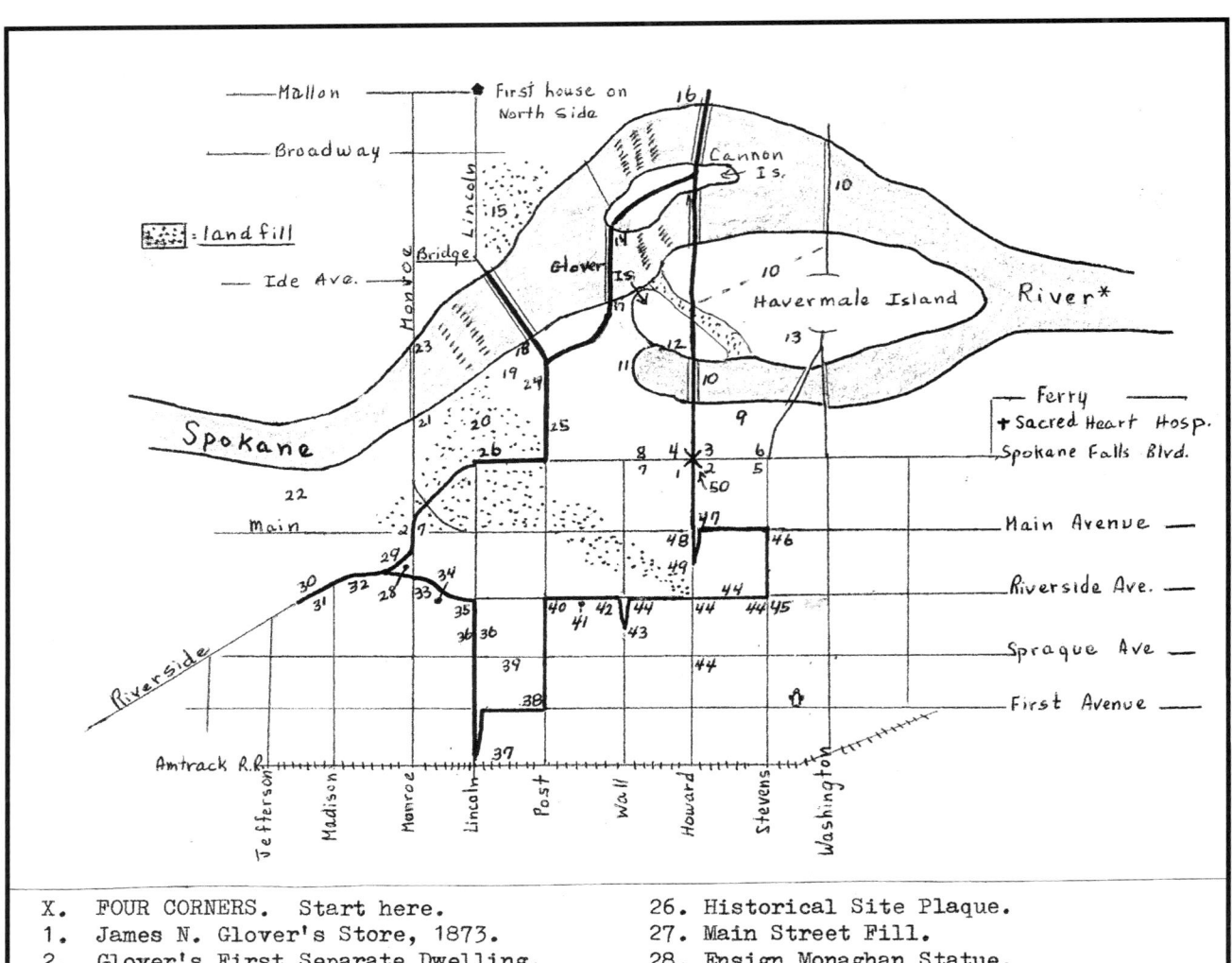

X. FOUR CORNERS. Start here.	26. Historical Site Plaque.
1. James N. Glover's Store, 1873.	27. Main Street Fill.
2. Glover's First Separate Dwelling.	28. Ensign Monaghan Statue.
3. California House.	29. Spokane Club.
4. Glover & Gilliam Livery Stable.	30. "Dutch" Jake's Wheel of Fortune.
5. Masterson's Boarding House.	31. Our Lady of Lourdes Cathedral.
6. Hunsaker's Grocery Store.	32. 1923 - "Best money can buy."
7. Early Jail.	33. Spokesman-Review Building.
8. Army Officers' Quarters, 1877.	34. Crescent Building.
9. Carousel.	35. Empire State Building.
10. First Bridge, 1881.	36. Dead-end Alleys.
11. Scranton & Downing's Sawmill.	37. Fire of 1889 started here.
12. Havermale & Davis Roller Mill.	38. Davenport's Restaurant, 1893.
13. Gt. Northern Clock Tower, 1902.	39. Davenport Hotel, 1914.
14. First Water Pumping Plant, 1884.	40. Peyton Building.
15. Land Fill & 1st Hydro-electric Plant.	41. Kuhn Building, 1890.
16. Flour Mill.	42. Jamieson Building, 1890.
17. Historical Marker, Suspension Bridge.	43. Sartori's.
18. Clark & Curtis Flour Mill.	44. 1890 Office Buildings.
19. Bassett Cabin.	45. Glover's Second Residence, 1881.
20. Land Fill.	46. 1889 Building, Bodie Block.
21. Second Power Plant, 1889.	47. Bennett Block, 1889.
22. Glover Field & Peaceful Valley.	48. "Dutch" Jake's Lavish Saloon, 1889.
23. Piers from 1894 Monroe St. Bridge.	49. Duffy & Butler's Saloon.
24. Washington Water Power Sign.	50. Coeur d'Alene Hotel.
25. Gondola.	⚑ Fire Station, No. 1.

Map of the walking tour of early Spokane from Barbara F. Cochran's book *Exploring Spokane's Past, Tours to Historical Sites*, published by Ye Galleon Press, 1979.

The Glovers' financial situation began to improve with the arrival of people, such as the Brownes and Cannons, interested in buying his land. Consequently, they built a new residence on the southeast corner of Riverside and Stevens (see arrow), which was completed in November 1880, and is shown above after a fire on August 20, 1886, that destroyed a millinery shop and grocery store (salvaged belongings were piled in the lot in the foreground). The following year, Glover sold his lot for business purposes (the Tull Block was built on that site in 1888 and is now occupied by the Paulsen Building) and the house was moved to First and Oak in Browne's Addition, where, radically remodeled, it is still standing. The houses surrounding the Glover home were early pioneer-style houses and represent the first frame homes in Spokane. *(Patsy Clark album, courtesy Mark Danner)*

Semi-weekly mail service connected the town to the outside world. Supplies to furnish the little businesses were brought in over rutted wagon roads, but a bridge across the river at the town site was still a year away. The U.S. Army Signal Corps established three stations in Washington Territory, including one in Spokane Falls, that began keeping the area's first weather records. The Signal Corps also began construction on the first telegraph line connecting Spokane Falls to other communities and military forts. The military Fort Spokane was established at the confluence of the Spokane and Columbia rivers during the year, and James Monaghan and Clement B. King constructed a telegraph line that connected it with Spokane Falls. Around this same time, they also started a stage line connecting Spokane Falls with Colfax. It wasn't much, but it was a good start. Although still lacking in some of the basic services, such as running water, electricity, and public transportation beyond the one stage line, people were moving to Spokane Falls. The 1880 federal census in June listed well over 500 names. This included over a hundred Chinese who were either railroad laborers or servants. (Most sources list Spokane's population in 1880 as 350, so it is quite likely the Chinese population was not considered. During that era, there was tremendous racial enmity toward Asians, especially the Chinese.)

The law that created Spokane County stipulated that an election was to be held in a year to select the permanent location for the county seat, which set off an immediate lively competition with the town of Cheney. The outcome of the election, held in November 1880, was cloudy. Although Cheney appeared to be the winner, the results were disputed by the residents of Spokane Falls. As a result, in the dead of night a few months later, some of Cheney's residents, with the assistance of the county auditor who wanted the county seat to be at Cheney, forcibly obtained the records. Cheney remained the county seat until another election was held in 1886, which returned it to Spokane. By that time, Spokane's population far exceeded Cheney's.

The Northern Pacific arrives from the west

Construction of the Northern Pacific's line was from both the east and the west, eventually joining in Montana. In 1881, it reached Spokane Falls from the west. When the first train pulled in on June 25, 1881, the celebration was such that, according to one account, the few people who didn't get drunk were not to be seen. Instead of fireworks, dynamite was set off, raining rocks over the area.

The railroad's arrival in 1881 was a major benchmark for Spokane. The town had languished after the removal of the county seat to Cheney, but the railroad connection sparked an increase in population, reaching nearly 1,000 that year. The rugged little settlement along the falls of the Spokane River quickly began to evolve into a city of reckoning. The 1880s were a time of new developments, largely fueled by the demand for real estate.

Evident signs of growth included a second newspaper, the first brick building, and a series of bridges across the river. Spokane's second newspaper, the *Spokane Falls Chronicle*, was founded as a weekly on June 29, 1881, by Glover, Browne, and Cannon. The first brick building was a storage warehouse built by I. T. Benham for J. N. Squire, owner of the Pioneer Saloon. The first story was of rock, the second of brick "laid herringbone fashion," as Benham phrased it. It was laid on edge with a header, which created a partially hollow wall. The first bridge across the Spokane River at the town of Spokane Falls (at Howard Street) actually consisted of three spans that zigzagged over the islands (see image on page 21). The next bridge, built at Post Street, followed two years later.

An enlargement of downtown Spokane Falls from an 1884 artist's sketch. The Post Street Bridge is at the center foreground and, on the left, the first span of the Howard Street Bridge. Opposite each other at the south end of the Post Street Bridge is the first flour mill and the sawmill. The Northern Pacific tracks skirt the top of the drawing (the train is in the upper left). *(Published by J. J. Stoner, Madison Wis., 1884)*

Spokane Falls incorporates

With the rapid growth, community leaders realized the need for formal city government and the means to meet the growing demand for services. As a result, the city of Spokane Falls was incorporated by an act of the Territorial Legislative Assembly during the 1881 session. It was signed by the Council on November 22, 1881, by the House of Representatives on November 25th, and approved by Washington Territorial Governor William A. Newell on the 29th. This new charter created the governmental framework and foundation upon which the city could begin building toward the future. Official city positions were created, and Robert W. Forrest was appointed mayor. The first city council was comprised of Samuel G. Havermale (council president), Anthony M. Cannon, L. H. Whitehouse, F. Rockwood Moore, William C. Gray, Lorenzo W. Rima, and George A. Davis. The lengthy charter spelled out the departments to be established and their respective responsibilities, laid out the legal boundaries of the town, the services to be provided, and countless other official matters. It also established the police department. Prior to this, law enforcement was handled by the county sheriff and a justice of the peace. (In the first territorial election for the Spokane Falls precinct, which was held in the fall of 1874 in Glovers' home, James Glover had been elected as a justice of the peace.)

The original city limits extended south from the north riverback between Cedar and Hatch streets to Sixth Avenue. This included the land Glover purchased from Scranton and Downing, as well as lands previously acquired by others. Two years later, an amendment to the city charter extended the city limits to two square miles and divided it into four wards. It provided for the mayor to preside over the council, which was comprised of two aldermen from each ward, and changed the city attorney, assessor, treasurer and chief of police to elected positions.

The spelling of the town's name was a matter of some controversy from the beginning (see the "Naming Spokane" sidebar, page 35), and the new

Eugene B. Hyde
First Police Chief of Spokane Falls

(Courtesy Washington State Archives)

Eugene B. Hyde, 32, became the first marshal of Spokane Falls when the city incorporated in 1881 and established the police department. (The term "marshal" is synonymous with "police chief," but generally is reserved for smaller towns.) Although the amended city charter in November 1883 specifically stated "chief of police," the election that followed on April 1, 1884, still listed the office as city marshal. Hyde was elected to the position by an overwhelming majority, which gave Chief Hyde the distinction of being both the first appointed and the first elected police chief of Spokane. In his new profession as marshal, Hyde was described as a stalwart man who had an accurate aim and was quick with a sidearm. He was later elected as a Washington State senator.

After Hyde moved to Spokane Falls in the spring of 1881, he immediately became involved in the real estate business and invested in a number of commercial buildings. His three-story Hyde Block was destroyed in Spokane's 1889 fire, but he rebuilt on the same site. His six-story Hyde Block was one of the largest constructed right after the fire. Although he and his wife, Florence, left Spokane in 1912, he still owned property in Spokane at the time of his death on May 29, 1917.

Hyde's brother Rollin, his sister Martha "Mattie" Blalock (one of Spokane's first school teachers), and his sister Clara Olmsted all dealt successfully in real estate. Rollin built the Fernwell Block and Martha's husband, John Blalock, built the Blalock Block. The Hyde, Fernwell, and Blalock blocks were all designed by architect Herman Preusse.

The islands at the town of Spokane Falls in the early 1880s. A city ordinance on May 1, 1889, officially named the main islands on the Spokane River: Havermale, Glover, and Cannon. The island in the foreground is Havermale, originally called Big Island. On the left, originally called Middle Island, is Cannon, but it became known as Crystal Island because the Crystal Laundry was located there from 1905 to 1973. As the site used by the Canadian provinces during Expo '74, it was officially dedicated by the city council as Canada Island. This photograph was probably taken from Glover Island, which became part of Havermale Island after the channel in the foreground was filled in. *(Courtesy SPLNWR)*

Spokane mayors. The first mayor, Robert W. Forrest (inset), was appointed by the territorial governor upon the incorporation of Spokane Falls in 1881. The others are (front row from left) David Fotheringham (10th), James N. Glover (2nd), Daniel Drumheller (11th), Charles F. Clough (9th), (back row) Charles A. Fleming (23rd and 25th), Charles M. Fassett (22nd and 24th), Herbert Moore (19th), and William J. Hindley (21st). James Glover, the Father of Spokane, is at the right. *(From the Patsy Clark album, courtesy Mark Danner)*

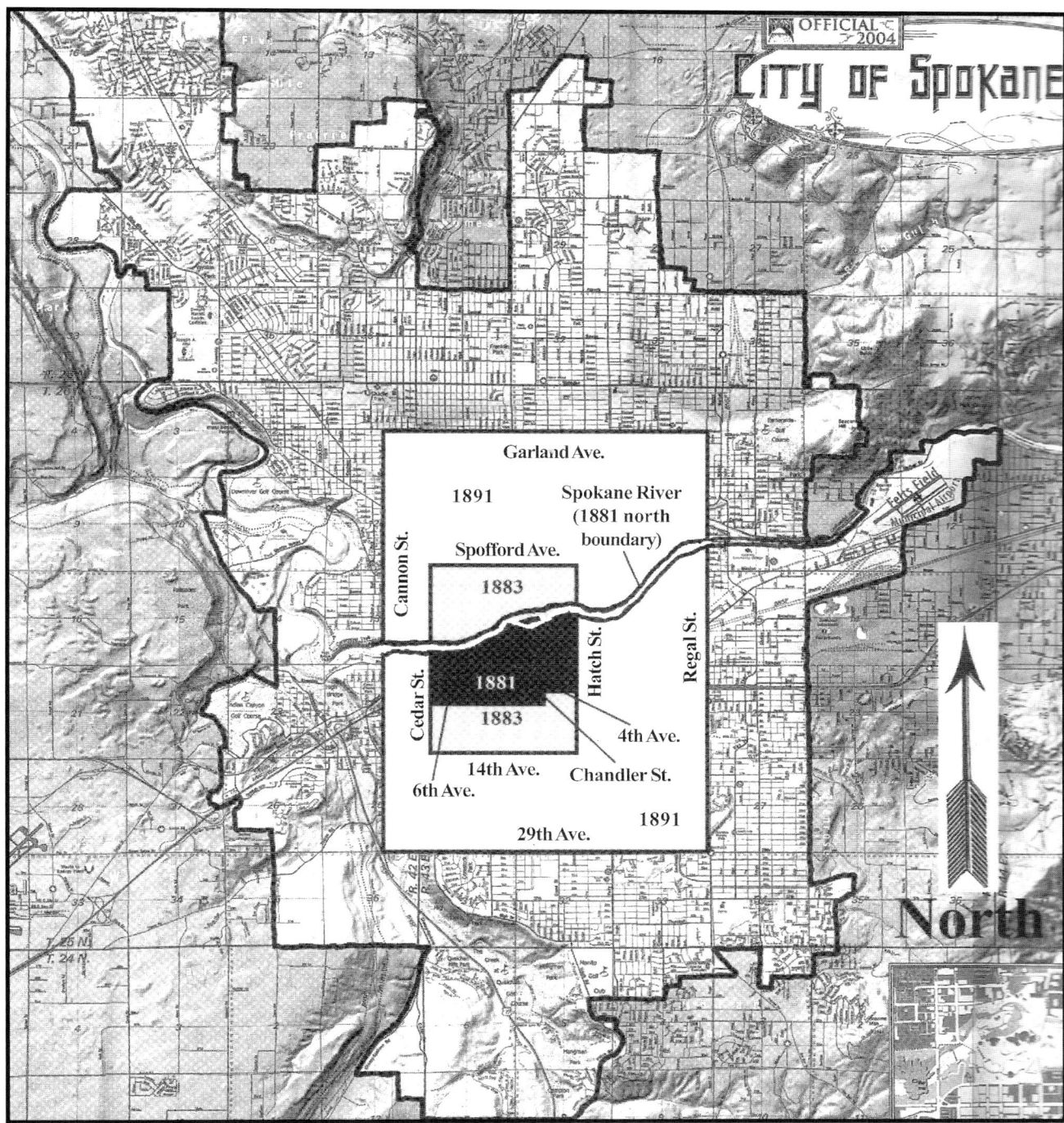

When Spokane Falls incorporated on November 29, 1881, the original city limits (the blackened area) encompassed 1.56 square miles. The boundaries extended south from the north riverbank between Cedar and Hatch streets to Sixth Avenue. At the southeast corner, the area south of Fourth and east of Chandler included land given by the Spokane Indians to Rev. Henry Cowley for an Indian school. The title to that land was somewhat clouded, which accounts for why that corner was not included in the original incorporated city limits. Delineated within the larger boundaries are annexations made in 1883 and 1891. In 1907, the boundaries doubled the size of the city. At the time this map was prepared in 2004, there had been 68 annexations since the original incorporation. The present incorporated city encompasses about 60 square miles, which means the city limits have increased to more than 38 times its original size. *(Boundaries for map created by Tony Bamonte in 2004 for* Life Behind the Badge: The Spokane Police Department's Founding Year, 1881-1903 *by Suzanne and Tony Bamonte)*

Articles of Incorporation only served to complicate the matter. The handwritten document submitted to Olympia by the town officials spelled the city's name "Spokane," but the territorial printing office left the *e* off. Although the "Spokan" spelling was used by some, most businesses that included the town's name as part of its own name or on its letterhead used the "Spokane" spelling.

The long-awaited day

Daily change was visible from the ceaseless activity in the growing town. By the time the east and west ends of the Northern Pacific's line met at Gold Creek, Montana, for the golden-spike ceremony on September 8, 1883, Spokane Falls had a second flour mill (Echo Roller Mills) that had just begun producing flour, an opera house of sorts (Joy's Opera House), six hotels (which included the Sprague House situated along the Northern Pacific tracks opposite the depot), and

The Glover Block, at the southwest corner of Front and Howard, in 1883. *("Spokane and the Inland Empire")*

even its first professional architect, Herman Preusse. In 1883, Glover gave Preusse, who arrived the prior year, his first commission in Spokane, the design of his two-story brick Glover Block on the southwest corner of Front and Howard. Glover had founded the First National Bank in 1882, which he moved into this new building. It also provided an office for the new police department.

The Sprague House, at Railroad and Post, was built in 1882 and burned in 1884. *(MAC, L89-267)*

Naming Spokane

The names of the city, county, and river were adopted from the name of the local native peoples, possibly given by the first Euro-Americans to visit the area. Although the name has become simplistically distilled and generally accepted to mean "Children of the Sun," the origin of the name from which it was derived, *Spokanee*, and the subsequent spelling, have been the subject of much controversy.

In regard to the origin of the name, the website of the Wellpinit School District on the Spokane Indian Reservation offers the following:

> The Spokanes (Spokans) maintain that their name originated when a native beat on a hollow tree inside of which a serpent made a noise that sounded like "Spukcane." One day, they say, as their chief pondered the noise, vibrations radiated from his head, which gave the word the vague meaning "power from the brain." In early times the Spokanes called themselves the Spukanees, which is translated "sun peoples," or more freely, "children of the sun." Others maintain that the tribal name derived from that of one of their chiefs and from nothing else.

Some tribal members question whether their ancestors called themselves Spokanes, but when the whites first arrived, the chief of the Spokane Tribe was Illim-Spokanee (*Illim* means "chief" and *Spokanee*, pronounced with a long *e* sound at the end, refers to the sun). Another theory suggests the name may have been derived from the sunny plains on which they resided, as opposed to the wooded, mountainous habitat of many of the neighboring tribes. Whatever the origin, the three major bands of native inhabitants living along the Spokane River became known as the Spokanes. Some of the primary encampments of the Upper Spokanes were around the falls where the city of Spokane took root and present-day Peaceful Valley.

In time, the second *e* was dropped from Spokanee, as was the long e sound. The Anglicized translation and interpretation of this word from the local tribes' native Salish language came to be Spokane (or Spokan), although earlier spellings also included "Spokein" or "Spokain." When Rev. Samuel Parker visited the region in 1836, he was corrected by members of the tribe who had apparently adopted the name by this time, when he called them Spokans, saying the pronunciation was closer to "Spokein." The new settlers, however, began pronouncing the name Spo-kan (with a soft *a*), and a controversy ensued about the inclusion of even one *e* at the end, arguing it would be pronounced "Spokayne" by those unfamiliar with the name. Francis Cook, the owner and publisher of Spokane's first newspaper, was a vocal proponent of that argument and named his paper the *Spokan Times*.

In the early days of the postal service, the local postmaster was required to purchase his own equipment. While the city founders wrangled over the spelling of Spokane, postal officials simply looked the other way in regards to the postmaster's choice. The town's first post office opened on July 5, 1872, in one of the tiny cabins clustered together near the falls, with Seth Scranton serving as the first postmaster. Initially, Scranton opted for "Spokan" without the *e*, but later postmarks indicate "Spokane" was also used. Both included "Falls" in the name until officially dropped in 1891. By this time, Spokane had grown sufficiently to reincorporate as a first-class city and a new charter officially changed the name to Spokane (the argument for dropping the *e* had long since died). The falls, which had enchanted James Glover upon his arrival, were now congested and clogged by industrial operations and were no longer a beautiful selling feature. Dropping "falls" from the name also met with the approval of the postal service in its nationwide effort to simplify city names.

Spokane has been variously referred to by such descriptive slogans as the City Beautiful, Heart (or Gem or Hub) of the Inland Empire, Gateway to the Pacific Northwest, the Power City, the Lilac City, and the Friendly City.

A sketch of the California House, Echo Roller Mills, and Glover and Gilliam's livery stable, as they appeared in 1884. The livery stable was operated by John W. Glover, James Glover's younger brother who had moved to the area in 1879, and Lane C. Gilliam, who had been a deputy sheriff assigned to enforcing the law in Spokane Falls prior to the formation of the police department. Gilliam and Glover built their livery stable around the time Gilliam moved to Spokane Falls in 1881. After the stable was destroyed in the Great Fire of 1889, Gilliam found real estate and mining promotion to be more lucrative pursuits. The Howard Street Bridge, the first bridge over the Spokane River in downtown Spokane Falls, is at the center of the photo. *(From* Westshore, An Illustrated Journal of General Information Devoted to the Development of the Great West, *April 1884)*

In July 1882, the *Spokan Daily Times* had reported: "There were two or three well laid out streets with substantial buildings, a great many of which are two stories high." Unfortunately, a fire in January 1883 had destroyed a number of these buildings. And the "well laid out streets" typically were ankle deep in dust in the summer and even deeper in mud when it rained. There were also mounds of basaltic rock, which created uneven terrain, that later had to be leveled for street development. But by the end of 1883, the *Spokane Falls Review* had a favorable report:

> Nearly all the principal business blocks [then a common term for commercial buildings], of which there are quite a number, are built of brick, and have plate glass windows and doors, and nice wide sidewalks in front. We have a number of churches, nice, neat frame buildings, mostly well-attended. There is now being completed a large opera house and a [roller] skating rink [the Casino Rink, which opened in November 1884] which is very much needed for exhibitions and concerts.

The townspeople of the "Gem City of the Inland Empire" had reason to be proud. Although the town's population was only about 1,500, the Fourth of July celebration had attracted about 6,000 from around the Inland Northwest. The railroad's completion promised to be another memorable occasion, and the town took its anticipated role seriously. Spokane Falls would be the first town to welcome the Northern Pacific's esteemed entourage, which included Ulysses S. Grant, to Washington Territory.

The planned celebration for this event was to be of a more sophisticated nature than the one in 1881. The town was cleaned and decorated, invitations were sent to nearby military forts and towns, an elaborate program of entertainment and speeches was to be held on a specially constructed stage at the new Echo Roller Mills, and every suitable carriage was on standby for guests to tour the town and the falls.

A crowd gathered early that Sunday morning, September 9, 1883, in eager anticipation. Five trains en route from New York were carrying German-born Henry Villard, NPRR's president since 1881, and an impressive entourage of noted dignitaries and capitalists from both the United States and Europe, an estimated 300 people. The American excursionists were due to arrive about 8:00 a.m., and were to be entertained by the townspeople until the arrival of Villard and his foreign guests.

Sadly, the first train did not arrive until 7:00 p.m. Villard's train was close behind, but only stopped long enough for him to make a quick apology. About the only reward for the elaborate, but futile, plans was the half hour General Grant spent greeting the crowd. However, what mattered most was the exhilarating realization that Spokane Falls was finally connected by rail to the outside world.

The effect of the mines on early Spokane

The population of Spokane Falls took a sudden jump when, in the fall of 1883, news of gold discovered in the Coeur d'Alene Mountains of northern Idaho reached the press. Although there were earlier mineral discoveries, including some scattered gold, in what are now Stevens and Pend Oreille counties, this isolated and rugged area attracted a limited number of prospectors.

Announcement of this new discovery coincided with the completion of the Northern Pacific's cross-country line, which suddenly provided easier access to the Northwest. The railroad capitalized on this news to promote the use of its line, and promote it did! Handbills played up the gold discovery with great exaggeration, and word spread quickly. With easier access made possible by the railroad, thousands flocked, many in the dead of winter, to the region of Eagle and Prichard creeks, some 30 miles northeast of the city of Coeur d'Alene. Numerous hastily built towns grew up nearly overnight, the first of which, and also the most prominent for the first few months, was Eagle City. (Today, no trace of that community remains. The only surviving gold-rush town of the region is Murray.)

The hordes of prospectors heading to the gold fields had to pack in all needed supplies as the area was completely uninhabited. Most secured their supplies from the nearest communities along the railroad. Together with regularly featured reports from the gold mines, the local newspapers pointedly promoted the route through Spokane Falls as the most direct and emphasized its importance as the premier outfitting location. The town was suddenly teeming with life as a major supply point and hub for the mining activity. Some fortune seekers were just passing through, while many others chose to seek refuge in the town to await the spring thaw. Because the Coeur d'Alene Mining District was devoid of any settlement prior to the gold rush, there were huge opportunities for merchants and those offering other services. Some made fortunes while others, discouraged in

The Paragon mining camp near Murray, Idaho, soon after the 1883 gold rush began. *(Courtesy Butch Jacobson)*

Daniel C. Corbin Channeled Wealth From the Coeur d'Alene Mining District to Spokane Falls

Daniel C. Corbin
(Jerome Peltier Collection)

Daniel C. Corbin headed west from his New Hampshire home at age 19 to pursue various financial and commercial interests, eventually including mining and railroad ventures. At the time of the great Bunker Hill and Sullivan discoveries in the Coeur d'Alene Mining District in 1885, he set his sights on that region. Along with a group of investors, he began making some monumental investments in the mining district, the first of which was constructing a concentrator mill for the Bunker Hill and Sullivan mines.

Corbin quickly recognized the need for a rail line to haul the ore from the mining district. Although John J. Browne and investors were already in the planning stages for a railroad from Spokane Falls, Corbin forged ahead with plans to run a line from Montana. As the result of some governmental technicalities, and by shrewdly cutting through restrictive red tape, Corbin gained the necessary permits to build into the district from the west instead, giving him a jump on Browne's contingent.

In the summer of 1886, Corbin, a vibrant man in his mid-50s, began supervising construction of two railroad lines. One connected the town of Coeur d'Alene with the Northern Pacific Railroad at Hauser Junction, and the other ran from the Cataldo Mission, the head of navigation on the Coeur d'Alene River to the mining district. These railroads, connected by a steamboat line, placed Spokane Falls in direct contact with the great Coeur d'Alene Mining District. This railroad was the first to connect the Coeur d'Alenes with the outside world and, fortunately for Spokane, the line ran west instead of east. By the late 1800s, the tremendous richness of the Coeur d'Alene district was being realized and soon earned its place as a world-class silver ore producer. As wealth flowed from the mines, a substantial portion of it was funneled into Spokane, financing many beautiful mansions and commercial buildings. The Coeur d'Alene mines quickly became the major player in the building of the Inland Northwest, especially the city of Spokane, where many of the key mining developers chose to live.

Building the railroad into the Coeur d'Alene Mining District heralded the fortuitous start of Corbin's lucrative career in railroad construction. In 1888, he sold his Coeur d'Alene line to the Northern Pacific and moved to Spokane Falls soon thereafter to supervise the construction of the Spokane Falls and Northern Railroad. He later built the Spokane International Railroad north through Idaho to Canada. Among other enterprises were a beet sugar factory south of Spokane at Waverly and an extensive irrigation system (which came to be known as the Corbin Ditch) stretching from Post Falls to the Spokane Valley. Daniel and his son, Austin, worked side by side on many of these enterprises. The senior Corbin was a rather stern, authoritarian businessman who played an enormous role in placing Spokane at the center of a network of railroad lines.

Corbin's first wife, Louisa, was in ill health when he came to Spokane. She subsequently sought treatment in Europe, where she died in 1900. In 1907, Corbin married his housekeeper, Anna Louise Larson. In addition to his son Austin, there were two daughters from his first marriage, Louise and Mary. For a short time, Mary was married to architect Kirtland K. Cutter, who designed his father-in-law's home on Seventh Avenue. Today that home, which is on the Spokane Register of Historic Places, is the Corbin Art Center. Daniel C. Corbin died on June 29, 1918. His ashes were eventually placed in the Peace Abbey Mausoleum at Fairmount Memorial Park.

their efforts, returned to Spokane in search of better opportunities. The demand for increased law enforcement was immediate, as the excitement of the gold rush not only attracted hard-working miners but also an unsavory element.

The gold rush played out quickly. By 1884, most readily accessible placer gold was exhausted, but the real wealth in the Coeur d'Alenes – silver, lead and zinc – was just being discovered. Between 1884 and 1886, almost every silver-lead ore deposit of importance in that region had been claimed. Each new mineral discovery brought large influxes of settlers and prospectors. It also attracted wealthy industrialists, as enormous amounts of capital were required to develop the mines and process the ore. Many of the newcomers intended to take their share of the wealth and move on, only to discover a newfound desire to settle in the beautiful Inland Northwest. A great number of them made Spokane their home, as well as corporate headquarters. The tremendous mineral wealth stimulated the expansion of the railroads and, thus, the development of the overall economy, which soon included the timber industry, agriculture, water-generated power, and other diverse industrialization.

As the railroad promoted sales of its properties, the U.S. government also seized every opportunity to distribute its land. The railroad sold land at a cheap rate, but the government not only matched that but also had free land to give away under the conditions of the Homestead Act. Homesteading in Washington began later than most other states, the majority following construction of railroads that connected Seattle and Spokane to the Midwest.

U.S. district land offices were conveniently situated and regularly advertised in the local newspapers. The U.S. Land Office located in Spokane Falls caused, as the *Walla Walla Union* reported in March 1884, "thousands of dollars to be expended there since last summer."

Everyone sold real estate

It wasn't long before the land investors or speculators who had purchased large tracts of government or railroad land, such as Glover, Browne, Cannon, Cowley, and Havermale, were platting and subdividing their properties and selling to the next wave of newcomers. Private land and real estate offices also placed ads, such as the following one that appeared in the *Spokan Times* on April 22, 1882:

> Land Office of J. T. Lockhart – Homestead, preemption and other filings made. Homestead and final preemption proof taken. Weekly corrected maps of the various townships; Special attention paid to special land cases before the local and general land offices, and buys and sells real estate on commission. Office over post office.

At this time, men who dealt in real estate did not call themselves realtors, and it was quite common for those with real estate for sale to open "investment offices" that also sold mining stocks and insurance or offered real estate loans. Although the above ad mentioned homestead and preemption claims, government land could only be purchased from official U.S. land offices. Lockhart may have been capitalizing on one of the many ways to make money on land deals, that of assisting others with the paperwork to file a claim. Because it was such a lucrative field, many who arrived in Spokane Falls with established trades or professions soon abandoned them in favor of dealing in real estate or land development.

The town's population simply exploded after the arrival of the railroad. In 1885, when the first Spokane Falls directory was published, it estimated the population at nearly 3,000. Two years later, it was estimated at 7,000, and the city was experiencing a major real estate boom, which was accompanied by inflationary housing prices. By May, there were 200 houses under construction. The following year, 600 new homes were built, and in July 1888, the *Morning Review* reported the city's population at 11,888 (a 60% increase over the previous 12-month period), of which 50 were "colored" and 213 were Chinese. The population reached a sufficient level to provide free mail delivery, precipitating a need for house numbers. An ordinance for numbering houses passed on February 24, 1888.

Northern Pacific Railroad Promotions

In 1883, the Northern Pacific Railroad published a guide book by Henry J. Winser titled *Guide to the Northern Pacific Railroad and Its Allied Lines*. It was prepared prior to the completion of the railroad and contained numerous inaccuracies. Consequently, in 1886, by the time many towns along the line of the road had developed, a corrected volume was published. The book covered a general history of the railroad and descriptions of the various geographical districts through which the line passed. Most important from the railroad's perspective was its value as a sales tool for the millions of acres of government lands they were granted through the Pacific Railway Act. There were still many inaccuracies in that volume, but it captures the flavor of the boisterous and exaggerated approach employed in the promotion of the railroad. The following excerpt – all geared to entice the reader to settle in Spokane Falls – is from the 1886 edition:

The Spokane Valley and Lake Coeur d'Alene. – One of the most singular districts of this country is the Spokane valley. It is thirty miles long, and three to six miles in width, surrounded by the western ranges of the lower Coeur d'Alene or Bitter Root Mountains. The Spokane river rises in Coeur d'Alene Lake, close under the timbered mountains, in Idaho, about ten miles south of the railroad. The lake extends south at least forty miles, and has long arms reaching in among the mountains. A rich agricultural region lies close to it on the west, in great part contained in the Coeur d'Alene Indian reservation....

The rivers that drain the western water-shed of the Coeur d'Alene Mountains pour immense volumes into the lake; but the Spokane river, the lake's only outlet, is comparatively small in size, with no tributaries of importance. Still, thirty miles below the lake, this stream becomes a roaring cataract at the town of Spokane Falls....

In spite of the gravelly character of the entire plain, there are many large patches and strips where a rich soil has been deposited. This is especially true of the upper end of the valley, and the people near Rathdrum are raising good vegetables and other crops. The railroad runs diagonally through this strange section, and soon reaches the fertile, well-wooded and well-watered region of the Palouse and upper Columbia ...

Spokane Falls (1,537 miles from St. Paul; population, 4,000). – This is the first point of importance reached in Washington Territory. It has, in some remarkable respects, more claims to consideration than any other place east of the Cascades. Its situation – upon the gravelly plains just above where Hangman's creek joins the Spokane river – is very beautiful, looking out upon the hills, with the grand, roaring waterfall in its midst.... Enterprising men were early attracted to the place, not alone by its natural beauty, but also by the wonderful water-power, so easy to control, and so abundant in a country that has very few water privileges. It will never be necessary to pave the streets of this city, nor will its people be troubled with mud. Its thoroughfares are macadamized sufficiently by Nature.

The educational facilities of the town are remarkably good. It has a large public school building; the Spokane Methodist Episcopal College, which occupies a handsome building on the north bank of the river; a Roman Catholic college [Gonzaga], having a large new brick building ... and also a number of private schools. There are six churches: Episcopal, Congregational, Methodist, Baptist, Presbyterian and Catholic.

The milling and manufacturing establishments include three flouring mills, the largest of which has a building six stories high, with a capacity of 800 bushels per day; a saw mill, a sash, door and blind works, a planing mill, fence works, carriage works, and a bottling establishment. There are thirteen brick blocks in the town for stores and offices. The press is represented by one daily and two weekly newspapers. The river is crossed by three bridges. There are water-works, with the Holly system of supply from the Spokane river. Stages leave Spokane Falls for Fort Coeur d'Alene and the mines, for the Colville valley and mines, for the Little Dalles of the Columbia ...

The falls, seen when melting snows swell the flow and the banks are brimming with the hurrying flood, are a sight never to be forgotten. Basaltic islands divide the broad river, and the waters rush in swift rapids to meet these obstructions. A public bridge crosses from island to island. The width of the river is nearly half a mile. There are three great streams curving toward each other, and pouring their floods into a common basin. Reunited, the waters foam and toss for a few hundred yards in whirling rapids, and then make another plunge into the canyon beyond. Standing on the rocky ledge below the second water-fall, and looking up the stream, a fine view is obtained of the wonderful display of force.

A Little-Known Fact

The construction of the Northern Pacific Railroad led to the General Custer defeat in 1876. The Indians had become increasingly disruptive to the construction of the railroad being built through their territory without their consent. As a result, on June 22, 1876, General George Armstrong Custer was assigned to lead his cavalry out of the valley of the Yellowstone in southeastern Montana on a five-day trip to scout for Sioux. He was to meet up with generals Terry and Gibbon at the Little Bighorn River and report his findings. The army hoped to trap the Sioux between the various U.S. forces somewhere in the valley of the Rosebud River and eradicate them. During his career, Custer relished the glory and publicity of killing Indians. For a short while, he thought he was going to accomplish another of his massacres of the Indian people. Instead, he was killed, along with his entire company, at the Battle of the Little Big Horn.

General George A. Custer *(Courtesy Library of Congress)*

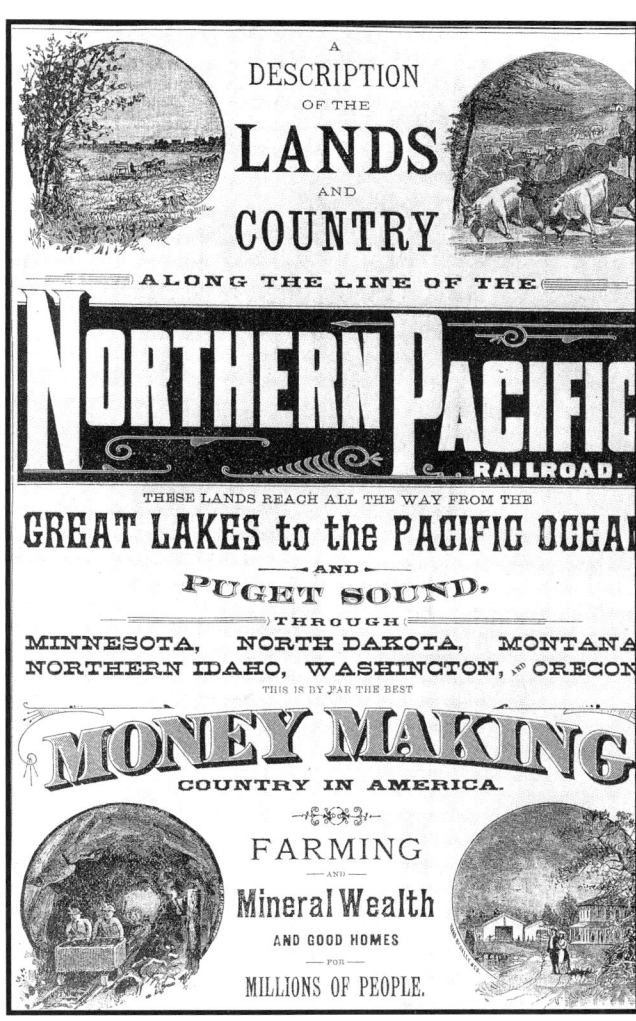

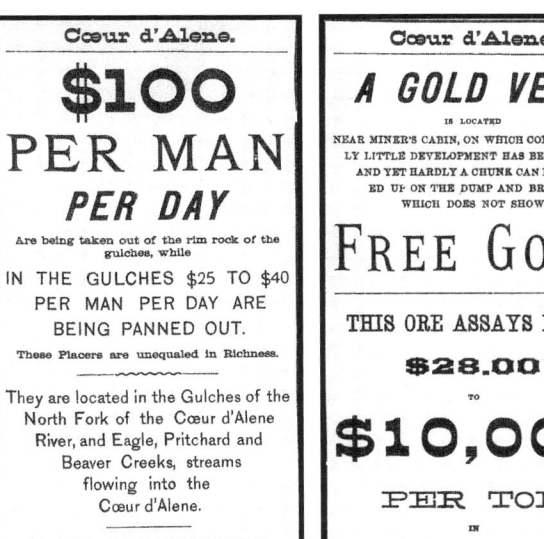

Samples of ads from the public relations department of the Northern Pacific Railroad. Unaware of the vast silver deposits, they only capitalized on the discovery of gold in the Coeur d'Alenes. The search for gold led to the subsequent silver discoveries.

The newspapers were filled with plentiful examples of how quickly land values escalated. On March 23, 1883, Cheney's *Northwest Tribune* printed a small article that stated:

> Spokane Falls is enjoying a real estate boom nearly equal to that of our own prosperous town.... Rev. Cowley lately sold fifty acres for $5,000, Geo. Brants sold one hundred acres for $5,000, Rev. Stratton [J. J. Browne's father-in-law] sold eighty acres adjoining town, in section 18, at $40.00 per acre....

If these lands were acquired through the Homestead Act, the land was free to the original owners. Through one of the other land acts, the per acre cost would have been around the $1.25 to $3.00 per acre range.

On August 11 1883, the *Morning Review* stated:

> If people living on the outside imagine that real estate in Spokane Falls is not worth hard money and plenty of it they are most woefully off the track. From the natural consequences of rapid and substantial growth, property has slowly and surely crept upward, and there is no telling how high it will reach as there is no abatement in the demand and no sign of weakening in prices. This week Ben Bravinder sold the lot upon which stands his livery stable at the southeastern corner of Main and Howard streets, without the building, for $11,000 to the First National Bank ... A couple of years ago it could have been purchased for a few hundred.

Even for those who bought and sold on a small scale, land was a tremendously profitable investment. On July 26, 1887, the *Morning Review* included this small article:

> A small lot 20x60 (twenty by sixty) feet, corner of Howard and Sprague streets, was sold in April, 1887, for $2,500, and a few weeks after for $2,750, and finally a few days ago for $3,700, each of these sales being made by our quiet, but enterprising real estate firm, Stroback & Munter. This shows a healthy and heavy increase in value of lots in our growing city.

Hazards of real estate booms

While many profited from the growth, others suffered at its hands. Indian title to non-reservation lands was extinguished in an agreement drawn up in 1886 and signed at Spokane Falls on March 18, 1887. The agreement was the result of demands by whites to force any non-treaty Indians onto reservations. In light of the unbridled development in and around Spokane Falls on Indian lands, extinguishing their rights was merely a formality. By this time, the resident Upper Spokanes were demoralized and degraded – expansive white settlement had encroached on their ancestral lands and their traditional means of survival.

Not only the Indians, but some of the white settlers of lesser influence, if they happened to cross swords with the wrong person in laying claim to the same piece of land, might find themselves in a dangerous position. One such case involved A. M. Cannon, an influential, respected civic leader who is considered one of Spokane's founding fathers.

According to one newspaper account, Cannon and another man both staked out property in what became Cannon's Addition. The other man allegedly staked his claim before Cannon, creating some animosity. Consequently, Cannon decided to handle the problem outside the law. One evening he invited a number of his friends and supporters to his home (at Fourth and Walnut) for a dinner party. During the course of the evening while the alcohol flowed, Cannon convinced many of the guests in attendance that he was being wronged. As a result, several men armed themselves and made their way to the cabin of Cannon's adversary. Yelling threats and firing weapons next to the cabin persuaded Cannon's opposition to leave the area that evening. He was never heard from again.

Another more extreme incident, which became known as the "Shantytown War," occurred in 1890. Spokane Falls was still in the heat of the boom following the railroad's arrival, but this incident was exacerbated by the loss of so many businesses and residences during the Great Fire of 1889. In April 1890, the demand for real estate fueled a frenzied and violent land rush to a valuable tract of land lying to the south of Sprague and west of Division that was at the center of a legal dispute between Rev. Cowley and the Northern Pacific Railroad. In 1876, when Cowley contracted to buy the land from the railroad, it wasn't worth much because of the distance from the tiny

Looking southeast at the budding town of Spokane Falls, circa 1886. *(Patsy Clark album, courtesy Mark Danner)*

Spokane Falls town site and the overabundance of land for sale. However, as its value had greatly increased, the Northern Pacific tried to find a way, albeit illegally, to reclaim it and, in fact, before the lawsuit was settled in 1898, it had sold lots on which some upscale homes were built.

As ensuing court actions dragged on, land-hungry citizens watched eagerly for the outcome. Following a rumor the land might revert to public domain and that squatters' rights could be established simply by taking possession, a rush to the area took place on April 16, 1890. Hundreds of shanties were hastily constructed that day, including many by citizens who had legally purchased lots from the Northern Pacific and wanted to be "on the safe side." In the frenzy, among the lots jumped were some owned by the Catholic and Congregational churches. The land rush and resulting violence was short-lived. The day after the frantic claim jumping, a group of bona fide owners rallied in force and demolished a large number of the shanties. Sheriff's deputies and special policemen stood guard to preserve law and order, and a number of claim jumpers were arrested.

At its peak, this Shantytown (not to be confused with the one along the north riverbank west of the Monroe Street Bridge) had about 400 flimsy shacks with hundreds of squatters living in filthy, unsanitary conditions. By the time the nearly two-decade battle between the Northern Pacific and Mr. Cowley was finally settled in Cowley's favor in 1898, Shantytown had long-since been replaced with homes and businesses. By that time, according to one estimate, the land was worth about a million dollars. Cowley received a $25,000 cash settlement from the Northern Pacific. The railroad was only allowed to keep the right-of-way. According to the *Spokesman-Review's* assessment of the lawsuit on February 28, 1898, the railroad had tried a bullying tactic on Cowley, but picked the wrong man of whom to make an example. Although the railroads were extremely powerful and formidable forces at the time, Cowley stood firm on his conviction that he was in the right.

The need for infrastructure

Accompanying the population explosion was a corresponding explosion in the development of Spokane's infrastructure. Following the events of 1883, so much happened at once that construction of the most recent commercial building, no matter how grand or costly, was hardly newsworthy. Consequently, the narrative following the sidebars on J. J. Browne and A. M. Cannon summarizes the developments by category instead of by year. Although there were too many "firsts" during the 1880s to cover in detail, a reasonable portrait is presented of how Spokane grew and developed during this period, and what it lost in its Great Fire.

John J. Browne and Anthony M. Cannon
Fortunes from Spokane Real Estate

John J. Browne, 35, and Anthony M. Cannon, 41, arrived in Spokane Falls on April 24, 1878. Both were living in Portland, Oregon, at the time. Having heard some news about the "upper country," and ripe for new opportunities, they decided to check out Spokane Falls, then a town of only 54.

It was evident there were potential fortunes to be made by the first land developers to the area. The railroad was again under construction and heading toward Spokane, and there were vast amounts of cheap government land available surrounding James Glover's property. They also quickly learned that Glover was willing to sell some of his property. Within two days, the two men had negotiated an arrangement with Glover to purchase half of his remaining town site (which excluded the land he had given to Frederick Post or had already built on) for $3,200 (this amount was according to Glover, but other accounts vary on the purchase price). They pooled the money they had with them, gave Glover $50 as a down payment, with a contractual arrangement for the balance, and returned to Portland for their families. This was the start of a partnership in many endeavors. Almost no aspect of Spokane's early development was left untouched by them, either jointly or separately.

Browne, an attorney by trade, opened the first law office, and Cannon, the first bank. Browne later founded the Browne National Bank, as well as banks in other Washington towns. Cannon also expanded his banking involvement. He founded the Bank of Palouse City, and constructed the Marble Bank at Riverside and Wall. Construction of the Marble Bank began in 1892, but Cannon's Bank of Spokane Falls failed in the Panic of 1893 before he had the chance to move into the new building.

In the fall of 1878, Cannon and his brother-in-law, Alexander Warner, purchased Glover's store. The following year, despite the lack of any capital with which to do so, he opened the Bank of Spokane Falls in the store. In 1880 or 1881, Cannon purchased Glover's sawmill, along with a partner (or partners, which changed over time as the sawmill grew and was reorganized).

Cannon and Browne continued to expand their real estate holdings, eventually gaining possession of the Middle Falls (now the Upper Falls) and a half ownership in the Lower Falls; in other words, a large percentage of the waterpower of the river. They eventually sold their property embracing the Lower Falls and their waterpower rights to the new Edison Electric Illuminating Company (later absorbed into the Washington Water Power Company).

Each established 160-acre preemption claims west and south of Glover's land. Browne's land adjoined Glover's on the east and roughly covered the triangle formed by the river and Hangman Creek, and Cannon's was on Spokane's lower South Hill. By 1883, they had platted and were selling lots in their respective Cannon's Addition and Browne's Addition. From their adjacent claims, they set aside a four-block section for Spokane's first city park, Coeur d'Alene Park. According to Barbara Cochran in *Seven Frontier Women and the Founding of Spokane Falls*, by 1890, Browne "was reported to be the largest property owner in town with an assessed value of $1,200,000 – three times what Cannon's property was worth."

On June 29, 1881, Browne and Cannon, along with James Glover, founded Spokane's second newspaper, the *Spokane Falls Chronicle*. This weekly paper was founded largely in opposition to Francis Cook and his *Spokan Times*. They only held it a year, but Browne bought it back in 1890.

Browne, as one of the founders in 1886, and later Cannon were involved with the Spokane Street Railway Company, Spokane's first street railway, which began with a horse-drawn trolley running from the center of town to Browne's Addition. In 1886, when the Spokane and Palouse Railway, Spokane's first branch rail line, was built in 1886, Cannon became its president.

Both men were also involved in civic matters as well. In 1885, Cannon was elected mayor of Spokane Falls, serving for two years. In 1888, he founded Greenwood Cemetery. Browne's legal skills were applied in drawing up the bill that organized Spokane County in 1879, and a decade later, he assisted in writing the state constitution prior to the formation of Washington State in 1889. Browne was also a huge proponent of education, and was involved in a number of capacities (see sidebar on the Brownes).

Prior to Spokane's devastating fire of 1889, Cannon and Browne had begun construction of the Auditorium Building, which would house Spokane Falls's premier opera house. Because Little Wolf Ditch stood between it and the raging fire, it was one of the few downtown buildings that did not burn, and it was completed the following year.

In 1892, the *New York Tribune* published a list of America's millionaires and the lines of businesses in which their fortunes were made. Six men were listed in Spokane Falls, two of whom were Cannon and Browne. The list gave credit to real estate and banking, and also railroads in Cannon's case. However, the Panic of 1893, during which many of Spokane's wealthy lost their entire fortunes and were left without resources, changed that status. The Brownes were hard hit, but Cannon's financial base completely collapsed. Overextended fiscally and mortgaged to the hilt, the Northwestern and Pacific Hypotheekbank (a Dutch mortgage company) foreclosed on about 60 prime residential lots and purchased the properties, his last remaining assets in the city, at a sheriff's sale. Within a decade, Browne had made a remarkable financial recovery, but Cannon's fate was not so fortunate. In an attempt to revive his lost fortune, Cannon sailed for South America to look into possible mining and railroad investments. During the return trip home, he was found dead in his New York hotel room on April 6, 1895, alone and bankrupt.

The red brick Auditorium Building and Theater, located at the northwest corner of Main and Post, was in existence from 1890 to 1934. The building was designed by Herman Preusse, and financed by owners Anthony Cannon and John Browne. With the theater's seating capacity of 1,750, all important city functions and events were held there during its time. Desiring a showplace to surpass all others, Browne and Cannon requested the stage be 61 feet wide and 46 feet deep, allegedly making it the largest stage west of the Mississippi River at the time. The building also had apartments and office space for rent. *(Jerome Peltier collection)*

The Personal Life of Real Estate Developer J. J. Browne

John J. Browne, circa 1874, and Anna W. (Stratton) Browne, circa 1895. *(MAC L85-45 and L87-99)*

John J. Browne, affectionately known as J. J., was born April 28, 1843, in Greenville, Stark County, Ohio. His first career was teaching, which began as a high-school teacher in Columbia City, Indiana, where he was raised. Although he found genuine satisfaction in that vocation, he felt there was more opportunity in the practice of law, and attended law school at the University of Michigan in Ann Arbor, where he graduated in 1868. He practiced law for a year in Columbia City and afterward for four years in Oswego, Kansas. While there, he also served for a time as Oswego superintendent of schools. In 1874, he married Anna W. Stratton, nearly 13 years his junior. Soon thereafter, they departed for Portland, Oregon, where J. J. again practiced law and served, first by appointment and later by election, as superintendent of the schools of Multnomah County.

During his first seven years in Spokane, J. J. continued practicing law, but because the population of the area was so slight, it was often necessary to travel, as court was variously held in the towns of Colfax, Colville, and Walla Walla. After about seven years, he closed his law office and devoted his full attention to his real estate developments and other business enterprises, including a number of investment firms, that were far more lucrative than his law practice. Despite his many career demands, J. J. still devoted time to serving the furtherance of education. When Spokane County was formed, he became its first county superintendent. He was appointed to the Board of Regents for the University of Washington and elected president. He was also a regent for the State Normal School at Cheney (now Eastern Washington University) and, later, for Washington State University, where he also was board president and vice president.

J. J. and Anna Browne moved to Spokane Falls in July 1878 with their eleven-month-old son, Guy. After spending the winter with the Frederick Post family, they built a small home at 1717 West Pacific, in what became Browne's Addition. It was a small four-room box structure with rough-board walls and floor. As each new baby arrived, they added on to the house. Finally, in 1886, with the birth of their sixth child (they had seven altogether, five of whom lived to adulthood), they began construction on a new home. It was located on First Avenue about half a block from Hemlock. The original estimate of $20,000 nearly doubled before the house was completed in 1888. At the time, it was claimed to be the finest residence between Helena, Montana, and the Cascade Mountains. They lived in the home until 1902, when they purchased a large farm on Moran Prairie, where they built another palatial home. By this time, Browne's Addition had become too crowded for their tastes.

Mr. Browne died March 25, 1912, a month before his 69th birthday. Despite being an attorney, and suffering from ill health, he left no will. Although financially solvent on paper, showing a net worth of nearly half a million dollars, much of the assets were invested in banks that were not doing very well. In order to keep the home on Moran Prairie and satisfy others' claims, Anna began trading or selling land, including 415 acres of the Moran Prairie farm.

In 1927, Anna Browne married Edward G. Taber, a well-known railroad engineer. She died September 2, 1936, at age 81.

The Browne Block (as commercial buildings were called in those days), one of Spokane's earliest brick buildings, was built in 1883 by J. J. Browne at Riverside and Post. It was primarily a real estate office until Browne opened a bank there in 1889. This building was destroyed in the 1889 fire. *(Maxwell photo, MAC L89-121)*

Looking southeast at the Brownes' farm at the base of Browne's Mountain on Moran Prairie in 1892. The Brownes purchased this property from Joseph Moran's family after he was killed by a bull. Moran had originally acquired it from Stephen E. Liberty, for whom Liberty Lake was named. Liberty had planted a large orchard there. *(Sketch from the* Northwest Magazine *June 1892)*

The Personal Life of Real Estate Developer A. M. Cannon

Anthony M. Cannon, circa 1890, and Jennie F. (Pease) Cannon, circa 1892. *("Spokane Falls and Its Exposition" and MAC L87-100)*

Anthony McCue Cannon was born in May 1837 and raised on a farm in Monmouth, Illinois. After a number of business ventures in various locales, some of which centered around prospecting for gold, by 1874, he ended up in Portland, Oregon. Sometime after moving there, he and his first wife, Julia Rupp, divorced. They had two children.

In Portland, Cannon went to work selling sewing machines for the Howe Sewing Machine Company. At the same time, Jennie (Pease) Clarke, who had become a widow in 1871, taught sewing classes for the Howe Company to support her five young children. By coincidence, they both lived in the Centennial Block. In July 1878, three months after Cannon and Browne had purchased half the Spokane Falls town site, Anthony and 38-year old Jennie were married. Cannon interested Jennie's sister Maria and her husband, Alexander "Jack" Warner, in a partnership in Glover's general merchandise store, put together the inventory to stock the store, and sent the Warner family on ahead to Spokane Falls. The Cannons followed several weeks later. During those early years, various other family members on both sides joined the Cannons in Spokane Falls, some stayed, others lasted only a brief time. A. M.'s brother Aniel R. Cannon acquired land on the north side, which became Cannondale's Addition.

The Warners and Cannons took up residence in the two box-houses previously occupied by Glovers, Yeatons, and Glover's store. After living there for two years, Cannon built a small home for the family near Fourth and Walnut on his preemption claim. In 1883, he commissioned Herman Preusse to design their mansion (shown opposite page), which appears to have been the first mansion in Spokane Falls.

Both A. M. and Jennie were very active in the community. There was no business enterprise A. M. was unwilling to tackle, no matter how slim the odds for success seemed. Jennie was the consummate hostess, and the person many came to if they needed help on any committee or to nurse the sick. Unfortunately, her own health began to fail in the early 1890s, and the same year Cannon lost his wealth in the Panic of 1893, Jennie passed away. Four months after her death, Cannon shocked friends and family when he married a divorcee with three small children. Jennie was very beloved in Spokane, and many old acquaintances ostracized him as the result of his hasty marriage. But he was not in good health either and died two years later.

Cannon's sawmill (the small building at the far right), formerly owned by Scranton and Downing, then Glover. This image is a detailed enlargement from a photo of Spokane Falls, circa 1886, shown on page 43. *(Patsy Clark album, courtesy Mark Danner)*

A. M. Cannon home designed by Herman Preusse and built in 1883, occupied the block bounded by Third and Fourth streets and Walnut and Cedar avenues. *(From* Spokane Falls and Its Exposition*)*

Cannon's Marble Bank, circa 1905, adjacent to the Crescent store, at the northwest corner of Riverside Avenue and Wall Street. *(From* Vintage Postcards From Old Spokane *by Duane Broyles and Howard Ness)*

Chapter Two

~ Development of the Basic Utilities ~

On the night of January 19, 1883, the residents of Spokane Falls became painfully aware of the need for a water system and a fire department. A fire along the south side of Front Street destroyed F. R. Moore & Co.'s store, Charlie Carson's restaurant, Forrest's grocery, a drug store, doctor's office, and the post office. Rima's jewelry store, in the path of the fire, was torn down to stop its advance.

Following the fire, building with brick reached a new level of importance, and the next year a volunteer hose company formed. In addition, a local company developed a Holly water system located in Samuel Havermale and George Davis's new Echo Mills on Glover Island (eventually part of Havermale Island after the channel separating the two was filled in). The company ran out of funds and an association of 30 men formed to finance its completion. The city granted a waterworks franchise but reserved the right to purchase it once completed. This right was exercised in 1885 through the issuance of the first municipal revenue bond, authorized by a city election in April of that year, and the system became the Spokane City Water Works. Prior to its construction, a newspaper reported that "in the heart of the city there is but one well [at Howard and Main], and the business houses and private residences are compelled to rely on a water carrier for the liquid necessity." (The well was filled in the year after the new waterworks was built.) Obvious satisfaction regarding the new waterworks was expressed in the *Spokane Evening Chronicle* on August 1, 1885:

> The vast water power at the falls is used to force it to the highest point in the city. Hydrants are placed at every street corner, and in case of fire the hose is attached and a stream strong enough to cut a horse in pieces is turned on the flames; the water is taken to every house and everyone can use just as much as he pleases. Since it came into use there is already a great difference in the appearance of the residences; where of old "'twas all barren," are now pretty flower gardens, trees growing, all imparting a refined and more home-like look to the place.

A larger municipal waterworks facility, built in 1888 on Crystal (now Canada) Island, was in operation until the third one was completed in 1896 at the present site of Upriver Dam (sources vary on the date of completion, but the March 7, 1896, issue of the *Spokesman-Review* stated: "Now that

This scene of the Upper Falls (then called the Middle Falls) shows Spokane Electric Light and Water Power Company's plant in the foreground and the waterwork's pumping station on Crystal (now Canada) Island, in the early 1890s. *(Libby Studio photo, MAC L86-1093)*

the new waterworks are finished and the old station ... is to be abandoned."). Philip Buehner supervised construction of all three of the first waterworks plants.

Sanitation an issue

During construction of the Upriver facility, an inordinate amount of water was encountered. Unbeknownst at the time, the great Spokane Valley-Rathdrum Aquifer had been tapped into, but it wasn't until 1907 that this huge source of pristine water was identified as such. An extensive official report of a river-water analysis printed in the November 24, 1888, issue of the *Morning Review* claimed: "River Water is Good, Well Water Bad and Unsafe." Unfortunately, as industries developed along the river and the population increased, the Spokane River and its tributaries became the main disposal channel for garbage and waste from developing sanitation systems. In an article titled "Doctors on Horseback: The Practice of Medicine in Washington Territory" in the fall 1989 *Medical Bulletin,* Norman Bolker, M.D., wrote: "Typhoid fever was endemic in Spokan Falls until the villagers stopped taking water directly from the river and began drawing it from wells tapping the aquifer." There were typhoid outbreaks about twice a year during Spokane's early days.

By 1887, according to Spokane County Health District records, major health problems were generally associated with a gross lack of sanitation. The city began installing the first sewer mains that year, channeling sewage directly into the river. The following year, city officials became concerned about garbage piling up in streets, alleys, and yards after the city garbage platform below the falls had been carried away by high water the previous year. Dr. A. S. Campbell, the city health officer, recommended a system of "cremating garbage" instead of dumping it and sewer waste directly into the river. (It finally happened in 1904.)

At this time, the health officer's primary duties were to survey the community for environmental problems, issue public health orders and provide smallpox immunizations. If the health officer issued an order that was not followed, the chief of police, who also had the "sanitary policeman" responsibility, would enforce the order. Because contagious disease was a primary cause of death in the early years, physicians were required to report any known cases to the local health officer within 12 hours. The chief of police collected weekly reports from each physician.

Developing the waterpower

The mighty waterpower potential of the Spokane Falls was evident from the beginning, but George A. Fitch was the first to tap its power to light the town. On September 2, 1885, Fitch was granted the first city permit to develop electric power. The original Scranton and Downing sawmill, by this time Spokane Falls Lumber & Mfg. Co. (owned by Cannon and partners), and other smaller ones, as well as the flour mills (the Echo and the C and C), were already using the waterpower to run their operations when Fitch powered up his generator in the Echo Mills. A string of about 10 arc lights (sources vary on the number) throughout the little business section and the one at the north end of the Post Street Bridge presented a curious sight to the Indians who lived in and around the town.

The following year (1886), a group of local businessmen bought out Fitch and organized the Spokane Electric Light and Water Power Company. The company began developing a power plant – a crude system of heavy timbers and rough-cut planks – on the north river channel in a bay (since filled in) near the Post Street Bridge. Through a subsequent reorganization, the Edison Electric

Another view of the Spokane Electric Light and Water Power plant. The Centennial Flour Mill, at the upper left, was built in 1888. *(Courtesy SPLNWR)*

This clipping from the July 8, 1910, *Spokesman-Review* shows the Howard Street Bridge with a large pile of garbage directly below, a common site when the river was low. At the time, many of Spokane's bridges had trapdoors for disposing of rubbish into the river.

Even as recent as the 1960s, it was quite common for sewage from towns and cities to be piped directly into the river. In the March 18, 1902, *Spokesman-Review* a front-page article read "City Must Stop Quick, Notice Served That It Must Not Throw Refuse Into the Spokane River After the Middle of June." This article went on to say:

> This city and Post Falls, Idaho, have destroyed one of the most beautiful streams in America. I consider this stream, if it had not been so badly abused, would have been worth $10,000 alone to the city as a sort of resort. They have been dumping sawdust and refuse at Post Falls until the eddies along the stream are perpetually filled with it, which gives a bad taste to the water in the summer and makes it smell bad. By dumping so much sawdust they have nearly destroyed all the spawning bars of the river between Post Falls and Spokane Falls.... and nearly ruined the river so far as fish are concerned.... Now below the city the river is just as handsome and just as important to the city as it is above, and yet along the bank, when the weather gets warm or the water is low, it is almost impossible to travel because of the stench.

The headline in the November 26, 1906, *Coeur d'Alene Press* read: "Can Dump Sewage in River, That Is Opinion of Spokane City Attorney." The city attorney referring to Coeur d'Alene's sewage that would be carried downstream to Spokane was James M. Geraghty.

Illuminating Company emerged, which, during the winter of 1887-1888, began construction on a new plant with four times the capacity of the previous one. It was located at the rear of the C and C Flour Mill in order to utilize the water from the mill operation. With the increased capacity, residential lines were strung into Cannon's and Browne's additions. William Pettet was the company president and William S. "Billy" Norman the general manager. (Norman played an instrumental role in the future development of waterpower and the Inland Northwest telephone system. He was also the owner, along with his brother Ben, of a successful chain of hotels, which included the Hotel Spokane.) The Spokane Falls Gas Light Company, which incorporated in 1887, also built a plant that offered another source of lighting.

Even as the new Edison plant was completed, it was evident that it would not equal the demand for electricity. Developing industries, streetcar lines, and residents were all becoming eager consumers. This demand gave rise to a new company, Washington Water Power (WWP, now Avista Utilities), headed up by F. Rockwood Moore and incorporated on March 13, 1889. WWP purchased the Lower Falls and property on both sides of the river, including that owned by A. M. Cannon and J. J. Browne, and built a power plant, completed in 1890, at the base of Monroe Street for Edison Electric's use. WWP soon dominated the waterpower industry throughout the Inland Northwest and beyond. A number of the esteemed, wealthy investors who signed the original articles of incorporation, including Pettet and Norman, were also investors in Edison Electric. The two companies worked closely together until 1891, when WWP bought out Edison Electric and began to systematically build new dams and absorb its competitors along the Spokane River.

~ Public Transportation – the Key to Developing Real Estate ~

Ferries and bridges

Prior to the settlement at Spokane Falls, crossing the Spokane River was possible by way of a few ferries or bridges some distance away, the nearest being about 18 miles upriver at Spokane Bridge and about equal distance downriver at LaPray's Bridge. However, none of the options were convenient for those living near the Spokane Falls. Because the falls created a treacherous flow, there were only a few attempts made to operate a ferry in the vicinity, but some at least tried.

Sometime before Scranton and Downing arrived, a man by the name of Joseph Payne was alleged to have operated a ferry in the area between the present sites of the Division Street Bridge and Gonzaga University. The source of this information came from an article published in the *Spokane Daily Chronicle* on June 10, 1972, following an interview with Rowland Bond, author of *Early Birds in the Northwest*. Bond had apparently come by his information from a statement prepared in 1930 by Alexander McLeod, who was born at the Hudson's Bay Company's Fort Colvile in 1854.

According to McLeod, Payne had the ferry as early as 1868, likely in response to the foot traffic of prospectors in search of gold after it was discovered in the upper reaches of Northeastern Washington. He said that Payne had "a crude hut and a couple of tents on the north side of the river where he lived with his wife and small child – a boy." In his *Reminiscences,* Glover stated that, after his arrival in May 1873, he crossed the river in a makeshift skiff, a pine log about 10 to 12 feet long that was hollowed enough for two people to ride in if they sat very still. It was located near the present Division Street Bridge. Quite possibly this was Payne's "ferry." About 1879, Robert W. Forrest, who became Spokane's first mayor, also operated a "ferry" (another man-powered boat) around the same location until the first bridge was built at Spokane Falls.

The pressing need for a bridge was met in 1881 with the construction of three spans that zigzagged across the islands, connecting the nucleus of the town at Howard Street to the north bank at Washington Street. An additional bridge was built at Post Street in 1883. They were financed by the

The first Post Street Bridge, built in 1883, and the lower Spokane Falls in the late 1880s. In 1885, F. Lewis Clark and Frank Curtis purchased the old Post flour mill on the south bank of the river and incorporated it into their new, much larger C and C Flour Mill, shown at right. Below it is the Edison Electric Illuminating Company plant. *(Courtesy SPLNWR)*

local residents. Early bridge construction was not what it is today and, as a result, a law was put into effect following the construction of the first bridges that levied a $5 fine for crossing at a speed faster than a walk! By the end of the decade, three other bridges had been built at present-day crossings from downtown to the north side: Division Street in 1888, Monroe Street in 1889, and Washington Street (south channel) in 1889. All were initially wooden bridges and have since been replaced by steel and/or concrete construction.

Trolleys and streetcars

With the successive waves of immigration, the demand for real estate in and around Spokane necessitated the need for public transportation to the outlying developments in the process of being platted into building lots. By 1883, stagecoaches, the principal means of transportation, were running in all directions, connecting Spokane Falls to Fort Spokane, Colville, the Coeur d'Alenes, the Big Bend Country and the Palouse. But when land developers first began platting additions to the city, the only modes of transportation available within the city, aside from walking, were by horseback or horse-drawn carriage. Developers realized early on that providing streetcar transportation to building lots was a significant enticement, as was the presence of a nearby park. Browne and Cannon were the first to incorporate the idea of a park in the midst of their developing residential neighborhoods. They set aside a four-block section straddling their adjacent additions for Coeur d'Alene Park, and offered it to the city on the condition it would develop the site. (Official title passed to the city in 1891.)

Three women and a horse-drawn surrey. *(From the Don Neraas collection)*

Spokane's first streetcar line, the Spokane Street Railway Company, was incorporated on December 17, 1886, by Henry C. Marshall, Andrew J. Ross, and J. J. Browne. (Cannon and Browne became the sole owners in 1889, but sold their stock soon thereafter.) On April 15, 1888, two fine horses made their appearance, pulling a trolley along the tracks laid from downtown Division Street out First Avenue to Browne's Addition. It looped around Coeur d'Alene Park before returning to town. The void filled by the first streetcar line was evident by a statement from the superintendent of the Spokane Street Railway Company, printed in the *Spokane Falls Review* on November 18, 1888, just seven months after beginning operation: "We have carried on an average of 12,000 passengers a month up to date."

By the time the horse-drawn trolley began operating, another streetcar line was under construction. The other line, the Spokane & Montrose Motor Railroad, was powered by a wood-burning steam engine, making it Spokane's first motorized streetcar. It was a new concept at the time.

The Spokane Falls City Council granted the franchise authorizing construction of this motor line on December 20, 1887. It was given to Francis Cook (the initiator and president of the line and founder of the *Spokan Times*), T. J. Dooley, Horatio Belt, and E. A. Routhe for a period of 30 years. Cook intended to develop a residential neighborhood on the plateau south of town, called Spokane Heights (today's South Hill), where he owned land (eventually nearly 700 acres). It would be connected to town by the new motor line (see page 58).

With a $25,000 loan made by the Provident Trust Company, construction began in the spring of 1888. Its inaugural trip on November 16, 1888, ran from downtown to an area of his planned neighborhood not well suited for building lots but ideal for a park. He called this park Montrose, which evolved into today's Manito Park.

The Spokane & Montrose looked more like a train than the current concept of a streetcar. Traveling on a narrow-gauge track, the nine-ton square-

PAID FIRST FARE ON LOCAL STREET CAR

George K. Stocker, Prominent Realty Dealer, Had Initial Ride on Old Horse System.

PAY-AS-YOU-ENTER PLAN

The above caption was accompanied by the following narrative in the Sunday, June 12, 1910, *Spokesman-Review*:

Workman Pulled Car For Length of Few Rails Around Lincoln and Sprague Curve.

While in the last few years the local real estate men, especially those handling new additions, have been the leading factors in securing additional streetcar lines and improved car service, back as far as in 1888, when the first horse or mule car was put into operation in Spokane, it remained for a real estate man to be the first to pay fare on the public service property. That real estate man was George K. Stocker, one of the pioneers of Spokane, who was in the real estate business in Spokane then as a member of the firm known as Tilton and Stocker.

It was in March, 1888. A. J. Ross was the president of the streetcar company, and the track was being laid ... towards Browne's addition. Mr. Ross himself was superintending the construction work and four or five rails had been laid and spiked down when Mr. Stocker happened along. That part of the city then was little better than a wilderness, and when Mr. Stocker saw that the work was progressing and that within a few hours the experimental car would be started, he had a consultation with the workmen and insisted that he be allowed to pay the first fare and have the first ride on the new spur.

The pay-as-you-enter system was then in vogue, and Mr. Stocker boarded the car, dropped his nickel in the slot, and four or five of the workmen grabbed hold of the car and by pushing and pulling rode Mr. Stocker the length of several rails, and the first fare had been donated to the company for a ride of less than 10 yards.

This little episode was recalled by Mr. Stocker a few days ago in remarking about the building development on the North Side during the last few years. ... Mr. Stocker recalled that it was he, in conjunction with the firm of Tilton, Stocker & Fry, about that time, built the first store building on the North Side. The store building, a frame structure, was on the southwest corner of Mallon avenue and Monroe street.

This photo of Spokane's first trolley line, the Spokane Street Railway, which connected Browne's Addition to downtown Spokane, was taken at the time of the streetcar's first trip, April 15, 1888. Bill Shannon was the driver and John Simonson the conductor. *(Jerome Peltier collection)*

Spokane & Montrose Motor Railroad, circa 1889, on Washington Street, just south of Spokane's first viaduct, which provided passage under the Northern Pacific Railroad tracks. When the line began operations in 1888, the viaduct was not yet completed, so early trips began near this point. *(E. E. Bertrand photo, MAC L86-1040)*

The first Monroe Street Bridge, which opened in 1889 and burned in 1890. *("Spokane and the Inland Empire")*

shaped engine burned wood to get up a head of steam. Going downhill to town, the locomotive led, but on the return uphill trip the engine had to push the passenger coaches. The line had two cars, each designed to carry twenty passengers.

Following quickly on the heels of the first two lines, which were making their way into developing upscale neighborhoods, were the cable and electric lines reaching out in every other direction to areas slated for development. Because of its intended route, the Spokane Cable Railway, incorporated in 1888 by a group that included a number of the large shareholders in Washington Water Power, was the prime mover in the construction of the first Monroe Street Bridge. Private subscriptions and the City of Spokane Falls also contributed financially.

The line was completed and cars began running on both sides of the river after the Monroe Street Bridge opened in 1889. One route went south on Monroe to Fourteenth and another crossed the river, heading west on Boone. Its destination was the new Twickenham Addition (owned by Washington Water Power) and the future Fort Wright grounds. (Twickenham Park, later renamed Natatorium, became an added attraction by 1892.) After the bridge burned the following year, the company had to resort to having horses pull the cars across the Post Street Bridge.

The Ross Park streetcar line, with G. B. Dennis as president, was the first in Spokane to use electricity. It started running in mid-November 1889, giving Spokane Falls its fourth streetcar line since April 1888. It was a first-class operation. Thirty-foot power poles had been installed at 100-foot intervals in the center of Main Street to support the trolley lines between double tracks. Because of the gilt balls on top of the center poles, the Ross Park line was dubbed the "gold plate" line. The cars, built by the Pullman Company, were heated by a small coke-burning stove and contained red plush seats running the length of each car.

The route began at Post Street and ran east on Main, then Front until it reached its own wooden bridge across the river into the Dennis and Bradley's Addition. From there it headed north, then east into the Ross Park Addition.

Ross Park Railway streetcar. *(Jerome Peltier collection)*

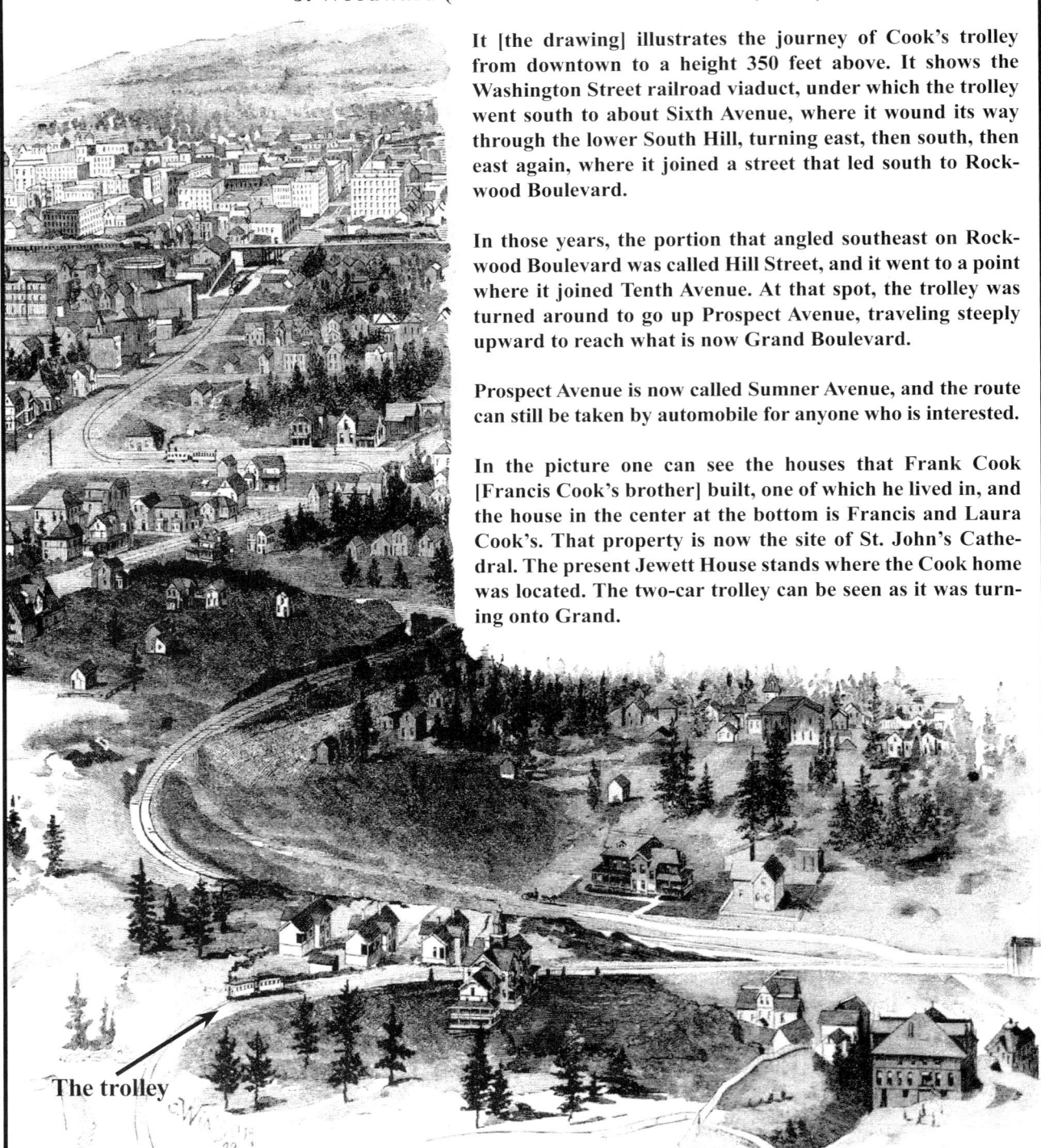

The following narrative describing the route of the Spokane & Montrose Motor Railroad line in reference to this drawing is from *The Indomitable Francis H. Cook of Spokane: A Man of Vision* by Doris J. Woodward (Tornado Creek Publications, 2011):

It [the drawing] illustrates the journey of Cook's trolley from downtown to a height 350 feet above. It shows the Washington Street railroad viaduct, under which the trolley went south to about Sixth Avenue, where it wound its way through the lower South Hill, turning east, then south, then east again, where it joined a street that led south to Rockwood Boulevard.

In those years, the portion that angled southeast on Rockwood Boulevard was called Hill Street, and it went to a point where it joined Tenth Avenue. At that spot, the trolley was turned around to go up Prospect Avenue, traveling steeply upward to reach what is now Grand Boulevard.

Prospect Avenue is now called Sumner Avenue, and the route can still be taken by automobile for anyone who is interested.

In the picture one can see the houses that Frank Cook [Francis Cook's brother] built, one of which he lived in, and the house in the center at the bottom is Francis and Laura Cook's. That property is now the site of St. John's Cathedral. The present Jewett House stands where the Cook home was located. The two-car trolley can be seen as it was turning onto Grand.

This drawing of Spokane Falls and the Spokane & Montrose trolley to Spokane Heights was published in the April 1890 issue of *The Northwest Magazine.* It was captioned "The trail of Francis Cook's Montrose Line." Cook purposely built the line to promoted his planned real estate development on the South Hill. Unfortunately, he was heavily mortgaged at the time of the 1893 economic panic and was forced to sell his South Hill property. It was purchased by others who later developed the area much as he had planned.

This sketch from the April 1890 issue of *The Northwest Magazine* provides a view of the Ross Park line as it crossed its wooden bridge into the Dennis and Bradley's Addition. After this bridge washed out in 1894, it crossed at the present Trent (formerly Olive) Avenue Bridge about 100 yards downstream. The line then traveled north on Hamilton to Illinois Avenue, where it followed the curve of Illinois, bisecting the Ross Park Addition and ending at about Regal Street.

As mentioned earlier, parks were an enticement to a development, but they also attracted riders on the streetcar lines. Within a developing neighborhood's boundaries, it was quite common to set aside a substantial parcel of ground that would be donated to the city for a park. In return, the city would develop the roads, water systems, and other services necessary for development. This turned out to be a good thing for both the city and the developer, although the city did not accept every offer because of the associated costs. Some of Spokane's most popular neighborhoods, such as Browne's Addition and Manito Park, developed around parks donated by the original property owners. Natatorium Park was the most popular of the destination parks and entertained crowds of visitors for three-quarters of a century, though it ceased to be a trolley park in 1929.

During the late 1880s and early 1890s, many Spokane businessmen left established trades to invest in and develop streetcar lines and residential real estate, and many reaped handsome rewards. By the spring of 1890, Spokane Falls had almost 17 miles of streetcar tracks to serve the public. An addition of 25 more miles was anticipated by the middle of summer, some of which was provided by a second electric line, the City Park Transit Company, which opened that year. Electricity was the

The Ross Park car barn on Desmet Avenue. The building was later purchased by McGoldrick Lumber Company and used in their sawmill operation. *(Courtesy Jim McGoldrick)*

An 1890 sketch of an elegant streetcar on the Ross Park Railway, the first electric line in Spokane Falls. *(From the April 1890* Northwest Magazine*)*

cheapest way to power the lines, and in December 1890, even the horse-drawn line began converting to electricity. The *Electrical World*, a weekly publication printed in New York, carried an article on the electric railways in Spokane Falls in their issue of May 10, 1890. In conclusion it stated:

> This is one of the very few successful attempts to supply electric energy from water power, and our neighbors in the Northwest are to be congratulated upon having accomplished that in the trial of which so many have failed.

Despite the glowing reports, trouble was on the horizon. Fierce competition between the existing streetcar lines (with more franchises pending) and disputes over joint use of some streets or bridges often required the police or other city officials to intervene. In addition, City Hall and the mainline railroads were often contentious forces. The city objected to the streets being perpetually torn up (partly due to replacement of original track with that suitable for electric lines), and the railroads, with safety and scheduling concerns, did not want the streetcars crossing at grade. Many court battles ensued. Meanwhile, Washington Water Power entered the competition. By the end of the 1890s, WWP absorbed the competitor lines, which by then had all converted to electricity, and developed a temporary monopoly. It had the decided advantage of being a full-service utility company with almost no competition.

Cook's Spokane & Montrose was the only early streetcar line that remained independent of Washington Water Power. In 1902, Jay Graves acquired the line and much of Cook's South Hill property, which he reorganized the following year as the Spokane Traction Company.

A navigable river?

In addition to power, the river was also considered for transportation. On March 3, 1888, an announcement was made in the *Spokane Falls Review* that a steamboat was to be put into operation on the Spokane River. It would require the river bed to be deepened and cleared out in several places. The route was to begin near the Division

The Spokane Street Railway trolleys, after converting to electricity, crossing the second Monroe Street Bridge. This bridge lasted from 1891 to 1910. *(Jerome Peltier collection)*

Road construction on Riverside Avenue, circa 1885. *(Courtesy SPLNWR)*

Street Bridge and would travel upriver, stopping at all landings that property owners might see fit to erect. The company that originated this enterprise was known as the Suburban Rapid Transit Company. The steamer was to have a 40 horsepower motor with twin screws, capable of traveling 12-13 m.p.h. with a capacity of 50 passengers and baggage. The boat was expected to be making regularly scheduled trips by the end of June. This plan never developed, and the river was never used commercially as a navigable channel near the city of Spokane.

Streets

In 1885, the *Spokane Falls Review* reported that "one of the most extensive public improvements is the grading of several of the principal streets." About two years later, grading really began in earnest. Numerous ordinances were passed each year authorizing grading in different sections of the city. It was newsworthy when the basaltic rock outcropping at the intersection of Riverside and Howard, the town's center, was cut down to grade.

A city ordinance passed on June 10, 1885, authorized the use of male prisoners to work "upon the public squares, lots, blocks, engine houses, streets, sewers, or other property of the city, or in clearing the crossings of streets, and streets and alleys in the city." In 1889, to help defray some of the costs of the road construction, the mayor urged Police Chief Joel Warren to exercise that right. Apparently prisoners were put to work on the streets, but not always with the desired results. On July 12, 1889, the *Morning Review* reported the escape of two prisoners who were part of a chain gang doing work on Mallon Avenue. Although they were linked together, they solicited something to eat from one of the neighbors, then "traveled so far that no one has yet been able to find them." Neighbors complained that "the prisoners appeared to be free to wander wherever they pleased, so long as they traveled by twos."

An artist's drawing of Gonzaga's first building, constructed in 1885. Fr. Cataldo named the school after St. Aloysius Gonzaga, an Italian Jesuit saint of the 16th century. The inset shows St. Joseph's, the first Catholic church in Spokane, located at the northwest corner of Main and Bernard. *(MAC L93-18-124)*

~ Places to Gather, Worship, and Learn ~

As some in the community were attending to the physical needs of the new settlers, others began making strides to offer nourishment for their minds and souls, or provide resources for assistance. The founding of libraries, literary clubs, and other social or fraternal clubs provided respectable places and occasions to gather. The YMCA and the Ladies Benevolent Society, which provided assistance for needy people, were founded in 1884. The organizations helped many who found life in the "promised land of milk and honey" to be a lot more difficult than anticipated and lacked necessary survival skills or resources.

Schools and churches, which had established a toehold in the 1870s in service to the native peoples, began expanding to meet the needs of the growing white population. The Methodists and Congregationalists had organized in 1879 and the Episcopalians about 1880. In 1881, the Baptists organized, the Congregationalists built their first church building (at Sprague and Bernard), and Fr. Joseph Cataldo, Superior of the Jesuits' Rocky Mountain Missions, converted a 15-by-22-foot carpenter shop on the northwest corner of Main and Bernard into the Church of St. Joseph, the town's first Catholic church. Construction of other churches soon followed and, by 1883, the Presbyterians, Methodists, Baptists and Episcopalians also had their own church buildings. The Episcopal Church at the southwest corner of Lincoln and Riverside was moved in 1887 preparatory to the construction of new city offices, a jail, and city morgue at that location. That year, Spokane Falls received its first female minister, Rev. May C. Jones, who became the pastor of the First Baptist Church.

To accommodate the influx of population, Fr. Cataldo soon purchased two more lots adjacent to St. Joseph's. In 1886, Our Lady of Lourdes Church was built to the west of the little chapel. The chapel was later used as a preparatory school for Gonzaga College. Two years later, a parochial school, under the tutelage of the Sisters of the Holy Names, was built next to the new church. When Our Lady of Lourdes Cathedral was built on Riverside at Madison (dedicated on Thanksgiving Day 1908), the original church and school buildings at the old site were sold and converted to commercial use.

The Jesuits' original priority was to the Indian people, but they soon were pressured to provide schooling for the white children as well. In 1881, Fr. Cataldo negotiated the purchase of two 320-acre parcels of land. The third St. Michael's Mission Church for the Indians was built on one parcel, later becoming the site of Mt. St. Michael's Scholasticate (now St. Michael's Academy and Convent). The other parcel became the home of a private school for white Catholic boys. As plans progressed, Cataldo weathered opposition on several fronts: dissension among the priests on whether the school should be for the Indian or the white children; pressure from church officials to build the school in a more promising community; and concern that this gravelly ground on the north bank of the river (with 40 acres in the river) was worthless.

Cataldo remained undaunted and, with some financial assistance from many prominent local businessmen, began construction of the first building at Gonzaga College (now University) in 1885. The school opened for classes in 1887. This marked the beginning of the college's struggle for survival, but today the esteemed university occupies a beautiful 108-acre campus. Its oldest surviving structure is the 1894 administration building. The remaining land purchased by Cataldo was parceled out in various ways. Sites were donated for the construction of Holy Names Academy (a private Catholic school for girls) and St. Joseph's Children's Home. Other parts were developed and houses built, which were sold through the Jesuits' nonprofit corporation, the Pioneer Educational Society, to provide financial support for students preparing for the priesthood. Land was also granted to the Oregon Railway and Navigation Company, which was built through Gonzaga's property in 1889. In those early years, with the pressure from the town's residents to be connected to the outside world, no one dared deny a railroad right-of-way. However, the priests granted it somewhat begrudgingly because the rail traffic disturbed their peaceful environment and cut the college off from their river bay.

By the time Gonzaga opened, the Methodists' Spokane College, also a private school, had already been in session for five years. Classes commenced in 1882 in the Methodist Church while the college was under construction. The school, completed in 1883, was located west of Monroe Street on College Avenue (thus, the name) on land donated by Col. David P. Jenkins, the first settler on the north side of the river. Jenkins largely subsidized construction of the first building (a second one was completed west of it by 1887) and later donated the land for the present county courthouse.

Isaac C. Libby, who later became superintendent of schools and also taught at Spokane and Lewis & Clark high schools, was the college's first president and his wife was the primary department principal. An ad in the November 3, 1883, *Spokane Falls Review* read: "Spokane College, the Collegiate, Preparatory and Primary Departments will accommodate all grades." Accommodating all grades was typical of the private colleges of the day, including Gonzaga (which required that students be at least ten years of age).

Gonzaga eventually prospered, but Spokane College lasted for less than a decade. In 1891, the property reverted back to Col. Jenkins and operated as Jenkins University for a brief time. The buildings were abandoned in 1904 and torn down in 1910. Just prior to this, another Protestant school, also named Spokane College, opened at 29th Avenue and Garfield on the South Hill.

The white children's basic educational needs were also met through the public schools and, in 1883,

The Central School opened for all grades in 1883. In 1891, it was moved from this site to make room for the construction of Spokane High School, later replaced by Lewis & Clark High School. *(Jerome Peltier collection)*

a new four-room, two-story schoolhouse (the Central School) was built in the block of present-day Lewis and Clark High School, bounded by Howard, Stevens, Fourth, and Fifth. The public school system expanded to meet the needs, sometimes just barely, of a growing community. In July 1888, the *Morning Review* reported an enrollment in the two public schools (which, by this time, included the Bancroft Elementary School) of 1,230, with an average daily attendance of 522. Other public schools were built in rapid succession, which by the end of the decade, included Lincoln, Logan, and Bryant.

Spokane Public Library

Many of Spokane's founding residents, including the women, were highly educated, no doubt a factor in the early efforts to start a library even before many other services were established. In 1880, the Ladies Library and Aid Society began holding fund-raisers to start a library in Spokane Falls. One of the motivations was to provide a more respectable place for men to congregate than the saloons. A library association was formed and a small quantity of books were purchased. Unfortunately, this library's existence was rather short lived (possibly a casualty of the January 1883 fire). In 1884, a newly formed library association opened a reading room in Mr. and Mrs. Eugene J. Fellowes's store in the new brick Central Block, designed by architect Herman Preusse and built in 1883 on Riverside between Mill and Post. This library also lasted for only a few years. Both efforts had been funded by membership subscriptions and, in the case of the second one, stock sales of $10 each, which entitled the purchaser to a lifetime membership of unlimited use.

A few years passed before further concerted efforts produced another library. This one, however, took root and evolved into the present Spokane Public Library system. It began with the merger in 1891 of two separate libraries, one of which was started by the Sorosis Club (one of Spokane's first women's social clubs) and the other by local labor unions whose reading rooms were for members only. The merger resulted in the Union Library Association, which opened in the Auditorium Building in April 1891. It was supported solely by donations and subscriptions, until an 1891 city ordinance authorized $50 a month for the library. Dr. Mary Latham, Spokane's first woman doctor, was one of its greatest benefactors and a member of its first board of directors.

In 1894, the Spokane City Library, a municipal tax-supported institution, was formed. It acquired the books from the Union Library Association and moved into the new city hall building on Howard at Front. On June 14, 1895, the *Spokesman-Review* reported that, although the library's growth was slow due to reliance on the city's coffers, an average of 350 men were using the library on a daily basis. It also stated, "Comparatively few ladies patronize the ladies' reading room." A little over a year later, the paper pointed out that "city hall is not central, and a great many ladies object to coming down here." Though not explicitly stated, the building was in a rough section of town and in the midst of the "red light" district.

By the turn of the nineteenth century, the library's collection had outgrown the space at City Hall. In 1901, in hopes of a more accommodating building in a better location, Spokane contacted wealthy industrialist Andrew Carnegie, who was in the process of donating millions of dollars to establish libraries across the nation. He initially turned down the request, but in 1903, he gifted the city with $85,000. He also donated money in 1911-12 for the construction of three branch libraries: Heath, Union Park (Altamont) and North Monroe.

The Carnegie Library, designed by architects Preusse and Zittel, was completed in 1905 on Cedar between First and Riverside, on land donated by mining magnate Amasa B. Campbell. Before long, expansion modifications were made to the Carnegie to accommodate the growing library. In less than 60 years, the library had totally outgrown the beautiful Carnegie and, in 1963, moved into the old Sears building, donated by the Comstock Foundation and renovated by funds from a $300,000 bond issue passed by the voters.

In 1990, citizens approved a $28.9 million bond issue to build a new downtown library and five branch libraries. The old Sears building was demolished for construction of the new downtown library on the same site, which was completed in 1994. In the 103rd year of its continual existence, the main branch of the Spokane Public Library moved into its current facility overlooking the beautiful falls of the Spokane River.

The Carnegie Library, designed by Preusse and Zittel, on Cedar between First and Riverside. It is on the national and Spokane historic registers. *(From* Vintage Postcards of Old Spokane, *courtesy Duane Broyles and Howard Ness)*

~ Glimpses of Spokane's Early Medical Profession ~

Pioneer doctor Joseph Gandy, a member of the Washington Territorial legislative body responsible for creating Spokane County, moved to Spokane Falls about 1879. In an interview in his later years, Gandy stated there were then about seven or eight families and enough bachelors to make up a population of nearly a hundred residents.

On a lot purchased from James Glover, Dr. Gandy erected one of the first two-story buildings in Spokane Falls and set up a medical practice. According to Gandy, Spokane Falls "was then composed principally of men and women in their prime and didn't require a great deal of medical attention." Although the population reached 300 within several months of his arrival, Gandy was not the only doctor, and there likely was not enough business to support them all. In 1881, Dr. Gandy accepted an appointment as a surgeon for the U.S. Army and, for the next two years, spent most of his time at Fort Spokane before returning to Spokane Falls to resume his medical practice.

Dr. Gandy's building was one of the casualties of the January 1883 fire. Gandy and others who had lost buildings in the fire, including Robert Forrest and Eugene Hyde, formed a partnership and constructed the brick Union Block on the site of the fire. In terms of ground-floor area, it was the largest building in town before the 1889 fire. (After that fire, Gandy built a smaller Union Block, which still exists, on the east side of Howard between Main and Spokane Falls Boulevard.) Dr. Gandy retired from practicing medicine in 1889, but remained active in political and civic affairs, helping to raise capital for improved roads, railroad construction, and to secure the land for Fort George Wright.

By 1885, with about 20 doctors of varying degrees of education and experience practicing medicine in Spokane Falls, the Spokane Medical Society was organized. Shortly thereafter, it was reorganized into a professionally oriented organization, largely through the efforts of Cyrus K. Merriam, a military surgeon assigned to the eastern region of Washington Territory. According to the Fall 1989 *Medical Bulletin*, the Spokane Medical Society predated the Washington State Medical Association (WSMA) by four years. The *Bulletin* stated:

> It included a dentist and physicians from as far away as Colville, Cheney, Rockford and Deep Creek ... the apparent primary purpose of the organization was blatant, but honest – to set up a schedule of fees for services by which the membership could be guided.

Sacred Heart Hospital

About the same time, due to the rapid growth of the city and need for charities, Mother Joseph and Sister Joseph of Arimathea of the Sisters of Providence heeded a plea from the Jesuit fathers and traveled to Spokane Falls in 1886 to build Sacred Heart Hospital. It was located on land purchased from S. G. Havermale on the south bank of the river between Browne and Bernard. The sisters raised money to build the hospital by soliciting donations from local saloons and gambling halls, as well as from the rugged mining and railroad camps, which were reached by horseback. Mother Joseph (at age 63) supervised the entire construction project. Having learned carpentry from her carpenter father, she was known to personally tear down faulty construction and sometimes rebuild it herself. (In 1980, Mother Joseph became Washington State's second representative in Washington, D.C.'s National Statuary Hall. The inscription reads: "She made monumental contri-

Sacred Heart Hospital on the south bank of the river between Browne and Bernard opened on January 27, 1887. This photo was taken in 1901, after the first wing was added in 1889. A second wing was built in 1902. *(Courtesy Sylvia Mowery)*

This view looking southeast across Havermale Island and the Spokane River (carrying logs to the sawmill) was taken from the roof of the Echo Mills on Howard Street about 1888. In the left foreground is a shingle mill. Spokane's first hospital, Sacred Heart (marked with an "X" at the top of the photo) was at the approximate site of the present Double Tree Hotel on Spokane Falls Boulevard. *(Jerome Peltier collection)*

butions to health care, education, and social work throughout the Northwest.")

Sacred Heart Hospital opened in January 1887 as both a hospital and a facility to care for the poor and homeless. Soon after the hospital opened, the need was so great that new wings were added in 1889 and 1902. The first wing doubled the hospital's previous capacity. With the burgeoning railroad and industrial activity along the river, accompanied by a growing demand for a larger facility, the sisters sought out another location. In 1910, a new hospital was built on Eighth Avenue, where it continued to expand and evolve into the present Sacred Heart Medical Center.

Dr. Mary Latham

In 1887, the same year Spokane Falls received its first female minister, the first woman doctor, Mary Archard Latham, also arrived. She was accompanied by her three sons. Her husband, Dr. Edward Latham, joined the family two years later. Mary opened a combination office and residence in the fall of 1887. She specialized in the treatment of diseases affecting women and children. Her charitable works on behalf of the poor and helpless were noteworthy and, in addition to her large practice, she was closely involved with the founding of the Spokane Humane Society and the public library. Meanwhile, Edward accepted a position as resident physician on the Colville Indian Reservation in January 1891. Sadly, Mary's life began to unravel following the tragic death of son James in 1903 and, by all accounts, she appears to have suffered from severe psychological problems that manifested in some bizarre and destructive behavior and resultant lawsuits. Despite having divorced 22 years before her death in 1917, neither Mary nor Edward had remarried and are buried side by side at Spokane's Greenwood Memorial Park. Although Mary's accomplishments in Spokane outshone Edward's and she had created a name for herself as a professional woman during a time when few women had careers outside the home, the headstone reads: "Edward Latham and Mary his wife." In 2007, a monument was erected near their graves that honored Dr. Mary Latham's contribution to Spokane.

Dr. Mary Latham
(Courtesy SPLNWR)

The photos on this and the opposite page, which provide a panoramic view looking toward the South Hill over the heart of the town in the mid-1880s, are among the earliest photos of Spokane. This photo was taken from one of the islands in the Spokane River. The large building at the upper center on Front Street (later Front Avenue, and later still Trent and now Spokane Falls Boulevard) at Howard Street (the street running through the center of the photo) is the California House, the town's second hotel, but the first formal one. The first bridge at the town of Spokane Falls was built in 1881 and actually consisted of three spans that zigzagged across the islands, connecting the nucleus of the town at Howard (as shown above) to the north bank at Washington Street. *(Courtesy SPLNWR)*

~ Spokane's First Newspapers and Telecommunications ~

From its inception, Spokane's news industry has abounded with excitement, competition, and sometimes violence. Printing the news can result in emotional trauma for those on the receiving end of a negative news release. Reactions to what has been published have been known to endanger the lives of those on the reporting end. A few of the more sensational incidents involving Spokane's newspaper past were a shooting in the *Spokan Times* office in 1881 (see sidebar, page 70), the murder of a *Spokesman-Review* editor in the Review Building in 1912, and attempts have been made to blow up the Review Building.

The following summary highlights the major participants in Spokane's newspaper industry during its formative years, an era characterized by the rapid emergence, and sometimes an even more rapid disappearance, of newspapers. Those fortunate enough to survive for any length of time experienced frequent changes in ownership, including mergers with other papers.

As discussed in earlier text, regular reporting activity in Spokane Falls began with Francis Cook's *Spokan Times* in 1879, and the second newspaper, the *Spokane Falls Chronicle*, founded as a weekly on June 29, 1881, by Glover, Browne, and Cannon. The *Chronicle* employed C. B. Carlisle, an experienced newsman from Portland, Oregon, to run their operation. Factional politics of the era had pitted Cook and his supporters against Glover, Browne, Cannon, and their followers. The *Chronicle* was founded as a voice of opposition to and with some malice towards Francis Cook and his *Spokan Times*.

Shortly after its inception, the *Chronicle* was purchased by Charles B. Hopkins and Hiram Allen. Hopkins was cofounder of the Inland Northwest's first newspaper, Colfax's *Palouse Gazette*. In 1882, the *Chronicle* was sold to Arthur K. Woodbury, formerly with the *Cincinnati Commercial Gazette*, who sold it to the Rev. H. T. Cowley in the spring of 1883. (Cowley had sustained a leg

This view is looking southwest from the Spokane River. In the foreground are Front (running east and west) and Mill (now Wall) Street, which curved along the river to the sawmill. The two-story building facing Front (arrow) was the Carter Brothers' machine shop. In 1887, Elijah Davenport, uncle of Louis M. Davenport of the Davenport Hotel, converted it into the U.S. Hotel. *(Don Neraas collection)*

injury that interfered with his former livelihood, forcing him to find a new line of work.) During Cowley's ownership, the *Chronicle* was changed from a weekly to a daily. Over the years, variations in the name reflect the changes from weekly to daily (and whether morning or evening).

In 1883, about the time Cowley bought the *Chronicle*, with its Democratic perspective, Frank M. Dallam started the *Spokane Falls Review* to offer a Republican voice. Although he had hoped to buy an existing newspaper, Dallam was an experienced newsman who was well qualified to start his own. As the first to regularly report news of the North Idaho gold rush, it was an immediate success.

The *Review* was originally located in Spokane's first schoolhouse, which was no longer in use following construction of the Central School. On March 31, 1889, the *Review* moved into new quarters, the former First Presbyterian Church building on the southeast corner of Riverside and Monroe. This proved to be a serendipitous move as Spokane's devastating fire a few months later spared this block. The old church building was moved several months later to begin construction of the Review Building, the city's first office tower. By the time of the fire, the controlling interest in the *Review* was held by the owners of Portland's *Oregonian*. They transferred Nelson W. Durham, a dynamic and competent news reporter, to Spokane Falls to assume responsibility for the newspaper. In addition to his years in the newspaper business, Durham left a lasting legacy as the author of *Spokane and the Inland Empire* (also known as *History of the City of Spokane and Spokane Country, Washington*). This three-volume set chronicling Spokane's early history was published in 1912.

The *Spokesman* was founded in 1890 in opposition to the *Review's* control by outside interests. The next year, William H. Cowles, a 24-year-old police reporter for the *Chicago Tribune*, of which his father was secretary-treasurer, became the business manager. The ensuing rigorous and costly competition came to an end in 1893 when the two papers merged. The *Spokesman* was suspended for a little over a year until Cowles purchased the controlling interest in the *Review* (which included the Review Building) and resurrected the name. Durham continued as editorial director of

A Shooting in the *Spokan Times* Office

Although Cook was Spokane Falls's most ardent and vocal supporter and promoter, his opinions often provoked some of the early Spokane community leaders. During his final year with the *Times,* he expressed negative opinions about the character and actions of some of these leaders, arousing their ire. An article on October 25, 1881 stated:

> The interest of the ring [Cook's reference to a group of city leaders, namely J. N. Glover, A. M. Cannon, and J. J. Browne] are not identical with those of our citizens. J. N. Glover & Co. must rule the property for which they have already received a price, or do their best to ruin the prospects of the real owners. They are a blight upon the place, standing between our city and the prosperity to which it is entitled. They foster no experience but such as pays them tribute.

This article appears to have escalated an ongoing feud between Cook and "the ring" that was carried on between these opposing forces in their respective newspapers, the *Spokan Times* and the *Spokane Falls Chronicle*. On March 31, 1882, this "newspaper war" erupted into violence. Anthony Cannon and future son-in-law, B. H. Bennett (who built the Bennett Block and, before the Great Fire, was proprietor of the Grand and Arlington hotels), stormed into Cook's office to confront Cook about an article he had written that Cannon felt was uncomplimentary toward him. Both Cannon and Bennett were armed with pistols. Their purpose was to demand that Cook print a retraction. Shots were fired, despite the presence of Cook's wife and baby, and a confrontation followed that left both Cannon and Bennett severely beaten. Cook remained unscathed, although a bullet pierced the chimney of the stove in his office.

B. H. Bennett
(*"Spokane Falls Illustrated"*)

Following this incident, Cannon and Bennett were ordered to appear before a grand jury on charges of attempted murder. By all accounts, there seemed to be sufficient probable cause to support the charge, including motive, witnesses and evidence. However, the grand jury, whose foreman was James Glover, ruled that Cannon and Bennett did not intend to assault Cook and dismissed the charges.

As might be expected, the two newpapers' accounts of this incident varied somewhat. Cook's summation after the trial, which he titled "A Grand Farce," appeared in the *Spokan Times* on April 22, 1882, excerpts of which follow:

> The fact A. M. Cannon and B. H. Bennett were not indicted was not owing to a lack of all the evidence necessary under ordinary circumstances. In older settlements, where law is properly respected and rigidly enforced, such a crime as they committed would have been punished by imprisonment in the penitentiary for a fixed number of years. The names of witnesses placed in the hands of the proper authorities, could truthfully testify Cannon stated before he made the attack, when remonstrated with, that he "had the law in his pocket," and that Cannon and Bennett left the bank when they expected and probably knew no one was to be present in the office but their intended victim and his wife and child....
>
> ... That Cannon and Bennett were not indicted is no evidence that they were not guilty, because the above facts are well understood by the residents of this city, and are commented upon by people all over the Northwest. We are almost ashamed to tell the world that such an atrocious crime goes unpunished, but such is the history of all new countries....

Within weeks of the trial, both newspapers changed hands. Obviously disenchanted, Francis Cook retired from the field of journalism.

A full account of this incident, with perspectives from both newspapers, can be found in Doris J. Woodward's book *The Indomitable Francis H. Cook of Spokane: A Man of Vision*.

Looking east along Riverside Avenue from Monroe Street in 1889 (before the Great Fire of August 4th). The buildings (from left) were Elijah Davenport's Commercial Hotel, the City Offices Building (including the police department headquarters), the Crescent Block, and the Review Office. Behind the Review's small frame building at the corner, which was used as the business office and editorial room, the former First Presbyterian Church building served as the newspaper's mechanical department since March 31, 1889. Their earlier move spared the newspaper from the Great Fire, because the fire's progress was arrested just east of the Commercial Hotel. The Crescent Store, located in the Crescent Block, was able to open for business on August 5, 1889, the day after the fire. Although the Crescent's owners were in a position to take advantage of the city's misfortune, they did not raise their prices. In 1899, the City Offices Building and the Commercial Hotel were demolished for the construction of the Empire State Building.
("Spokane and the Inland Empire")

the *Spokesman-Review* until 1910. Today it is Spokane's only daily newspaper. In 1897, Cowles also purchased the *Chronicle* and moved its operations into the Review Building. Though under the same ownership, the *Chronicle* was published as a separate paper until its termination in 1992.

The *Spokane Press*, Spokane's third longest-running newspaper, was in business from 1902 until 1939. It was with the working man and openly antagonistic towards William Cowles and his newspaper. However, without any public forewarning, the final issue, on March 18, 1939, abruptly announced its permanent suspension. Over the years, numerous smaller or special interest papers have come and gone, but since the 1890s, the *Spokane Press* has been the only one to seriously compete with or challenge the *Spokesman-Review*.

The first telephone company

Pioneer newsman Charles B. Hopkins became interested in the telephone for news purposes, and soon took the lead in establishing the telephone system throughout the Inland Northwest. Most considered his venture a waste of money, certain this new invention would never catch on. Nevertheless, in 1884, he began purchasing the old military telegraph lines connecting the region's forts and started converting them to telephone lines. His primary interest was to connect his newspaper office in Colfax to the outside world, but by December 1886, he had secured the necessary equipment and opened an exchange in the Hyde Block in Spokane Falls.

While the exchange was being established, Thomas H. Elsom installed the first telephone set,

Francis H. Cook, a Man of Many "Firsts"

Laura (McCarty) and Francis H. Cook *(Courtesy great granddaughters Laura Poulin and Jan Edmonds)*

Francis H. Cook was born in 1851 in Marietta, Ohio. He learned the printing trade and purchased his first newspaper at the age of 16. Four years later he set out for the Pacific Northwest and began working for the *Puget Sound Courier* in Olympia. He later bought the *Olympia Echo*, which he operated for three years before starting Tacoma's first newspaper, the *Tacoma Herald*.

While in Tacoma, Cook became aware of the Northern Pacific Railroad's blatant violations of the Pacific Railway Act. Driven by a sense of justice, he spoke openly about its illegal actions and corrupt influence. His fortitude and ethical reputation in standing up to the corruption of large corporations gained him popularity with the general public, and he was urged to run for the Washington Territorial Legislature. Although the Northern Pacific supported its own candidate and vigorously campaigned against him, Cook was elected to serve in the 1879 session. By a unanimous vote, he became presiding officer of the joint session, the youngest to ever attain that position. While serving in that capacity, the bill was passed to create Spokane County.

Cook was so inspired by Eastern Washington's beauty and potential after a visit in 1878 that he decided to start a newspaper in Spokane Falls. In 1879, Cook set up his printing operation for the *Spokan Times* in a small wooden building on Front Street, between Post and Mill, where he lived until his marriage in June 1880 to Laura McCarty from Sumner, Washington. Shortly thereafter, Cook built a two-story building on the southeast corner of Howard and Riverside (later the site of the Rookery Building, recently demolished for a parking lot). The printing office and their living quarters were on the second floor and, ironically, the Northern Pacific located its office on the ground floor. Laura assisted with the newspaper until she was too busy with new babies, which eventually numbered eleven.

An energetic and enterprising man, Cook was always looking ahead. After leaving the newspaper business, he purchased nearly 700 acres of land on the South Hill, and set his sights on a neighborhood development. He began laying out his plan, which included the beginnings of Manito Park, and with some partners, started the first motorized streetcar line. Although he had engaged a man by the name of T. J. Dooley in a partnership on the project, that was short-lived, and Cook forged ahead on his own.

In 1890, the Cooks moved into their beautiful new mansion overlooking Spokane. Unfortunately, they did not fare well in the Panic of 1893. Defaults on contracts Cook was carrying for lots he had sold made it impossible to make his own mortgage payments. Consequently, Cook lost the streetcar line, most of the South Hill property, and their home. Nevertheless, he forgave many of the contracts he was carrying.

Fortunately, the Cooks still owned property on the Little Spokane River (now the site of Wandermere Golf Course), where the family moved. Cook developed that area and built the road to the top of Mount Spokane, opening it for public use. For this, he is known as the "Father of Mount Spokane State Park." Francis Cook died at their home on Wabash on June 29, 1920, and Laura died August 31, 1941. They are buried at Riverside Memorial Park, where a monument was erected in 2007 to commemorate Francis Cook's lifetime of contributions to Spokane.

A telephone crew raising a pole in Spokane in 1899 without the aid of hoisting equipment, which Thomas Elsom designed later that year. *(Thomas Elsom collection, courtesy Dean Ladd)*

located in Walker L. Bean's grocery store in the Union Block on Howard at Front. (Bean had arrived on the Northern Pacific's first westbound passenger train through Spokane Falls in 1883.) Twenty-five-foot native pine telephone poles were raised along the north side of Riverside between Post and Stevens and along Howard from Front to First and to Browne's Addition.

Upon completion of the exchange, Hopkins sold it, along with the remnants of the telegraph line connection to Fort Missoula, to William S. Norman and his partners. Norman then negotiated with the military to also secure the line between Fort Sherman in Coeur d'Alene and Spokane Falls. As Norman began stringing a telephone line along the route of D. C. Corbin's narrow gauge railroad into the Coeur d'Alene Mining District, Hopkins continued building telephone lines from Colfax to Spokane Falls, reaching the latter by 1887.

The next year, Hopkins and Norman partnered in securing the military telegraph line between Spokane Falls and Fort Spokane and converted it to telephone lines. The preexistence of the military telegraph lines clearly expedited long-distance service in Eastern Washington. By the end of the year, Spokane Falls was connected by telephone to Fort Spokane and nearly every town in the mining district (at $1.00 per minute) and throughout the Palouse.

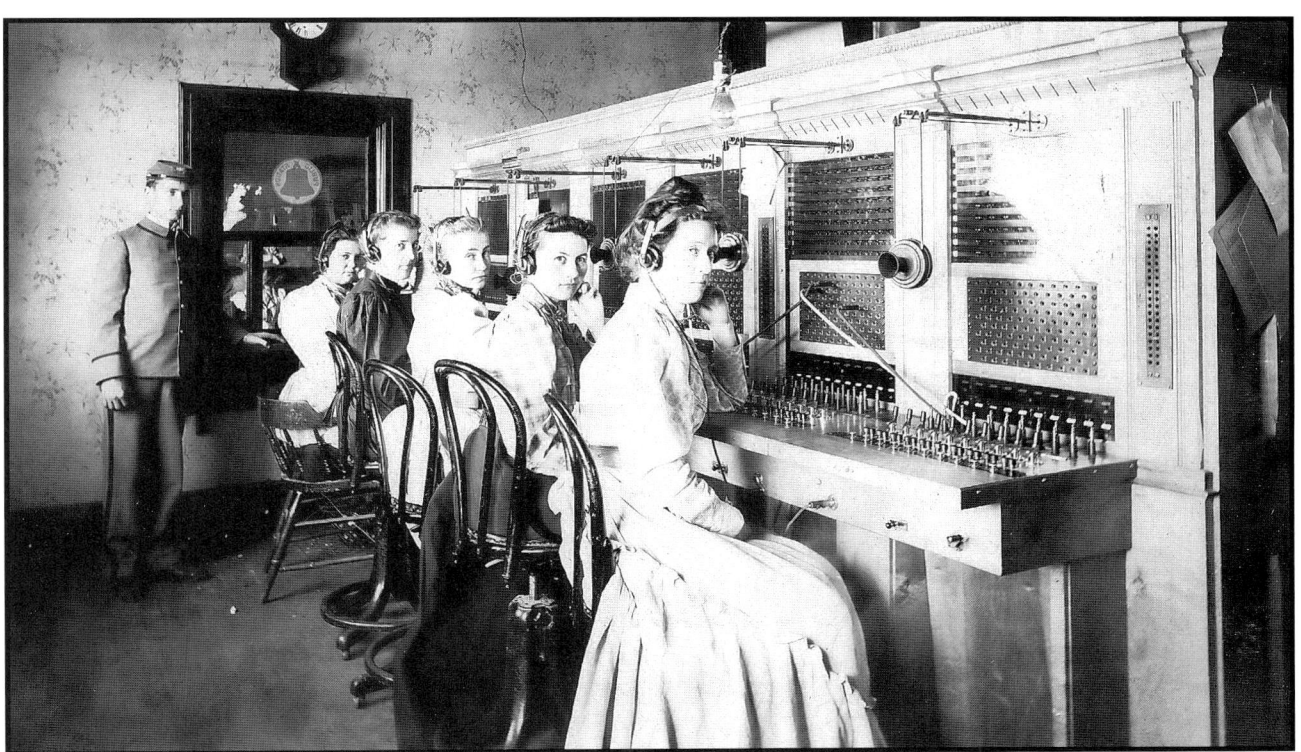

An early telephone exchange. *(Thomas Elsom collection, courtesy Dean Ladd)*

In the spring of 1889, Hopkins and Norman combined Spokane's first telephone systems into the Inland Telephone and Telegraph Co., with the exchange located in the First National Bank building at Riverside and Howard. Polk's *City Directory* published a few months later listed half a dozen telephone companies. Although a great deal of the telephone system was destroyed in Spokane's Great Fire that August, it was quickly rebuilt and consolidated under the Inland Telephone name. Hopkins was the first general manager. In 1890, the number of subscribers was reported to be 410.

Charles Hopkins, William Norman, and Thomas Elsom, all enterprising and accomplished men, continued to play significant roles in the development and expansion of the telephone system throughout the Inland Northwest. Elsom had a long career in the telephone business, retiring in 1930 after nearly 44 years of service. As referenced earlier, in addition to the telephone business, Norman also pursued other enterprises, including development of waterpower and a chain of hotels. Hopkins had wide ranging interests and was involved in many civic and social activities, but bracketed his newspaper-and-telephone career with law enforcement service.

The Inland Northwest's first telephone installation crew. Thomas Elsom is seated at the right. The others were only identified by their last names: (from left) Sultzman, Black, Blanton, and Kollo. *(Thomas Elsom collection, courtesy Dean Ladd)*

Telephone and telegraph offices shortly after the fire of 1889. This same building served as the "Electric Light" facility. *(Thomas Elsom collection, courtesy Dean Ladd)*

~ Entertainment and Recreation ~

Every frontier town had its share of saloons, variety theaters, and gambling halls, and Spokane Falls was no different. The Spokane directory that was published just prior to the 1889 fire listed 50 saloons. These establishments offered a ready source of entertainment and could easily relieve the miners, loggers, and other frontiersmen of their hard-earned wages. Gambling had long been a favorite pastime of the Indians, who also frequented these establishments despite the fact that it had become illegal to sell alcohol to them.

By the end of the decade, the names Jacob "Dutch Jake" Goetz and Harry Baer began to appear frequently in association with the aforementioned types of entertainment. Immediately after the Great Fire of 1889, they opened a huge saloon and gambling hall in a tent on Riverside, reportedly having an attendance of 600 men on slow nights and up to 1,000 on Saturday nights. For years to come, amidst great outcries from "respectable citizens" and law enforcement's efforts to curtail some of the "wicked activities" associated with their business ventures, they – and others – continued to prosper. However, many townspeople were eager for more refined entertainment, as was evident when actor John Maguire, who was celebrated throughout the United States for his popular one-man show, came to Spokane Falls in the early 1880s. During a visit to Spokane in 1903, he recalled the event. His comments, which now provide an interesting glimpse at what was likely a familiar scene at the time, appeared in the August 11, 1903, *Spokane Press*. It claimed his was the first show in Spokane:

> It was a Saturday night. I opened to an audience of about 100 people at $1 per," said the pioneer actor. "The conditions under which I acted were not the best, the low roof forcing me to remain in nearly one position for fear of bumping my head. [His show was held in a room above a drug store across from the California House.] However, they gave me a great hand and I was well satisfied. The next day, Sunday, the lawn in front of the hotel was like a country market. There were hundreds of gaily bedecked Indians ... trading with the whites, and the picturesque scene in front of the hostelry is one that has ever remained in my mind in connection with my initial appearance in this city.

Spokane's first theaters

London-born, part-time actor Harry C. Hayward came to Spokane in 1881 to take a job with the Northern Pacific Railroad. He subsequently opened a sporting goods store, but seeing the potential for success, he also became involved in the theater business. Eager response to the professional acts he brought to Spokane Falls led him to a full-time occupation. Hayward managed most of the early theaters, including Joy's Opera House, Falls City Opera House, Concordia Hall (built by the Concordia Singing Society, a German organization), and the Auditorium Theater.

Recorded history of Spokane's first theaters is full of contradictions. In the beginning, Spokane Falls did not have a suitable hall or opera house for theatrical performances. The town had plenty of variety theaters (the Globe is said to have been the first) associated with the drinking and gambling establishments. The entertainment was usually provided by the "ladies of the night." Consequently, these places were often looked upon with disdain.

For the more professional entertainment, various makeshift theaters sufficed for a few years, but frequent references in the newspapers called for a much-needed opera house. Little is known about Joy's Opera House, believed to be the first "opera house," which was described as little more than a wooden barn built by a Mr. Joy in 1882. It provided a place for acts that could be enticed to come to Spokane Falls, although some threatened to sue for booking them into a "cold storage house instead of a theater."

The Casino Rink, a new roller skating rink (also referred to as an opera house at the time of construction), opened in November 1884 on the northeast corner of Riverside and Post. A month later it collapsed under the weight of heavy snow, but was rebuilt and soon became the primary venue for theatrical productions. It reopened in time for a grand ball, a fund-raiser for the new volunteer fire department, on February 17, 1885. A newspaper article the day before the ball stated the Casino Skating Rink was the largest building in town. As such, it was also a popular place for dances, another favorite pastime of the era. Dances often were hosted at private residences, especially after construction of the larger mansions with private ballrooms.

On September 16, 1885, the *Spokane Evening Review* announced the fire department's plans for its first annual ball to be held on October 22nd and stated: "It will be remembered that the firemen's ball given in the rink last winter was one of the largest, most successful and most enjoyable public dances ever given in the county." The ball would be held at the same location, but the name had changed to Star Skating Rink. The facility's use as a theater was apparently more lucrative and, as time passed, it was referred to as simply "the opera house." Recollections from early settlers occasionally refer to this as Joy's Opera House, but newspaper references to Joy's precede the construction of this building.

An oft-reported, erroneous claim states the first theatrical production in Spokane was *The Bohemian Girl* starring Emma Abbott, a highly acclaimed stage actress of the day, and said to have taken place in 1883 in a leased warehouse, where "the audience reserved seats on gang plows and farm implements." The newspapers, however, clearly establish a sequence of events leading up to Abbott's performance in *The Bohemian Girl* in 1887 (by which time Hayward had booked numerous other productions).

On January 22, 1887, the *Morning Review* reported Hayward had received notice from landlord J. N. Van Dorn that the opera house building had been sold. This was bad news for Hayward, who was in the midst of negotiations with the Emma Abbott opera company and had no alternate facility in which to book the performance. In February 1887, following what was to have been the last performances held there, the new owners began converting the building into an agriculture implement warehouse. However, Hayward was able to negotiate an extension, and on February 15, 1887, the *Morning Review* announced: "The one great operatic event in the history of musical matters in Spokane Falls will be the appearance for the first time of the famous American prima donna, Emma Abbott and her grand English opera company at the opera house, Saturday, February 19th." Although the opera house subsequently became an agriculture implement warehouse, it was not until after Emma Abbott mesmerized her Spokane Falls audience, who definitely were not sitting on "gang plows and farm implements," as often stated.

Following this performance, the movement to secure for the city a "proper" opera house gained momentum, and the Falls City Opera House, built by Daniel Dwight, was completed in November 1887. The new opera house was on the third floor of the Falls City Block, located on the southwest corner of Riverside and Post. Although not a particularly large facility, it was well equipped and, for a short time, met the pressing need for an opera house. Of note, it was the first public building in Spokane Falls to be illuminated by gas lights. Concordia Hall on West Second, built by the German Singing Society, was also used as a theater. Because Spokane Falls was growing with such force, by the time of the Great Fire of 1889, J. J. Browne and A. M. Cannon were constructing their larger, elegant opera house, the Auditorium Theater, at Main and Post. It was completed in 1890.

Falls City Block and Opera House (third floor) at Riverside and Post in 1887. *(MAC, L94-40.22)*

Women's foot race at the Crescent employees' picnic in Spokane, circa 1913. *(MAC L97-63.110)*

Foot and horse races

Then as now, competitive sports such as baseball and any type of racing were other popular forms of recreation and entertainment in the 1880s. Foot races have always been a common attraction in downtown Spokane, which today annually hosts what has become the largest timed foot race in the world (Bloomsday). In the 1880s and 1890s, races that generally consisted of sprints between 20 to 150 yards occurred on a regular basis. Most were widely advertised and the betting was heavy. Amusing handicaps often made the races quite interesting. For example, on October 17, 1885, a much-anticipated race took place between hometown favorite Hal Odell and Charles Watson, a newcomer to town. The previously agreed-upon handicap allowed Odell a 15-foot head start with Watson starting the race on his stomach. As advertising commenced on what was touted to be the best foot race ever to take place in the territory, both men began rigorous training. Wagers on the 100-yard race totalled between $1,000 and $1,500. Odell, the hometown favorite, emerged victorious and took the $50 prize.

Horse racing vied with foot races in popularity and involved both the new settlers and the Indians. One of the first recorded horse races in Spokane Falls was during the Fourth of July celebration in 1879. Contestants raced along the bluff above the Spokane River from the site of the present Review

Foot racing has always been popular in Spokane. Although this race on Riverside Avenue took place in 1910, it was not unlike those popular in the 1880s. *(Courtesy SPLNWR)*

Building to the J. J. Browne home in Browne's Addition. The following quote in the June 2, 1883 *Spokane Falls Review* described Spokane's first official racetrack and some upcoming races:

> From an interview with J. M. Grimmer, who has charge of the arrangements pertaining to the promised horse racing on the 4th, we are enabled to lay before our many readers some idea of that exciting feature of the day's sports. The race course will be thirty feet wide and extends from the belt of timber near J. J. Browne's residence in an air line directly to the Review office, making a track just three-quarters of a mile in length. The land is almost as level as a floor and the whole course can be plainly seen from any quarter. The grass is about to be cut from the track and a plow run over to both the outlines. It is proposed to have a three-quarter, one-half and quarter mile dashes. In the first two, five entries are to be required an entrance fee of ten percent of the first being charged. [Though confusing, this is precisely as the sentence was written.] The prize will be $100 in coin, best two in three. For the half mile dash there is first and second money, $40 and $15, best two in three heats. The quarter mile race will be for a purse of $50, free to all without entrance charges. A number of persons have signified their intention to put horses in the race, and we have every reason for believing that the running will not only be excellent but exciting, and prove a successfully [*sic*] drawing card. No efforts will be spared to have the races go off in good shape, and justice and fairness will mark the rulings of the judges.

In the early 1880s, no significant community event was complete without a horse race. Rich and poor, young and old, all enjoyed watching the serious riders, the buggy races, and the Indian free-for-alls with the same degree of enthusiasm. Participation in the wagering was all part of the fun. Even when it became illegal to play any game of chance with Indians or to hold races on Sundays (in violation of the Sunday Laws), horse racing remained a lucrative pastime in Spokane. Violations, which were punishable by hefty penalties and/or imprisonment, were largely ignored by the citizenry and law enforcement alike.

In 1886, the Washington & Idaho Fair Association was formed and Spokane held its first agricultural fair in September of that year. It was hosted by Francis Cook on his property south of town. Horse racing was to be an integral part of the fair, and Cook gave prior notice that whips, spurs or anything abusive towards the horses would not be allowed. Following this event, the community began to raise capital to purchase land and build a public racetrack. Spokane's second agricultural fair, held in 1887, was at the new facility about two miles north of downtown, now Corbin Park. The fairground featured a mile-long oval racetrack that attracted some of the finest race horses in the country. At the center of the track was a baseball field where innings of baseball entertained spectators between horse races. The fairground also included a large pavilion for agricultural displays, a long line of stables, and a large grandstand. Due to financial difficulties, the fair association was forced to sell the land a decade later.

During these early years, a man's stature in the community was measured in part by the quality of his horses. The local riding clubs catered to the elite. Even as the mode of transportation began to change, horse racing remained an established part of Spokane's culture. An era came to a close when, after more than 100 years in operation, Playfair Racetrack (in the East Central area of Spokane) closed and the buildings were demolished in 2004.

Baseball craze

Baseball was also an early source of entertainment in Spokane Falls. Whenever enough players could be assembled to form two teams, typically a baseball game soon followed. Games drew large crowds who placed bets on their chosen team. Most towns and military forts had their own teams, as did many businesses. Being a good ball player often provided an edge in securing a job with these businesses. The following statement recorded in the May 11, 1885, *Spokane Evening Review* offers a sense of the interest generated by local games:

> No sporting event ever took place in this city that created so much excitement as the game of baseball Saturday afternoon between Coeur d'Alene and Spokane clubs ... The game was called at 2 o'clock, several hundred spectators being present. Both clubs appeared in uniform. [The Spokane team won the game. The final score was 17 to 14.]

Baseball teams, electricians versus streetcar men, beside a Natatorium Park trolley. *(Jerome Peltier collection)*

During the 1880s, baseball became a national craze and, in July 1889, Herbert Bolster, one of the original founders of Washington Water Power, organized and served as president of Spokane's first official baseball club (the Spokane Baseball Club). They played their first professional game the following year. With the growing interest, as the Spokane Cable Railway built its line into the Twickenham Addition, a new baseball field, with a grandstand seating capacity of 1,000, was built adjacent to the line. This became the first attraction for what would become Natatorium Park.

The Spokane Cable Railway's bridge across the Spokane River to Twickenham Addition. *(Source unknown)*

Alice A. Houghton, Spokane's First Female Real Estate Agent

Alice (Ide) Houghton and Horace E. Houghton
(From History of Washington, *1893 (left) and* Spokane Falls and Its Exposition *souvenir book, 1890)*

The New Year's Day 1892 supplement of the *Spokane Spokesman* included a biographical sketch of one of the city's leading real estate agents, and the only woman in the field, Alice A. (Ide) Houghton. She was an anomaly at the time because the real estate field was dominated by men. Following is a quote about Alice Houghton from *Seven Frontier Women and the Founding of Spokane Falls* by Barbara Cochran:

> Mrs. Houghton's venture into real estate began in the spring of 1887 with little or no capital. It might have been in conjunction with an uncle, Chester D. Ide, and a cousin, Clarence W., who opened a real estate office in the Jamieson Building at that time. Alice proved very adept at selling, and by the next year when the Ides withdrew for other pursuits, she became a partner in the firm of H. M. Williams & Co.
>
> Alice's executive ability, shrewd judgment, unflappability, and unwavering persistence led to almost instant success. In the first two years she was associated with Williams, sales exceeded two million dollars. It was said her personal worth was over $100,000 [*Spokane Falls Illustrated,* 1889] – not a small accomplishment for two and a half years as a neophyte businesswoman. In the summer of 1889, the firm of Williams and Houghton rented rooms 24 and 25 in the prestigious Frankfurt Block....

Alice Ide was born in Montreal, Canada, in 1848. At the age of 16, she married 32-year-old Horace E. Houghton, an attorney from Wisconsin. The Houghtons moved to Spokane Falls in 1884, joining other members of the Ide family who preceded them to the area. Houghton opened a law office and soon gained a reputation for his legal acumen. In 1886, he went into partnership with Frank H. Graves and was also elected as city attorney, serving three terms. He later served in the state senate.

To help with their finances after Horace began experiencing some health problems, Alice began dabbling in real estate investments, but soon discovered her innate talent in such matters. Financial success and noteworthy accomplishments were soon being recognized. Although a retiring person by nature, she never missed an opportunity, especially when traveling away on business, to promote Spokane. Surprisingly, despite excelling in the business world, she became president of the anti-suffrage movement in Washington Territory in the late 1880s. She was quite traditional in her views on her role as a wife and the mother of a son and a daughter. Also very civic-minded, she contributed both her time and her financial resources.

Although the business office burned during the 1889 fire, most of her assets were in residential real estate. After the fire, Alice opened her own real estate firm in the Eagle Block, and branched into mining, timber, and town-site investments, as well as insurance. Her business soon became one of the largest and most profitable of its kind in the Northwest. But despite her soaring success, the Panic of 1893 took a personal toll, and she began pursuing possible opportunities through contacts made in Chicago during the recent world's fair, where she served on the Board of Lady Managers. By 1895, she had essentially made Chicago her home, where she again engaged in the sale of real estate and continued to promote the Pacific Northwest.

Three years after Horace's death in 1897, Alice married her business partner, Archibald Brownlee. Although he was nine years her junior, she outlived him, too. Her husbands were buried side by side in Chicago's Rosehill Cemetery. Following her death one day after her 72nd birthday in 1920, she was buried on the other side of Horace.

The interior of the Frankfurt Block outside the real estate office of H. M. Williams and Mrs. Alice Houghton before Spokane's Great Fire. *(Sketch from* Spokane Falls Illustrated, *Hook and McGuire, 1889)*

An interior view of Alice Houghton's real estate office in the Eagle Block, which she opened after the 1889 fire. *(Sketch from the April 1890 issue of the* Northwest Magazine*)*

In 1888, with their newly acquired wealth from the Coeur d'Alene mines, Jacob "Dutch Jake" Goetz and Harry Baer built the Frankfurt Block at the southwest corner of Main and Howard. It was designed by architect Herman Preusse, and named for Dutch Jake's birth place, Frankfurt, Germany. As it was the finest commercial building in Spokane Falls to that date, many businesses and professional people rented office space. A number of real estate companies and architects opened offices in the building, including Alice Houghton and Herman Preusse. Dr. Mary Latham also had her medical practice there. Of course, it also housed Goetz and Baer's saloon and variety theater. The building was completely destroyed in the Great Fire, after which Goetz and Baer opened a "chop house," tent saloon, and gambling hall in a huge tent, one of the largest tent businesses in the burned district. *(Jerome Peltier collection)*

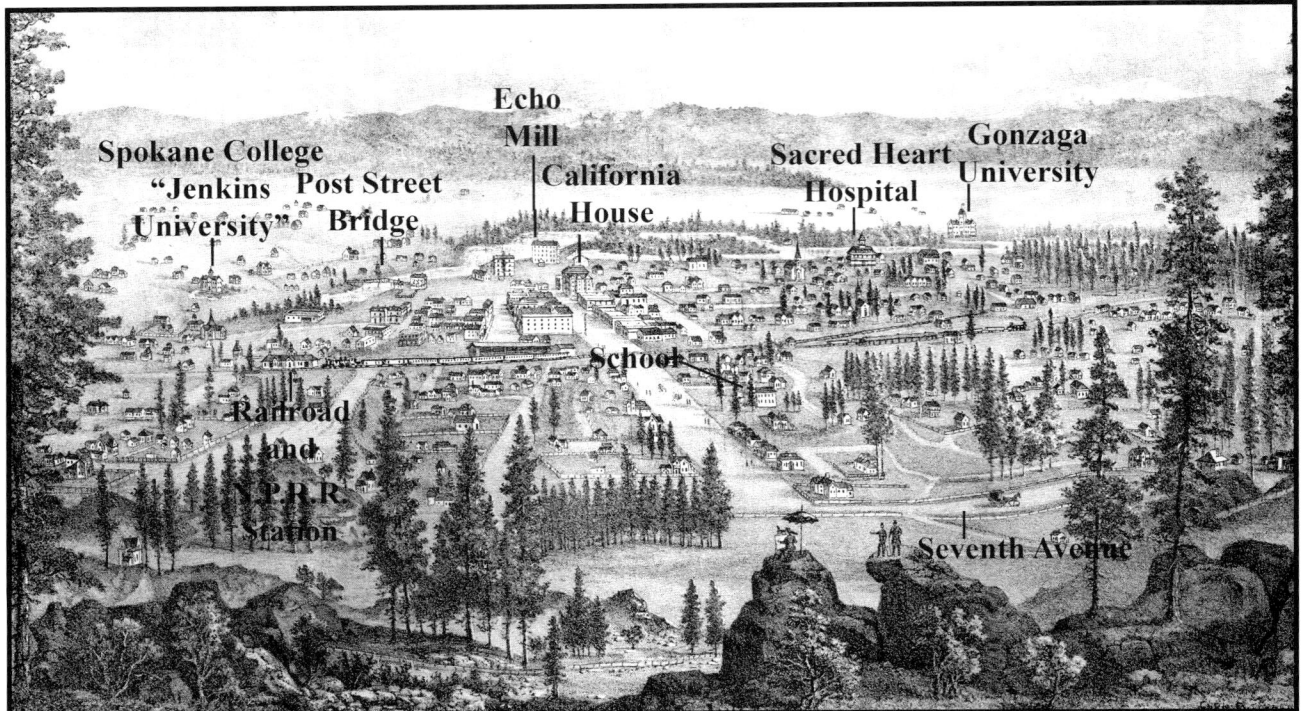

Sketch of Spokane Falls, Washington Territory, before much of the development seen here was destroyed by the Great Fire of 1889. *(Sketch from Taylor and Jefferson, Real Estate and Investors' Agents, courtesy SPLNWR)*

~ A City of Note ~

By the end of the 1880s, Spokane had become a major railroad hub. In addition to the Northern Pacific's cross-country connections, there were three branch lines and two independent railroads (Spokane Falls and Northern, under the direction of D. C. Corbin, and the Seattle, Lake Shore and Eastern). These lines snaked north through Stevens County, east into the Coeur d'Alene Mining District, south into the Palouse, and west into Big Bend Country. In late 1889, the Oregon Railway and Navigation Company reached Spokane Falls, thus placing the city on the route of a second transcontinental line.

To stimulate the use of its lines, the transcontinental railroads initiated aggressive promotional schemes, not just in the eastern states but across Europe. Reduced fares and discounted land prices enticed families to migrate out west, where the railroads and the federal government had abundant land for sale. As a result, many Europeans migrated to Spokane. There was also a significant Chinese population, but due to growing discrimination, Spokane, like many other U.S. cities at the time, did not provide the most friendly, welcoming environment for them. Because of the demand by the railroads for cheap labor, Chinese and Japanese immigrants constituted a large part of the work force in the construction of the transcontinental lines. Yet, despite this demand, Congress responded to the escalating discrimination by passing a series of Exclusion Acts, beginning in 1882, denying Asians from entering the U.S.

During this period, the newspapers were also doing their part to encourage western migration and were using a great many superlatives to describe Spokane Falls. They boasted of Spokane as a mining center that "will stand without a peer in the country," of the uninterrupted waterpower, the picturesque beauty, and phenomenal growth. In July 1889, just a month before the Great Fire, one newspaper printed a partial list of buildings under construction but said the city was getting so large that no one even paid attention to the new buildings as "one cannot look in any direction without seeing some kind of a structure under way." Most of them were substantial brick structures. The use of bricks had taken on greater importance after the January 1883 fire. In response to the increased demand for building materials, in 1887 the Spokane Mill Company, under the management of E. J. Brickell, built a new sawmill at the foot of Wall Street to replace the old Glover mill. The demand for laborers also gave rise to the city's first unions. The first in Spokane Falls, the Knights of Labor, had formed in 1885, but around 1889, labor unions and trade organizations began organizing in earnest.

As a result of the abundant opportunities for success, many of today's prominent businesses and institutions had taken root before the Great Fire. One of these is Dodson's Jewelers. George Dodson and Daniel Wetzel opened a jewelry store in 1887. Their partnership dissolved after the store burned in the fire of 1889, but Dodson started over and today Dodson's Jewelers is one of the oldest existing retail stores in Spokane.

The value of the great mineral deposits and vast stands of timber were also just beginning to be tapped. The Coeur d'Alene and Colville mining districts (and a short time later the Metalines) were producing, and Spokane was quickly becoming a thriving mining center. In addition, another natural resource was being realized. Although early reports lamented a lack of good farm land in close proximity to Spokane, the region actually proved to possess some of the richest and most diverse agricultural land in the nation.

The positive attributes of Spokane and the region were summed up in a glowing account published in the *Seattle Post Intelligencer* and reprinted in the October 18, 1888, *Morning Review*. Some excerpts follow:

> Already has it out-run in the race for population and wealth, towns and cities many years older, and today bids fair to rival even the Queen City of Puget Sound. The population is not far from 15,000, while on all sides are seen evidences of wealth and refinement far exceeding other communities of that number. Its growth is phenomenal; indeed, it is questionable if its parallel can be found in America. In few cities of 50,000 can be seen more palatial residences; more substantial, costly or commodious business structures; larger or better hotels; while the schools, hospitals, churches, etc., will compare favorably with those of cities much older and more populous than Spokane Falls.

The article continued with several more paragraphs, praising the town's layout, its businesses and industries, commercial buildings, street railways and so forth, finally capping the article with:

Downtown Spokane Falls street scene, circa 1885. By the end of the decade, people were still arriving by whatever means available, but stagecoaches such as this would rapidly become a thing of the past.
("Spokane and the Inland Empire")

Chapter Two

With the constant and increasing demand for lodging facilities, a three-story addition, built in 1887, converted the former Frederick Post house (two-story portion at right) into the Falls View Hotel. It was on the site of Spokane's present City Hall. The stagecoach was from to the Keystone House directly across the street. That hotel burned in the 1889 fire, but the Falls View was spared. *(Courtesy SPLNWR)*

> To adequately describe the surroundings of this beautiful city – to speak fittingly of the lovely natural parks, the boiling, foaming, rushing waters that furnish the motive power for the industries mentioned, with other matters worthy of note, would require more space than can now be spared ... Spokane Falls is the cleanest, the brightest, the handsomest, the livliest [*sic*] and most attractive, the most enterprising, the most hospitable city of Washington territory – save alone the Queen City of Puget Sound.

Polk's *1889 Spokane Falls City Directory* (for the year ending June 30, 1889) estimated the population to be 17,340. It listed 10 banks, 16 churches (with 10 denominations represented), 10 newspapers (including a weekly German paper and the YMCA's monthly bulletin), some of which issued both daily and weekly editions, and numerous "secret and benevolent societies," unions, clubs, and associations.

The 1889 directory also listed two cemeteries, Greenwood and Fairmount, both of which had incorporated and opened in 1888. Five years earlier, Mountain View Cemetery had been established in Cannon's Addition (between Cedar and Ash, Tenth and Fourteenth) as the city's official cemetery. At that time, bodies were removed from the original pioneer cemetery at the west end of Browne's Addition and moved to Mountain View. However, with the city's rapid growth and expansion, the value of the land for building lots quickly overshadowed its importance as a cemetery, just as it had in Browne's Addition in 1883. When Greenwood and Fairmount opened, the process of moving bodies once again took place.

Spokane Falls was a classic boom town, and as an earlier quote pointed out, it had reached a level unequaled by many larger and older towns. But there was a downside to this rapid growth. Although the town attracted the genteel, it also drew the unsa-

Looking south on Howard at Riverside in 1888. The corner building on the left is the Spokane National Bank. It was built earlier that year on the former site of Francis Cook's two-story building where he published his *Spokan Times*. The building on the right is the Keats Block. *("Spokane and the Inland Empire")*

84

Looking east along Riverside Avenue from Post Street at the heart of the business district, circa 1888. Many of the important business blocks lined this street: Vandorn & Bentley, Cannon, Wolverton, Ziegler, Hyde, Jamieson, Van Valkenburg, and Central, as well as a couple of banks. *(Jerome Peltier collection)*

vory and every type of person in between, making it a rough – and sometimes dangerous – place to be. In the very early days, the tough characters who were drawn to the rugged wilds were generally transient, often prone to frontier vigilante justice, and were comfortable using their fists, knives or firearms to settle a dispute. The array of people looking to make a quick fortune during the North Idaho gold rush included not only raw-boned, hard-working miners but also opportunists, swindlers, thrill seekers, and prostitutes. Simultaneous with the development of a growing metropolis was a flourishing underworld of gambling, drugs, and prostitution. The town also had its share of infamous outlaws and dangerous gunmen.

The mix of cultures also produced frequent clashes as the town grew and prospered. In terms of hardships, the Spokane Indians, who for centuries had lived a peaceful life along the Spokane River, paid the biggest price for the development of the region. Among the newcomers, the Asians fared almost as poorly. Completion of the Northern Pacific Railroad in 1883 put hundreds of Chinese laborers out of work. Many pursued honorable means of supporting themselves doing gardening and running stores, tea houses or hand laundries; but in the hands of others, the opium trade suddenly began to flourish, which would give the police department problems for years to come.

Because of the transient nature of the opportunities that attracted the influx of people, it was a challenging era for Spokane's police officers. The police department rapidly increased in size, but lack of sufficient funding often hampered its best efforts at enforcing the law. In response to various social ills, especially unbridled use of alcohol in some circles, organizations began forming to stamp out the "depravity." By 1889, the Woman's Christian Temperance Union had three chapters in Spokane Falls (the first one had formed by 1883) and the Young Woman's Christian Temperance Union had two. Still, despite attracting its share of the lawless element, according to some recorded reminiscences of early residents, most of the town's citizens were law-abiding, hard working, and respectable.

A History of Spokane's Early Brick Industry

It has frequently been written that the uncontrollable inferno that destroyed downtown Spokane Falls in 1889 was largely due to the majority of buildings being of wood-frame construction. However, it is clearly evident by looking at the photos following the fire, and the number of burned-out brick buildings, that simply was not the case. Following the much smaller fire in January 1883, the residents of Spokane Falls had realized the importance of building with more durable and fire-resistant materials. As a result, the choice building material for new construction was brick. Because of its significance to Spokane, a summary of its early brick-making history follows.

John T. Davie, who arrived in 1879, is credited with firing the first usable bricks in Spokane Falls. Davie was born in Scotland in 1851 and came to America in 1872. After learning the brick trade at Martha's Vineyard, he moved to California in 1874 and then to Spokane Falls after hearing about the activity there. The following quotations were taken from N. W. Durham's *Spokane and the Inland Empire* (1912), which contains Davie's lengthy and detailed account of the area's brick business. It also chronicled the construction of the brick buildings during this period.

> I walked into Spokane Falls just before noon, November 15th [1879], and made my quarters at Sam Arthur's hotel and restaurant near Howard and Front. I dined sumptuously and then commenced asking questions, the only one of which I now remember was, "Is there a brickyard here?" to which I got two replies, there was, and there wasn't. Some one had been trying to make brick but was not successful in some essential particulars. I said that I would go and see for myself and would report on my return. I found the yard on the homestead of the Rev. H. T. Cowley.... My report was that the brickyard and kiln were not gems of the first water ... A very small portion of the brick next [to] the fires [was] being burned, but very imperfectly.

> A few days afterwards I ran across the proprietor of the yard, a man by the name of Roberts, a bricklayer by trade.... We agreed that I would make the brick and he would lay them as of yore in our new home. I took up a homestead in February, '80, and the location was about eight miles west of Medical Lake....

Davie went on to recount his struggle to make a living from his first brick operation, located on Latah (Hangman) Creek. There was little demand for bricks, but he could produce 1,000-1,200 a day. By 1881, business began to pick up, and his account continued, as follows:

> Roberts, the bricklayer, left town in the spring of '80 and I. T. Benham, a contractor and builder, still well remembered among the old-timers, came in. Benham was thoroughly up in his business and built quite a number of the best business blocks that went up before the big fire of '89.

> In 1881 I made about 200,000 brick and I. T. Benham built out of them the first Wolverton block (the first all-brick block) for W. M. Wolverton, at the corner of Mill and Riverside....

> In 1882 I made 400,000 brick ... In August, J. N. Glover bargained for 250,000 brick for the construction of the First National Bank building at the corner of Front and Howard.... Henry Brook [a contractor and builder] also came to town about the same time and next year superintended the brick work on the bank.

> 1883 was a stirring year in the manufacture of brick and the construction of buildings. Wright [his partner] and I made about 850,000 during the season. A man by the name of Taylor started a large yard southeast of town on the Moran prairie road and went broke about the middle of summer....

> A man by the name of Adams late in the season of '83 burned the brick for the old Gonzaga College. Adams was up a stump for a hand moulder.... We had a good moulder, a Colfax boy by the name of Monte Bickford, that we were paying $90.00 a month [$3.00 a day] and board. Monte went over to Adams yard to see how the clay worked. He found that it moulded first-class and came back and reported. He also said that the fathers over there offered him $5.00 [a day] and board to do the moulding, but that he had hired for the season to us and he did not want to break [the] bargain. I told him to take it in and I would do the moulding on our yard for the rest of the season. Monte went to the college, and moulded up all the

material that had been hauled up from the bank of the river to the site of the prospective building. The old building still stands and it was moved a few years ago a considerable distance from its original site....

But I am getting ahead of my story. The building was put up the next year and I have still to mention that among the buildings put up in 1883 were the First National Bank, the Union block situated across Howard street from said bank, Henry French's block, Jamieson block, and the Browne block on the corner of Riverside and Post. Over 1,500,000 brick were laid in the wall in 1883 and the town for the first time was overbuilt. There were all kinds of vacancies and it, was about two years before there was much more done in the way of brick-building.

In 1884 I was the only one in the brick-making business and the only building that went up was the Gonzaga College building [other accounts give 1885 as the year]. Henry Brook and Preusse, the architect, were the officers in charge, and both of them took a hand with the trowel in its construction. There was about 250,000 brick used in the building.

At this point in his narrative, Davie went into an overly detailed account of how he happened to supply the brick for Spokane's first Catholic church, which was built on Main at Bernard by the Jesuit priests responsible for the founding of Gonzaga.

Later in the season of '85 I sold D. M. Drumheller brick for a residence on the corner of Second and Mill streets, and Mr. Van Valkenburg for his block adjoining the Jamieson block on Riverside avenue.

In 1886 I moved my plant from Latah creek up to the present location of Cannon Hill Park. Henry Brook and I bought eighty acres of land up there from Calvin Robertson.... Mr. Brook handled all of the brick I made, using most of them himself for the buildings for which he contracted. Among the buildings that he erected this year were the Keats block [another account credits this to contractor Frank Johnson], corner Riverside and Howard, the old Hyde block, adjoining, and the First Presbyterian church on the present site of the Review building.

This year, with one hand moulder I made over 1,000,000 brick. I moulded the last two months myself, which was the last of my hand moulding. In this year N. Triplet, my first co-worker that stayed in the clay working craft for any length of time, started operations. His yard was first located on Downer's ranch, or the present location of Liberty Park. Wm. Reddy ran a yard for several seasons on the same site some time after. Next year Triplet moved down to Hangman creek to the site of one of my old yards and he stayed in the business altogether for nearly twenty years ... and made brick for a good many of the substantial blocks put up after the big fire....

In 1887 the first machines were introduced into Spokane for the manufacture of brick. That year I made 3,000,000 brick.... There was great difficulty in early days in getting skilled help, and that year so much of the higher mysteries of the craft fell to my lot that I overworked myself and my health broke down.... Early in 1888 I sold out all of my interests in the business, including the land, to Mr. Brook ...

Mr. Brook ran the yard under the superintendence of George B. M. Rambo, and after a short time sold out to two men from the east, Messrs. Spear and Belt. Belt went out of the business that year, and Messrs. Brook and Spear formed the company that certainly came to stay, the Washington Brick and Lime Company. Mr. Brook died some years ago, but Mr. Spear is still at the head of one of the greatest industries of the northwest and a clay-working establishment of national note.... [The manufacturing operation had since moved to the town of Clayton in Stevens County.]

In 1889 I came back to the business, taking in Mr. P. Erickson as partner....

After the big fire of August 4, 1889, brick makers crowded into Spokane from all over the United States. Next year there must have been about two dozen concerns pouring brick into the city by wagon and rail. The business was entirely overdone and the burg was as badly overbuilt that year, which, of course, resulted in the inevitable and world-old struggle among the clay workers, the survival of the fittest, and in about two years after, when the smoke of battle had cleared, away, only the four old firms that were here before the fire, though much dilapidated, were still in the ring.... Three of the old yards survived [the 1893 Panic]: The Washington Brick & Lime Company, N. Triplet, and J. T. Davie & Co....

To this day there still exist quite a number of commercial buildings and homes in Spokane that were built of brick during the late 1800s and early 1900s, certainly a testament to the local significance of this industry.

~ The Volunteer Fire Department ~

Because Spokane's devastating fire is such a significant piece of its history, a brief background on the city's first fire department is warranted. Despite the ever-present risk of a destructive fire, Spokane Falls did not have a viable fire department until 1884. The Hook and Ladder Company of Spokan Falls (its official name) had been organized in 1880, for which the *Spokan Times* published the complete articles and bylaws on April 22, 1880. The detailed nature of the constitution suggests considerable time was invested in its development. Although citizens expressed the need for an efficient fire department, Spokane Falls experienced several fires before one was finally developed. A June 2, 1883, article in the *Spokane Falls Review* confirmed the existence of "the hook and ladder company," but pointed out "the material in use is entirely inadequate to prove even an apology for a protection againt [sic], or a means of extinguishing, the most trivial fire."

In 1884, the city waterworks system was developed, and a functioning volunteer fire department was formed. Two hose companies organized within a month of each other. The first one, Rescue Hose Company #1, began on August 24, 1884, with the town's marshal, Eugene Hyde, appointed as its president. Spokane Hose Company #2 was organized in September. The volunteer fire department was much like a fraternal order. Membership had to be approved, regular meetings were held, officers were elected, and dues were collected. Badges and uniforms soon gave the firemen an official appearance. A fund-raising ball was held in the spring of 1885 and in the fall, they held their "first annual ball."

An ordinance passed in October 1884 authorized the formation of the fire department, and on May 29, 1885, the city council passed a second one outlining the department's powers and duties. One section specified each hose company to have no less than 15 active members and no more than 30. Hook and ladder companies could have up to 40 active members. It also mandated the election of the chief engineer by the firemen. The city council had appointed Eugene Hyde in December 1884 to act as the temporary fire marshal, a position he held until an election among the firemen in June 1885. Because their vote was tied, the city council decided the outcome, naming Frank M. Dallam, founder and editor of the *Spokane Falls Review*, as chief engineer. Horace L. Cutter followed him for a one-year term, at which time Hyde was elected to fill the position again. Hyde was reelected in 1887 for a second term, but resigned in June 1888, likely for health reasons. The council chose veteran volunteer William W. Witherspoon to complete the term, and in December 1888, Witherspoon was elected as the last chief of the volunteer fire department. During his term, the need for a professional, full-time, salaried fire department became obvious.

Members of the Spokane Falls Volunteer Fire Department in 1886. From left: Frank Aiken, Lt. S. K. Harrison, Dennis Sheehan, and Capt. William W. Witherspoon. Witherspoon became fire chief in 1888 and police chief in 1899. To date, he and Eugene Hyde are the only two people in Spokane's history to have served as both fire chief and police chief. *(Patsy Clark album, courtesy Mark Danner)*

One of the volunteer fire department's hose carts in 1886. Hose-cart races became a popular source of sport and entertainment. Two teams from Spokane Falls consistently won trophies in both local and Pacific Northwest tournaments. *(Patsy Clark album, courtesy Mark Danner)*

Following the organization of the hose companies, finding a building was next on the agenda. The arrival of the equipment, consisting of two hose carts and 1,500 feet of hose, presented the dilemma of where to house them. The carts were stored temporarily in Glover and Gilliam's livery stable until a building on Howard between Main and Front became available in December of 1884. This was the first official fire station.

The following summer, both companies moved into their respective facilities, which served the basic needs of housing equipment and providing a meeting place. Later stations had sleeping quarters, but during this era they were often cold and damp, and hoses often froze. Spokane Hose Co. #2 occupied an old lumber office that was moved to Howard near Railroad Avenue. A bell tower was constructed for the new fire bell that arrived on September 9th. By this time, Company #1 had moved into its facility on Main near Howard (later relocating to Riverside west of Wall). In 1885, Company #2 moved into its quarters, which were claimed to be large enough to accommodate both a hose cart and a much-needed hook and ladder truck. However, when the city finally purchased one, which arrived in August 1887, they "had no place to keep it." A new building was erected adjacent to Hose House #2, and the Tiger Hook and Ladder Company was formed to man it. By July 1889, a third hose company, called Washington Hose Company #3, was organized. It was the first fire station on the north side of the river.

Despite the dedication of the volunteer fire department, its adequacy in the face of a major conflagration was a concern. A city the size of Spokane Falls (nearing a population of 19,000) needed paid firemen on regular duty and horses to haul the heavy hose carts. The alarm system consisted of a fire bell, to which church bells would join in, a common practice in the West at the time. This was by no means an efficient, integrated system. Also, there was no telephone at the pumping station, and an 1888 fire had proven the water pressure to be insufficient.

Such was the state of affairs at the close of that quiet Sunday afternoon of August 4, 1889. When the alarm was sounded about 6:00 p.m., volunteer firemen rushed from their homes to man the hose carts. Although the fire chief had been requesting horse-drawn equipment since 1887, none had been received. When the firemen attached the hoses to hydrants, there was only a trickle of water, then nothing.

Fire Station No. 1 at 418 West First Avenue, built after the 1889 fire. It was occupied by the end of December and, because both fire stations located on the south side of the river were destroyed in the fire, it became the department's headquarters. This building was abandoned as a fire station in 1938 but is still standing. *(From* Spokane Police and Fire Departments *by the Spokane Police and Fire Department Pension Board, 1902)*

~ Spokane's Great Fire of 1889 ~

The tremendous growth and development experienced during the decade was dealt a cruel blow that hot summer evening. The fire started at Railroad Avenue between Post and Lincoln in an area of flimsy wooden structures. Although accounts vary, the likely origin of the fire, according to the most credible sources, was at Wolfe's Lunch Counter, across the street from the NPRR depot. What started as a small, seemingly manageable fire soon turned into a raging firestorm. The summer of 1889 had been exceptionally hot and dry, forest fires were burning out of control in Washington and Idaho, and the prevailing conditions put everything at risk.

Following earlier fires, most of the large commercial buildings had been built of brick and stone. Many observers were certain the fire's progression would be blocked by those solid structures, but watched in disbelief as fire overtook them. A primary means of arresting the fire's progress was to destroy buildings in its path with dynamite. According to the eyewitness account from Dr. Gandy's son Lloyd, before the fire in one section could be extinguished, it leapt to another area, and soon the whole city was engulfed in flames. The fire raged on for almost four hours, devouring nearly everything from Railroad Avenue to the river and from Lincoln to Washington, causing an estimated $5-10 million in damages (an exact amount could not be determined because many homes and small business were not insured and did not file claims).

The day after the fire, the heat was still so intense that when some of the surviving safes were opened, the contents immediately burst into flames. As a result, most were allowed to cool for four or five days before being disturbed. Fortunately, there was only one death. George I. Davis, a civil engineer, died in Sacred Heart Hospital from severe burns. Shortly after the fire, the hospital reported an admission of 37 people (representing a 45-percent increase in patients) who had been suffering with illnesses at home and had nowhere else to go after being burned out by the fire. Countless others fled to the north side of the river and watched helplessly as their homes and businesses went up in flames. Among the losses were two of the three fire department hose houses. The men were demoralized, but a week later a letter appeared in a local newspaper from former Seattle fire chief Gardner Kellogg, who was in Spokane Falls at the time of the fire, applauding the efforts of the firefighters. He was aware of criticisms aimed at the fire department and stated, in part:

> I saw no mistakes made that night. Every officer and man did his whole duty ... no department could have done more with the means at their command ... I have had many years' experience in fire matters, served in every capacity from torch boy to chief of the department ... and I am not saying too much for your department when I say had the same intelligence been displayed by the officers in command of the Seattle fire department at the time of our great fire [June 6, 1889] as was shown by yours, Seattle would not have been in ruins to-day.

Outrage and blame were also leveled at Rolla A. Jones, superintendent of Spokane's new water-

The Arlington Hotel Block, built in 1887. Civil engineer George I. Davis was the only person to die in the 1889 fire. When the Arlington became engulfed in flames, he leaped from the burning building. He later died at Sacred Heart Hospital from severe burns. This was Spokane's first four-story building. *(Sketch from the 1890* Spokane Falls Illustrated*)*

This rare perspective of the aftermath of the fire, photographed from Havermale Island, shows a good-sized portion of the burned district of the Great Fire of 1889. The fire began on the north side of the NPRR tracks and consumed nearly everything between Lincoln and Washington to the Spokane River, essentially the entire business district and downtown core. Logs in the Spokane Mill Company's pond (foreground) caught fire, as did the first span of the Howard Street Bridge, but fortunately the fire did not jump to the north bank of the river. *(Patsy Clark collection, courtesy Mark Danner)*

works, who was in Coeur d'Alene at the time of the fire, leaving, as reports contended, an inexperienced individual in charge who failed to turn on the pumps. Newspapers as far away as New York repeated the charge. However, an in-depth investigation ordered by the city council presented an entirely different picture. The man in charge was, in fact, sufficiently experienced and competent, and the lack of water pressure was due to equipment malfunction. Nevertheless, unduly vilified, Rolla Jones resigned. The false accusation has persisted and has been repeated in numerous publications over the years. In reality, there were a number of contributing factors to the widespread devastation, some of which were discussed earlier. The city of Spokane Falls realized the reconstruction process needed to include a full-time professional fire department equipped with proper horse-drawn equipment and a city-wide alarm system.

The fortitude of the residents was triumphantly demonstrated in the aftermath. The following excerpt from an article entitled "Rising Spokane" in the *Spokane Falls Review* on August 10, 1889, illustrates, although perhaps somewhat exaggerated, the prevailing attitude:

> Nearly every available man was at work clearing away debris to commence excavating for new structures, and teams are hauling it away. More of the walls were blown down yesterday. The booming of the blasts, together with the sights of soldiers patrolling the city, gives the appearance of war times.
>
> The hour of sadness has passed and everyone is jubilant over the brilliant prospects for the immediate rebuilding of that portion of the city that passed so quickly away in smoke. Of course the loss sustained by our business men is keenly felt, but they say that this is no time for mourning, and their minds are engaged with only the one important thing, that is the work of reconstruction.
>
> Real estate is not in the least affected, but on the other hand, has increased in value. This was evident by the busy time enjoyed by real estate dealers and by the private sales ... The records show that $25,000 worth of property changed hands yesterday, but this don't [*sic*] include all the deals, as the instruments were not all filed.

Condolences, assistance, and supplies poured in from all over the country, with an especially strong outpouring from the surrounding Inland Northwest communities. National Guard troops were stationed around the fire district, not only for safety reasons, but also to guard against looting. The August 10, 1889, *Spokane Falls Review* posted a notice that all unclaimed and unidentified goods salvaged from the fire were to be delivered to Chief Joel Warren at city hall. It went on to say that Warren proposed a search of the city

Main Avenue, looking west from Stevens.

Howard Street, looking north from Sprague.

Riverside Avenue, looking east from Lincoln Street.

Looking north from Railroad Avenue. *(All photos from the Pasty Clark album, courtesy Mark Danner)*

and "all parties found in possession of goods that do not belong to them will be dealt with according to the law."

It was later learned that three city officials had misappropriated wagon loads of donations meant for the homeless, delivering them to the homes of other officials or private citizens who were untouched by the fire. This caused an outcry of indignation from the community and the three men – Major Sidney D. Waters, councilman and former Indian agent for the Colville Reservation, Councilman Peter Deuber, and Police Officer William Gillespie – were indicted by a grand jury in December 1889. Unfortunately, the cases dragged on for years, and the indicted were never brought to trial, allegedly because the main witnesses had left the area. The following May, Deuber was forced to resign his council position as the result of a bribery charge, but Waters remained in his position as councilman, and Gillespie continued to serve on the police force.

Most post-fire efforts, however, were productive. The townspeople wasted no time rebuilding, with every able-bodied person pitching in to help. Most did this willingly, but to encourage those otherwise inclined, the city council adopted a motion that "any person offered employment and refusing to work, be notified to leave the city." Harry Hayward efficiently supervised the relief work. As clean-up efforts progressed, debris was dumped into a large gully that fanned out in a 'V' shape from the block where the Crescent Court now stands (between Main and Riverside at Wall) to the river. After the gully was filled in with fire debris, buildings were later constructed over the fill, including the main Spokane Public Library and the newer addition to the Spokane Club.

Insurance adjusters moved in, most of whom set up desks in Concordia Hall on Second Avenue. Although many businesses carried insurance, a lot of the coverage was inadequate, necessitating the need to finance reconstruction. Much of the capital to rebuild came from Dutch investors. One of the largest Dutch companies was Northwestern and Pacific Hypotheekbank (the Dutch word for

A typical scene in Spokane Falls, which quickly became a tent city after the fire. Business resumed nearly overnight. The Crescent Block is visible at the upper right. *(Patsy Clark album, courtesy Mark Danner)*

mortgage). In the wake of the national depression in the early 1890s, the company foreclosed on the properties of many of Spokane's wealthy, heavily mortgaged businessmen who were unable to make their payments. As a result, the Dutch subsequently owned a large portion of downtown Spokane.

Devastating as it was for most, the disastrous fire provided career or business opportunities for many. Within days, commercial enterprises were conducting business in tents. The F. O. Berg Company (originally Omo and Berg), pioneer tent and awning manufacturer, supplied many of these tents or the canvas to cover new buildings. Today, they are one of the oldest continuously operating businesses in the state.

The fire did not cross Lincoln Street to the west, thus sparing the city offices, police station, jail, and the newly erected three-story Crescent Block, so named for the crescent-shaped curve of Riverside Avenue at its location. This building immediately filled up with businesses and boarders burned out by the fire. James M. Comstock and Robert B. Paterson had just stocked their new store, the Crescent, and were ready to open for their first day of business on August 5th. As the only surviving retail dry goods store in town, success was guaranteed. The entire stock sold out immediately, and the Crescent began building a good name by not taking advantage of the situation and raising prices. (Although the Crescent had done this by choice, a few days later, Mayor Furth announced that any businessman attempting to take undue advantage by raising prices would have his business license taken away and be closed down.)

Rebuilding the city commenced immediately. Naturally, architects and builders were in great demand. Herman Preusse, who had arrived in Spokane Falls in 1882, was already well established as an accomplished and talented architect, the city's first professional in that field. Having designed many of the commercial buildings lost in the fire, he was quickly overwhelmed with new reconstruction projects. Kirtland K. Cutter's business also flourished. His name is now associated with many of Spokane's greatest historical mansions and commercial buildings, and is one of the most recognizable names in Northwest architecture.

Louis M. Davenport, an unknown 20-year-old at the time, would play a significant role in bringing attention to Spokane in years to come. He had arrived in Spokane Falls in March 1889, and had gone to work for his uncle Elijah Davenport, who had established himself in the local hotel and restaurant business. After working for a few months in Elijah's restaurant, the Pride of Spokane, Louis had assumed ownership just prior to the fire. Following the loss of the Pride of Spokane to the fire, Louis soon opened a small restaurant, called the Waffle Foundry. It was a small start, but this enterprising young man would eventually be at the helm of Spokane's finest historic treasure, the Davenport Hotel. During his rise to the pinnacle of Spokane's hospitality industry, Davenport turned to Kirtland Cutter almost exclusively as the architect of choice for both business and personal projects. Consequently, Cutter and Malmgren received the commission to design the grand hotel.

At the time of the fire, a great promotional book produced by local businessmen (published through the Board of Trade) titled *Spokane Falls Illustrated* was at the press. The book boasted of the city's rapid growth, prosperity, and development, and included synopses of the primary industries, prominent businesses, civic leaders, businessmen, commercial buildings, and homes. Still believing heartily in the city's future, the writers quickly added a section summarizing the fire. It was followed by "A Word To Investors," which offered reassurance that the "handsome city Spokane Falls" would be "far handsomer than the old one" and would provide great investment opportunities. Their optimism is to be applauded, but a dark reality settled over the town before it would, like the legendary Phoenix, arise victorious from its ashes.

As the decade came to a close, snow fell early on the pitiful city that lay in ruins from the fire's devastating blow. Winter settled in with an oppressively cold and snowy season; temperatures dipped as low as 23° below zero. Spirits sank, but the townspeople remained undaunted. Spokane stood at the center of a region rich in abundant natural resources untouched by the fire. And, with the residents' determination to rebuild, the land beneath the rubble was as valuable as ever.

The Crescent Block, located on Riverside between Lincoln and Monroe, after the 1889 fire. As one of the few downtown buildings that escaped destruction, it filled up immediately with boarders and businesses, many of which hung their advertisements out front. Some of the advertisers were Arthur D. Jones and Co., real estate and insurance; Bower and Sawyer, real estate and insurance; Adams and Co., real estate brokers; and a number of mortgage and loan offices and banks. The Crescent Store, which took its name from the building, was a new store slated to open on August 5th. It opened as scheduled the day after the fire. Although it was the only surviving dry goods store in town, the proprietors did not take undue advantage of the situation by raising their prices, endearing them to the public. Their stock sold out immediately. The store quickly outgrew its space and relocated the following year. Three moves later, in 1899, the store settled into its own newly constructed building at 700 West Riverside. As the Crescent grew and prospered, its owners built a big addition on Main and absorbed other buildings on the block, resulting in what is now the Crescent Court. One year shy of a century in business, the Crescent Store was bought out by the Frederick and Nelson chain, which subsequently filed for bankruptcy. *(MAC, L88-362)*

Three

Fire Could Not Destroy This Town (1889-1899)

Spokane Hardware in its temporary quarters two weeks after the fire. Underneath their sign was a handwritten one stating "Open Day and Night." *(MAC, L98-122)*

Although the downtown core of Spokane Falls had been reduced to skeletons of burned-out brick buildings, and piles of rubble and ash, the residents were resolute in their determination to rebuild. Business resumed in tents, which quickly began to line the streets, giving the town the appearance of a war zone. Nearly every type of business enterprise, including about a dozen selling alcohol and offering gambling options, was represented. As the remaining building frames were dynamited, every able-bodied person labored to assist in removing the debris. Building construction was underway as soon as the ground cooled.

But as the town struggled to regain some sense of normalcy, snow began to fall and the temperatures plummeted. That winter, snow lay on the ground for three solid months. A comment was made that "all Spokane is on runners," as every means of conveyance had been fitted with them. At one point, even the railroads into Spokane Falls were blocked by snow.

Nevertheless, by the end of the year, there were about 500 buildings under construction, the list of which filled 20 columns in the newspaper. During each of the next two years, an estimated five to six million dollars was spent on new construction, and real estate transfers in 1890 were reported to have totaled $18 million. (In today's dollars, the amounts would be roughly 25 times the value in 1890, so in this case, about $450 million.) A large

Looking east along First Avenue after the fire. (*Courtesy SPLNWR*)

percentage of this construction was financed at eight to ten percent interest by the Northwestern and Pacific Hypotheekbank, which had been chartered two months before the fire. Still, this was only the beginning.

Accompanying the arrival of spring was a plan to show the world the spirit of Spokane was untouched. The city of 20,000 was going to host a grand industrial exposition, designed to acquaint the outside world with the enormous potential of the extensive natural resources found in the Pacific Northwest. Spokane Falls needed to present a respectable image for its month-long Northwestern Industrial Exposition scheduled to open on October 1, 1890. With this goal as motivation, the speed and degree to which the city rebounded was nothing short of remarkable.

In early 1890, the city council issued an edict that any remaining temporary structures from the tent city erected after the fire were to be vacated and removed by the first of August. Simultaneous construction of the massive exposition hall and an inordinate number of downtown commercial buildings created a high demand for laborers, especially

Dutch Jake and Harry Baer's tent saloon, constructed shortly after the fire, was reported to contain 14 bars, a gambling hall, and a variety theater. This structure was built over an existing gully that stretched from the river to where the Crescent Court now stands (between Main and Riverside Avenues at Wall Street). The empty beer kegs behind the men in the photo is evidence of the brisk business it conducted until it closed in June 1890. Up to a thousand men packed the place on the weekends. In January 1890, following an altercation outside the saloon, Baer shot and killed a man. He claimed self-defense, was tried and found not guilty. (*E. E. Bertrand photo, MAC L93-66.278*)

carpenters and bricklayers. The list of buildings completed in the early 1890s are too numerous to include here, but a number still exist and are on either the local or national historic register (see appendix). A perspective of the building activity was offered in a letter published in the June 17, 1890, *Spokane Falls Review*. It was written by Mary J. Holmes, a best-selling author who sold over two million copies of her books before her death in 1907. She had recently visited Spokane Falls, and likened the activity she witnessed to an ant hill that had been disturbed, saying:

> ... Spokane impressed me just like that – a human ant hill, uprooted from its foundation; and as I saw the people – men, women and children – all busy, all in a hurry, all eager and determined to repair the waste places and make them more fair and substantial – I had a great respect for the place which has received so terrible a baptism of fire and still was neither discouraged nor dismayed ...

Spokane Falls began to emerge more impressive than ever, and claimed its position as the second

The Hotel Spokane, located on the southwest corner of First and Stevens, in 1890. It was Spokane's finest hotel and a choice venue for elite functions. It also hosted visiting dignitaries, including Vice President Adlai Stevenson, who spoke to a large gathering in front of the hotel during a visit to Spokane in 1893. Among other things, it became known for its restaurant, the Silver Grill. Around 1908, another floor was added and the Lamona Block (arrow at right) was incorporated into the hotel. The hotel was demolished in 1962 to make room for the construction of the Ridpath Motor Inn, connected to the Ridpath Hotel by a pedestrian bridge. The Lamona was built in 1889. Among its early occupants were the Chamber of Commerce, the Spokane Club (formed in 1890), the Spokane Amateur Athletic Club (SAAC, formed in 1891), and the University Club. *(From* Spokane Falls and Its Exposition, *1890)*

largest city in the state (Washington had just become the Union's 42nd state on November 11, 1889). In 1891, the former Spokane Board of Trade reorganized as the Spokane Chamber of Commerce. During the year, its secretary, John R. Reavis, authored a booklet titled *The City of Spokane: Its Tributary Country and Its Resources*. It had been underwritten by the real estate firm of Clough and Graves in an attempt to stimulate sales of property. The publication boasted of the major structures in downtown Spokane and their costs at the time. Among those listed were the Exposition Building, $100,000; Hotel Spokane, $240,000; the Lindelle Block, $115,000; and Auditorium Building and Theater, $300,000. The latter had opened in 1890 with a production of *Nanon*. The first performance was attended by the majority of Spokane's elite and wealthy.

The Auditorium Theater. *(Jerome Peltier collection)*

Spokane's downtown core offered the usual mix of businesses or services of a growing town in

First (now Westminster) Congregation Church, located at the southeast corner of Fourth and Washington. Construction began in 1890 but was not completed until 1893. It is now listed on the National Register of Historic Places. The church was chartered by Rev. Henry Cowley in 1879. The first building was constructed in 1881 at Sprague and Bernard. By 1891, this was one of Spokane's 30 churches. *(From* Spokane, A Tale of a Modern City, *Fifth Edition, published by the Spokane Chamber of Commerce in 1907)*

this era, including retail stores, restaurants, real estate brokerages, mining and stock exchanges, pharmacies, hotels, bakeries, doctor and dental offices, markets, grocers, tobacconists, ice cream parlors, banks, and law offices. The commercial buildings typically housed retail stores and banks at street level, with printers, real estate companies, and finance companies occupying the basements. Second and third floors held business and professional offices, and apartments were located on the upper levels.

Although many people lived within the downtown city limits, neighborhood development beyond those limits continued to grow in popularity, and the streetcar lines serving those areas were capitalizing on the great opportunities. However, this was not without incident, and as mentioned in the previous chapter, it often involved City Hall. One such incident arose in early 1890 over an issue with the first Monroe Street Bridge. The city, the Cable Railway Company, and the private property owners who most benefited by the bridge had a shared arrangement to cover its construction costs. After the bridge opened in 1889, the city withheld its payment, stating the bridge was unsafe and not built to specifications. In response, the Cable Company closed both entrances and attached signs stating "Private Property; No Crossing." Although some subsequent efforts were made to strengthen the bridge, it soon burned down, creating larger and more pressing problems.

There was also heated competition between the various lines, sometimes to the point of becoming violent. However, in the early 1890s, the Washington Water Power Company (WWP) began consuming the competition. It had the decided advantage of generating the electricity on which the streetcars operated. The company purchased the stocks and bonds of the independent trolley lines, such as the Ross Park line (purchased by Spokane Street Railway, which had become a WWP subsidiary by 1892), the Spokane Cable Railway, the East Sprague line of the City Park Transit Company, and the Lidgerwood Cable. By 1899, WWP consolidated them into one system known as the

The Review Building, which was designed by architect Chauncey Seaton. When it was completed in 1891, an estimated 8,000 people attended its grand opening. *(Courtesy SPLNWR)*

Spokane's Northwestern Industrial Exposition Building as it appeared several years after the exposition that was held in October 1890. This massive building was designed by architect Chauncey Seaton and was located six blocks east of Division on the north side of Sprague (across the street from where Becker Buick is presently located). *(Courtesy SPLNWR)*

Washington Water Power Railway System. The company held a monopoly on the city transportation system for the next decade.

The Northwestern Industrial Exposition

The exposition's massive building was located on the north side of Sprague Avenue in the east 600 block. Some of the land had been donated by one of the exposition's directors, L. C. Dillman, a successful, wealthy real estate and mining capitalist. Free electricity was donated by Washington Water Power, and the architectural design was created by Chauncey Seaton (also the architect for the Review Tower simultaneously under construction).

Around the end of August, the union carpenters employed by the Spokane Mill Company went out on strike. It soon became a general carpenters' strike in protest of low wages and long hours. Just two weeks before the exposition was due to open, the carpenters working on its building, who made $3.00 a day, walked off the job and joined the strike to reduce the 10-hour workday. This threatened to doom the highly publicized (and, according to some, overly ambitious) project.

The directors of the project promptly issued a general appeal for help, asking those who could assist to report to the Exposition Building "... with or without tools, to do whatever is within your power to aid in completion of the building." Because of the popularity of the project, 350 citizens offered their services. Some people contributed by serving meals to the workers. A number of business owners also reassigned about 200 carpenters engaged in their respective building projects to work on the expo building.

The event opened on schedule with the presentation of hundreds of mining and agricultural exhibits. Exposition President F. Lewis Clark and Mayor Charles F. Clough both delivered welcoming remarks to the crowd of over 12,000 attending the opening-day ceremonies. The fair was a success, and with intentions of making it a permanent location, the city purchased the building and grounds in November of that year for $75,000.

Unfortunately, the building had been constructed with green lumber and, following an inspection by Seaton only six months later, the building was reported to be unsafe due to the amount of shrinkage in the unseasoned lumber. The problem took care of itself a few years later when the building was completely destroyed by fire. This exposition was a monumental task for a city the size of Spokane Falls, but history repeated itself in 1974 when Spokane overcame impossible odds and, as the smallest city to that date to host a world's fair, presented Expo '74 to the world.

Spokane's worst tragedy

Spokane has a history of generously reaching out during times of need and coming to the aid of the less fortunate, examples of which stem back to its very early days. As just mentioned, the residents stepped forward to help during the construction of the Expo building, but earlier in the month, they had also responded to a horrific tragedy. In terms of lives lost, this tragedy is unparalleled in the history of Spokane.

The Northern Pacific Railroad had a large labor crew working on a rock-cut at the intersection of Sprague and Division, where it was building new freight yards. On September 6, 1890, just minutes before the shift was to end at 6:00 p.m., over 200 pounds of dynamite prematurely exploded, instantly killing and wounding scores of workers and horses. A concentration of workers had been in the immediate area. Most had no chance to run and were buried under as much as 15 feet of falling rocks, some weighing several hundred pounds. An eyewitness reported seeing the two men who were setting the blast – foreman James McPherson and powderman Joseph Rhea – blown into the air in a dense column of smoke. The scene was one of horrify-

From the *Spokesman*, September 7, 1890

Another tragic incident involving the Northern Pacific occurred on July 13, 1891, when its trestle at Sixth and Cannon collapsed, causing numerous injuries and a death. This incident was the main focus of the city council meeting on July 16, 1891. The council president, Paul J. Stroback, expressed disgust that an inquest had not been held regarding this accident. He felt it was caused by the railroad's neglect of the trestle, which had been unsafe for some time and should not have been in use, emphasizing that it was located over one of the city's busiest streets and had been an ignored public hazard for some time. *(MAC, L87-321)*

The New Arlington Stables and Carriage Depository (the name they used to differentiate between this one, built shortly before and spared by the Great Fire, and their Arlington Stables on East Front Street). This building stretched along Washington between Sprague (the street in the foreground) and First. The YMCA building (at right) was built in 1891, and was one in a string of YMCA buildings. *(Jerome Peltier collection)*

ing terror and confusion, and the air was pierced by the agonizing cries of the injured survivors. One observer likened the aftermath to a "battlefield with dead men lying around, broken carts and mangled horses."

An alarm was sounded and the police were enlisted to hold back the well-intentioned crowd that quickly gathered. Several hundred volunteers, including almost every physician in town, worked feverishly to save lives and rescue those who were trapped. Many family members lined the rock-cut and crowded outside the morgue in total despair. Sadly, the blast claimed about 26 lives (24 were positively accounted for).

During this era of cross-county railroad construction, many hazards and poor working conditions contributed to a substantial number of industrial deaths. Little concern was placed on workers' safety or well being. In life, these laborers, mostly immigrants, were little more than numbers to their employer. Each wore a brass tag etched with his identifying number. When the foreman wished to summon a man, he called him by number. Now in death, a majority of the laborers were buried in unmarked graves in a common section of Greenwood Memorial Terrace, and the families who depended on them were left with no means of support. In 1996, Fairmount Memorial Association placed a monument at the site to acknowledge the uncelebrated contributions of Spokane's early laborers who, as these men, often risked their lives during the upbuilding of the city.

Although negligence was suspected, a grand jury investigation found no fault. Within a few days of the explosion, investigations and newspaper reports ceased, and work resumed at the site. No exact death count was ever reported. There would be no fight against the powerful corporation the city was so eager to please.

A new city charter

In 1891, a new city charter was drawn up to cover the changes of the times. "Falls" was officially dropped from the city's name. Now lined with industrial establishments and a key component of Spokane's waste-removal system, neither the falls nor the river offered quite the enticing visual allure of days past. In addition to the name change, the size of the city council was increased to provide representation from each of the city's wards. The city limits were also expanded, nearly quadrupling its size. The new boundaries were Garland Avenue on the north, 29th Avenue on the south, Regal Street to the east, and Cannon Street to the west. It also changed the location of Spokane's axis from Howard Street and Sprague Avenue to Division and Sprague, which required complete renumbering of all east-west addresses.

Hill's Great Northern Railroad scheme

By 1891, Spokane was already the most significant railroad hub west of St. Paul and Omaha when the Great Northern Railroad's president, James J. Hill, began making the necessary arrangements and procuring the land in order to include Spokane on its main line. The first passenger train with its single coach, carrying three passengers, arrived in Spokane from the east on May 27, 1892. Because the tracks into the city were still incomplete, the passengers were transferred to the Ross Park streetcar line for transport to their destinations. The last spike, signaling the line's completion, was driven on January 6, 1893, on the western slope of the Cascades, 13 miles below the summit.

In just slightly over a decade, Spokane had gone from having no railroad connection to seven significant lines passing through the city. Although the railroads were a boon for the whole area, the greater Spokane region suffered from unfair shipping rates because of its inland location. The inland rates were often higher than to ship to coastal ports, especially so if a railcar was only partially filled. When James Hill began procuring land for the Great Northern, he led the Spokane area residents to believe he would be offering fair rates

The Great Northern Railroad Depot, built on Havermale Island, was completed in 1902. *(Postcard from* Vintage Postcards From Old Spokane *by Duane Broyles and Howard Ness)*

in exchange for donated rights-of-way along the line's proposed route through the city. This was of considerable importance to Spokane businessmen, many of whom played right into Hill's hands and donated the sought-after land.

This turned out to be one of the most controversial business dealings in Spokane's history. In the beginning, Hill's shrewd negotiations gained him great popularity, and almost all the property along his chosen route was donated by the various owners, who believed in his promises. Once he acquired the desired property and his lines were in, the truth was realized. He had never signed binding documents to hold him accountable for any "promises." Although he gained nearly free passage through Spokane, the anticipated lower rates never materialized. He had misled the entire community, and the land donors received nothing in exchange.

Hill also purposely built his rail yards beyond the Spokane city limits so he would not have to pay city taxes. Nevertheless, it was an economic benefit for Hillyard, the town that grew up around the

Great Northern's machine shops and rail yards, and was so named because of this connection (literally "Hill's Yard"). Later, when the residents of Hillyard pushed for incorporation, Hill threatened to move his rail yards to another location. The town eventually was incorporated, but the yards were not included within the city limits.

In 1924, Hillyard was annexed to Spokane. Despite the amount of wealth generated by and funneled through the town because of the Great Northern's industrial complex, the community is now one of the poorest per capita in Spokane and the state of Washington.

The Panic of 1893

By 1892, Spokane was on its feet again, and according to a list in the *New York Tribune* that year, the city was able to claim six millionaires among its ranks. Along with the list of names were the sources of their wealth. They were Frank Rockwood Moore (silver mining and real estate), John J. Browne (real estate and banking), Anthony M. Cannon (real estate, banking, and railroads), James N. Glover (real estate and banking), Robert W. Forrest (real estate and banking), and the estate of E. J. Brickell (real estate and local waterworks). Unfortunately, their status and the city's newfound sense of stability would be short-lived.

The reasons were many and complicated, but in 1893, an economic panic threw the country into a downward spiral, plunging it into the greatest depression it had yet to experience prior to the Great Depression of the 1930s. The rolls of unemployed spiked out of control, businesses closed, and banks began to fail in Spokane. The town's first bank, Anthony Cannon's Bank of Spokane Falls, was also the first to fail. After its closing on June 5, 1893, like dominoes, the other ten banks closed, seven of which never reopened. The Browne National Bank managed stay open until November 22, 1894, but it, too, succumbed to the ravages of the depression. Four of Spokane's most significant early developers – Glover, Browne, Cannon, and Cook – lost nearly everything. Glover and Browne eventually repaid their bank depositors and, in time, recovered their fortunes. Cook pursued other endeavors, and Cannon died in 1895.

Many others among Spokane's class of wealthy and elite also lost their fortunes. After the Great Fire, Spokane was rapidly overbuilt and overfinanced. Those most affected by the Panic had large mortgages and deep debt. Foreclosures followed inability to repay mortgages, a large percentage of which were held by the Northwestern and Pacific Hypotheekbank. For a considerable time thereafter, much of Spokane's valuable real estate was owned by the Dutch mortgage company and its investors. It had taken over millions of dollars worth of buildings, commercial sites, thousands of acres of farm land for which there were no buyers, and many private homes.

There were others who also profited during this time – those with capital to invest. The investment opportunities seemed nearly endless. Despite the Panic, the city continued to show growth. A number of new homes were built in 1893, and attendance in the city schools was 3,326 compared to 2,880 the year before. Near the close of 1894, the real estate records for the previous 11 months totaled over four million dollars.

The new high school, completed in 1891, called Spokane High School. By this time, there were nine public schools. The high school occupied the same site as the present Lewis and Clark High School. This building burned in 1910. *(Courtesy SPLNWR)*

Northern Pacific Railway Depot at First and Bernard, circa 1894. The depot was built in 1890 to replace the one that burned in the Great Fire. Today it is the Spokane Intermodal Facility. *(MAC, L88-371)*

For most, however, it was a trying time. During the dark days of the depression, some of the unemployed working class resorted to such acts as stealing chickens to feed their families, while some from the upper class were known to opt for equally illegal white-collar crimes. Even the Northern Pacific Railroad was not immune from the effects of the depression and went into receivership on August 15, 1893.

Possibly also a result of the depression, at midnight on November 30, 1894, Spokane was plunged into darkness when the contract expired for electrical service to the city. A local electric company had been providing service, but when the company and the city council were unable to agree on the terms for a new contract, all power for the city was shut off. Prior to this, the city had been paying for 200 arc lights. Following two nights of darkness, the city agreed to pay $475 per month, but they reduced the number of arc lights to 50.

A new public safety building

A couple of major city and county construction projects provided some work and an economic boost during the depression. One was the Spokane County Courthouse, and the other was a new public safety complex. With the increase in the city's population, overcrowding in the municipal offices, and the deteriorating condition of both the public safety building (then on Riverside) and the adjacent jail, there had been a growing need to build a larger and stronger facility. The jail had become so inadequate that prisoners were able to escape from it almost at will. A contract was negotiated to begin construction in the fall of 1892 on a new facility, designed by architect Willis A. Ritchie. The impressive Romanesque-style brick edifice at the northeast corner of Front and Howard was built on the site of the Windsor Hotel (formerly the California House), which was destroyed in the Great Fire. The new building stretched approximately 100 feet along the east side of Howard Street and 75 along Front Avenue. It had three full stories plus an attic with numerous dormers. There were two 14-foot diameter round towers at each corner on the main entrance side, which faced Howard. The building was designed to accommodate the city offices and municipal courts. In addition, among the other occupants were the Chamber of Commerce and the Spokane City Library.

A two-story annex facing Howard Street on the north end of the building was built for the fire department (presently the site of the Looff Carrousel in Riverfront Park). Being the largest fire station, and designed to house the fire engines and the horses, it became the department's headquarters. The police department was sandwiched in between the fire station and the main building. The city jail, a two-story facility made up of cage-type cells, was located in a separate building behind the fire station. It was state-of-the-art for its time, and had four distinct units, two of which were intended for women and minors (a relatively new concept as all prisoners had previously been housed together). The total cost for this complex was estimated at $100,300, not including furnishings.

Construction was nearly complete on the main building when a fire of unknown origin destroyed the entire structure on September 13, 1893. Fortunately, the building was not yet occupied and the construction workers were able to escape the fiery inferno without casualty. Although the annex sustained some damage and was badly scorched, it remained intact. Within a few weeks, the contractors began clearing the debris and resumed working on the building.

Despite the original plan to move the police headquarters into the new annex, in February 1894, during the throes of the depression, the city commissioners began squabbling over whether it would be financially sound to move the city departments from their present locations. This caused an outcry because the old jail had been declared a "public nuisance" and essentially condemned by the public health officer. In March, the police and fire departments were given the go-ahead to move into the annex. The main building was completed that fall.

Spokane's new public safety complex was plagued with a problem from its inception – it was located well within the heart of Spokane's Tenderloin (red light) District. According to the *Spokane Weekly Chronicle* on November 19, 1896, within about a two-block radius, there were a "nest of saloons" and numerous houses of ill-repute. It stated, "Within the past two or three months these latter places have become so numerous in the vicinity of the city hall that within one block there are no less than seven large houses of bad repute and innumerable small ones." This became part of what later was known as "skid row" (or "skid road"), stretching from Wall to Division, between Trent and Main. The area was cleaned up in preparation for the Expo '74 World's Fair, but by then, the public safety building had long since been demolished.

The Spokane Public Safety Building, designed by architect Willis A. Ritchie (inset), was completed in 1894. This photo was taken just before demolition in 1913 to make way for the Union Station, a passenger depot used jointly by a number of railroads. The fire department occupied the annex with the four ground-level arches at the left (north side). The Great Northern Depot clock tower is visible upper left. *(Courtesy SPLNWR)*

The Spokane County Courthouse, completed in 1895. In 1893, the voters approved a $250,000 bond issue to build a new county courthouse on land donated by Civil War veteran Colonel David P. Jenkins. The Board of County Commissioners officially opened a competition for the best design. They offered a $1,000 prize and a lucrative contract to the architect who would come up with the "grandest symbol of sophistication and stability." The winner was Spokane architect Willis A. Ritchie, 29, who had also designed the Spokane Public Safety Building. The construction contract was awarded to former mayor David B. Fotheringham. Groundbreaking began in late fall of 1893. During the ensuing depression, the construction project provided a stimulant for Spokane's faltering economy. *(Courtesy SPLNWR)*

Fort George Wright

In the fall of 1894, as the residents of Spokane struggled through the dark days of the depression, a glimmer of light suddenly appeared on the horizon. News of the federal government's plan to build another military post in the Northwest thrust Spokane business leaders into action. Confident that Spokane's odds of being selected were as good as any other contender, they sent Arthur A. Newbery, a prominent city leader, to handle the negotiations in Washington, D.C. Six weeks later, Newbery returned with hopeful news; Spokane would be the site of the new fort if, in addition to certain financial obligations, it could donate 1,000 acres of land with a dependable water supply.

The public was undaunted by the present lack of cash or capital, because they knew securing the military fort would have a huge impact on the local economy in terms of additional jobs and government funding. Once again, the city would prove, as it had with the Industrial Exposition, that it was capable of accomplishing remarkable feats under seemingly impossible odds.

At the time of the economic panic, Spokane was still a young town in a constant state of flux. People had been arriving in such large numbers that many were still strangers to their neighbors, often feeling alone in their personal struggle for survival. Now there was a reason to unite as a community and work towards a common goal.

The few men who still had the means to do so contributed land or cash donations, but the real capital campaign began with the women. Several smaller fund-raisers were met with moderate success, but the idea of donating whatever a person could for a Christmas raffle quickly gained momentum. Every conceivable item was donated to later be distributed from a huge Christmas tree on the stage of the elegant Auditorium Theater. Sales of $1 admission tickets, which doubled as raffle tickets, evolved into a contest that was highly successful. Preparations for the event grew to such proportions that it was postponed until New Year's Eve.

The excitement and fun lifted spirits – and the event was a huge success. From a mince pie that brought 25 cents to a $125 shotgun, the vast array of donated items netted $4,500 in cash, enough to secure the fort for Spokane. The first federal appropriations were still a year and a half away, so there was no immediate impact on the economy, but the effect on community spirit and morale was immeasurable.

Northwest Milling and Power Company

In the mid-1890s, Simon Oppenheimer, a prominent and wealthy Spokane businessman, recognized some fertile opportunities that were ripe for productive cultivation. The sawmill owned by the Spokane Mill Company (on the original Scranton and Downing mill site), with which he was connected, burned in 1892, tragically taking the lives of four men. The first order of business was to build a bigger, better mill in its place. In addition, he had plans for a grand new flour mill west of Howard on the north bank of the river and an electric light plant to compete with Washington Water Power's near-monopoly.

A 21st Infantry wagon train at Fort George Wright in 1919. After Spokane was approved as the site of the new fort in the Inland Northwest, in 1896 Congress authorized construction and appropriated $100,000. The first buildings were completed in 1898, and the fort was commissioned the following year. The first troops were the 24th Infantry, Company M, a regiment of African-Americans. *(Libby-Graff photo, MAC, detail of L87.1-16408-19)*

The C and C Spokane Flour Mills, located on the north bank of the Spokane River at 621 W. Mallon Avenue, in 1931. Sometime after the mill started operating, the C and C, which had sold its mill on the south side of the river, became involved with this one. *(Frank Guilbert photo, MAC, L97-63.85)*

After being unsuccessful in securing backers for the projects in New York, Boston, and San Francisco, probably due to the depression, Oppenheimer traveled to Holland, where he succeeded in raising a sizable sum ($300,000). Dutch investors were already quite familiar with the opportunities in Spokane through the Hypotheekbank, which may have helped Oppenheimer secure a good portion of the necessary capital for the project from the Amsterdamsch Trustee's Kantoor. (*Kantoor* means "pool" in Dutch, so roughly translated, a "pool of trustees" – a type of trust company.) Upon his return, he formed the Northwest Milling and Power Company through which the projects would be built.

The new sawmill, named the Phoenix, was constructed of solid timbers, brick, and stone, and was in operation by September 1895 (see photo on page 10). It was so well built that when it was dismantled in September 1945, the demolition contractor described it as "the most solidly bolted building he has encountered in years of experience ..." (*Spokesman-Review,* September 6, 1945).

The five-story flour mill, called Spokane Flour Mills (today known simply as the Flour Mill), was also constructed in 1895. In addition, the Northwest Milling Company had purchased about 27 acres of land in the heart of the city, plus the waterpower rights and some existing buildings from the Spokane Mill and the Spokane Water Power companies. This included some of the best river property in the city. It was anticipated the new

The Spokane Falls Fruit Fair, October 6-18, 1896, during which the attendance topped 56,000. The implement building to the right of the tents housed the first Fruit Fair, which was held October 24-27, 1894, and had 150 exhibits. Spokane was most proud of its apple production. Its first train-car shipment of apples from Spokane, which were grown on Moran Prairie, to an eastern market was in 1894. By 1901, the Fruit Fair had become the Spokane Interstate Fair. The photo also shows the Spokane Flour Mills (arrow at left) shortly after its construction, and the Auditorium Building (just beyond the tent). *(MAC, L94-9229)*

Looking north along Post Street in the 1890s. The Auditorium Building is visible at the end of the street, and Louis Davenport's restaurant, prior to the addition in the early 1900s of the Mission-style facade, is on the left. Davenport had moved into this location a few months after the Great Fire. The restaurant quickly reached great acclaim, and Davenport commissioned Kirtland Cutter to assist as he expanded and remodeled the restaurant. Because of his success, Davenport was later backed by a group of local capitalists responsible for building the first-class Davenport Hotel. The Hazelwood Dairy's creamery (far left) was on the main floor of the Bellevue Block (later the Pennington Hotel, also owned by Louis Davenport). The horses and delivery wagons belonged to the Hazelwood Dairy. *(Courtesy SPLNWR)*

power plant would have sufficient water flow to produce an abundance of electricity year around. A 50-year franchise had been approved in July 1895 for this company, called the Consumers' Light and Power Company.

The buildings were rising as quickly as the labor pool could construct them, and according to George E. Morse, a company director quoted in San Francisco's *Morning Call* on March 26, 1896, an estimated $425,000 had been expended by the company. Although the sawmill was operating, the flour mill had been completed, and construction of the power company was well underway, in March 1896, the Northwest Milling and Power Company went into the hands of a receiver (James Glover was appointed by the Exchange National Bank). Oppenheimer quickly left Spokane, allegedly, according to Mr. Morse, to try to sell the company's stock in New York. In spite of Morse's contention that Oppenheimer was "as honest a man as I ever met" and that he would soon return with additional capital, others suspected that he had fled with no intentions of returning. They proved to be right.

Apparently it had been known for some time the company was in some financial trouble, but as the reports from the bankruptcy proceedings began to unveil financial dealings and records, it was revealed that Mr. Oppenheimer had left the company in a deplorable state. The financial statements had been "balanced," but assets were overinflated and ledger entries and transfers so convoluted that little sense could be made of them. The entire $300,000 from the Amsterdamsch Trustee's Kantoor was gone, as well as the proceeds from loans with various banks and the city's rather sizable stock investment. However, Oppenheimer's personal bank account was suspiciously flush.

Company and personal assets, including Oppenheimer's home, were seized, but the ensuing

Looking north over the second Monroe Street Bridge in 1895. The newly constructed Spokane County Courthouse is visible at the upper left and the Spokane Flour Mills at the upper right. *(Courtesy SPLNWR)*

lawsuits, complicated by the international component, dragged on for the next five years. According to the City-County of Spokane Historic Preservation Office, the Spokane Flour Mill "did not come into operation, however, until 1900 because the property became mired in a complex international lawsuit that was one of the most explosive and long-fought battles in the city's legal history." It is now on both the Spokane and the National Historic registers, and for the past four decades has been the home of a number of popular restaurants and retail shops.

Considering the magnitude of Simon Oppenheimer's trail of deceit, as well as the productive results of his efforts, until recently there was surprisingly little available material about him. However, after his curiosity was piqued, Chuck King, an inveterate local history buff and researcher, has since compiled an impressive amount of information on him and other Oppenheimers in the area. Among his findings was a newspaper article following Oppenheimer's death in San Antonio, Texas, on July 18, 1926, at the age of 64.

The following information was extracted from that article. After Oppenheimer's hasty departure from Spokane, he went to South America, but also spent some time in New York, where he and his wife separated in 1910. Following their separation, he then changed his name to Juan O. Simmons "for business purposes," and moved to Mexico, where he "amassed a fortune of $1,500,000 through management of Mexican lotteries." Although the newspaper article used the terms "separated" and "estranged" from his wife, it appeared they did not divorce, yet he apparently married another woman in Mexico and had a son with her.

Oppenheimer's life followed a much different course than what the residents of Spokane might have expected in 1895. In his *Spokane and the Inland Northwest,* N. W. Durham wrote:

> For several months in 1895 Simon Oppenheimer was quite the 'biggest man in Spokane.' People paused in awe of him as he passed along the street and bankers stood deferentially around when he discussed finance and the great achievements he had in store for Spokane.

An improving economy

While most of the country remained in the grip of the depression until 1897, Spokane fared considerably better. Much of the capital backing for various British Columbia mining ventures had come from Spokane investors and, by the spring of 1895, the mines were producing enough to begin paying dividends. Because the mining region was tucked between two mountain ranges, access to Spokane via the recently completed Spokane Falls and Northern Railroad was more direct than crossing the mountains. Consequently, the city profited, as supplies to meet the needs of a booming mining district were funneled through Spokane. Almost simultaneously, production picked up again in the Coeur d'Alene Mining District, which also affected Spokane's economy. The stranglehold of the depression began to loosen by mid-1895, but the *Spokesman-Review* warned investors to use caution against the wild speculation that ensued.

By 1896, the population had increased to around 27,000, and there was a brisk demand for well-built houses in the range of $1,000-$3,000. Over 100 such houses were sold within a six-month period. The new wealth coming from the mines in the Coeur d'Alenes and other districts was creating many new millionaires, many of whom displayed their wealth by constructing extravagant mansions in Spokane's two upscale neighborhoods – Browne's Addition and "The Hill" (generally the area skirting the lower South Hill around Seventh Avenue). The first of these, which included the residences of D. C. Corbin (now the Corbin Art Center) and his son Austin, were built in 1897.

Many industrialists and the *nouveau riche* also invested their new wealth in major commercial buildings in the downtown area, typically bearing the owner's name. In 1897, a reported total for commercial building construction was around $1.3 million. The Spokane Lumber Association reported that, for the first time in seven years, the

Riverside Avenue looking east from Post Street in 1897. Streetcars were serving all the outlying developments, but a new competitor, the automobile, would arrive in Spokane within a of couple years. Street paving was already taking on new importance and was completed on Riverside in 1899. *(MAC, L90-132)*

The fire on January 26, 1898, which destroyed the Great Eastern Block at the southeast corner of Riverside and Post, was Spokane's most disastrous in terms of lives lost. The origin of the fire, which started around 11:30 p.m., was believed to be in the John W. Graham & Co. store, located in the basement. It spread quickly, filling apartments in the upper stories with smoke. Firemen rescued many of the tenants, but one man, four women, and four children perished. (Some accounts claim eight deaths, but when the recovery efforts were completed a week later, the newspaper listed nine victims.) Extinguishing the fire was difficult because freezing weather caused the sprays of water to form a casing of ice around the building. Only the exterior framework was salvageable. Col. Isaac N. Peyton purchased the property, restored and expanded the burned structure, and renamed it the Peyton Building. On May 16, 1916, another fire started in about the same location of the building as the 1898 fire. There were no deaths but over 50 firemen were overcome by smoke inhalation. On June 6, 1956, in yet another fire in the Peyton Building, Fire Captain Leonard W. Doyle was killed and 42 other firemen were overcome by smoke. The Peyton Building and the Peyton Annex (built in 1908) are listed on the Spokane and the National Historic registers. *(Jerome Peltier collection)*

supply of dry lumber was exhausted in the Inland Northwest. It was most timely that, having exhausted the stands of timber on the East Coast, capitalists in the timber industry began looking to the Northwest and sending representatives to purchase timberlands and layout plans for large-production sawmills. In addition to other valuable species, the largest stands of remaining white pine in the country, the most valuable species on the market, were in the Northwest.

Around this same time, another opportunity presented itself when the tables turned on the Hypotheekbank. The following quote is from Barbara Cochran's book *Seven Frontier Women and the Founding of Spokane Falls:*

> With this fresh income [from mining and logging], men began buying up real estate from the Northwestern and Pacific Hypotheekbank at depressed prices. The mortgage company had fallen on difficult times; as was the case with those who earlier were the subjects of foreclosures, the company had expenses on the properties it held with no related income. It declared bankruptcy on March 30, 1898. Some who took advantage of the opportunity to purchase real estate from Hypotheek were: F. Lewis Clark, Charles Sweeny, D. C. Corbin, Patrick Welch, Aaron Kuhn, James Comstock, Robert Paterson, James Monaghan and David Ham. As Spokane author John Fahey has pointed out, the Panic did what the fire had not. It closed out the pioneer builders, and turned over their ground to a new group of men, largely speculators and developers, who would influence Spokane for the next thirty years. With Sweeny's purchase in 1904 of the Rookery, Riverside, and Spokane National Bank buildings, the Hypotheekbanks's ownership of the central business district came to an end [although the bank continued operations in Spokane for many years].

Around the time Hypotheekbank declared bankruptcy in 1898, the Northern Pacific Railway's real estate division announced a reduction in the per-acre price (two to four dollars an acre) in hopes of stimulating sales of its undeveloped grant lands. This created a renewed rush to the Inland Northwest and additional fortunes from real estate.

Growing pains

As Spokane's rapid growth continued, its future was full of hope and promise, but it also suffered its share of growing pains. Despite a more refined appearance, Spokane was still a young

Bicycles began gaining popularity in Spokane in the early 1890s. A bicycle club known as the Spokane Wheel Club formed in 1893, and took its first run on May 14, 1893. It was to Cowley's Bridge 18 miles east of the city. By 1904, there were about 10,000 bicycles in Spokane. The cyclists shown here, as they prepared for a race around 1899, were Loren Eastman, Art Cowley, Joe Richards, and Will Jobes. *(MAC, L83-59.1)*

Interior of the Monogram Bar at the northwest corner of Main and Bernard, in the 1900s. In 1901, Spokane had 123 saloons and the numbers continued to grow. *(Don Neraas collection)*

frontier town with plenty of rough edges. Gun-toting, bank-robbing criminals and those bent on pursuing illegal means of grabbing their share of the excitement and wealth moved in alongside the hard-driving capitalists and the laborers eager for legitimate new opportunities.

During the 1880s, the police were regularly called out for burglaries, drunkenness, and disorderly conduct, but duels, armed robberies, or brutal murders placed demands on law enforcement in the 1890s. The police department also dealt with ongoing vice-related crimes and disturbances in the saloons, bawdy dance halls, variety theaters, opium dens, and houses of prostitution. Although vice-related crimes will probably always plague law enforcement, this era was marked by wide open, rampant immoral and/or illegal practices.

By the fall of 1898, after two months of frequent burglaries and armed robberies, sometimes two or three a night, the community had become practically immobilized by fear and frustration. The robbers were becoming bolder, fearing no consequences. The streetcars were especially vulnerable and became prime targets for nightly holdups.

Cutbacks in the police department's budget during the depression, coupled with a rapidly increasing population and the related crime, had left the department with a lack of sufficient resources. Mayor Elmer D. Olmsted acknowledged the need for drastic action and called a session with Police Chief Joel Warren and the city commissioners.

All agreed the situation warranted the declaration of an emergency. Emblazoned across the front page of the November 3, 1898, *Spokane Daily Chronicle* was the following headline: "SHOOT DOWN THE THUGS. Every Able Bodied Man in Spokane Is Called to Take Arms in Defense of Life and Property. REIGN OF TERROR MUST BE ENDED." Every man over the age of 21 who met with Chief Warren's approval was then sent to the offices of the mayor and city clerk, where they secured a permit to carry a firearm and were sworn in as special officers. A $500 reward was offered for the arrest and conviction of anyone involved in the recent holdups. The response was immediate and, over the next few days, nearly 200 special officers were sworn in. While the new officers prowled every conceivable hiding place, other residents joined in by leaving their home lights burning all night and hanging lanterns in dark corners. The emergency plan had the desired effect, resulting in a radical decline of robberies and burglaries.

The Age of Elegance

In the late 1890s, while Chief Warren's department struggled to pull a respectable mask over the darker side of Spokane, high society ushered in an "Age of Elegance" that extended into the early 20th century. It was a time of excessive opulence and formality, a sort of celebratory response to the recovery from the recent depression and the massive wealth being extracted from the nearby mines and forests. It was reflected in the magnificent commercial buildings and the palatial homes with their beautifully landscaped grounds. Architect Kirtland Cutter's familiarity with European design, coupled with his artistic talents, placed him in great demand. The finest building materials and furnishings were hand selected in Europe, sometimes by Cutter himself, and shipped to Spokane.

Many of the mansions had private ballrooms, where the homeowners would entertain lavishly. Formal attire, replete with flowing gowns, elaborate hats, gold watch chains, topcoats with satin-lined capes, high starched collars, and fashionable canes, created the desired look. The "look" coupled with proper etiquette lent an air of sophistication. Many early residents, both men and women, had been steeped in culture and well educated in the eastern states and had traveled in Europe. Despite the backdrop of a young frontier city with its prickly edges, they enjoyed nearly the same degree of social life in Spokane as in the East.

It was certainly a time of interesting extremes. While some celebrated their good fortunes, the laborers in the Coeur d'Alene mines wearied of poor working conditions, long hours, and low wages. The unrest had been festering for some time. Violence had erupted in 1892, but what became known as the mining war in 1899 captured national attention. About 1,000 of the area's miners were imprisoned, forcing the mines to close.

Though some impact was felt in Spokane, signs of progress and expansion were everywhere. Streetcar lines, which aggressively vied for routes and the right to use primary streets, continued to reach farther into the outskirts. As the lines competed for customers, they developed enticing destination spots, especially parks that provided some kind of

A southeasterly view of Spokane's Natatorium Park, which originated as a trolley park called Twickenham. Its primary purpose was to stimulate ridership on the new Spokane Cable Railway, the park's owner, which built its line to the Twickenham Addition in 1889. The first attractions were a baseball diamond, a zoo and, in 1893, Spokane's first public swimming pool, called a "natatorium" (a Latin word for pool). The natatorium was such a popular attraction that, in 1895, the park was officially renamed Natatorium Park, soon known simply as Nat Park. By this time, it had become the property of Washington Water Power. In 1905, Audley Ingersoll began installing amusement facilities, patterning the park after New York's famous Coney Island Park. Dances, vaudeville productions, open-air concerts, along with a zoo and beautiful gardens, were added attractions. During the first decade of the 1900s, Buffalo Bill's Wild West Show, which appeared all over the United States and Europe, was a featured attraction on several occasions and drew thousands of spectators. Spokane's most beloved entertainment park became a choice place for all types of family, social, religious, political or business gatherings. It remained in existence until 1968. This site is now a mobile home park called San Souci West. *(MAC, L63-65.133)*

F. O. Berg, pioneer tent and awning manufacturer in Spokane, in his new car, the third in Spokane. *(Photo courtesy SPLNWR)*

entertainment or recreation. Natatorium Park was, by far, the city's favorite.

Spokane's first automobiles

Spokane's early automobile history is clouded by conflicting information. Although businessman F. O. Berg is often credited with owning the first car, the article on the opposite page clearly refutes this claim and establishes both the arrival date and the correct ownership.

Roy L. Boulter was the proud owner of the first car, a Haynes & Apperson, but he didn't know anything about operating such a machine. One of the few people in the city who did know something about the automobile was George Bartoo, who soon opened the first garage and "held the first automobile agency" in Spokane. With some difficulty, Bartoo helped Boulter get it running, and they took a 50-mile drive.

Residents were excited about the prospects of seeing this car "speeding about the streets of Spokane," but it failed to meet those expectations. Two months after the car's arrival, the *Chronicle* reported: "The automobile was seen downtown once. It was being drawn along through a back alley and was tied to a good old-fashioned horse and wagon, on the way to the repair shop ... After two trips to the repair shop, the automobile is now in the barn of its owner ..." Accounts conflict regarding the car's ultimate fate but do agree it was a miserable failure. It did, however, stimulate plenty of discussion regarding the pros and cons of steam versus gasoline engines.

The first three cars

On March 5, 1911, an article in the *Spokesman-Review* summarizing Spokane's early automobile history stated that Roy Boulter's car was followed by a second one on April 9, 1900. It was owned by Fairmount Cemetery. The third, according to an article on September 11, 1900, had arrived the previous day and belonged to businessman F. O. Berg.

In 1901, its first year in business, George Bartoo's agency sold a grand total of five cars. Typical of the times, these sales were transacted at Bartoo's bicycle shop. Within two years, gasoline-powered cars began to arrive in noticeable numbers and the first electric car made its appearance.

On July 26, 1903, the *Spokesman-Review* claimed: "No other town in the northwest can boast of as many automobiles as Spokane." During the early years, one of the newspapers published annual reports listing the make of every car in Spokane and the owners' names.

Years later, Berg recalled the first drive in his new car and was quoted in the February 11, 1926, issue of *The Spokane Woman* magazine as saying: "I'll never forget the night I brought it to Spokane. I started from the old O.W.R.&N. depot on Cataldo Street, and before I got uptown I had succeeded in startling five runaways [horses]. They didn't have any arrest laws in those days, but I got plenty of abuse." Police Chief Witherspoon was on hand to help remedy the lack of motorized vehicle laws.

William W. Witherspoon, chief of police from 1899 to 1902. *(Courtesy Spokane Law Enforcement Museum)*

Fire Could Not Destroy This Town (1889-1899)

SATURDAY MORNING, SEPTEMBER 16, 1899.

AN AUTOMOBILE HERE

FIRST IN SPOKANE ARRIVED LAST EVENING.

Comes Direct From the Factory to the Owner, R. L. Boulter—Will Carry Nine Passengers—Operated by Gasoline Engine—Trial Trip Today Probably.

The first automobile carriage ever in Spokane reached the city last evening over the Northern Pacific. It came direct from the factory, consigned to the owner, R. L. Boulter, who resides at the corner of Fifth avenue and Haven streets. It was seen last evening at the Northern Pacific express office.

It will be turned over today to Mr. Boulter, who will have it set up and probably make a trial trip this evening. If everything works smoothly an extensive trip about the city will be taken in the carriage by Mr. Boulter and a party of friends Sunday.

The carriage weighs between 1600 and 1800 pounds, and is to be operated by a gasoline engine. It is geared to maintain an average speed of 18 miles an hour. It has three seats, and is intended to carry nine passengers, including a driver. The four wheels have each a diameter of 36 inches, and have inflated rubber tires, which are about three inches broad.

So far as known there is no one in the city who has handled such a carriage, but Mr. Boulter expects little difficulty in operating it successfully so soon as it is put together.

On May 25, 1902, a "horseless carriage" moving along Riverside at a rapid clip caught the chief's attention. He jumped from the streetcar he was riding and caught up to the offender as the man reached his destination. Estimating the auto driver to be going at least 12 to 15 miles per hour, the chief issued a citation for speeding. Exceeding six miles per hour on horseback within the city was a misdemeanor punishable by a stiff fine. There were a few other traffic-related ordinances, which pertained primarily to streets and horses, including restrictions against riding a horse or bicycle on the sidewalks. But, because there were no city ordinances under the topic of automobiles, the charge was dropped. Witherspoon wasted no time initiating an ordinance to restrict the automobile's rate of speed within the city limits. Beginning with this single law, the body of vehicle ordinances multiplied exponentially.

An electric car

On July 31, 1910, an article in the *Spokesman-Review* described a trip H. G. Hawkins, manager of the Spokane agency for the Baker electric car, and Richard Howard made from Spokane to Hayden Lake, Idaho, in a Baker electric roadster. The trip took a little over three hours each way. Considering the state of the roads in 1910, they made good time. Remarkably, they made the entire round trip, about 80 miles, without recharging the batteries. In 1910, with the few gasoline-powered cars, the demand for gas was low, but at .7 cents per gallon, the electric car stood little chance of success at that time.

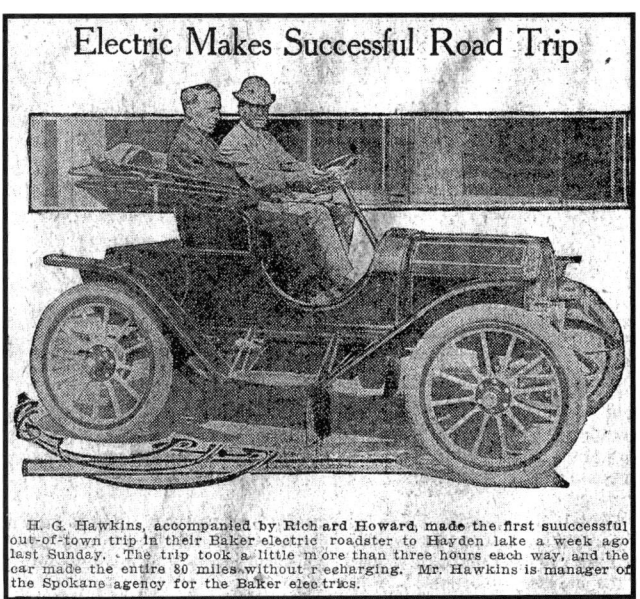

This newspaper clipping, found in the July 31, 1910, *Spokesman-Review,* described a road trip from Spokane to Hayden Lake, Idaho, in a Baker electric car. The entire approximately 80-mile round-trip was accomplished without recharging the batteries.

Street paving on Riverside Avenue in 1898. As this took on a higher priority, prisoners from the city jail were put to work sweeping the newly paved streets. *(MAC, L85-224)*

At the center of its universe

In 1899, Spokane set another record for construction. Contractors estimated about 1,200 to 1,300 new buildings were constructed that year. The next year, the U.S. census placed the city's population at 36,848, nearly doubling what it had been just after the Great Fire. Its geographical location, surrounded by great stores of natural resources all within a 100-mile radius, had secured its position as the economic, social, and cultural center of what was then called the Inland Empire. Many men continued to leave their chosen professions to pursue big-monied opportunities in real estate, mining, and other resource-extraction-based ventures. It appeared the sky was the limit.

The funeral procession on June 27, 1899, of war hero Ensign John R. Monaghan, who was killed in action in the Samoan Islands on April 1, 1899. He was the son of a prominent Inland Northwest pioneer family, among the first students at Gonzaga, and the first person from Washington to be appointed to the U.S. Naval Academy at Annapolis. In 1906, a statue at Monroe and Riverside was erected in his honor. *(MAC, L94-40.106)*

Four

Setting the Stage for the Formation of the Spokane Association of Realtors (1900-1911)

Looking southeast over the west end of downtown Spokane, circa 1903. At the center of the photo is the Vincent Methodist Church and, left of it, the Auditorium Theater, whose plain, boxlike exterior was a dramatic contrast to the ornate interior. Conjoined at a right angle on the east is the Auditorium Building (with its identifiable conical tower). The land between the Auditorium and the second Monroe Street Bridge (foreground) was formerly part of the huge gully, now filled. In 1905, the Terminal Building was built there to service the electric rail lines, and is now the site of the main branch of the Spokane Public Library. Note that power poles lined the bridge. By this time, all the streetcars had converted to electricity. Spokane High School, with its tall, slender clock tower, is visible at the upper right. *(Jerome Peltier collection)*

By the dawn of the 20th century, Spokane's pioneer epoch was fading and the city began taking on its new metropolitan persona. The first decade was marked by the largest and most diverse influx of people the city ever experienced, either before or since that time. It reflected what

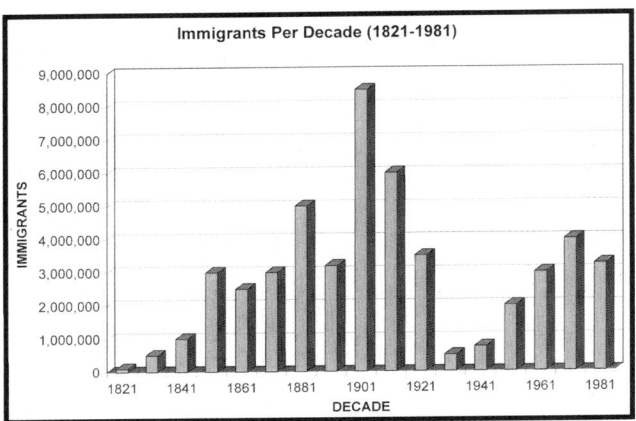

This U.S. immigration chart from 1821 to 1981 illustrates the dramatic influx in the early 1900s.

was taking place nationwide. The United States was rapidly gaining a worldwide reputation as a land of untold possibilities and promise. Between 1900 and 1909, over 8.8 million immigrants arrived, representing the largest influx in the nation's history. Although some immigrants came from Asia, the majority were from Western Europe. Many were fleeing poverty, religious persecution, or political upheaval in their native homelands, and believed America offered answers and solutions.

This dramatic increase in the immigrant population coincided with a new wave of building and development in Spokane. "Progress" was the city's watchword at the turn of the century. After building construction had essentially been halted by the 1893 financial panic and following depression, it was again gaining momentum. The county courthouse and the public safety complex, built during the mid-1890s, were the last significant projects during the post-fire building boom. During the early years of the 1900s, the mines were paying stockholders millions in dividends. In 1900, the Empire State Building became the first in another string of new buildings constructed in Spokane as these dollars were being invested during this post-depression rebound.

Since many of the mine owners or stockholders lived in Spokane, some sectors of the population luxuriated in opulence during the city's Age of Elegance. A number of mining, railroad, and real estate magnates, including Daniel C. Corbin, John A. Finch, Patrick "Patsy" Clark, Amasa B. Campbell, F. Lewis Clark, and Jay P. Graves, were already comfortably settled into their exquisite mansions in Browne's Addition or the lower South Hill. Others with money to invest in Spokane were close on their heels. Among those were Charles Sweeny, August Paulsen, and Levi and May Hutton. The greatest silver discovery in the Coeur d'Alene Mining District during that era was made in 1901 by August Paulsen. It was at the Hercules Mine, in which Paulsen and the Huttons were partners. They and the other partners, all of whom had been working this mine for about a decade, became millionaires nearly overnight. Employment and every facet of Spokane's economy were affected in some way by wealth from the area mines.

Many of the big-monied railroad builders – Frederick A. Blackwell, D. C. Corbin, Jay P. Graves, and Robert Strahorn – were also actively investing in

The Empire State Building, at the southwest corner of Riverside and Lincoln, was completed in 1900. Built by wealthy capitalists F. Lewis Clark and Charles Sweeny and designed by architect John K. Dow, this brick office building was Spokane's first large commercial building with a steel frame. The Commercial Hotel and the old City Offices Building were demolished to make room for the Empire State. Early tenants included Spokane's Weather Bureau, Washington Water Power, Eilers Piano House, Arthur D. Jones & Company, and Joyner's Drug Store. The Great Western Savings and Loan Association acquired the building 1961, renamed it the Great Western Building, and refinished the first floor exterior facing the streets. It is now on the National Register of Historic Places *(Courtesy SPLNWR)*

Inside the Hercules Mine bunkhouse, some of the mine owners and friends are examining the ore from August Paulsen's silver strike in June 1901 that made the owners wealthy. Paulsen is third from the right. Seated to his left is Myrtle White, whom he later married. On the other side is Levi Hutton and at the far left is May Hutton. (*Barnard Studio photo, courtesy Joel Moore*)

Spokane and the Inland Northwest. Railroads and electric railways were expanding either within or extending from the city of Spokane. Emphasis on interurban connections took on new importance. The railroads had become a key component of the city's economy, and collectively, they were the largest employer by 1902.

Although Spokane was the largest railroad center west of St. Paul and Omaha, it remained at the mercy of the transcontinental railroads' high inland freight rates. At that time, Spokane was primarily a supply and service center for the Inland Northwest, and unfortunately, the inequitable rate structure persisted through the era of greatest growth. Although the freight rates may have hampered the city's ability to recruit or establish more manufacturing enterprises, the number of manufacturers tripled in the first decade of the 1900s. Consequently, Spokane never developed into a factory town. The upside was that it wasn't subjected to major labor strikes such as those that affected the towns in the Coeur d'Alenes.

By 1903, Spokane had fully recovered financially from the Panic of 1893, and according to an article published in the *Spokesman-Review* on October 15, 1903, it had a new set of millionaires. The only name that appeared in both this article and the list published by the *New York Tribune* in 1892 was James Glover. The wealthiest was D. C. Corbin, whose estimated net worth was around two million (the conversion to 2010 dollars using a GDP deflator equals about $41 million). Although a few of the millionaires mentioned in the article were wealthy to begin with, most had been men of little means just a decade earlier. Such lists were published periodically, clearly indicating the region's growing wealth. Spokane's economy was booming, and in 1906, the tax assessed valuation of property surpassed the 1891 total of the post-fire boom. Even as an economic downturn swept the eastern portion of the U.S. in 1907, the West continued to prosper and Spokane was left largely untouched, principally because by this time the timber and agricultural industries were prospering.

Influx creates communities within the city

The exceptionally high demand for laborers, especially for craftsmen and those with other skills in the building trades, was attracting scores of newcomers. This demand was coupled with the attraction of cheap, available land, the easy access to the region the railroads now provided, and what appeared to be potentially unlimited wealth from the area's natural resources. By 1905, the city's population had nearly doubled since 1900. All these newcomers needed places to live, and many were interested in buying or building homes of their own.

Integrating people of widely different cultures and languages into a new community always presents challenges for both the established residents and the newcomers. Consequently, it is not uncommon for immigrants to band together with fellow countrymen and create their own community where they speak their native tongue and form their own newspapers, schools, grocery stores, social halls, and churches.

Spokane has always been more insular than some larger metropolitan cities, but over time, it has developed wider ethnic diversity. In the 1906 *Raymer's Dictionary of Spokane,* only three primary groups of immigrants were named: Chinese, Italians, and Japanese. The dictionary overlooked quite a few other nationalities represented in Spokane, and interestingly, featured the three toward which there was the greatest prejudice at that time. The dictionary failed to include the large Scandinavian population, which had settled in the East Central neighborhood and in Peaceful Valley. A great many of the skilled craftsmen who

Looking slightly southeast over Peaceful Valley toward downtown Spokane and the Monroe Street Bridge, circa 1918. Many of today's outstanding buildings are visible along the skyline. The Great Northern Depot's clock tower is above the north end of the bridge and the Davenport Hotel is at the far right. The tallest building (right of center) is the Old National Bank (ONB) Building. Also visible, moving right from the ONB, are the steeple of Our Lady of Lourdes Cathedral, the Paulsen Building, and the Review Tower. Most of the buildings at the south end of the bridge have since been replaced. The long light-colored one was the electric railway's Interurban Terminal Building. In its early days, Peaceful Valley was occupied largely by a thriving Finnish community. Part of the old Shantytown is barely visible below the north end of the bridge. *(Courtesy SPLNWR)*

Carl Nelson driving the Spokane City water wagon, circa 1900. Before the streets were paved, watering the streets was necessary to keep the dust down. Nelson was the father-in-law of Bob Briley, one of Spokane's most recognized television broadcasters. *(Courtesy Bob Briley)*

contributed to the building of Spokane during the early years were from the Finnish community in Peaceful Valley. In 1910, the *Spokane City Directory* listed 184 men living in Peaceful Valley who were employed in the building trades. They were stonemasons, lathers (who prepared the lath base for plaster, which required a great deal of skill to make it uniform), bricklayers, plumbers, carpenters, mill workers, and general laborers.

The home of William Sigg, who was a lather, at 2316 West Clarke Avenue in Peaceful Valley, February 1907. *(Courtesy SPLNWR)*

The challenges for those who did not speak English were obviously more difficult, but because the city was growing so rapidly at that time, even those already settled in Spokane were experiencing the ups-and-downs of a rapidly changing environment. Services were often sorely lacking because the city and other providers could not keep up with the demand. It was the same with the roads. In 1902, the Spokane Street Committee voted to pave all the downtown streets in brick, as asphalt was more expensive and often was of poor quality. But this was a slow process, especially since the demand continued to grow. The next year, it was reported that Spokane led the Northwest in car ownership. Depending on the model, the cost of a new car ran between $700 and $3,000, and the local car dealers were thriving.

Marquerite Motie and a friend washing the family car. Motie was Spokane's first "Miss Spokane," the official city hostess. *(Dorothy Marchi collection)*

The inability to provide adequate roads and services was not the only problem the city faced, and many people struggled to find their place within the community. Vagrancy had become such an issue by 1901 that, in an attempt to control it, the police department temporarily returned to an earlier practice of using of the ball and chain and putting prisoners to work on the rock pile adjacent to the jail. (This also accomplished a secondary purpose. The work on the rock pile produced crushed rock needed for the street paving that was in such demand.) The town was even more wide open than ever, and the police and city leaders struggled to gain some control over the illicit activity that was spiraling out of control in the saloons, variety theaters, gambling halls, and brothels.

In response, a moral crusade began to develop during this time to combat the social ills and overindulgences. The Anti-Saloon League formed in 1902 and the Ministers' Alliance in 1904. Both applied pressure on the city leaders and police to strictly enforce the laws against drunkenness and vice. William J. Hindley, who served as pastor of the Pilgrim Congregational Church, arrived in Spokane in 1903, and became active in this crusade. His involvement ultimately led him into politics. He became Spokane's mayor in 1911. A city ordinance passed in 1900 banning the sale of alcohol between the hours of 2:00 a.m. and 5:30 a.m. already had the saloons in an uproar when, in 1906, a law was passed to close certain businesses (explicitly targeting saloons) on Sunday. The following year, the citizens elected Mayor C. Herbert Moore, whose campaign platform had emphasized the need for reform. After taking office, he demanded the Sunday law be enforced.

The Woman's Christian Temperance Union became more vocal in its fight against alcohol, and other high-profile protests against Spokane's wide-open policy were increasingly more common. Following an invitation in 1908 from the city's ministers, the flamboyant, nationally known evangelist Billy Sunday held a six-week-long revival campaign to "convert the sinners." In 1910, Carry A. Nation, another nationally known figure who was equally as dramatic in her approach, paid a visit to Spokane. Although she had become famous for smashing saloons to make her point about the evils of alcohol, she spent her time in Spokane giving lectures and left the saloons untouched.

Jimmie Durkin's most recognized saloon, opened in 1897, was located at the northwest corner of Sprague and Wall. Durkin was in the business of selling liquor, both wholesale and retail, but was also an advocate of moderation. In the early 1900s, during the movement to curtail liquor consumption, he agreed to letting Rev. Charles A. Braden of Grace Baptist Church put a display in one of his window avowing the evils of liquor. Rev. Braden provided Durkin with a slogan that "he was a man of his word" (which he had etched on his headstone) and "If your children need shoes, don't buy booze." His obtrusive advertising made him a target for the anti-saloon, anti-alcohol reformers, but he was well-liked and respected. *(MAC, L98-46.7)*

The large building left of center, at the southeast corner of Broadway and Lincoln, was built by the Galland brothers, Julius, Adolph, and Samuel, and opened in 1892 as the Galland-Burke Brewery. This photo was taken after it was sold to the Spokane Brewing and Malting Company in 1902. With a substantial customer base to support production, the breweries in Spokane thrived until prohibition went into effect in Washington State on January 1, 1916. In the mid-1960s, the old brewery was converted into new quarters for the YWCA when its building was demolished for construction of the U.S. Court House. *(Don Neraas collection)*

Other changes resulting from the city's rapid growth and development were of a more positive nature. Up to this time, it had been typical for private residences to have gardens, barns to house a milk cow and a horse or two to pull a buggy or carriage, and outhouses. But by the end of the first decade of the 1900s, sewers were replacing outhouses and cars replacing horse-drawn transportation. Another notable change during this time was Spokane residents' dependency on grocery stores and meat markets for their food. Plus, a modern amenity was now making its appearance in private homes – electric lights. The Washington Water Power Company had established a commercial electricity department, and the company began installing the first meters in 1902. In addition to the convenience within the home, porch lights now helped light the city.

Additional sources of employment were created as more businesses opened and services expanded. The main employers at the start of the 20th century were the railroads, followed by wholesale and retail outlets, theaters, the building trades,

Wadham & Bartlett grocery and feed store. Grocery stores were becoming common during the early 1900s. *(MAC, L86-1043)*

The Manito Grocery at 3003 South Grand Boulevard in 1907. *(Elinore Biermann collection)*

Farmers' market at 400 West Second Avenue in 1908. *(MAC, L90-208.2)*

St. Luke's Hospital and its beautiful sunken garden, circa 1913. The hospital on Summit Boulevard and A Street opened in 1904. Because of the need for additional space, a second wing (on the left) was added the following year. *(Postcard from* Vintage Postcards From Old Spokane, *courtesy Duane Broyles and Howard Ness)*

schools, and city, county, and federal government. A sure sign of how Spokane was being perceived beyond the Inland Northwest was its regular inclusion on the theatrical road show circuit. The road shows were at their peak between 1901 and 1910, and were well patronized in Spokane.

Providing help for the less fortunate

Unfortunately for many, the stark reality of residing in this city on the move did not always measure up to the hopeful expectations. By 1906, the city was being so flooded with homeless and indigent the hotels and lodging houses could not accommodate them. There was an ever-widening extreme between those with conspicuous wealth and those who struggled to survive. Sadly, at that time, there was little by way of organized relief to assist the latter.

Hospitals during that era frequently provided a place for the needy as well as treating the sick. In the first decade of the 1900s, the demand on the hospitals was so significant that three new ones were constructed. St. Luke's (first known as Spokane Protestant Sanitarium) and Deaconess (originally the Maria Beard Home and Hospital), both founded in the later 1890s, were housed in cramped quarters they quickly outgrew. In 1904, St. Luke's opened its new hospital at Summit Boulevard and A Street, on land donated by John Finch. The following year, a second wing was added to meet the growing need. Deaconess built

The Savoy Hotel in 1909, which occupied the upper floors of the Bennett Block (built in 1890). It was one of the hotels struggling to accommodate the vast influx of people at this time. *(MAC, L97-4.12)*

a new brick hospital on Fourth Avenue, west of where the present Deaconess Medical Center is located today. Even though the construction was not quite yet complete, the hospital opened to the public in the fall of 1907. To make way for the growing railroad development in the vicinity of Sacred Heart's first hospital building, they were offered monetary enticement and sufficient pressure to move to a new location on Seventh near Division. Construction began in 1905, and they opened their new facility in 1910. It has since grown and expanded to encompass what is now the Sacred Heart Medical Center.

Other charities began to form shortly after Sacred Heart opened its new hospital. In 1911, Mayor Hindley established the City Charities Commission, and ordered major housecleaning in the arenas of both civic and social services. To assist in the latter, the mayor appointed May Hutton as Charity Commissioner. She already had a reputation for her compassion and as a benefactress to the poor. Although Hindley and Hutton were often at odds, she was the perfect person for the job. According to Lucile F. Fargo in her book *Spokane Story* (Columbia University Press, 1950):

> Both enjoyed a good fight and no tears were shed. Grinned the mayor when his militant Charity Commissioner's first term was up: "There is no love lost between us. I have had my share of public roasting. But I'd have to look a long time to find a more useful person for the job. I'm inviting her to stay." Stay May Arkwright Hutton did, to go on joyfully breaking a lance for the public good as she saw it.

By 1912, the whole community was beginning to assume more responsibility for the proper care of the needy. Some examples include a charity ball; the appropriation of funds by the commissioners for use by charitable organizations, and Warren Latham, Dr. Mary Latham's son, opened a Christian Home for Men to which the City Charities Commission contributed three cents per meal for the men. Aid also came from some of the organizations and individuals fighting the battle against alcohol and other vices.

Looking west on Riverside Avenue from Bernard, circa 1905. The tallest building on the right, on the northeast corner of Riverside and Washington, was F. Lewis Clark's newly constructed Spokane Club Building. The Temple Court is the next building west (across Washington). *(MAC, 87-1.285)*

Looking east on Riverside Avenue from Howard Street, circa 1907. At the left, on the northeast corner of Riverside and Howard, is the Ziegler Block. The Paulsen Building, under construction, is in the next block on the other side of Riverside. *(Jerome Peltier collection)*

Touring cars in front of the Interurban Terminal Building, located on the northwest corner of Main and Lincoln (now the site of the main branch of the Spokane Public Library). The terminal was designed by architect Albert Held and built in 1905 to provide a central depot for the Spokane and Inland Empire electric railway system. The Vincent Methodist Church is visible at the right. *(MAC, L93-18.178)*

Expanding the electric streetcar lines

With a new set of developers, another wave of expansion in the street railway system marked the first decade of the 1900s. The changes were extremely important to the region's development, primarily because the emphasis was on building connections to other Inland Northwest cities. It involved major construction and considerable capital, but by the end of the decade, the electric lines were already beginning to feel the effects of the popularity and prevalence of the automobile.

Washington Water Power had nearly gained a monopoly in the streetcar business when Jay P. Graves and his associates secured their foothold with the 1902 purchase of Francis Cook's Spokane & Montrose Railway. They subsequently became a formidable competitor. In 1903, the company was reorganized as the Spokane Traction Company. The same year, Frederick A. Blackwell, of Coeur d'Alene, organized the Coeur d'Alene & Spokane Railway Company with capital stock of $500,000. The company planned to build an electric train route between the two cities and began acquiring rights-of-way. By 1904, the two men had joined forces, and began making plans to extend the interurban system into the Palouse, as well as to Liberty Lake and Hayden Lake.

Washington Water Power was also actively extending its electric lines and power production. In 1905, the company built a line to Medical Lake and a new dam and powerhouse at Post Falls, Idaho. It then drew up and finalized 10-year contracts to provide power to a number of the competitor electric lines.

Also in 1905, construction began on the Interurban Terminal Building at Main and Lincoln to provide a central depot for the ever-expanding electric streetcar lines owned by Graves and Blackwell.

The following year, the two men consolidated their three lines (Spokane Traction, Spokane & Inland, and the Coeur d'Alene & Spokane), as well as the Spokane Terminal Company that had formed to build the terminal, into the Spokane & Inland Empire Railway (the S&IE). Because their lines were among those that had contracted with WWP, and further expansion of the lines seemed inevitable, Graves began formulating a plan to develop a private source of power. In 1906, construction began on a power plant on the Spokane River at Nine Mile Falls. The power plant went on line in 1909, and subsequently came under ownership of WWP (Avista Utilities).

By 1909, the S&IE was experiencing financial difficulties. The situation was further compounded on July 31, 1909, when a tragic head-on collision of two of its passenger trains occurred on the outskirts of Coeur d'Alene (at Gibbs). The trains were crowded that day as the Coeur d'Alene Indian Reservation had just been opened for non-Indian settlement, and people were rushing to register for land openings. Numerous deaths and injuries resulted. In October of that year, the Spokane & Inland Empire Railway was sold to the Great Northern and Northern Pacific railways.

Washington Water Power Substation, located on Post Street above the Lower Falls dam. It was designed by Cutter and Malmgren and completed in 1909. *(Courtesy SPLNWR)*

Jay P. Graves
(From Spokane Falls and Its Exposition, *1890)*

Jay P. Graves came to Spokane from Illinois in 1887. His initial business dealings were in real estate, but he then ventured into the mining industry. His involvement in the development of the Granby Mining, Smelting and Power Company in British Columbia (the largest copper producing mine in Canada at the time) was fortuitous and timely. It buffered him from the effects of the financial panic, and with his newfound wealth, he invested in Spokane when there was an abundance of abandoned, foreclosed or tax-delinquent properties for sale. He seized some choice opportunities, especially in the purchase of Francis Cook's streetcar line.

By 1912, at the age of 52, Graves had divested himself of controlling interests in both the S&IE and the Granby. Once again, his timing proved profitable. With his proceeds, Graves hired Kirtland Cutter to create the plans for a beautiful estate on a bluff overlooking the Little Spokane River, which he named Waikiki. The Olmsted Brothers firm landscaped the grounds. (Today, it is Gonzaga University's Bozarth Conference and Retreat Center.)

Through the development of the electric railway system, Graves played a major role in Spokane's transition from horses to motor vehicles. He also left his mark on the development of the South Hill, and because of his generous land donation, Whitworth College moved from Tacoma to Spokane in 1914.

Although Graves escaped the ravages of the depression in the 1890s, during the Great Depression, he experienced financial difficulties and, in 1937, had to sell Waikiki at a deflated value. After his death in 1948, at age 88, his ashes were scattered on Whitworth's campus.

~ Some Significant Buildings From This Decade ~

The Spokane Club's second headquarters which opened in 1901. It was later various known as the Chamber of Commerce, the American Legion, and the Metals Building. The original roof line was altered after a fire, and the building fell into a state of disrepair. In 2002, Steve Schmautz of SDS Realty purchased the building and invested millions on a restoration that included returning the roof line to it original design. *(From* Vintage Postcards of Old Spokane, *courtesy Duane Broyles and Howard Ness)*

The Spokane Club

The Spokane Club was founded on February 28, 1890, as a club for the city's leading business and professional men. It began as just an association, but incorporated in 1899. Article I of the club's constitution stated: "This society is incorporated for literary, mutual improvement and social purposes ..." Prospective members had to be "proposed and seconded" in writing by two members, and then be approved by the nine-member Board of Managers. Only one dissenting vote was enough to deny membership. Even if approved, five members could submit a written objection to a proposed admission, depriving the person of membership.

Once approved, members were expected to adhere to the club's rules and standards. Violation of the rules or regulations, or conduct "unbecoming a gentleman," would be cause for suspension and, if deemed serious enough by the board, expulsion from the club. The house rules, enforced by a steward, included matters such as no conversation in the library, no non-members allowed in any room except the one for visitors, and no gambling on the premises. When all the conditions of membership were met and admission fees paid, annual dues kept a person in good standing.

Though not explicitly stated in the club's Constitution and Rules, the exclusive club was designed for prominent men of a certain social class, and becoming a member of the Spokane Club was looked upon as a measure of considerable worth. The membership list included in the 1909 Constitution and Rules showed a concentration of members in the western states and Canada, but also included people from as far away as Texas, New York, and Washington, D.C. An annual event included wives and children, but women were not allowed to use the club facility. That changed after the move into the present building in 1911, but even then, until the 1980s, women had to enter or leave through the lower front entrance.

The November 29, 1898, *Daily Chronicle,* announced the Spokane Club "May Buy a Site and Build a Handsome Club House on Riverside." (Being on Riverside was important because it was the financial center of the city.) Since 1890, the club had met on the second floor of the Lamona Block, but they had outgrown that space. Plus, they were looking to increase their membership. The paper went on to report:

Will Help the Town

The fact that Spokane has one of the finest clubs in the country will be an excellent advertisement for the city, both from a financial and social point of view. By extending the list, merchants, lawyers, well-to-do mining men and all of the most desirable classes of the city will be admitted. The result cannot be otherwise than beneficial.

Some members had reservations about constructing their own building, so they were receptive to F. Lewis Clark's proposal the following April to expand a building he was preparing to construct at the northeast corner of Riverside and Howard. Clark, who had been the club's second president (A. A. Newbery was the first), was planning for a three-story building, but was offering to add another three floors to accommodate the club's space requirements. They would also be allowed to design the interior of their floors.

Clark's proposal, presented by his agent, Arthur D. Jones, was published in the *Daily Chronicle* on April 25, 1899. The newspaper's summation of the proposed accommodations were:

This will give the Spokane Club such apartments as the members have hardly dreamed could be secured so soon, and which will be among the most perfect in America. With the beautiful balconies overlooking the grand hall and the town below, the elegant fireplaces, and the handsomely decorated ceilings, it seems that nothing will be wanting to give Spokane club rooms of which she may well be proud....

The three lower stories of the building will be used for offices, and the upper three for the club. There is also a half story more which will be used as a gymnasium. On the sixth floor will be suites of bachelor apartments, where a person can press a button and have his trousers pressed, his hair cut, his face shaved, his boots blacked, can telegraph, telephone, get a messenger boy, or have his supper served without moving from the room.

The following excerpt from F. Lewis Clark's proposal is exactly as it was printed in the paper, including the punctuation:

Looking west on Riverside Avenue near Washington Street, circa 1910. The Spokane Club is visible above the trolley at the right. The photo illustrates the gradual transition from the horse-and-buggy days to the automobile. It includes a horse and wagon, three horse-drawn carriages, a streetcar, and an automobile.
(MAC, L86-754)

To: F. H. Mason, President Spokane Club

Dear Sir: I will lease to you the premises as per memorandum attached and signed by me for 10 years from completion at $500 per month, payable in advance first of month. You to give me a surety bond of $10,000 or cash in my hands (not a C. D., but actual cash) $5000, as liquidated damages for failure on your part to carry out any agreement you make.

I should be willing after you are in possession of premises with all your furniture and fixtures to relinquish said bond or cash and take a first mortgage on your furniture and fixtures, understanding that they are sufficient to properly furnish the premises.... As I shall be unable to discuss the matter with you personally, I beg leave to submit the following remarks:

For $35,000 I can build on this ground a three-story building that will rent for $800 per month, and without any elevator expense. This is a very much better net return to me than I can possibly hope to get from a six-story building which will cost between $90,000 and $100,000, and very likely more. I have a great deal of vacant ground that is crying for improvement.

I admit, however, that I am quite enthusiastic over the plan of building for you. I should take pleasure in making it a handsome building, but from the standpoint of money alone it does not make me eager.

I should be the last to wish for action on your part without due deliberation. I should hope that at least two-thirds of your club favor the plan, or that you drop it. But I respectfully state that it is of great importance to me to know your decision at an early date, so that I may go and finish my three-story building before winter, as I originally planned, or that I may get a six-story undercover before winter, if you wish it. I further respectfully request that you do not waste time in making counter-offers. This offer is subject to withdrawal at any time before acceptance. Very truly yours, F. Lewis Clark

Clark obviously meant business and clearly had the upper hand. Specifications for the proposed six-story building, outlined and presented by Arthur Jones, were printed in the same article, as follows:

> The building is to be six stories high, with the sixth story being in the roof of the building. The plans of the fourth and fifth floors, together with a part of the sixth floor, which can be used without unusual cost in preparing the same, shall be arranged to suit the requirements of the Spokane Club. The building may be called the Spokane Club building.

The Spokane Club on Riverside at Monroe in 1920.
(Thelma Shriner collection)

> Owner to determine whether the principal and general entrance to the building shall be on Washington street or Riverside avenue [Clark subsequently chose Washington]. Passenger elevator to be located in this entrance, an elevator service to be both day and night. [When the building was completed, the elevator was claimed to be the "first high speed electric elevator in the city."] The freight elevator to be accessible from the alley and the dumb waiter in kitchen to run one floor either up or down.
>
> The owner to have the right to modify the design of the exterior of the building, and shall provide only such decorations for the exterior as are part of the construction of the building.
>
> The interior finish shall be for all halls and general rooms of oak or hardwood not more expensive, not to exceed 3 feet high wainscoting, and in all servants' rooms, rear halls and kitchen departments to be of pine. The private rooms of the members on the fifth floor to be of oak finish, not to exceed 3 feet high wainscoting, of hardwood not more expensive. [They chose pine instead.]
>
> The floors in the dining rooms, billiard room and card room, library and main hall on the fourth and fifth floors to be of hardwood, all other floors to be of pine or fir....

This offer was unanimously accepted. Mr. Mason, the club's president, told the *Chronicle* reporter they had plans to immediately increase their membership to 250 members at the present initiation fee of $50, after which the fee would be increased to $100.

A rather detailed description of the interior design as it was being completed appeared in the *Chronicle* on April 9, 1901. Most of what was described matched what had been proposed. The main differences in the club's space had to do with the

Because of his mysterious disappearance in 1914, F. Lewis Clark has become one of Spokane's most intriguing historical figures. He was born into a wealthy Bangor, Maine, family in 1861, and educated at Harvard. After moving to Spokane Falls in 1884, he became involved in real estate, mining, milling, banking, and lumber production. He married Winifred Wyard in 1892, and they had one son, Teddy, born in 1895. The Clarks built a mansion designed by Cutter and Malmgren and named Undercliff, at 601 West 7th Avenue. It later became Marycliff High School and is presently an office building.

Clark had a passion for sailing. In 1907, he purchased a yacht, christened *Spokane*, and with his family and a crew of 16, sailed to Europe to represent the U.S. in the summer regattas. They won a number of first-place awards, but in Germany, came in second to Kaiser Wilhelm. At a banquet hosted by Wilhelm that evening, Clark was among the guests of kings, princes, heads of state, and royalty from all over Europe. Clark desired to build a summer house similar in design to the Kaiser's summer palace, so with the Kaiser's permission, sent architects to Germany. In 1910, from the architects' drawings, the Clarks built a palatial mansion, called Honeysuckle Lodge, on 1,400 acres along the shores of Hayden Lake. It was the site of many lavish parties until F. Lewis Clark became ill.

By 1913, at the age of 52, Clark was down to 135 pounds and he knew he was dying from his cancer. He was also experiencing financial difficulties, as his real estate holdings had lost value and the mines were not producing. They spent Christmas in Santa Barbara, California. On January 16, 1914, Winifred was returning home to Hayden Lake.

F. Lewis Clark
(From Spokane Falls and Its Exposition, *1890*)

Clark, accompanied by his chauffeur and valet, drove her to the train station for her 11:30 p.m. departure. He kissed her goodbye, walked to the limousine, dismissed the chauffeur and valet, and walked away into the night. He was never heard from again, nor was his body found.

Winifred waited, but by 1922, she had to auction everything, including her beloved Honeysuckle Lodge, to meet financial obligations. She then moved to a small apartment in Spokane. After becoming ill in 1940, she left Spokane to be with Teddy and his family Boston. Ten days after her arrival, she was dead. She had not remarried and, at the time of her death, her estate, once valued in the millions, had dwindled to around $10,000.

apartments, which were on the fourth and sixth floors. The proposal had indicated a limited number of "toilet rooms," but they ended up with about 25 apartments, most of which had "private baths, and there are basins with hot and cold water in every room." In addition, they were quite proud that all the rooms had been wired for the latest technology – the telephone. The rooms were also wired for electric lights and fitted for gas.

As proposed, the building was called the Spokane Club Building during the years of the club's occupancy. It was designed by John K. Dow, and at the time of its completion, it was considered one of the most artistic structures in the city. Like the Empire State Building completed the previous year, it was a steel-frame structure.

The club moved into its new quarters in 1901. At the end of the 10-year contract, they built their own facility, designed by Kirtland Cutter, at 1002 West Riverside Avenue. Since moving into the building in 1911, they have relaxed some of the membership requirements (including accepting women as members), largely a function of periodic financial difficulties and dwindling membership. They also merged with the University Club in 1936, and added a new athletic complex in the 1960s.

The Paulsen Dental and Medical Building (left) nearing completion in 1929 and the adjacent Paulsen Building, completed in 1908. The two buildings are on the south side of Riverside and stretch from Washington to Stevens. The Paulsen Building was designed by Dow and Hubbell (John K. Dow and Clarence Z. Hubbell) and the Dental and Medical Building by Gustav A. Pehrson. Both buildings are steel-frame brick structures with glazed terra-cotta trim, produced by the Washington Brick and Lime Company. The general contractors were Frederick Phair on the first building and Rounds-Clist Company Inc. on the second one. The 11-story brick Paulsen Building was the tallest in Spokane until the 15-story Old National Bank was built across the street in 1910. *(Libby Studio photo courtesy Joel Moore, Paulsens' grandson)*

Mighty Hercules Contributions to Spokane: The Paulsen and Hutton Buildings

One of the most colorful stories involving Inland Northwest mining history, the Coeur d'Alene Mining District, and the building of Spokane was the discovery of North Idaho's richest silver vein during the mining boom days of the Coeur d'Alenes. That discovery was at the Hercules Mine and the discoverer was August Paulsen.

The mine had been staked in 1889 by Harry L. Day. It was a mile and a half north of Burke, Idaho. Harry, his father, and other family members, had come to the Coeur d'Alenes in 1886, and had engaged in the stock and the dairy business. But they also turned their attention to prospecting.

After staking the mine, Day sought out men he had come to know and trust to enter into a partnership with him. Among them were railroad engineer Levi W. "Al" Hutton and dairy hand August Paulsen. Among Day's partners were some other local businessmen – Paulsen's employer, a butcher, a barber; and a Burke storekeeper.

Having little capital with which to develop the mine, the partners had to compensate by doing the manual labor themselves. Most of Paulsen's contribution to the Hercules development was in the form of labor. He was the only one of the partners who worked five to six days a week in the mine; the rest had to work around other employment obligations and usually worked at the mine on the weekends. For 12 years, the partners followed a small vein of ore in search of a major discovery.

During the early part of 1901, while working at the mine alone, Paulsen was visited by a dynamite salesman. While at the site, the salesman requested a tour of the mine. As they walked to the face of where Paulsen had been working, the salesman

Some of the principal owners at the Hercules Mine the day August Paulsen confirmed his discovery of what would prove to be one of North Idaho's richest silver strikes. Paulsen is on the wood pile holding his cat, his faithful companion as he worked alone in the mine. Myrtle White is standing directly below him. Levi Hutton is at the right and May Hutton is seated in front. The two mean standing in back are Jerome Day and Eugene Day. There are conflicts on the other names. *(Barnard Studio photo, courtesy Joel Moore)*

noticed a slight mineralized rock formation on the side of the main drift. He suggested Paulsen stop where he was working and follow the ore showing he had just noticed. Paulsen took his advice, and on June 1, 1901, he discovered the vein of silver that turned the owners of the Hercules Mine into millionaires.

The history of the Hercules is especially unique among the major mines in the Coeur d'Alenes because, typically, the mines were developed by large companies with a lot of capital to back them. The prospectors who discovered the mines usually did not have the kind of capital required to develop a mine and sold their mineral rights early on in the process. However, with the Hercules, the same group of people responsible for the discovery of the mineral veins were also the ones to develop and operate the mine.

Of the original partners, Harry Day and his family became one of the most powerful families in the Coeur d'Alenes. Their influence extended over a period of more than 30 years. They continued to expand their mining interests, purchasing and operating numerous other mines in the area. Three of the other original partners (Paulsen, Hutton, and Frank M. Rothrock) moved to Spokane and invested in the future of the city.

The Paulsens

August "Gus" Paulsen came to the United States from his native Denmark in 1888, at the age of 17. He eventually made his way to Spokane in 1892. He worked on a dairy farm until he saved enough money to fulfill his ambition of moving to the Coeur d'Alene Mining District, which was still in the discovery period. After arriving in the Coeur d'Alenes, he again found employment on a dairy farm. In June 1896, with money he saved from his dairy job, he bought into the Hercules Mine partnership.

August Paulsen, age 20. *(Courtesy Joel Moore)*

The Paulsen Building during construction in 1907. *(Courtesy Joel Moore)*

While living in the mining district, he met and married Myrtle White, originally from Colfax. After striking it rich, they subsequently moved their family of five to Spokane. A fourth child was born in Spokane. The Paulsens were among Spokane's early self-made pioneer families who returned their wealth to the community in many ways.

Their name is most recognizable because of the two major downtown structures that bear the Paulsen name. But, in 1915, August Paulsen also built the Clemmer Theater, which is now one of Spokane's premier performing arts theaters. It was built in the early days of motion pictures, when theaters were designed to look like opera houses and seat large numbers. Howard S. Clemmer operated the Clemmer, which later became the Audian, then the State Theater, the name when it closed as a movie theater in 1985. It was subsequently renovated by Paul Sandifur Jr. of Metropolitan Mortgage, and reopened as the Metropolitan Performing Arts Center, simply known as The Met. It was subsequently purchased by Mitch Silver, and became the Bing Crosby Theater in 2006.

Construction crew working on the Paulsen building, circa 1907. *(Courtesy Joel Moore)*

August Paulsen's wife, Myrtle, was a remarkable individual in her own right. Construction had recently commenced on the Paulsen Dental and Medical Building when August died on March 11, 1927, but Myrtle carried the plan out to its completion in 1929. During her lifetime, she devoted countless hours to various charitable organizations. Among them, her favorite was the Spokane Chapter of the American Red Cross. She began her volunteer service with them in 1918 and served as Spokane director and chairman of volunteer services through two world wars, from 1918 to 1947. She also provided free office space in the Paulsen Buildings for the Spokane chapter. Myrtle died on January 5, 1959. Their beautiful home at 245 East 13th Avenue, which they built in 1911, was donated to the Cathedral of St. John, and is presently the headquarters for the Episcopal Diocese of Spokane.

The Huttons

Levi W. "Al" Hutton and his wife, Mary "May" Arkwright Hutton, made significant and lasting contributions to the Inland Northwest. Of all the people who made fortunes in the Coeur d'Alenes, these two individuals probably did the most to help others in need.

May Arkwright came to the Coeur d'Alenes during the 1883 gold rush. She first worked as a cook in Eagle City. In 1886, after the major mining activity moved to what is now known as the Silver Valley, she opened her own boardinghouse in Wardner Junction (now Kellogg). Levi Hutton was an engineer for the Northern Pacific Railroad's Wallace Division. Because May had a reputation for being the best cook in the Coeur d'Alenes, he became a regular diner at her boardinghouse. It

The Hutton Building, on the east side of Washington between First and Sprague, in 1920. It was designed by Dow and Hubbell and completed in 1907 as a four-story building. It initially became known as the Chamber of Commerce Building as the chamber leased the second story for five years. The Huttons moved to Spokane the year the Hutton Building was built. They lived in a comfortable apartment on the fourth floor until 1914, when they moved to a home they had built on 17th Avenue. Three additional floors were added in 1910. The building north of the Hutton Building was the Lindelle Block, built shortly after the fire and demolished in 1963. Just beyond it (the tallest building at the left) was the former Spokane Club, by this time known as the Chamber of Commerce Building. *(MAC, L87-1.17866-20)*

was a popular gathering spot for many in the region, and the Days and August Paulsen were also some of her customers.

The Huttons married on Thanksgiving Day, 1887, and subsequently moved to Wallace. In 1895, the Huttons bought 3/32 of the Hercules for $880. In addition to the monetary payment, Levi began working at the claim between runs on the railroad. Having developed an interest in politics at her grandfather's knee as a child, May became politically active as an adult and was instrumental in women gaining the right to vote in Idaho in 1896. Both Huttons were well-known and respected members of the community. Because of their standing and May's involvement with politics, when President Teddy Roosevelt visited the Northwest in 1903, their home in Wallace was one of his stops.

In 1907, with their fortune from the Hercules, Al and May Hutton moved to Spokane. They built the Hutton Building, where they lived until 1914, when they moved to their new home at 2206 East 17th Avenue, adjacent to Lincoln Park.

Although May only had a third grade education, she was intelligent, and had a strong and forceful nature. When engaged in causes she was passionate about, she was unstoppable. After moving to Spokane, she lost her hard-earned right to vote. Within a year, she picked up the cause in Washington, and once again, was an instrumental force in securing the right of women to vote in Washington in 1910. She fought tirelessly for other women's issues as well. She became a vocal activist against conditions in the Spokane city jail and the need for a police matron. The Florence Crittenton Home for unwed mothers benefitted from her philanthropy, as did the Spokane Children's Home, and other similar charities.

May Hutton died on October 6, 1915, at age 55. By the time of May's death, the Huttons had donated nearly half a million dollars to various charities. But for Levi, that was only the beginning. In 1918, he purchased 384 acres and spent $750,000 building the Hutton Settlement at 9907 E. Wellesley Avenue. Levi was orphaned before the age of seven and was then shifted from one relative's home to another, never feeling quite se-

Levi and May Hutton working in the yard of their home in Wallace, Idaho, circa 1905. *(Courtesy Butch Jacobson)*

cure or loved. His wife's childhood had been similar. Through the Hutton Settlement, Levi was able to provide a safe and healthy home for orphans or other children in need. The Huttons never forgot their humble beginnings, and did everything they could to help the less fortunate. Levi Hutton died on November 3, 1928, at age 68. Through the Hutton Settlement, he left behind a lasting legacy.

The Hutton Settlement, circa 1921. In 1918, Levi Hutton commissioned Spokane architect Harold Whitehouse to design the complex. Hutton spared no expense in the construction of the Settlement, which includes four brick-faced Tudor Revival cottages, each designed to house up to 30 children, on a college campus type of setting. The campus is surrounded by farmland, which was used in the early years to grow gardens and raise animals to help provide food for the Settlement. Upon Hutton's death, virtually his entire estate was placed in a perpetual trust endowed to the settlement. The Hutton Settlement continues to provide a home for deserving children in need of a safe and healthy environment. It is a living tribute to what wealth can accomplish in the hands of compassionate and caring people. *(Courtesy the Hutton Settlement)*

Chapter Four

Levi Hutton and children at the entrance to the Hutton Settlement Administration Building, circa 1921. *(Courtesy the Hutton Settlement)*

The Hutton Settlement Administration Building. *(Courtesy the Hutton Settlement)*

This photo was taken on Father's Day the year after Levi Hutton's death. It was held at the Huttons' graves at Fairmount Memorial Park. The Settlement's Boy Scout troop and a Camp Fire girl bugler led a grave-side service in his honor. In 2008, a monument was erected at this site by the Fairmount Memorial Association to commemorate the untold contributions made by the Huttons during their lifetimes, which continues through the ongoing service of the Hutton Settlement. *(MAC)*

The Richmond Hotel in the Mearow Block, 225 West Riverside, built in 1905. The photo was taken after the Spokane Everitt Motor Co. (at left) was built in 1911. *(MAC, L83-72.3)*

Built as the Kemp and Hebert Department Store in 1908, this building at the corner of Main and Washington was later occupied by Liberty Furniture Co. and is now Auntie's Bookstore. *(Courtesy Shannon Ahern)*

Left: Holley, Mason and Company, wholesale and retail hardware, located on the east side of Howard south of Railroad Avenue. It was designed by Albert Held and built of reinforced concrete in 1906. *(Courtesy SPLNWR)* **Above:** Our Lady of Lourdes Cathedral, at the southwest corner of Riverside and Madison. Construction began on this brick and stone cathedral in 1904. It was dedicated in 1908. *(From* Vintage Postcards From Old Spokane *by Duane Broyles and Howard Ness)*

The dedication of the Masonic Temple on Riverside Avenue in 1904. The estimated cost was $100,000. Barely visible behind the trees at the right is Elijah Davenport's Merchants Hotel. *(MAC, L93-66.271)*

The Pfister Block, built around 1904 and demolished in 1912 for the construction of the Davenport Hotel on this site, and Davenport's Restaurant showing the first phase of its new Mission-style facade. *(MAC, L93-80.1)*

Davenport's Restaurant opened on July 10, 1890, in a small portion of a very plain building (see page 109) at this corner (Post and Sprague). Louis Davenport rapidly expanded until the restaurant occupied the entire building. He also purchased the Bellevue Block adjoined on the south (at left), which became the Pennington Hotel. In the late 1890s, Kirtland Cutter was hired to remodel the restaurant, which included a new Mission-style facade. At its completion, shown here in 1909, the entire exterior of his two buildings had been completely transformed into a work of art. *(Courtesy Louis Davenport III)*

In 1904, Louis Davenport hired Kirtland Cutter to design this beautiful ballroom, the Hall of the Doges, which was built above his restaurant. *(Courtesy Walt and Karen Worthy)*

~ Special Events and Developments During the Decade ~

The town was decorated and crowds gathered on Riverside at Howard to greet President Theodore Roosevelt during his stop in Spokane in 1903. *(Public domain)*

President Teddy Roosevelt Visits Spokane

In May 1903, the city was abuzz with excitement over the forthcoming visit of President Teddy Roosevelt. This stop was part of the president's 14,000-mile, two-month journey through 22 states and two territories. Roosevelt was given the royal treatment by the over 100 cities and towns he visited, and Spokane was prepared with its own celebration. This would be the first time a sitting U.S. president would visit Spokane.

The President disembarked from an O.W.R.&N. train the afternoon of Tuesday, May 26, 1903, after having spent the morning in Wallace, Idaho, and was taken on a grand tour of the city. A row of mounted police officers escorted the entourage of horse-drawn carriages and a contingent of Rough Riders. Mayor L. Frank Boyd accompanied Roosevelt in the first carriage, which was followed by a carriage of secret servicemen. Among other prominent members of the entourage was Spokane's first chief of police, Eugene B. Hyde.

Along the route, the President graciously greeted excited well-wishers and visited with military veterans, thanking them for their service. As the carriages passed the Monaghan home, Roosevelt stood up, uncovered, to honor the fallen Ensign John R. Monaghan. At the public safety building on Howard, the patrol and fire department wagons were hitched and manned, and all officers present proudly paid their respects. The sightseeing tour also included Gonzaga College, the bluff overlooking Fort Wright (from where Roosevelt was given a 21-gun salute), a slow drive over the Monroe Street Bridge, which prolonged the President's appreciative view of "the mighty water power," a loop around Coeur d'Alene Park, and a stop for refreshments at the Seventh Avenue home of former U.S. Senator George Turner and his wife, Bertha. (Their property is now part of the historic Corbin-Moore-Turner Heritage Gardens.)

The President participated in a ground-breaking ceremony for the Masonic Temple on Riverside and was supposed to have done the same for the new Spokane Amateur Athletic Club, but didn't due to an oversight in scheduling. The only other major disappointment during Roosevelt's three-and-a-half hour visit was the omission of a talk to the throngs of school children who had gathered at Coeur d'Alene Park with banners in hand. Apparently a last minute telegram from the President's secretary informed Spokane officials that Roosevelt had time for only one speech, which was given to 25,000 people at Lincoln and Main. Unfortunately, it was too late to notify the children, who watched with disbelief and deep disappointment, many to the point of tears, as the parade of carriages circled the park and drove out of sight.

As the parade of carriages entered the final leg of the tour, troops from the Grand Army of the Republic (GAR), cadets from Washington State College (now WSU) and Gonzaga, and regular troops, along with several bands, fell into formation and marched down Riverside to the speakers' platform. The final approach had been kept secret and, according to a following day newspaper account, Police Chief Edward Woydt had personally overseen keeping it clear. Following his rousing address, President Roosevelt was presented with gifts and mementos to remind him of Spokane,

The Spokane Amateur Athletic Club, on Main at Monroe, designed by Albert Held and built in 1904. President Roosevelt was to have participated in a ground-breaking ceremony during his 1903 visit, but due to an scheduling oversight, it didn't happen. The building was demolished in 1966 for construction of the U.S. Court House. *(Courtesy SPLNWR)*

and quickly driven to the Northern Pacific Depot to board his 6:05 p.m. eastbound train. It was a day that would not soon be forgotten by residents of the Inland Northwest.

Theodore Roosevelt would visit Spokane again in 1911, when he participated in laying the cornerstone for Lewis & Clark High School, and in 1912. President William H. Taft visited in 1909 and was honored at a banquet in the Hall of the Doges.

This photo was taken just before the unveiling of the Ensign John R. Monaghan statue at Monroe and Riverside on October 25, 1906. During President Roosevelt's tour of the city, as they passed the Monaghan home, he publicly paid his respects to the fallen Ensign Monaghan. *(MAC)*

The McGoldrick Lumber Company, adjacent to Gonzaga University, became established in Spokane in 1905, and was its largest employer for the next 40-plus years. By 1908, it had an annual production of 40-million feet of lumber. The millpond in front of the sawmill, shown above filled with logs, is now called Lake Arthur. As a young boy, Bing Crosby and his friends would often swim there. *(Courtesy Jim McGoldrick)*

McGoldrick Lumber Company

By the time James Patrick McGoldrick, a lumberman from Minneapolis, Minnesota, and his associates purchased the recently established, but floundering, A. M. Fox Lumber Company in 1905, other lumber mills were making their appearance around the region. Small mills had been present from the beginning, but by the early 1900s, the little mills were growing into larger ones, and well-established Eastern timber companies were moving west and building high-volume operations. The Eastern Washington & Idaho Lumbermens' Association formed in 1902 with 30 members. Huge tracks of acreage were being purchased from the Northern Pacific Railroad at $2.50 an acre. In 1902 alone, Eastern capitalists invested $30 million in Northwest timber. McGoldrick was able to gain a solid base by also purchasing, for $450,000, all of A. M. Fox's timber holdings in North Idaho's Benewah and Shoshone counties. From this, the company grew and flourished.

James P. McGoldrick, founder and president of McGoldrick Lumber Company. *(Courtesy Jim McGoldrick)*

Young J. P. "Jimmie" McGoldrick photographed by a reporter at his grandfather's sawmill (see arrow). This photo appeared in a book published by the Chamber of Commerce. During their tenure as a business in Spokane, the majority of McGoldrick employees owned their own homes (see opposite page) as it was something the company stressed. *(Courtesy Jim McGoldrick)*

The above photo montage shows Spokane homes owned by employees of McGoldrick Lumber Company. J. P. McGoldrick made it a point to see that all of his employees were able to own a home. He was one of Spokane's most beloved employers. *(Courtesy Jim McGoldrick)*

The McGoldrick crew and staff posing at the mill in the late 1930s. The inset photo is of J. P. and his son Milton McGoldrick. *(Courtesy Jim McGoldrick)*

Looking north over the Spokane River at the McGoldrick Lumber Company's operation adjacent to Gonzaga University at left. *(Courtesy Jim McGoldrick)*

This 1940 aerial photo gives a perspective of the size of the McGoldrick operation. *(Courtesy Jim McGoldrick)*

Custom-sawn "green" timbers from the McGoldrick mill loaded on a wagon en route to a construction site. *(Courtesy Jim McGoldrick)*

Billy Sunday, the Evangelist, Attempts to Convert Spokane's Sinners

One of the most significant and publicized events in 1908 was the arrival of nationally renowned evangelist William Ashley "Billy" Sunday. As part of the city's moral crusade to bring the rowdy behavior and illicit activities of the "sinners" under control, the Spokane Ministerial Association solicited Sunday to conduct revival meetings in Spokane.

Billy Sunday was born in 1862 and raised in poverty in Iowa, but in his early 20s, he gained nationwide fame for his success as a major league baseball player. He became the first player to run the bases in 14 seconds, and set records for stealing bases. Someone said he was "one of the swiftest diamond runners that ever crossed the plate."

Following a life-changing religious experience at the Pacific Garden Mission in Chicago in the mid-1880s, he became inspired to preach the gospel. In 1891, he turned down a lucrative baseball contract (sources vary from $3,000 to $6,000 annually) for an $85 per month ministry position. After a few years of assisting one of the best known evangelists of the time, in 1896 Sunday went out on his own. He soon learned how lucrative evangelistic preaching could be, and endorsed his new career with remarkable enthusiasm.

Sunday developed a fiery style of preaching hellfire and brimstone, becoming known in religious circles of the times as "the devil's worst enemy." He was handsome, energetic, flamboyant, athletic, and employed a lot of theatrics to make his points. His impassioned sermons would be punctuated by pounding his fists on the lectern, striking unusual poses, and the most dramatic, breaking furniture (usually chairs). Consequently, he was often described in the same terms used for vaudeville and theater idols. He was on his way to becoming the most sought-after evangelist of his era.

At the time Spokane extended its invitation, Billy Sunday was preaching mostly in the Midwest, but had preached in just about every state in the Union except in the Pacific Northwest. Attracting larger crowds than what most churches could accommodate, his revivals were held in circus tents or spacious temporary wooden structures, called "tabernacles." The one in Spokane, which cost $4,200, was built to accommodate both the revival campaign and the apple show held the previous month. It was designed to seat 8,000. An unplanned use was as a temporary homeless shelter during some unusually cold weather in January. The city was bursting with the homeless and unemployed struggling to stay warm, and in his compassion, Sunday opened the tabernacle for a place to sleep. Other charitable souls provided food. The shelter was soon overflowing, and in an effort to draw further awareness to the pitiful situation, Sunday appealed to Police Chief Ren Rice to take some action.

A Billy Sunday baseball card.
(Public domain)

The campaign began on Christmas night and lasted into February 1909. The first night, the tabernacle was filled to capacity. According to the *"Billy" Sunday Spokane Campaign* souvenir booklet printed after the event, two days later, on December 27, 1908, the 46-year-old evangelist "... was heard by 25,000, while multitudes were turned away for want of even standing room in the great tabernacle." This was the largest religious revival ever held in Spokane. Nearly every day for six weeks, Sunday preached against Spokane's social evils, and exhorted the habitual sinners to change their ways. He mixed humor and hellfire in a way that made his listeners take notice. As an influential advocate of Prohibition, he often stated:

> I am the sworn, eternal and uncompromising enemy of the liquor traffic. I have been, and will go on, fighting that damnable, dirty, rotten business with all the power at my command.... Whiskey and beer are all right in their place, but their place is in hell.

Billy Sunday's revival "tabernacle" at Second and McClellan. It was built for this occasion and for the first National Apple Show in November 1908, but it also doubled as a homeless shelter during Billy Sunday's six-week revival campaign, held from December 25, 1908, into February 1909. *(Public domain)*

He also decried the evils of dancing, gambling, and the theater (probably referring to the raucous variety theaters that were still prevalent). Many listened with rapt attention and donated generously. In addition to $15,000 the Spokane supporters had previously given to cover expenses, goodwill donations were collected, which on the final day alone amounted to $10,871. In terms of the number of attendees, the excitement generated, and the enthusiasm felt by participants, the revival was declared a success. However, once the intensity of the moment faded, there seemed to be little lasting effect. Of the thousands, only hundreds turned in cards swearing to never touch alcohol again. Of those, it's impossible to know how many actually kept their promise, but Spokane's wild side did not appear to be much tamed by the whole experience.

In 1924, Billy Sunday was invited to return to Spokane, this time to speak on "Americanism." The Spokane Advertising Club had recently formed a subcommittee, called the Civic University Bureau, "for the purpose of establishing a medium through which our citizens might obtain at first hand authentic information on subjects of vital importance in the civic life of our community and nation." With that purpose in mind, Sunday was to be one of a number of speakers. In advance of his arrival, the *Spokane Press* referred to him as "the famous and spectacular orator." However, his performance was disastrous and publicly embarrassed the Ad Club. The next day, on August 21, 1924, the *Spokane Press* stated:

> Foul-mouthed, filthy-minded, lying and blasphemous, Billy Sunday was back on his Oregon ranch [at Hood River] today, after having indulged here in the most remarkable orgy of villification [*sic*] ever heard from a Spokane platform....
>
> Much of his tirade was utterly incoherent. In one breath he denounced Soviet Russia, in another he condemned the labor movement ... and from that to an attack on President Samuel Gompers ...
>
> Liberal preachers in the churches and those friendly to reform and labor movements were characterized as "weasel-eyed, hog-jowled, sniveling Judases" who have no right to preach from the pulpit their "doctrines of anti-America and anti-Christ."

His tirade continued to spew vitriolic jabs at one thing or another, making little sense of anything. The Ad Club spokesman interviewed by the *Spokane Press* said they had explicitly told Sunday not to give a political speech, and on the front page of the paper, within a framed text box, was the heading "Ad Club Isn't Responsible."

Sunday's lasting legacy

Sunday left an indelible mark on American evangelicalism, if not for his preaching, for breaking furniture. His appeal came from his energetic preaching style and large, successful evangelistic campaigns across the United States. In his lifetime, it has been estimated Billy Sunday addressed over 100 million people without the aid of loud speakers, TV, or radio. For good or bad, he came to epitomize what many Americans thought of as an "evangelist." His wife, Helen (Nell), played a major role in his success. After years of Sunday traveling the preaching circuit alone while Nell cared for their four children, she became his manager. Leaving the care of their children to a nanny, she began traveling with him and proved to be a remarkable asset in the development of his career.

Sunday was often accused of being a tool used by the ruling elite to defuse lower class discontent. Suspicions were expressed or inferred in newspapers that Sunday was little more than a grafter getting wealthy from his temporary congregations. In 1915, famed author, poet, and Pulitzer Prize winner Carl Sandburg wrote a 21-stanza poem titled "To Billy Sunday." It leaves little question as to Sandburg's impression of Billy Sunday. Following are the first six stanzas:

> You come along... tearing your shirt... yelling about Jesus.
> I want to know... what the hell... you know about Jesus.
>
> Jesus had a way of talking softly and everybody except a few bankers and higher-ups among the con men of Jerusalem liked to have this Jesus around because he never made any fake passes and everything he said went and he helped the sick and gave the people hope.
>
> You come along squirting words at us, shaking your fist and calling us damn fools so fierce the froth of your own spit slobbers over your lips – always blabbing we're all going to hell straight off and you know all about it.
>
> I've read Jesus' words. I know what he said.
> You don't throw any scare into me. I've got your number.
> I know how much you know about Jesus.
>
> He never came near clean people or dirty people but they felt cleaner because he came along. It was your crowd of bankers and business men and lawyers that hired the sluggers and murderers who put Jesus out of the running.
>
> I say it was the same bunch that's backing you that nailed the nails into the hands of this Jesus of Nazareth. He had lined up against him the same crooks and strong-arm men now lined up with you paying your way.

Not everyone shared Sandburg's sentiments. After Billy Sunday's death on November 6, 1935, the following article, which appeared in the *Moody Church News,* indicated he was revered by many:

> Three thousand one hundred and fifty-seven persons filed past the casket of the great evangelist. Many were in tears. Many exclaimed: "He led me to Christ." As the funeral service began there were some 3,500 people seated in the great auditorium of the Moody Memorial Church. Many of Mr. Sunday's former associates in his great campaigns were present.... A large number of ministers, Salvation Army officers, and other Christian workers were in the choir loft....
>
> The front of the platform was literally banked with magnificent floral offerings and among these most noticeable was one from the Cubs, Chicago's well-known baseball aggregation, formerly known as the "White Stockings," with which Mr. Sunday was connected at the time of his conversion.

Billy Sunday about to destroy a chair. *(Public domain)*

The International Workers of the World, the Free Speech Movement, and the Assassination of Former Acting Police Chief John T. Sullivan

The era of Spokane's greatest population growth and inpouring of massive wealth from the mines and forests was cause for celebration by many, but it was also an era of great social unrest and agitation as the poor became more downtrodden and the ranks of the unemployed multiplied. The plight of industrial laborers, especially the unskilled, became more desperate and disgraceful. This situation in Spokane and the Inland Northwest was a microcosmic reflection of what was taking place across the nation.

Many industrialists were concerned only about their profits, often at the expense of their workers. Unfair labor practices, long hours, deplorable or unsafe working conditions, and lack of benefits and decent living wages prevailed. Because the pool of unemployed laborers was so high following another economic downturn in 1907-1908, workers were essentially expendable. Malcontents were simply replaced by the next in line who was desperate for a job. Unfortunately, exploitation of the situation was allowed to persist without fear of retribution – at least for a period of time.

By the early 1900s, Spokane was already known as a strong union town. In February 1903, a large newspaper headline stated "Spokane Strongest of Union Cities" continuing on to state "in the country." In 1905, Spokane's Central Labor Council formed with 24 unions participating. Efforts were being made to rectify some of the poor labor practices, but with modest results.

Largely in response to the unhealthy conditions in many mining and lumber camps, the International Workers of the World (IWW) formed in 1905. Volumes have been written about this era of unrest and the IWW, an international union advocate commonly known as the "Wobblies." Its methods of dealing with the impasse between unskilled laborers struggling to make an honest living and the greed of big industry were controversial. The IWW gave the masses hope for the future, but the large employers who were being targeted to effect some change in the treatment of their employees perceived the organization as too revolutionary, radical, and militant. Ultimately, the dire need for improving the labor situation was so extreme that revolutionary tactics may have been the only successful way to bring about the desired changes.

As the IWW became more vocal, the issue of free speech began to take center stage. Government was in the pocket of big business, and as a means of suppressing labor agitation, cities and towns were passing ordinances banning open-air speaking, which violated the constitutional right to freedom of speech. The IWW responded with a radical approach of provoking those charged with enforcing the laws. In turn, law enforcement frequently reacted with outright brutality.

One of the objectives for bringing Billy Sunday to Spokane was to quell the labor agitation that was beginning to occur in 1908. However, igniting the people with religious passion did nothing to ameliorate the situation of growing unemployment or unbearable working conditions. To compound the situation, in the summer of 1909, Spokane passed its own ordinance banning speeches on downtown streets. An exception was made, however, for religious purposes.

By fall 1909, the smoldering discontent erupted, and Spokane became a center of the fight for workers' rights and freedom of speech. November 2, 1909, was set as Free Speech Day, and the IWW leaders rallied recruits from across the nation, calling on supporters to fill the jails and overwhelm law enforcement. As a result, hundreds of workers and activist converged on Spokane, and within weeks, over 500 people had been arrested. When the jail filled up, the vacated Franklin School at Trent and Grant was converted into a makeshift jail, and permission was granted to house prisoners in the guardhouse at Fort Wright.

Among those who responded to the call to assist in Spokane's fight was 19-year-old Elizabeth Gurley Flynn. She was a full-time organizer for the IWW, and fearless in her dedication to their cause. Even at this young age, Flynn had become legendary for her fiery and witty eloquence. While in Spokane, she assumed the editorship of the Wobblies' paper, the *Industrial Worker,* "the voice of revolutionary industrial unionism." Her first edition referred to one of Spokane's judges as a "lackey of the parasites." She also referred to the Spokane police as "hired thugs" and "hired clubbers."

Elizabeth Gurley Flynn, circa 1910.
(Courtesy Library of Congress)

Flynn was soon arrested for speaking on the streets, and spent a night in jail. She bonded out the following day, and proceeded to expose the filthy conditions and the absence of a matron in the women's jail. This was confirmed by other women with the same experience. As a result, the following year, the police department finally hired a police matron. The absence of a full-time matron had been an ongoing issue, and even though by this time it was required by law, city officials and the police department chose to ignore it. Their reasoning was that fees for violating the law were less than a full-time matron's wages. Flynn also accused the jailers of exploiting some prostitutes that had been arrested by hiring out their services. This later proved to be true.

Following this article, the office of the *Industrial Worker* was raided by the police, who seized over 7,000 copies of the December issue. Days later, five of the ringleaders, including Flynn, were arrested on charges of conspiracy and sentenced to three months in jail. Flynn immediately hired an attorney to appeal her conviction, and was subsequently acquitted. She continued her fight for human rights, and was one of the founders of the American Civil Liberties Union. She also eventually joined the American Communist Party.

As the demonstration in Spokane raged on, it was followed in the newspapers. Both the *Spokesman-Review* and the *Chronicle* were unsympathetic toward the IWW, but the *Spokane Press*, which was known as the "people's paper," sympathized with the workers' causes and the violation of free speech. Although the IWW was prepared to stay and fight, the situation in Spokane was brought to a peaceful resolution in March 1910, and a settlement was negotiated. The IWW agreed to drop all damage suits against the city in exchange for release of the IWW prisoners, freedom to distribute their materials and speak publicly, and repeal of the ordinance that had banned it.

Some lasting statewide reform came out of this uprising, but the fight for free speech and fair and humane labor practices continued for years. Spokane's IWW labor demonstrations were the first in Washington, and it led the way for other cities to stage their own rallies. As more extremists were drawn to the organization, demonstrations often became violent. However, except for some minor incidences, the demonstration in Spokane remained peaceful. Ironically, although the city and police fought against the IWW, union activism would later ensure police officers had good working conditions, and received comfortable wages and retirement benefits.

Fallout from inhumane treatment

During the demonstration, those who were arrested were generally sentenced to 30 days on the rock pile or confined to jail on just bread and water. Conditions in the jail were a frequent topic in the newspapers, especially because a number of prisoners either starved to death or later died from illnesses they developed from insufficient nutrition or the unsanitary conditions. One such case was reported in the March 10, 1910, *Spokane Press* titled "Victim of Police Dies." The following story blamed Acting Chief John Sullivan's mandate that "prisoners live on only bread and water."

CHINN, WHO WAS STARVED, DEAD
In a little cot at the Deaconess hospital this evening a poor wasted body lies stretched in its last sleep ... S. O. Chinn, because of Chief Sullivan's mandate that

he should live on bread and water 35 days, died at the hospital at about 4:00 o'clock this afternoon. Because he lived up to his convictions, even as the did the Puritans of old, he was thrown into prison a few months ago, and orders were given that he should be fed only bread and water, so that he could be starved into weak submission.... He went to jail a healthy man; he left fatally sick, and went to the hospital to die....

On March 12, 1910, *Spokane Press* followed with:

S. O. Chinn did not die in vain. The funeral of this victim of Sullivan's brutal methods occurred yesterday, and while Chinn was but a simple worker in the ranks, his cortege was one of the most imposing the city has seen in months. It was not an I.W.W. demonstration, for hundreds were there who were not followers of the union; it was the respect of honest men for another man who died for what he held to be principle.

Chinn's death appears to have been the turning point in the sentiment of Spokane regarding the police system. Before Chinn died the recent conflict was generally a fight between authority and anarchy; now that the dust has settled, the average worker is discovering that it was a fight between brutality – senseless brutality run amuck – and devotion to a principle by men who had nothing to gain and everything – even life itself – to lose.

The Portland (Ore.) I.W.W. local on Saturday passed strong resolutions on Chinn's death, condemning Mayor Pratt and Acting Chief Sullivan. While these resolutions will have no especial effect in Spokane they will in Oregon, and as they are being sent out to every city and town where the telegraph goes, the result will be that this city will be given a most unfortunate name for needless brutality; all because it had a chief of police, a mayor and a prosecuting attorney who could think of nothing but brutality to quell a disturbance. The I.W.W. conflict could have been settled in two days had the commonest principle of sense and humanity been used. They were not, and a great flare of scandal arose.

During his career with the police department (1890-1911), Captain Sullivan, who was acting chief during Spokane's IWW demonstration, had developed a reputation of being heavy-handed. There were frequent allegations of questionable conduct in the performance of his duties as a police officer. Sullivan already had his share of detractors, but his endorsement of the ordinance banning speeches on downtown streets and his handling of the labor demonstration made matters worse. In general, this was an era of police lawlessness and corruption, and the public was getting fed up and frustrated. On September 27, 1910, two of Sullivan's associates, both former policemen, were sent to prison for theft. It was alleged that Sullivan covered for them. In November 1910, a grand jury investigation was called to look into Sullivan's actions. He was found guilty of gross violation of police regulations that allowed ongoing corruption. As a result, he resigned as acting chief.

Acting Police Chief John T. Sullivan
(MAC, L84-361.08)

On January 5, 1911, at 8:45 p.m., an assassin fired a shot through the window of Sullivan's home at 1314 West Sinto. Sullivan was sitting in a chair near a window reading the paper. The .32 calibre bullet passed through the chair, and pierced his right lung. Although Sullivan was mortally wounded, he crawled to the phone and called the police station for help. Following the attendance of numerous physicians at his home, he was taken to Sacred Heart Hospital, where he died in the morning hours of January 7th. Sullivan's list of enemies contained many potential suspects. In 1912, an arrest was made in the Sullivan murder, but he turned out to be the wrong person.

The murderer is caught 13 years later

Thirteen years would pass before the case was solved. Two articles in the *Spokane Press* (see opposite page) provided information about the murderer, Victor C. Miller of Alabama. He had been shot by his wife, Florence Miller, in self-defense. Prior to the shooting, he had frequently boasted to both her and one of his closest friends that he had gotten away with killing Spokane's police chief in 1911. Chief Wesley Turner and Captain Martin Burns did a thorough investigation and found the claim to be true. They also learned that Miller was responsible for an number of other murders. Whether or not a motive for the murder was ever established or publicly stated was never disclosed, but Captain Sullivan had obviously upset the wrong person.

Captain John T. Sullivan's funeral possession on January 9, 1911. *(Courtesy Spokane Law Enforcement Museum)*

SLAIN BY OWN WIFE IN SOUTH!

Mystery of Murder of Spokane Police Chief 13 Years Ago Believed Solved by Shooting in Alabama.

After having evaded justice for 13 years, the slayer of John T. Sullivan, acting chief of Spokane police, has at last paid in full his debt to society.

Strange to say, the murderer was punished in the identical manner in which he punished Sullivan. He was killed by the bullet of an assassin—his wife.

The man's name is V. C. Miller, and his confession is said to have been made to his wife before he died, after being shot by her on the government reservation at Muscle Shoals, near Florence, Ala., on the night of September 3.

SAID HE KILLED CHIEF

Arrested for the murder of her

IDENTITY OF MURDERER IS NOW CERTAIN

Alabaman Murdered by Wife Known to Be Slayer of John Sullivan.

Sworn affidavits received by police Tuesday evening from K. S. Skinner, acting police chief of Wilson Dam, Ala., have established beyond doubt that Victor Claude Miller, who was shot to death by his wife at Muscle Shoals on September 3, is the man who killed Captain John Sullivan, acting chief of Spokane police, at his home January 5, 1911.

Chief Wesley Turner and Captain Martin Burns have been investigating the case since they received word that Miller had told his wife of the murder before he died. Taxpayers objected to sending a Spokane officer to Alabama to investigate, and little hope of definitely clearing up the matter was had.

But after much correspondence one of Miller's pals was located, and Skinner cooperated with the Spokane officials in gaining the statements which have at last cleared up the case, which remained a complete mystery for 13 years.

The affidavit is sworn by W. E. Bennett, who has been Miller's friend and companion since 1912. Bennett, who was foreman in railroad yards at Nashville, Tenn., where both men were employed, said that Miller had asked him to keep a lookout for strangers coming onto the job, because he was wanted in Spokane for killing several Italians.

Later Miller confessed murdering a Spokane police officer before their acquaintance, and boasted that he "got by with it."

The iller had a long line of victims, and during his friendship with Bennett had illed two negroes. He was acquitted in one of these cases and was never arrested for the other.

Miller was an expert powder man, and during his stay in the northwest, prior to his murder of Sullivan, had been employed in railroad construction work on the Great Northern, Union Pacific and Oregon Short Line.

His wife, Florence Miller, who illed him in self defense, has been acquitted and has returned to her home in Tracy City, Tenn.

Miller married her there in 1918 when she was 16 years old. She has ben in no way connected with his many crimes, according to Alabama officials, who state that her character is above reproach.

The article on the left appeared in the *Spokane Press* on September 23, 1924. The article on the right appeared on October 8, 1924.

Spokane's First Airplane Flight

The "Flying Machine" began making history in Spokane in 1910. The March 27th *Spokesman-Review* announced:

> Charles Keeney Hamilton, the famous aviator, who will give exhibitions of his skill at the Interstate Fairgrounds April 1, 2 and 3, will arrive in Spokane this morning from Vancouver, bringing his Curtiss biplane and accompanied by his manager, Nat Reis, and two machines.

A promotional photo of Charles Hamilton, c. 1910.
(Courtesy Library of Congress)

Charles K. Hamilton was born in Connecticut in 1885. By the time he was 18, he was doing hot-air balloon and parachute jumping stunts at circuses and fairs. This quickly evolved into piloting dirigibles and performing daring flight exhibitions throughout the United States. He was perhaps the best-known American flyer at that time, and had gained a reputation as a daredevil who would fly anything, anywhere, frequently crashing his biplane, the *Hamiltonian*.

Hamilton delighted his audiences with daring stunts. Airplanes were still very much a novelty, and not understanding the concept of gliding, people were convinced that if the engine stopped, the machine would crash. One of Hamilton's first, and very successful, stunts was to climb to some 1,500 feet above the exhibition grounds and cut his engine. He would then take a steep dive, pulling out at the last possible moment before landing. The public loved his skill and bravado. The risk involved was made apparent by pilots who plunged to their deaths while attempting the stunt. However, if successful, the financial rewards were very lucrative. Two or three flights of 10 or 15 minutes duration could net $10,000.

In 1909, Hamilton became an exhibition pilot for the Glenn Curtiss Airplane Company. He was winning prizes and gaining notoriety for his flight accomplishments, which is how he happened to be booked for a three-day event at Spokane's fairgrounds (later the Playfair Racetrack). Hamilton arrived with his Herring-Curtiss biplane, but something had apparently not been packed correctly and he could not get it running for the first day's performance.

On the second day, April 2, 1910, despite being a rainy day, he thrilled the crowd with two flights. In the first one, which lasted about five minutes,

The front page of the Sunday morning March 27, 1910, *Spokesman-Review*, announcing the introduction and forthcoming arrival of the first airplane to fly in Spokane.

he circled the racetrack in front of the grandstand twice. The second flight lasted about seven minutes, but he encountered a dangerous obstacle. The fairgrounds, located off Sprague between Altamont and Regal, were surrounded by a network of power lines, making it a very hazardous place to fly. During the second flight, Hamilton encountered a 12,000-volt power line in his flight path. Without time to attain the necessary altitude to fly over it, he flew just a few feet above a street to pass under it. Word traveled quickly, and the estimated crowd that watched his show on the third day was about 20,000, although only about 3,000 were paid admissions. People covered roof tops, were in trees, and on telephone poles – anything that would give them a viewing advantage.

Hamilton was definitely a showman, albeit frequently with reckless abandon and foolhardiness. A glimpse of this was expressed by the following quote in the *Spokesman-Review* on April 3, 1910, the day after his first flight in Spokane:

> The only extra protection he wears while in the air is a leather coat, and the only reason he wears this is because in an accident last fall his leather coat saved his life by preventing one of the broken stays of the machine from piercing his body....

A promotional photograph of Charles Hamilton in a Curtis biplane, circa 1910. *(Courtesy Library of Congress)*

> Aviator Hamilton is always smoking a cigarette, and before each flight he always lights a fresh one to smoke while in the air. He smokes all the time, even when around the engine or gasoline cans, whether the cans are open or the gasoline is being vaporized by the engine.

Hamilton's aviation career was thrilling, but like that of many other early pilots, it was cut short. He was not quite 29 years old when he crashed on January 22, 1914. At the time of his death, he reportedly already had two replaced ribs and metal plates in his skull and one ankle.

Hamilton's show was followed the next year by two young aviators, one of whom had just be-

The Spokane Interstate Fairgrounds in 1907. This was the site of the first airplane exhibition in Spokane. It later became the Playfair Race Track. *(From* Vintage Postcards From Old Spokane *by Duane Broyles and Howard Ness)*

Aviator Hamilton (fourth from left) and his airplane at the Spokane Fairgrounds in 1910. *(Courtesy SPLNWR)*

come nationally famous two days prior to his first scheduled show at the Interstate Fair on October 2, 1911. Nineteen-year-old Cromwell Dixon Jr. of Columbus, Ohio, the youngest licensed aviator in the world, had just been the first to fly across the Rocky Mountain Continental Divide, which earned him a $10,000 prize. Unfortunately, fate was not so kind when he took off from the Spokane Interstate Fairgrounds. As he began to ascend, a gust of wind caught his Curtiss Pusher, plunging him to his death on the railroad tracks just north of the racetrack. In his book *The Spokane Aviation Story, 1910-1941* (Tornado Creek Publications, 2007), James P. McGoldrick II wrote: "It is a sad page in history when a young man becomes famous, and rich, and dead, all in a span of three days!"

In 1913, some local men interested in aviation began using a field east of the city near Parkwater for

A. D. Smith's Curtis Pusher-type aircraft taking off from Glover Athletic Field, circa 1912. *(Jerome Peltier collection)*

flying instructions. This later became Felts Field. Some other sites were used as landing strips early on – Glover Field in Peaceful Valley and the fairgrounds – but Felts Field was improved, largely

The Spokane Airport Terminal Building was constructed in 1932 and is part of the Felts Field Historic District. *(Wallace Gamble collection)*

through the labor of a work gang from the county jail, and became the airfield of choice. It was the original home of the Washington Air National Guard and, in the early 1930s, became Spokane's first municipal airport.

From this humble beginning, aviation became a major institution in Spokane and the Inland Northwest in the form of Fairchild Air Force Base, which is now a key component of the local economy. Prior to Fairchild, Sunset Airport became a military base during World War II, then named Geiger Field, and is now the Spokane International Airport.

Sonora Smart Dodd and the Founder of Father's Day

Sonora Smart Dodd presented a resolution to the Spokane Ministerial Alliance on June 6, 1910, to dedicate a day each year honoring fathers. The measure was immediately accepted. Dodd had been inspired to do this out of respect for her father, who after his wife's death, was left alone to raise six young children. A decision was then made to observe the first Father's Day on the third Sunday in June 1910. Sons and daughters were asked to wear a red rose in honor of the living father and a white rose if deceased. In 1916, President Woodrow Wilson acknowledged National Father's Day by pressing a button that unfurled a flag on a platform at a celebration in Spokane.

By 1918, the day was internationally recognized by a heartwarming exchange of letters between stateside fathers and their sons and daughters in the U.S. Armed Forces in France. In 1924 President Calvin Coolidge commemorated Father's Day by expressing, "The widespread observance of Father's Day is calculated to establish more intimate relations between fathers and their children and also to impress upon fathers the full measure of their obligations." It wasn't until 1971 that Congress officially declared Father's Day a national holiday.

In 1948, a plaque was placed on a boulder at the corner of the recently demolished YMCA Building in Riverfront Park that bears the inscription: "Within this building June 6, 1910, Father's Day was founded by Mrs. John Bruce Dodd as a tribute to her Father, William Jackson Smart, a Pioneer, and to all devoted Fathers. This plaque is a kind gift from the Spokane County Pioneer Society. June A.D. 1948."

William J. Smart died in 1919. At the time, he was living on his farm near Wilbur, Washington. From 1907 to 1913 Sonora Dodd and her husband, John, lived at 610 West Sharp Avenue, until their new home was built at 603 South Authur (placed on the National Historic Register in 2010). John Dodd was a barber during his early years, but later became an agent for Prudential Life Insurance.

Sonora Dodd at the time she founded Father's Day. At the time, she lived at 610 West Sharp Avenue.
(Newspaper clipping from the Spokesman-Review, *June 16, 1910)*

A drawing of William Smart, the inspiration for Father's Day.
(Public domain)

The main entrance to Manito Park at 20th Avenue and Grand Boulevard in 1906. The arch over the entrance, designed by Park Superintendent Charles Balzer, was covered with multicolored ivy trained in the words "See Spokane Shine." The other side had "150,000," referring to the 150,000 Club, which was ambitiously promoting Spokane and targeting an increase in population to 150,000 by 1910. *(Courtesy Bill Stewart)*

Spokane's Greatest Promotional Era

During the excitement of the first decade of the 1900s, many of Spokane's civic and business leaders stepped up efforts to enhance the business climate and attract even more people to the city. It was an era of ambitious promotion and boosterism. The Chamber of Commerce, initially the Board of Trade, reorganized in 1901, and began actively promoting Spokane. Two years later, the Spokane Advertising Club was organized. This club began with eight members, which by 1924, boasted a membership of 600. They had five principal objectives and purposes: (1) promote truth in advertising, (2) eliminate fraud in business, (3) educate its members and the public in modern business methods, (4) advance the interests of Spokane and the Inland Empire by proper publicity, and (5) originate and carry out enterprises conducive to public welfare.

The 150,000 Club

In 1905, the Spokane Ad Club was joined in its promotional campaign by the 150,000 Club of Spokane, which put forth the challenge of doubling the city's present population of about 73,000 to 150,000 by the year 1910. It had doubled between 1900 and 1905, so it seemed well within reason to double it again over the next five year.

Enthusiastic, civic-minded men were enlisted to actively promote Spokane. The club was designed to differ from the Chamber of Commerce in that its annual membership fee of $1 was within everyone's reach. The concept of this club caught on immediately, and within two years, the membership increased by more than 2,400. Upon joining, each new member received a booster button imprinted with the club's insignia. The organization became so popular that it was a disgrace to appear in public without it. The club's constitution provided for a 15-member board of managers, elected annually by the entire membership. The only paid position was the secretary. Meetings were held every Monday to discuss the club's business.

The 150,000 Club's aggressive advertising campaign touted the potential and greatness of Spokane. They contributed to the rapid development of Spokane's industries by attracting a number of new manufacturers. Their stated goal did "not encourage immigration of laborers and mechanics but sought to increase the city's growth by inducing eastern factory owners and commercial houses" to locate in Spokane.

They also focused on beautifying the city through their City Beautiful Committee, organized in 1907, which promoted the city park system and was instrumental in the formation of the first Spokane Park Board. Their accomplishments were quite varied, and on one occasion, when the city ran out of funds, they raised $60,000 in less than a week to complete the new YMCA Building.

Although the 150,000 Club was highly successful in promoting Spokane, it did not reach its targeted goal of 150,000 people by 1910. The 1910 federal census placed the population at 104,402. However, padding was not only suspected but confirmed by some inside City Hall. Years later, Mayor Charles A. Fleming, who was city clerk at the time, said it was fairly well-known that census enumerators copied names from hotel and boardinghouse registers even though the guests were only in Spokane temporarily! The reason for the padding was that Spokane was vying with Tacoma for the position as the second largest city in the state (and still does to this day).

Based on public school enrollment, the population in 1910 has been extrapolated to be around 87,000. The growth rate for the next 30 years was much more measured than it had been the previous 30. The 150,000 Club's targeted population figure was not reached until the 1940s.

Other boostering efforts

At the end of its five-year campaign, the 150,000 Club disbanded, but other booster organizations quickly filled the gap. As business slackened, the Chamber of Commerce began a vigorous campaign to "Buy at Home," with an emphasis on producing or raising more locally to decrease the need to import so much from the east and Midwest.

In 1912, the Spokane Ad Club came up with a new concept, which quickly became the most intense and active promotional campaign the Inland Northwest has ever witnessed. It began as a drawing-and-design contest to capture a symbol that would be representative of the area. The winning drawing was of an Indian princess, "Miss Spokane." Immediately, another contest was held to put a live face to the drawing, the winner of which was 17-year-old Marguerite Motie. She was so poised and articulate the Ad Club decided to bring "Miss Spokane" to life. The young woman to hold the honored title served as a goodwill ambassador, the city's official hostess. The creation of Miss Spokane was considered a brilliant concept, and it continued until 1977. The program received both national and worldwide attention, and was copied by other cities.

Marguerite Motie held the position officially for eight years, but was periodically called upon to represent the city at major events until 1939. The program nearly folded during the Depression, but in 1939, it was revived when Catherine "Cay" Betts was selected as the next Miss Spokane. She served for eight years, but soon thereafter, the position was reduced to a one-year term. (For clarification, there were other Miss Spokane programs, but this one held the official city hostess position.)

Members of the Spokane Advertising Club presenting the city's first Miss Spokane, Marguerite Motie (later Mrs. Walter Shiel). Miss Spokane was the city's official hostess. *(Courtesy Dorothy (Shiel) Capeloto, daughter of Marguerite Motie)*

The second Miss Spokane, Catherine "Cay" Betts, presenting Bing Crosby with *Thanks Bing*, a book containing 20,000 signatures in appreciation for his continuous efforts to publicize his hometown. Crosby lived in Spokane from 1906 through the mid-1920s, when he moved to California and began his ascent to world fame as a singer and actor. Cay, later Mrs. Tom Williams, traveled to Los Angeles in 1941 to present this book. *(Cay Betts Williams collection)*

In September 1911, another organization formed, also largely as a booster organization. This organization was the Spokane Realty Association, the forerunner of today's Spokane Association of Realtors®. It was not the first real estate association to form in Spokane, but it was the one that survived as the present official association.

By the dawn of the 20th century, the stage was being set for the formation of this organization. During Spokane's founding years, almost everyone with the means to do so acquired real estate, then subsequently divided the land into smaller parcels, which they sold. Consequently, they all were, more or less, dealers in real estate. However, most handled their own properties and were not independent agents representing others who were buying and selling real estate.

As development progressed, so did the need for professional agents to represent others in land transactions. The was especially important as the situation evolved from selling undeveloped land to parcels that, by then, often contained a home or commercial building. The last chapter of this book contains a summary history of the Spokane Association of Realtors, but of significance here is that one of their original objectives was to be a booster organization to promote Spokane. The founders clearly understood that what benefited the region would equate to sales of real estate.

Despite the rapid progress at this time in history, some things still needed fine-tuning. In this 1911 photo, after this 20-horsepower car broke down, a two-horsepower towing operation rescued its Spokane owner. *(Courtesy Jim McGoldrick)*

Five

Spokane's Parks Were the Key to Developing Neighborhoods

Coeur d'Alene Park in the 1890s. This was Spokane's first park. *(MAC, L87.1-120)*

Public/private partnerships of Spokane's first parks

The majority of Spokane's early parks were donated by developers. They clearly understood the potential benefit of the city's development of the surrounding neighborhood infrastructure in exchange for land donated for parks. The city would construct the streets and avenues and other negotiable services, such as water and sewer, necessary for a development. In reality, this was not an equal exchange, as the value of the unimproved land was generally less than the cost of improvements. Typically, the men who were able to make the land donations were well-connected with the city fathers. Those who weren't so ingrained were often turned down when they requested the same special conditions. Although this exchange was clearly a serious conflict of interest with an illegal donative intent to the land owners, it proved to be quite popular with many of the town's successful developers and is how many of Spokane's early parks came about. (It is illegal for municipalities to make gifts of public benefits without fair compensation according to Washington State Law, which is backed by an attorney general opinion. In this case, the land trade for improvements would be considered a grossly inadequate return to the city.)

Chapter Five

The advantages of parks

In addition to the infrastructure provided, there were other real estate incentives to living near a park. One of these was the increased value of both real estate and homes located near parks. It was a financial advantage for the land developer to have properties near a park, especially if the city paid for all the improvements. The same still holds true today.

A front page *Spokesman-Review* article, under the headline "Park Improvements Add Fifteen Times Their Cost to Adjacent Property," stated on August 4, 1907:

> Property adjacent to a developed boulevard is 100 per cent more valuable than it would have been in the same district without the park or boulevard improvements having been made. This is the unanimous opinion of real estate men, who are in one accord in boosting for a better park and boulevard system.

Aubrey White and the City Beautiful Club

In the early 1900s, Aubrey White spent about six years on the East Coast on business matters. While in New York City, he joined the Municipal League, a civic organization concerned with parks and city improvements. During that time, he became aware of the challenges New York City had faced in securing park land after city development had consumed most of the open space suitable for parks. The cost to the city was far greater than it would have been had the land been secured while it was still vacant. When White returned to Spokane, he realized that at the rate the city was growing, if park land was not secured soon, in all probability, it would soon become completely unaffordable and, thus, unobtainable.

In 1905, to promote Spokane and increase its population, the 150,000 Club was formed. Two years later, White convinced the club to form

The Aubrey White family. Aubrey and Ethelyn (seated center) White and their daughters, (from left) Mary (Mrs. Henry) Hart, Dr. Elizabeth "Betty" White, Harriet (Mrs. Calhoun) Shorts, and Louise (Mrs. William) Willis. *(Courtesy Charlie Willis)*

Lilam, Lillian, and Lucy Hughes at the Bowl and Pitcher on the Spokane River. *(Magee photo, courtesy SPLNWR)*

a separate committee called the City Beautiful Club. Its function was to encourage the beautification of Spokane, largely through the promotion and establishment of a city park and playground system. His goal was to have a park or recreation area within walking distance of every neighborhood. White then organized and served as president of the City Beautiful Club.

Spokane's Park Board is approved and the park system developed

One of the club's first agenda items was to convince the city of the need for a nonpolitical park board. Prior to its creation in 1907, politics largely controlled how parks were developed and managed, often to the detriment of both the city and the parks. Upon formation of this board, Aubrey White was elected president at the first meeting. He served in this capacity from 1907 until 1922.

Upon becoming president of the park board, White convinced the city to hire the famous Massachusetts landscape architects, the Olmsted Brothers, to design a system of parks, parkways, and boulevards for the growing city of Spokane. He also persuaded the city council to buy and plant 80,000 trees along many of Spokane's streets. Because park funds were limited, he encouraged private citizens to plant deciduous trees as they were able, and to enhance the beauty of their homes and yards. Many of the trees planted by the city and the residents at that time still beautify Spokane's streets today. Grading, seeding, and planting of Manito Boulevard also began and, within three years, a $1,000,000 park bond was passed to expand and improve the park system.

Serving concurrently as park board president and president of the City Beautiful Club during its years of existence was fortuitous from the standpoint of helping to further the overall objective of creating and managing parks and park lands, and beautifying the city. White's foresight was remarkable, and he was tireless in his campaign to secure public park lands. He personally sought out property owners to obtain desirable land for parks and he acquired 1,000 acres through donations, trades, and low-cost acquisition. He acquired another 400 acres by convincing developers to donate their undesirable lands. Under his guidance as park board president, the Spokane park system grew from 273 to 2,272 acres. He also helped to secure, through various methods, the Bowl and Pitcher, 15 miles of parkway along both sides of the Spokane River, many golf courses, and areas outside of the city, including Mount Spokane park lands. Much of what he accomplished was through the help of his "powerhouse," an influential group that included William Cowles, Louis M. Davenport, John A. Finch, Joel E. Ferris, and Robert L. Rutter, whom he would invite for lunch and an afternoon drive to see proposed park acquisitions.

After 15 years as park board president, White and his family moved to a farm on the Little Spokane River. This move outside the city limits, according to a decision by the city council, disqualified White from serving on the Board of Park Commissioners. Thereupon, the park board passed a resolution declaring: "In the removal of Mr. White, the Park Board not only has lost its most valued member, but the city has been deprived of the services of a man who has done more for the up building of Spokane … to make it a better place in which to live, than any other individual or set of individuals." He later became known as the "Father of Spokane Parks." Under his leadership, the city came close to adopting the goal of a park within a 10 or 15 minute walk of every residence. White worked almost until his death in 1948 on the promotion of other improvements to enhance the quality of life in the community.

Formation of the park board

The initial park board was comprised of like-minded businessmen. With the objective of promoting a city park system, F. Lewis Clark, a wealthy real estate investor, William H. Cowles, publisher of the *Spokesman-Review*, Jay P. Graves, and other influential men joined Aubrey White in forming a park board that would be independent of city government. Consequently, in 1907, the voters approved a city charter amendment that established an unpaid 10-member Board of Park Commissioners.

Aubrey White and his four daughters, from left: Mary, Elizabeth (Betty), Louise, and Harriet. (*Courtesy Charlie Willis*)

The historical narrative of the *Report of the Board of Park Commissioners, 1891 to 1913* contributed the following additional information:

> The first public park of the city of Spokane, consisting of about 10 acres, and known as Coeur d'Alene Park, was donated to the city in 1891, by A. M. Cannon and J. J. Browne, and in the same year a charter provision was adopted placing the public parks under the joint supervision of the mayor, the president of the city council and the city engineer, subject to the direct authority of the city council.
>
> For several years thereafter, the city park area was gradually increased by voluntary donations of land, without particular reference to locality or public requirements. Under these conditions, park improvement and extension became a matter of secondary importance, proper administration was impossible, and efficiency

Who was Aubrey Lee White?

Aubrey White was born in Houlton, Maine, on February 17, 1869. His father was a farmer and he was one of 10 children, four girls and six boys. He was educated in the public schools except for one term at a preparatory school, Ricker Classical Institute.

In 1887, Aubrey followed one of his brothers to Spokane in search of new opportunities. His first job was for Arends and Kennard, a local bookstore. Following the Great Fire of 1889, he entered the mining business with his friend Jay P. Graves and moved to Montreal to promote the old Ironsides and Granby Mining properties in British Columbia. He also spent considerable time in New York and Philadelphia, where he raised funds for the Spokane Traction Company and Coeur d'Alene & Spokane Electric Railroad. During his time in New York, Aubrey joined the municipal league, a civic organization concerned with parks and city improvements. Following his return to Spokane in 1905, he became president of the "City Beautiful Club."

In 1907, the same year he became president, he married Ethelyn Binkley, daughter of Judge John W. Binkley. They produced four daughters. One of their daughters, Elizabeth (Betty), became a doctor, specializing in obstetrics and gynecology. She later became the first and only woman president of the Deaconess Hospital medical staff. Another daughter, Mary, married the longtime Lewis and Clark High School principal, Henry Hart.

In 1921, White moved to a small farm he named Montvale, located on the Little Spokane River north of the city, already the bucolic enclave of several other Spokane gentleman farmers, including his former employer, Jay P. Graves.

Aubrey White in his office in the Review Building.
(Courtesy Charlie Willis)

During the 1920s, White's business fortunes began to decline and, although far from destitute, he needed additional funds to live comfortably at Montvale, whose 15 acres gave extra space for his passion for gardening. He spent the last 26 years of his career as garden editor for the *Spokesman-Review*, a position created specifically for him by his friend William H. Cowles. White's garden columns and personal answers to inquiries of home gardeners were enormously popular. Under his guidance, Spokane residential gardens often won national competitions.

In 1948, Aubrey White died at his home at 617 East 13th Avenue, where he had moved in 1946 when his health began declining. Following an eye operation, he was sent home to convalesce, where he was overcome by weakness, suddenly losing strength daily until his death.

---

was sacrificed to political expediency with the usual unsatisfactory results.

In 1907 the public demand for systematic direction and control of public park affairs by some authority free from political interference, led to the organization by public spirited citizens of the city beautiful committee under the leadership of Mr. Aubrey L White, a sincere advocate of civil betterment, who is now completing his seventh consecutive term as president of the Board of Park commissioners. The efforts of this committee resulted in the adoption by popular vote on May 7, 1907, of a charter amendment placing the administration and control of all public park affairs under an independent, non-political Board of Park Commissioners of ten members, to serve without pay, with the mayor and ex-officio member thereof, also provided for a mandatory tax levy of not less than one mill for park purposes, to be expended only upon order of the Board of Park Commissioners; and on May 14, 1907, Mayor Floyd L Daggett appointed the following men to serve as a first Board of Park Commissioners of the city of Spokane: A. B. Campbell, Dr. P. S. Bryan, F. E. Goodall, A. W. Jones, E. B. Hyde, J. W. Wentworth, F. P. Holden, Charles Liftchild, A. L. White and A. M. Winston. From the organization of this park commission-based the present park, playground, and parkway system in the city of Spokane.

Olmsted Brothers hired

After White received permission to hire the Olmsted Brothers, John Olmsted agreed to prepare the plan, but he stated the value of his advice would be dependent upon a topographical map indicating trees and rock features. The map was to be furnished by J. G. Seupelt, park engineer. As Olmsted and James Frederick Dawson attempted to use the maps provided by Seupelt, they found them to be obviously incorrect. During the early 1900s, with his mentor, John Charles Olmsted, Dawson made numerous trips to the Pacific Coast, developing designs for the parkway systems of Portland, Seattle, and Spokane, the Alaska-Pacific-Yukon Exposition, the San Diego Exposition, and the campus of the Washington State Capitol. White knew the Olmsteds were engaged in designing projects in Seattle and Portland. As they were already in the Northwest, he was able to convince them to spend some time in Spokane preparing a report for the city.

Over several visits in 1907 and 1908, White accompanied John Charles Olmsted and his associate, Dawson, to Spokane's potential and existing

A group of girls at the Bowl and Pitcher. *(Magee photo, courtesy SPLNWR)*

Who were the Olmsteds?

During the 1900s, one of the nation's most sought-after landscape architectural firms was that of the Olmsted Brothers, who were descendants of Frederick Law Olmsted Sr.

A brief biography of the father, Frederick Law Olmsted, is important for Spokane's history as he was the patriarch of the family and gave the Olmsted name the original national recognition.

Frederick Law Olmsted Sr. (1822-1903)

Born in Hartford, Connecticut, in 1822, Frederick Law Olmsted Sr. moved to New York in 1848. In 1857, with no college education, he became superintendent of New York's Central Park, where he served as the administrator and then architect-in-chief of the park's construction.

According to information contained in Cynthia Zaitzevosky's book, *Frederick Law Olmsted and the Boston Park System 1982*, Olmsted took full credit for the New York park and other major projects, continuously failing to mention others who contributed. (Zaitzevosky teaches in the Radcliffe Seminars Graduate Program in Landscape Design. She is also consultant on the preservation of architecture and landscape architecture.)

Frederick Law Olmsted Sr.
(Public domain)

According to Zaitzevosky, Olmsted's partner, Calvert Vaux, should have received the majority of credit for Central Park. It was Olmsted's political connections, and the fact that he acted as the front man, that gained him the credit. From that point on, Olmsted's career flourished. Between 1872 and his retirement in 1895, Olmsted's firm completed 550 projects.

In late 1895, Olmsted suffered a mental breakdown and spent his remaining years in an asylum in Waverly, Massachusetts, where he died in August 1903.

Brief biographies of Frederick Law Olmsted Jr., John Charles Olmsted, and J. Frederick Dawson

Frederick Law Olmsted Jr. (1870-1957)

Frederick Olmsted Jr. was born on Staten Island, New York. He was the son of Frederick Law Olmsted Sr., following in his footsteps as an American landscape architect. He and his cousin, John C. Olmsted, were successors to their father's firm. He was best known for his wildlife conservation efforts with a lifetime commitment to national parks. He worked on projects in Acadia, the Everglades, and Yosemite National Park. Olmsted Point in Yosemite and Olmsted Island at the Great Falls of the Potomac River in Maryland are named after him.

He began his career as his father's apprentice in 1890, and worked on two significant projects: the 1893 World's Columbian Exposition in Chicago and the George Vanderbilt estate in North Carolina, the largest privately owned home in the United States.
In 1894, he earned his bachelor's degree at Harvard University, and in 1895, became a partner in his father's landscape architecture firm. Soon after, his father retired. Olmsted and his cousin John quickly took over leadership of the firm. For the next half-century, the

Frederick Law Olmsted Jr.
(Public domain)

Olmsted Brothers firm completed thousands of landscape projects nationwide. At their peak, the Olmsteds employed nearly 60 people.

He was a founding member and later president of the American Society of Landscape Architects. He married Sarah Hall Sharples in 1911. They had one child. Frederick Law Olmsted Jr. died on December 25, 1957. He is buried at Old North Cemetery in Hartford, Connecticut.

John Charles Olmsted
(1852-1920)

John Charles Olmsted, son of Dr. John Hull Olmsted and Mary Cleveland Perkins Olmsted, was born in Switzerland. By the time he was five, John Charles had traversed the Atlantic twice, lost his father to tuberculosis, gained a stepfather in 1859 (his uncle, Frederick Law Olmsted), and settled down in a house in the middle of Central Park.

John Charles Olmsted
(Public domain)

Following his graduation from Yale's Sheffield Scientific School, Olmsted began his professional career as an apprentice in his uncle's New York office. Early projects included work on the U.S. Capitol grounds and several park and institutional projects.

By 1884, when the firm moved to Brookline, Massachusetts, John had become a full partner with his uncle. After Frederick Olmsted Sr.'s retirement, John and his younger cousin, Frederick Law Olmsted Jr., formed Olmsted Brothers in 1898. John was senior partner until his own death in 1920; the firm continued until 1950.

Like his uncle, John was committed to the development of landscape art as a profession and to the education of communities and clients about the long-term benefits to be gained from careful, comprehensive planning. He, along with his cousin, was a founding member of the American Society of Landscape Architects, serving as its first president and establishing the standards of membership, while being active in other groups such as the American Park and Outdoor Art Association (later the American Civic Association) and the American Association of Park Superintendents.

For over 40 years, John Olmsted was a respected leader in the early landscape and planning professions. By the time of his death, the firm had completed more than 3,500 commissions, many of which he had originated. He was slowed in his last years of practice by the cancer that eventually took his life.

James Frederick Dawson
(1874-1941)

James Frederick Dawson was an American landscape architect. His father, Jackson Thornton Dawson, was superintendent of the Arnold Arboretum in Boston, and Dawson himself was actually born in that arboretum. Dawson graduated from Harvard University in 1896 and joined the Olmsted Brothers landscape design firm, where he led many significant commissions. He became a full partner in 1922.

Dawson studied agriculture and horticulture at Harvard's Bussey Institute. He apprenticed to the Olmsted firm in 1896 and traveled throughout England and Europe, observing the landscape and studying design and plant material. In 1904 Dawson was chosen by John Charles Olmsted and Frederick Law Olmsted Jr. as their first associate partner in Olmsted Brothers. Dawson spent his entire career with the firm. He supervised projects in Venezuela, Cuba, Canada, and Bermuda, as well as throughout the U.S., designing in a wide range of landscapes.

James Frederick Dawson
(Public domain)

park sites. Later, Olmsted and Dawson returned to their offices in Massachusetts and prepared a comprehensive park-related report. It began with their belief that every home, from humble to grand, should be within easy walking distance of a neighborhood park, and the more parks the better. They also believed that large areas of parkland should be left natural and undeveloped, especially large parks on the edges of the city.

Olmsted and Dawson completed their plan in May 1908, but the city fathers withheld it for five years to keep the general public from exploiting the land values around the park.

The firm's recommendations set off a rapid park expansion program. Their publication covered the years 1891 to 1913. It included the Olmsteds' philosophy and recommendations, and the board's progress towards implementation. The city was charged $1,000 for their work.

Spokane's parks

When the new Board of Park Commissioners took over the park department on June, 1, 1907, there were 12 parks with a total of 173.1 acres, only a third of which were improved. Currently, Spokane has 87 parks on 4,100 acres of land. Spokane's first parks included: Manito, Coeur d'Alene, Liberty, Corbin, Lidgerwood, Hays, Audubon, Cliff; Adams, Stracona, and Mission Avenue.

Today, there are a total of 36 neighborhood park, nine community parks; three major parks, 14 recreational parks, 10 community recreation centers; 12 conservation land areas, 11 parkways, one arboretum, and three recreational trails. A complete and thorough study of Spokane's parks would be a book unto itself. Consequently, only five parks are featured here by way of example. One is the city's first (Coeur d'Alene), three were designed by the Olmsted Brothers (Liberty, Cannon Hill, and Corbin), and one has become Spokane's premiere, award-winning park (Manito).

Coeur d'Alene Park
Spokane's first city park

The first effort in an attempt by Browne and Cannon to donate Coeur d'Alene Park was initiated by J. J. Browne. This proposal had numerous conditions attached, and proved to be very advantageous to Browne and Cannon. The following article appeared in the *Morning Review* on April 16, 1887:

> In reference to the Coeur d'Alene Park matter, which was laid over at the last meeting, Mr. J. J. Browne, who was present, stated to the Council that he was willing to convey his interests, and he thought Mr. Cannon would also do the same, if the city were to proceed to accept and improve the grounds. The property was now worth, figuring on a basis at which adjoining property was selling, at least $16,000.
>
> Mr. Hoover moved that the city accept the property and agreed to fence the same and convey water upon the land on or before November 1, 1887. Carried.
>
> Mr. Browne stated that he was ready to convey the property to the city as soon as the city complied with the conditions of the motion.

Browne's Addition developed around Coeur d'Alene Park

Most of Browne's property was located in the triangle of land formed by the Hangman Creek and the Spokane River. In 1883, this property was considered to be the most exclusive part of town. It included wide streets and a park, half of which was in Cannon's Addition. The addition was almost perfectly level, rising slightly from the original town site. Browne and Cannon each acquired 160 acres with the eastern boundary as Cedar Street and the southern boundary, which adjoined Cannon's, as Third Avenue through preemption claims.

It was always Mr. Browne's intention to have his property subdivided. Browne's Addition was surveyed and platted in 1883, at which time he began selling lots. By July of that year, Browne already had a force of men grading the streets and

Chapter Five

Coeur d'Alene Park, 1900. *(MAC, Libby L87-1.229)*

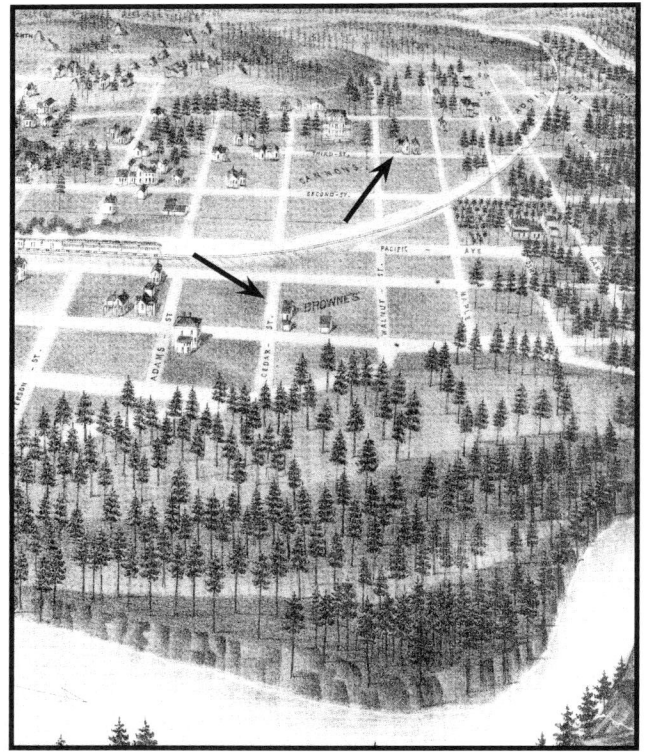

Map of Browne's Addition in 1884. The arrow on the left marks Cedar Street, and the one on the right marks Third Avenue. Coeur d'Alene Park was jointly owned by both Cannon and Browne. Third Avenue was the dividing line between their properties. Browne owned north of Third and Cannon owned south. *(Prepared by J.J. Stoner, Madison, Wis.)*

putting them in traveling condition. He stated he "intends to have his residence and surroundings equal to anything the territory has." This is corroborated in the July 21, 1883, edition of the *Spokane Falls Review*, which stated: "[Browne] has at last settled himself to the undertaking, and the result is that our local surveyor, Mr. Maxwell, has just completed a handsome plan of the addition. Mr. Browne is kept busy selling these lots, the demand for which surpasses all understanding." He also set aside a large plat of land containing several acres, where he intended to build his house.

The location of Browne's Addition attracted the more affluent. It had the first streetcar line of Spokane Falls, the horse-drawn line that traveled from downtown Spokane to the heart of Browne's Addition. Its main function was to promote real estate development in Browne's Addition. A selling feature was that the home owner could go to work downtown without worrying about his horse. This line marked the beginning of the streetcar era and an area of the majority of Spokane's first palatial homes centered in one geographical area. Many of the homes constructed in this area were designed by Kirtland Cutter during the late 1800s.

Another factor that came into play in Browne's Addition was the vast number of people living in this district whose money came from the Coeur d'Alene mining district, whose infancy began in 1883. Also, during the early 1900, a number of people involving the timber industry also were moving in that neighborhood.

Spokane Falls's first cemetery located at Browne's Addition

The northwest portion of Browne's Addition also contained Spokane Falls first cemetery. The May 26, 1887, *Spokesman-Review* provides a description and history:

> The Old Cemetery
> Movement to Remove One of Spokane's Landmarks
> –Pioneers Were Buried In it–
> Oldest Settlers Do not Remember When It Was Started–
> –Bodies to Be Exhumed–

A movement is on foot to remove one of the most important historical landmarks in Spokane. Last week a petition, prepared by J. W. Witherop and signed by W. J. C. Wakefield, John Finch, J. J. Browne, Dr. W. W. Potter and other residents of Browne's addition, was presented to the city council, asking that 17 bodies buried in the old cemetery near the end of the boulevard and Pacific avenue [Browne's Addition] be exhumed and reinterred in one of the modern cemeteries – either Greenwood or Fairmount. The petition stated the matter briefly, pointing out that the west end is rapidly becoming the most beautiful residence portion of the city, that the remains of most of those buried in the cemetery had been removed some time ago, and it would add to the attractiveness of the neighborhood if the remainder were removed.

This was Spokane's first cemetery. Here it was that many of the sturdy pioneers who came over the trail from Oregon, or from the far east, years before the Northern Pacific railroad was dreamed of, were buried, as were their wives, and in many instances their children. How the location was selected as a cemetery no one remembers. It was certainly a sublime spot, however situated on the abutting point of land, wrapt [sic] in the dense solitude of the primeval forest, commanding one grand, sublime view of rugged cliff and the valleys of Hangman creek and the Spokane.

The exact date of the cemetery's first burial is unknown, as were also the burials of later times. No tombstone was ever erected in the plot; only some plain wooden slabs, lettered by the hands of some loving father, husband or brother, told for a few brief months the name of the departed.

In speaking of the old grave yard yesterday, James N. Glover, Spokane's oldest pioneer, said: "Yes, I understand the old cemetery is to be removed. This was Spokane's first cemetery. I do not know just how old it is. It was there when I first came, and used for many years afterward. About 12 years ago most of the remains were removed. I thought all, but it seems not. No, I do not know the names of those buried out there, for I do not know how many or who were removed." J. J. Browne, on whose land the cemetery was located, was more familiar with the later history of the cemetery than Mr. Glover.

"This," said Mr Browne, "was Spokane's first burying ground. How it came to be selected I do not know; it was already located when I arrived. That was before it came to be surveyed, and was sold as government land. When I got the land from the government the cemetery was included in my purchase, and people continued to use it for many years afterward. That was probably 18 years ago. The cemetery was used until about 12 years ago, when the most of the bodies were exhumed by friends and taken to Spokane's second cemetery, the old burying ground in what is now known as Cannon's Addition, probably a half mile south of the Irving school. This latter cemetery was not used but a few years, the town growing so rapidly that the cemetery was abandoned and the bodies were again exhumed, most of them taken to Greenwood or Fairmount. I believe the number of bodies named in the petition as being still buried in the old cemetery is erroneous. The petition say 17, but I believe there are no more than six or seven. Do I know the names of those buried? No; or at least not many of them. I remember attending a number of the funerals, however; the first funeral I attended in the city was that of Mr. Lowry, a young man, 21 years of age, who worked in one of the mills, if I remember rightly. ...

"Another funeral I attended was that of Mrs. Evans... She remains buried in the cemetery. Another, and the only remaining case that I know of, is that of a Mr. Evans, who lost his life in a log jam up the river. He was buried there, and only last week his wife came to see me to learn if the remains could not be removed to Greenwood or Fairmount. I thought the proposal impossible, but she felt sure that she could identify the remains if they were exhumed. She said that Mr. Evans lost his life up the river, and that his skull was fractured in such a way that she could never forget it, or fail to identify the remains. The fracture was on the side of the head, and she still remembered how it looked. I also remember the burial of a number of men killed in a wreck on the Northern Pacific trestle, just north of the city, when that road was being built through the city... A number of the Havermale children were also buried there..."

In July 1897, W. H. Cowles, the owner of the *Spokesman-Review*, closed a deal with the Columbia Investment Company for the purchase of an attractive piece of property in Browne's Addition overlooking Hangman Creek (the site of Spokane's first cemetery). The purchase price was $12,500. According to the *Daily Chronicle*, dated July 22, 1897, "This was one of the best building spots in the city. It is located at the highest point in Browne's addition with the view of the city as well as Hangman Valley and Spokane River. In the same neighborhood, in close proximity to Mr. Cowles's purchase, Mr. Finch, Mr. Campbell, and Mr. Odell are currently erecting expensive residences."

In 1973 a permit was issued to Cowles Publishing Company for the demolition of the Cowles house. It was razed that same year along with several other adjacent Cowles-owned, Cutter-designed homes.

The land was vacant until 1986, when the new owners, Wendell Reugh and Harlan Douglas, built condominiums on the site. During the site preparation, prior to construction, a number of skeletons were uncovered, thought to be those of some early Native Americans. However, since this was the first burial site for the town of Spokane Falls, that conclusion is questionable.

The Ridge Condominiums at the former Browne's Addition Cemetery. This photo shows about a fourth of the buildings. It was one of the first gated communities in Spokane. *(Bamonte)*

Liberty Park

Liberty Park, Spokane's second municipal park, was deeded to the city in 1897 by F. Lewis Clark, one of Spokane's wealthy real estate speculators. At the time of his donation, he owned a considerable amount of land in that area.

On June 11, 1898, an article appeared in the *Morning Review* which stated: "It is now Liberty Park. Yesterday the City Park Commission anonymously decided on a name and legally affixed it to the site." According to the article, a petition had been signed by members of the community around the park requesting it be called Liberty because of its location in the Liberty Park District, which Clark owned. It was also announced in that article that the park would be extensively improved that year.

Under the terms of the deed by which F. Lewis Clark transferred the site to the city, the city was to spend $2,000 a year for three years to improve the park. It was proposed that the entire amount of work be done the first year. In addition to the $6,000 to be expended, the city was required to grade Fifth Avenue from Arthur Street to the eastern end of the park and the avenue running through it. The remaining work consisted of building rustic roads and bridges.

Liberty Park consisted of 19.5 acres of rocky hills and slopes. The park was bounded by Arthur and Perry streets on the west and east, and Third and Fifth avenues to the north and south. The highlight for the park was Springfield Lake, which was shallow and in the summer proved to be more of a swamp.

The park was situated in a small canyon bounded by sheer basalt cliffs and steep hillsides. Kirtland Cutter donated his services to the city to lay out a plan for the park's development. The plan included a narrow roadway across the park on the crest of its southeast-to-northwest ridge. It would also have walking paths and flower beds at the Fifth Avenue entrance.

A view of Liberty Park looking east. *(All photos of Liberty Park courtesy Charlie Balzer, grandson of Charles Balzer, Spokane's first park superintendent)*

When the grading of the surrounding roads was finished and water mains were installed, the eight-acre lake was able to be flooded for skating in winter. It opened in 1890 and at one time was the most popular skating pond in the city.

Because of a lack of money, the city workers were never able to complete the dredging and cleaning of the lake. By 1907, it again took on the term "mudhole." In 1913, when the park board report was revealed to the public, an article appeared in the *Spokesman-Review* stating Liberty Park was the most picturesque park in Spokane. The area of focus had been on the northwest corner, where a shallow wading pool and a children's play area were among the earliest improvements. To the southeast and above the lake a basalt wall and a

Springfield Lake at Liberty Park.

walkway were built, including built-in benches and a roof of peeled logs anchored by rustic pergolas at either end. The east end, which was concealed by a hill from the western part of the park, was graded for a hard gravel playground for boys' sports. Also, the need to dredge and maintain the lake was considered a major problem and dealt with in detail. A plan to plant vines and shrubbery to soften the many rock surfaces was also submitted. The Olmsted plan, as recommended in the 1908 report, was mostly implemented, and Liberty Park became one of Spokane's favorites.

In 1920, a swimming pool was added, and in 1950 Springfield Lake was filled in. By the late 1950s, plans for a freeway specified a downtown route for the proposed corridor. At the time, Liberty Park was in a state of disrepair, the swimming pool needed frequent repairs, and neighbors to the north complained they were cut off from the park because of heavy traffic on Second Avenue.

In the late 1960s, freeway construction began at Liberty Park. Only two acres at the eastern end of the park were kept intact. Because of neighbors' concern over the loss of the park, the park board bought 18 acres of adjoining property to the east. With both state and federal funding, the new Liberty Park officially opened in the summer of 1972. The original pool closed in 1981 and was replaced with another pool at the park's southeast end. The 1920 basalt bathhouse was demolished in 1984. With four more acres added at a later date, Liberty Park now consisted of 22 acres.

Portions of the old park ruins, which were separated from the rest of Liberty Park by the freeway, are now owned by the State Department of Transportation. They are accessible at Second Avenue and Arthur Street. Today, these ruins are called "Spokane's Stonehenge."

A survey crew at Liberty Park.

Spokane's Parks Were the Key to Developing Neighborhoods

This walkway was built at the southeast end of the park above the lake. A basalt wall and walk-way included built-in benches and a roof of peeled logs anchored at each end by rustic pergolas.

Liberty Park wading pool.

Corbin Park

Corbin Park was the location of Spokane's second agricultural fair. Although there is plenty of factual material to document that the first fair, which took place in 1886, was held on Francis Cook's property on the South Hill, most published accounts, concerning the history of Spokane's fairs, erroneously place the first one at Corbin Park.

Following the first fair, the community began to raise capital to purchase land and build a public racetrack. Spokane's second agricultural fair, held in 1887, was at the new facility about two miles north of downtown just west of Division Street. The driving park and grounds of the Washington & Idaho Fair Association were completed in time for the annual fair in the fall of 1887. D. C. Corbin carried a mortgage on the property. He had a particular interest in the new racetrack because he himself owned a number of race horses.

Due to financial difficulties, a decade later the fair association was forced to sell the lands, which Corbin purchased and developed into the Corbin Park Addition. He converted the former fairgrounds into Corbin Park, which he verbally offered as a donation to the city in 1899. The city accepted, and on January 25, 1900, the *Spokesman-Review* announced "City Now Owns Corbin Park" after D. C. Corbin formally handed over the deeds.

Several years later, the Olmsted Brothers firm made their recommendation for the 11.5-acre park, which was only 300 by 1,700 feet. As it was all level ground (which had been ideal for the race track), they suggested it be developed primarily as a play area for the neighborhood children. Their recommendation included a swimming "tank" with adjoining changing rooms, an outdoor gymnasium, tennis courts, ball fields, sandboxes, and a playground. The following quote was excerpted from the Olmsteds' recommendations (contained in their report published in 1913):

> The idea is that such a park, devoid of hills and valleys, woods and ledges and other marked beauties of nature, should be made as thoroughly useful to children as funds will permit, instead of being wholly given over to ornamental landscape gardening.
>
> The amusement apparatus in bare, hard gravel yards will of course be very ugly. If there were no remedy for that, we should, out of respect for the opinions of many neighboring householders as well as other citizens,

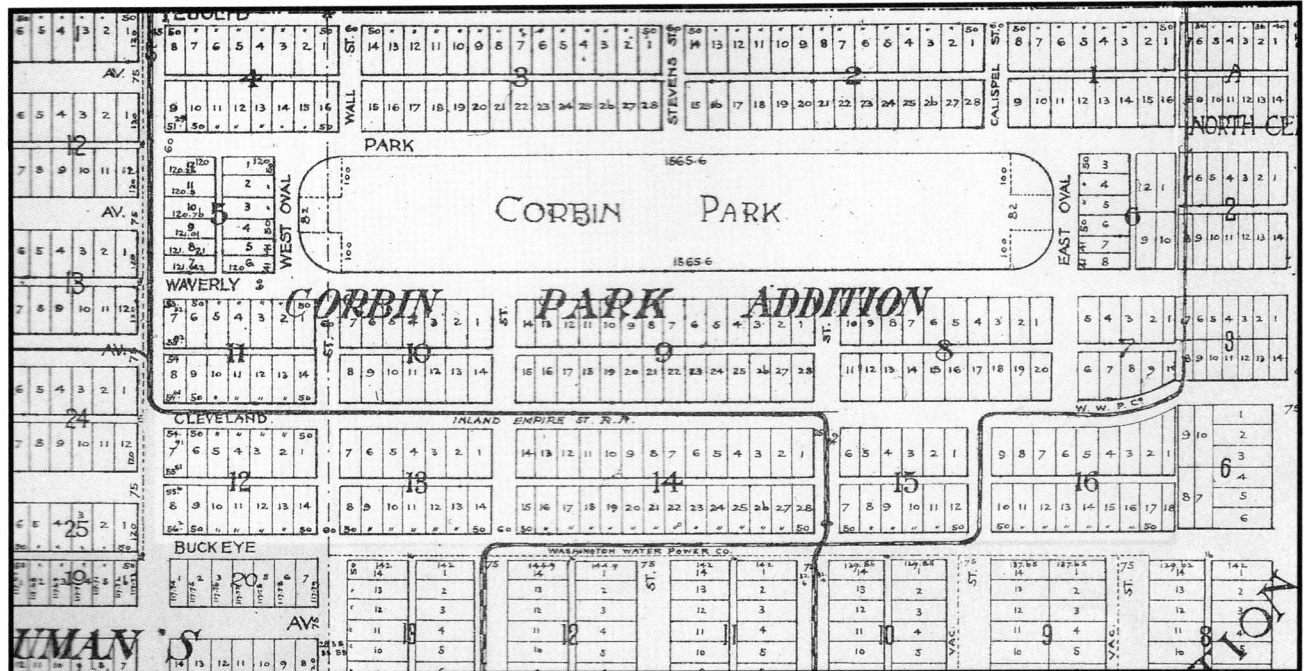

A 1912 map of Corbin Park, surrounded by land owned by D. C. Corbin. *(From the* Standard Atlas of Spokane County, Washington *by George Ogle and Co. Publishers and Engravers from Chicago)*

The driving park and grounds of the Washington & Idaho Fair Association were completed in time for the annual fair in the fall of 1887. This later became Corbin Park. (Spokane Falls Illustrated, *Hook and McGuire, 1889)*

hesitate to urge such arrangements in this park, considering the evident tendency to prettiness and neatness in the surrounding cottages; but we are confident that all this ugliness can be almost wholly concealed by beautiful planting. There is no reason why a high, fine-mesh, wire netting fence, covered with flowering vines, may not be as beautiful as a bed of colored foliage plants or other gardening decorations.

Because the majority of the neighbors around the park were in favor of a small "beauty spot," not a noisy play area, most of the recommendations were not followed. As a result, the Olmsteds prepared a revised design plan, which included a central fountain (never built), curved paths, and flower gardens. In 1913, the park board reported that two tennis courts had been installed, which were continually in use, walkways and driveways had been improved, and a great number of shrubs had been planted. In time, due to high maintenance costs, the city eventually chose to eliminate much of the formal design and flower gardens. Today, the park still has some of the oldest trees in the city, despite having lost the beautiful old elms to Dutch elm disease in the early 1990s. Many of the homes around the park reflect the large bungalow style that was popular when most of the homes were constructed in the early 1900s. There are also turn-of-the-century Victorian and Tudor-style homes.

In 1991, the Corbin Park Historic District, which includes more than 80 homes, was placed on the Spokane Register of Historic Places. It is also on the state and national historic registers, along with more than a dozen other historic districts in the city of Spokane. One of the longtime residents of this neighborhood, who died in 2002, was Robert B. Hyslop, who wrote *Spokane Building Blocks* (1983), an incredibly valuable resource to those interested in Spokane's history. His father, W. W. Hyslop, was a well-known architect who designed some of the early homes around Corbin Park. He also built the home his son lived in at 2913 West Oval.

In 2011, as part of their centennial celebration, members of the Spokane Association of Realtors partnered with the Northwest Museum of Arts and Culture (The MAC) in hosting the MAC's annual Mother's Day Home Tour, which featured the Corbin Park neighborhood.

Manito Park
(originally called Montrose Park)

There are conflicts amongst historians regarding the precise point of Manito Park's inception. A number of recorded events suggest a "park of sorts" as early as 1886, when the first fair in Spokane County was sponsored by Francis Cook and held somewhere on his "farm on the hill." The 1887 *Spokane Falls Directory* lists "Washington Fair Association (Francis Cook pres), grounds one mile south of city." For the years of 1896-98, the *Polk Directory* lists "Montrose Park, 2.5 miles S. of city on Cook's Electric Line" In the 1899 *Polk Directory*, only the Montrose Park Addition appears and, from 1900 to 1902, both Montrose Park and the Montrose Park Addition are listed.

The dance pavilion on the southern shore of Mirror Lake (Manito Pond) around 1907. *(1907 brochure, MAC, L93-31.3)*

A *Spokane Falls Review* article appearing in April 1888 highlighted Montrose Park as the destination for local picnics and family excursions. Another recorded event corroborating the early Montrose Park was an article appearing in the June 28, 1902, *Spokesman-Review*: "The old pavilion at Montrose park was burned yesterday. The building was not worth very much." The reference to the pavilion being "old" in 1902 corroborates the supposition it was built during Cook's ownership and development of the area, probably at the time of the fair in 1886.

Around the turn of the century, the stage was being set for Spokane's showcase neighborhood on the South Hill around Manito Park. Real estate was booming, and a new high-end neighborhood was about to rise in that addition. In the 1880s, Francis Cook had begun making plans to develop a neighborhood around his Montrose Park, but lost most of his South Hill property during the Panic of 1893. His original development project was destined for success, but without him.

By 1903, most of Cook's original properties on "Cook's Hill" had been acquired by a number of land speculators. Among them, the brothers Jay and Will Graves, formed the Spokane-Washington Improvement Company to develop and promote their new Manito Addition, bounded by 14th Avenue on the north, 33rd on the south, Hatch to the east, and Division to the west. Intent on providing reliable public transportation to the Manito area, Graves had acquired Cook's Spokane & Montrose street railway in 1902. He immediately began converting it from narrow to standard gauge track and improving the cars. The next year he reorganized it as the Spokane Traction Company.

Graves' next step was to organize the owners of the adjacent properties to offer a large tract of acreage to the city for a park. Along with the Spokane-Washington Improvement Company and Spokane & Montrose Motor Railroad Co., the Washington Water Power Company, Northwestern and Pacific Hypotheekbank, and real estate developer Frank Hogan collectively contributed nearly 95 acres to the city.

In exchange for this park acreage the city agreed to pave a road system around the new park, a water source, and a main waterline. The donors stipulated that this land was to be preserved forever as a park, and if the services and requirements were not met, it would revert back to the original owners. Although legal title was not transferred until the following year, Montrose Park took on new ownership, a new name and a definite sense of direction.

A July 31, 1903, article in the *Spokane Daily Chronicle* announced the proposed boundaries for the park. This article also proclaimed the new

The Manito Pond, circa 1925. *(Courtesy Spokane Parks and Recreation Department)*

name for the park "... Manita [*sic*] Park, referring to its elevation, which affords a fine view of the city."

The developers of the Manito Addition understood "Manito" to be an Indian word for "hilltop," as indicated in a brochure they published to promote their Manito properties. More specifically, it is an Indian word meaning "spirit," "Great Spirit" or "a supernatural force that pervades nature," still a fitting description for the area.

A point of interest regarding the stipulations was the lack of publicity regarding the city's future financial obligation in the acceptance of this land. A number of private interest groups, such as these Manito Park benefactors, had great influence on the local politicians and media, a practice common throughout Spokane involving many of the early parks. Today, this conflict of interest would likely receive much public criticism and challenge. However, at the time, it was key to the development of the parks and their surrounding neighborhoods.

Donating the land for Manito Park was clearly a successful financial move for all parties involved and marked the beginning of the real estate boom in that area. Graves would turn Cook's former holdings into an enterprise worth millions. Because of its rail access and the city's promise of new streets, Manito Park was at the hub of this rapidly growing neighborhood. Spokane's South Hill was now about to emerge with a mighty and lasting force. A real estate article in the June 24, 1903, *Spokesman-Review* stated:

> "Top Notch Hill" in the southern part of the town, is quite stable – very few changes in buildings, because people building homes there generally know what they want and can afford to pay for it; whereas the less fortunate ones often keep on enlarging on an originally small house.

"The Hill" was becoming a place of curiosity and awe. People enjoyed viewing the beautiful homes as they passed through this area on the way to Montrose Park (as Manito Park was still called at the time) and the new building lots on the plateau. For an up-and-coming family in the early 1900s, Manito was definitely the neighborhood in which to invest in property for a home. It had all the elements for success, situated directly above one of Spokane's already established elite neighborhoods immediately south of downtown (the area of the D. C. and Austin Corbin, F. Lewis Clark, Kirtland Cutter, F. Rockwood Moore/Senator George Turner homes).

Charles Balzer, first superintendent of Manito Park

About 1900, Charles Balzer, who was at the time, the city florist, was the city's first park superintendent. During Balzer's early years as superintendent, rapid changes took place in Manito Park, at-

Charles Balzer, circa 1905. *(Courtesy Charlie Balzer, Charles Balzer's grandson)*

Mirror Lake (the present Manito duck pond) in the early 1900s. The little foot bridge at the left crossed the canal that extended east to Grand Boulevard. *(Courtesy Bill Stewart)*

Looking southeast in 1909 from the intersection of Loop Drive, Tekoa Street and Manito Place showing the Owl Castle aviary (top right of photo), the swan house on the duck pond island and the bear cages with people standing in front (along the bottom of the photo). *(Courtesy Bill Stewart)*

tracting visitors by the thousands. People dressed in their Sunday attire packed a picnic basket, and gathered up the children to spend a day at the park. Beautiful flower gardens and floral sculptures adorned the park, and a growing zoo captured the attention of young and old alike. Regular weekend band concerts and baseball games entertained the picnickers. Money was tight, but Charles Balzer crafted swing sets and other playground equipment for the children out of old power poles.

In 1905, Charles Balzer began acquiring animals for a fledgling zoo in the park, which at times contained as many as 165. The zoo covered nearly a third of the park and became a major attraction.

During Balzer's tenure as park superintendent, his main focus was on Manito Park. Much of what he did was at his own expense and beyond the expected duties. Park records reveal his dedication to Manito and early photographs attest to his accomplishments, but the park board wanted more.

During the time the park board was pushing for Balzer's resignation, Aubrey White met the assistant park superintendent for the Boston Park System, John W. Duncan. An offer was made and Duncan accepted.

John Duncan became one of Manito Park's best known figures. He served as Spokane's park superintendent for 32 years, retiring in 1942 at the age of 77. Born in Aberdeen, Scotland, he moved to Boston with his family when he was a boy. He learned the nursery trade from his father. Although White and the Park Board Commission gave the appearance of seeking someone with a technical education to replace Balzer, there is no record in the available archives indicating Duncan ever received a formal education. However his experiences and his association with the Olmsted Brothers paved the way for him in Spokane. He was eager for the opportunity to implement some of their recommendations for Spokane, which over time extended the Olmsteds' influence.

During Duncan's tenure as superintendent, he made a number of trips to the eastern states to gather ideas from established parks in larger cities. His greatest contribution and lasting legacy was with the design of the formal European-style garden. In 1941, the year before Duncan's retirement, the park board honored his years of fine service as superintendent by changing the name of the garden from "Sunken" to "Duncan."

Under Duncan's supervision, the lake at Manito Park, called Mirror Lake during the Montrose Park era, also underwent the first of many alterations. The overall effect of these alterations was a reduction in its size to what is now the duck pond. In the early days of the park, the spring-fed lake extended to the edge of Grand Boulevard. The main body of water was at the present site, with a canal extending to the east. This canal would almost dry up in the late summer, leaving an unattractive mosquito-infested swamp. At the west end of the lake, the

John Duncan. *(Courtesy Spokane Parks and Recreation Dept.)*

The dedication of the Washington Monument at Manito Park on June 14, 1932. Mayor Leonard Funk officiated at this ceremony. In 2009, due to continued vandalism, it was moved to a safer area in the park across from the Park Bench Cafe. *(Courtesy Carmen Hagman)*

water would seep onto nearby lots. In 1912, in order to contain the water, a concrete wall founded on bedrock was built along the north and west sides of the lake. Water from nearby springs was also diverted to the lake to keep the water level up.

John Duncan initiated other changes at Manito Park during his tenure. As previously stated, during this stage of the park's development, he gradually incorporated some of the recommendations from the 1907 Olmsted Brothers' report. When Duncan retired in 1942, he was designated Superintendent Emeritus of the Park System. The park board minutes credited Duncan with "creating one of the finest series of gardens in the country out of barren rocks, lakes and bogs."

History Repeats Itself

Spokane Is No Exception To This Old Rule

The history of all cities in this and other countries is that the finest residence districts ultimately seek the higher levels. In Spokane the highest level is at

MANITO

It is the natural outcome of the development of any city of any size for the best residence district to be on the hill sections.

The railroads, the business houses and manufactories must of necessity be located on the lower levels and as time goes on and a city develops the "one-time" best residences give place to business houses.

Every resident of Spokane has implicit faith in the development of the city and believes that within a few years it will be one of the important cities of the country. When that belief has been fulfilled where will the choice residence section be?

TAKE TIME BY THE FORELOCK and get your home site where you think the choice residence section will be. Don't take any one's else opinion. Just use your own judgment. It will save you a great deal of money and make some for you, too.

Our Manito office is at 29th and Grand. Phone 3017.

The Fred B. Grinnell Company

TERMINAL BLDG.   PHONE 728.

By 1907, the Manito area had entered a steady growth pattern. During that year, Jay P. Graves hired Fred Grinnell, a seasoned real estate salesman, to sell his property. Grinnell owned one of the largest real estate companies in Spokane. His office was located at the intersection of Main and Lincoln streets on the main floor of the Interurban Terminal Building (now the location of the main branch of the Spokane Public Library). After Fred Grinnell assumed responsibility for the sales of the Spokane Washington Improvement Company's land for Graves and partners, he set up an office at the southwest corner of 29th and Grand, and later added a smaller office at the intersection of 21st and Grand, across from Manito Park. Grinnell had a reputation for aggressively pursuing the city to comply with the conditions of the park land donation. The economy was healthy in 1907, but most importantly, Manito Park was ready to receive its neighborhood.

Chapter Five

THE BEST DRINK IN TOWN
IS AT
MANITO

Visit MANITO this afternoon or evening and refresh yourself with a drink of the Manito spring water in the park. It is positively the finest water in the city.

Chemists who have analyzed Manito spring water say that it is chemically pure; that it is as fine a quality of water as it is possible to obtain anywhere.

ALSO

Manito is the coolest spot in town. In fact, you could not find a cooler one if you should journey many miles to some of the lakes. There is always a breeze, and the temperature is at least 10 degrees cooler than it is downtown.

In the afternoon there will be a band concert in the park from 2 until 5, and in the evening there will be a free moving picture exhibition under the pines. Bring your suppers with you and spend a Sunday that will really do you some good.

VISIT US

We have a branch office right opposite the park, on Twenty-first avenue, and another at Twenty-ninth and Grand. Call at either one if you are interested in the "Manito kind" of home sites, and we will drive you through the residence section of the addition and give you an opportunity to see what wonderful development has taken place in the past three years.

It won't cost you a cent—we just want to show you.

Manito Leads in Improvements

The Fred B. Grinnell Company
Terminal Building   Phone 728

BY ACTUAL COUNT
62
Houses Are Under Construction at
Manito Park

JUST STOP AND THINK A MINUTE WHAT THIS MEANS: Over $150,000 being spent for houses that are under course of construction within the boundaries of Manito Park addition today. By the way, that does not include the large number of houses that have already been completed at Manito this year.

Is there any other addition in the city with such a record? None that any one has heard of!

Where the most fine homes are being built is the place for you to build

Name your own terms on a Manito lot. We will do the rest.

The Fred B. Grinnell Company
TERMINAL BUILDING.   PHONE 728.
Manito Office, Twenty-ninth and Grand.

MANITO
HAS
- 62 houses now in course of construction
- 10 miles of cement sidewalks
- 12 miles of graded streets
- 7 miles of water mains installed
- 1600 shade trees planted along the streets
- Several miles of gas mains laid
- An improvement club, the members of which are boosters for a beautiful residence district

More Money---in Shorter Time

can be made in Manito property than in any other residence property in Spokane. Such has been the case in the past three years and it will continue to be so for years to come. *In all cities* the best residence districts seek the highest ground. *In Spokane* the highest ground is at *Manito*— that is one reason why Manito property is going to be so valuable. Another reason is that the owners of the addition are not afraid to spend money for improvements.

Visit the Park Today

We have a branch office at 29th and Grand and another one just opposite the park on 21st avenue. Our representatives will be at these offices all day prepared to show you about the park and let you purchase a homesite *on your own terms*.

The Fred B. Grinnell Company
Terminal Building   Phone 728

Another of Grinnell's Ads

No Other District But Manito Is Free From the Railroad Danger, We Now Have an Automobile in Which to Show You Around

The Manito residence section is known as one of the most desirable residence sections in the city.

The Way Is Made Easy For You

You will never have a better opportunity to secure a home site than today. We let you name your own terms, and Manito property is selling at the present time below its actual value. Only a small cash payment required and you can tell us how you want to pay the balance. Band concert at the park today. Come out. We have opened a new branch office at the park on Manito Place.

We have another office at Twenty-ninth and Grand and will have carriages at both in which to show you around.

To describe the building atmosphere around Manito Park, the above is a sampling of Grinnell's 1907 advertising campaign taken from various issues of the 1907 *Spokesman-Review*.

Hurry! Hurry! Hurry!

We mean the home lot buyer, the one who wants an ideal place to live; on the hill, in the heart of Spokane's best residence district.

McCrea & Merryweather's Addition to Manito Park

These lots are going fast; get in on this early and get a choice one; don't wait, but do it now; cheapest and best within two-mile circle.

$250 to $450   **$20 Down; $10 a Month**

LET US TAKE YOU OUT TODAY

McCrea & Merryweather
Insurance, Rentals

Phone 396   Sprague and Howard

Another company that dealt in real estate in the Manito Park area. From a series of ads in various 1907 *Spokesman-Review* newspapers.

Cannon Hill Park

Cannon Hill park is located east of Lincoln Street between Eighteenth and Shoshone Avenue. The park sits on about 13 acres and perhaps is one of the most picturesque neighborhood parks on the South Hill.

In 1886, John T. Davie, who produced the first bricks in Spokane Falls, purchased 80 acres with Henry Brook, a contractor and builder, at the site of present day Cannon Hill Park. They paid $30 for one of the 40-acre parcels and $50 for the other. Brook owned an additional 40 acres in the area.

Following their purchase, Davie moved his brick operation from Latah Creek and began producing the majority of the bricks used in the construction of the commercial buildings in downtown Spokane. In 1888, Davie sold out to Brook, who continued the operation for a short while before selling to a Mr. Belt and Joseph H. Spear. Belt soon gave up the business. Brook and Spear then joined in the formation of the Washington Brick & Lime Company, which was incorporated in 1889 and had an office downtown. In 1893-94, a plant was built at Clayton in Stevens County. It was probably at that time the operation ceased at the Cannon Hill Park site.

How Cannon Hill Park came about

The Adams family, represented by Charles F. Adams, owned a 60-acre tract surrounding the area of what is now Cannon Hill Park. Adams had plans to develop his surrounding land into a residential area along with the Cannon Hill Company. On February 14, 1908, Charles Adams deeded 13.18 acres to the city of Spokane. This property was specifically donated to the city for a park, which included the clay pit from the old brickyard.

In return, the city agreed to improve the land within one year from the date of this donation.

J. T. Davie and Company workers pose in front of bricks at what became Cannon Hill Park. *(MAC L86-1069)*

The improvements are not mentioned on the quit claim deed. Cannon Hill Park, prior to being donated to the city, was called Adams Park in honor of Charles Adams. It was later changed to Cannon Hill Park after Anthony Cannon.

When the Olmsted Brothers were in Spokane in 1908, Aubrey White, Spokane Park Board president, specifically requested they design a park at that site. The park was completed in 1910. The original plan called for two ponds, with the excess water from the numerous springs at Manito Park to be diverted to Cannon Hill Park.

Cannon Hill Park had one of the city's favorite skating ponds in the winter and wading pools in the summer. The smaller of these ponds, which was located on the west side of the park near 18th Avenue and Lincoln Street, is now gone. The only reminder a pond was ever there is a bridge made of basalt rock. Cannon Hill Park is a classic example of an Olmsted Brothers' design.

An article in the May 5, 1912, *Spokesman-Review* carried a headline that described the construction and facilities of the park:

> Miniature Lake will be feature of
> Cannon Hill Park Addition
> Improvements by park board will
> enhance beauty of rest spot.
> Many are building.
> Since the district opened up,
> 100 Homes worth $750,000 had been erected.

In preparation for the formal opening of Cannon Hill Park sometime in the latter part of the month, Arthur D. Jones and Company have had a force of more than 20 men at work for the last week smoothing off the graded streets, removing dandelions and other unsightly growths from vacant lots, mowing and trimming the miles of partnerships in the addition and planting new shade trees and shrubbery along the streets and in the parking strips that mark the center of 21st Ave., the Blvd., street of the park.

Final touches are being put upon the big lake in the center of the park by a crew of men employed by the park board, which has taken supervision of the new park. New lawn surfaces are being graded and seeded, and more than 12,000 shrubs and foliage plants are being planted along the shores of the lake, on the islands and the flowerbeds that are a part of the landscape work being done by the Park commission.

Build rustic bridges

A crew of stonemasons has been busy for a week laying foundations for the rustic shelter houses to be built around the lake and constructing the bridges that will connect the shores with several large islands a couple of arms of the lake. They are also arranging a rustic pool at the Northeast corner of the lake with a boulder waterfall, over which will fall the stream that will supply the lake.

Wading pools with sandy bottom, sand beaches for the children, and spacious lawns for playgrounds are among the features of the plans for the park. The Park commission has promised to have the landscape work, bridges and buildings all completed so the park can be thrown open to the public before the end of the month.

Stream feeds lake

The lake, when completed and filled, which has an average depth of about 30 inches with the constant current from the in-flowing stream there will be no stagnation, and the water will always be clear as a 12 inch double layer of clay and sand is now being laid at the bottom of the lake to ensure a minimum loss of water by seepage. This process is called puddling. On top of the six-inch layer of clay packed into the subsoil, which makes it a watertight covering, six cases of clean sand will be deposited. As soon as the park is completed the realty firm would hold a formal opening with the public as its guest and band concerts and a program of interest will mark the event.

Since the opening of Cannon Hill Park addition about two years ago nearly 100 houses with an average value of about $8000, have been constructed in the addition at an aggregate cost of approximately $750,000. There are 20 new dwellings now under construction, several of which will exceed $25,000 in cost.

Additional car services

The Cannon Hill Park Company keeps a force of men constantly at work caring for the lawns and shrubbery, and looking after the parking strip and vacant lots. All of the main streets and a number of the cross streets have been paved and the end of the season will see two car lines in the addition, as the cable Addition car line will be extended out Bernard Street from 18th to 25th avenues. A feature of the addition is the large number of Oriental plants or European sycamore trees that have been set out in the parking strips. This is a very hardy foliage tree, fast-growing and ornamental. Out of 1200 of these planted in the addition only 16 had to be replaced in the spring.

The Neighborhood

There are three separate parks within the Cannon Hill neighborhood: Manito, Cannon Hill, and Cliff parks. This area of Spokane is among the most desirable in the city. The majority of the houses in the area consist of bungalows, Queen Annes, Tudors, and a mix of eclectic styles.

By 1912, Cannon Hill Park neighborhood was in the process of a major expansion. An article in the May 12, 1912, *Spokesman-Review* describes three residences near completion. The beginning of the

---

—over $400,000 spent to make Cannon Hill Park the finest place to live in Spokane.

This money has been spent simply and solely for improvements, to add beauty and convenience, to make Cannon Hill Park a delightful place to live in; it does not include the price paid for the land.

Furthermore, this money has actually been spent to date or is represented in contracts now being carried out. It doesn't include what is planned. Before we get through there will be more than that. It is the actual cash investment in beauty and convenience to date.

It has been spent, or is being spent, in putting in cement sidewalks and cement curbs and concrete crosswalks on every street; in preparing wide parking strips on every street and planting shade trees; in laying out and beautifying a boulevard and a park; in installing the best water system on the south hill; in laying sewers to serve every lot.

And lastly, it is being spent in paving not only the main streets in the addition but also paving a street clear to Riverside avenue; so that there will be brick and asphalt paving all the way from the office to the home of Cannon Hill Park residents.

This work is now in progress and will be finished before winter.

We are doing a big work in Cannon Hill Park, one of the biggest pieces of work in point of elaborateness and completeness ever done in Spokane, and we offer homesites here with the assurance that they are just as fine as we know how to make them.

Don't attempt to see Cannon Hill Park alone now. The paving work has so blocked the streets that it is difficult to get about. Call at the office and a representative will go with you to direct you.

Prices $900 to $2500.   Easy Terms

ARTHUR D. JONES & CO.
Real Estate   Loans   Rentals   Insurance

907 RIVERSIDE AVENUE   EMPIRE STATE BUILDING

An ad in the *Spokesman-Review* boasting of the improvement to Cannon Hill.

article states: "Three attractive Cannon Hill homes soon to be occupied." That same article also made a point of expressing how popular the bungalow style was becoming in that area. It went on to state:

> Many beautiful homes are rapidly nearing completion in the Cannon Hill Park District and home sites on 21st., 22nd and 23rd avenues are rapidly building up with attractive residences. One of these is a seven room two-story residence, almost completed, built by Lewis Searle, on 21st Ave. near Howard Street.
>
> The house commands an excellent view of the city and the valley as far as Fort Wright. On the main floor of the big dining room and living room, with a massive fireplace and built-in bookcases in the latter, are features of the construction. The dining room has a built-in sideboard and the den has bookcases embracing the same features....

This article went on to describe more features of the house:

> Thomas and Jordan have nearly completed a seven room bungalow on 22nd Avenue, near Bernard Street on a view lot 50 x 140 feet. Particular attention has been paid to the original exterior into an artistic interior. Living room, dining room and Den are finished in white oak and have polished oak floors.

Another house was described as a house of English design. This "eight room English design house on 23rd Avenue, near Howard Street, erected by James Whitelaw will cost, when completed, $8000."

A June 30, 1912, article in the *Spokesman-Review* stated:

> Residential park boosts building
> Fine homes go up in Cannon Hill Park Addition
> Near new Park site
> Has artificial lake
> Rest spot on South Hill attracts builders of homes
> have many unique features
>
> One of the direct results of the beautiful Cannon Hill Park which the park board literally is building in the scenic Cannon Hill District is the erection of many new homes in the general neighborhood of the park. Visitors to the city have been impressed with the rapid development of the district, and no time probably has a development been brisker than this spring and summer. The new residences are all in keeping with the high standard of architectural beauty that has made this section of one of the most beautiful residential sections of the city.
>
> The park itself will be a marvel of beauty when finished. An army of men has been working all summer under the supervision of John W. Duncan, park superintendent, and the big undertaking is nearing completion. Practically the entire park has been converted into an artificial lake. This is studded with islands, planted to grass and shrubs and linked up with artistic bridges, four of them, built out of rustic stone with beautiful arches and approaches. The shelters and rest spots are being built largely of the same rock with blue cement pillars. James Whitelaw, M. L. Pershall and Jordan and Thomas have recently completed new homes.
>
> **Whitelaw Home Unique**
>
> The residence of James Whitelaw at 518 E. 23rd Avenue has many unique features. It is built in the old English style with the upper story finished in stucco and hip roofs characteristically of many of the old land homes. The most distinctive features the porch. Instead of being incorporated under the main roof the porch is built in front under its own roof. It is finished in severely plain lines almost on the California mission order with broad steps and walls adored by ornaments.
>
> The house has eight rooms. It is finished throughout in oak and white enamel. There is a fully equipped billiard room in the basement. Hardwood floors are in every room. The house has all the built-in features and a hot water heating plant. It cost $9000.
>
> **Builds Stucco Bungalow**
>
> One of the charming bungalows of the district is that just completed by M. L. Pershal on 21st Avenue near Bernard Street. It is built on a view lot and has seven rooms. The outside walls are finished in the stucco style, with trimmings in brown, and rustic stone is used as foundations of the porch and pergola over the automobile drive.
>
> The novel bungalow is finished in oak, curly fir and white enamel and the basement is fully subdivided and the walls are plastered. There is a sleeping porch and also two view porches. In the basement is a modern billiard room and hot water heating plant. The grounds have a cement driveway leading to the garage which will accommodate two cars the cost of the home was $8000.

Cannon Hill Addition promotion

A half-page article appearing in the June 5, 1910, *Spokesman-Review* showed photographs and described the Cannon Hill Park District real estate potential as an excellent investment. At the time, the Cannon Hill District was considered the "high grade district."

The district that sets the standard

These photographs of the streets of Cannon Hill Park are reproduced here to show the beauty of the district, its pines, its slopes and its street work.

Every street in the addition is like this, not only the front streets but the side streets as well. The improvements are put in or are being put in, and they are paid for. Walks, curbs, parking, trees, water and sewer – everything but paving is included with the lot. And this is the only addition in Spokane today where all the assessments for sewer, both trunk and lateral, and the improvements on the side, streets as well as the front streets are paid for.

Cannon Hill Park sets the standard. Today it is the best example of addition platting and district beautifying that can be found on Cannon Hill. It is the furtherest advance Spokane's fine home district has yet made.

It has every thing you can ask in a home locality; street work such as you see here; a 14-acre park of its own and a 96-acre park is a stone's throw; cool clear air; choice pines; elevation above the city; beautiful view; a boulevard; adequate building regulations; a water system that gives perfect satisfaction while other parts of the city experience drought; two car lines, and closer in than Corbin Park.

These are the reasons why there is more money being spent this season in Cannon Hill Park for homes than in any other addition in the city–over $125,000 represented in buildings either erected or are under construction since the first of the year; these are the reasons why purchasers are not offering their lots for sale, but are holding them for big profits they will accumulate.

Buy here now while the prices are still low. Lots here are the cheapest in the city, the same distance from the business center. You can get a full 50-foot lot with all the improvements – except paving – completely paid for as low as $900 – exactly the same kind of lots shown, in this picture and on Cannon Hill, and with even the sewer assessments paid. Lots out in the school section without the improvements are bringing more than that. The profits in the next few years in real estate are to be made in the high grade districts. Buy in Cannon Hill Park and when the prices of the high grade residence districts average uniformly as high as the poorer residence localities do now, sell out, and take your profit if you want to or hold for the big profit to come. $100 will start you towards the ownership of a Cannon Hill Park lot, and you can pay the rest on easy terms.

Arthur D. Jones & Co.
Real Estate, Rentals, Loans, Insurance
907 Riverside **Empire State Bldg.**

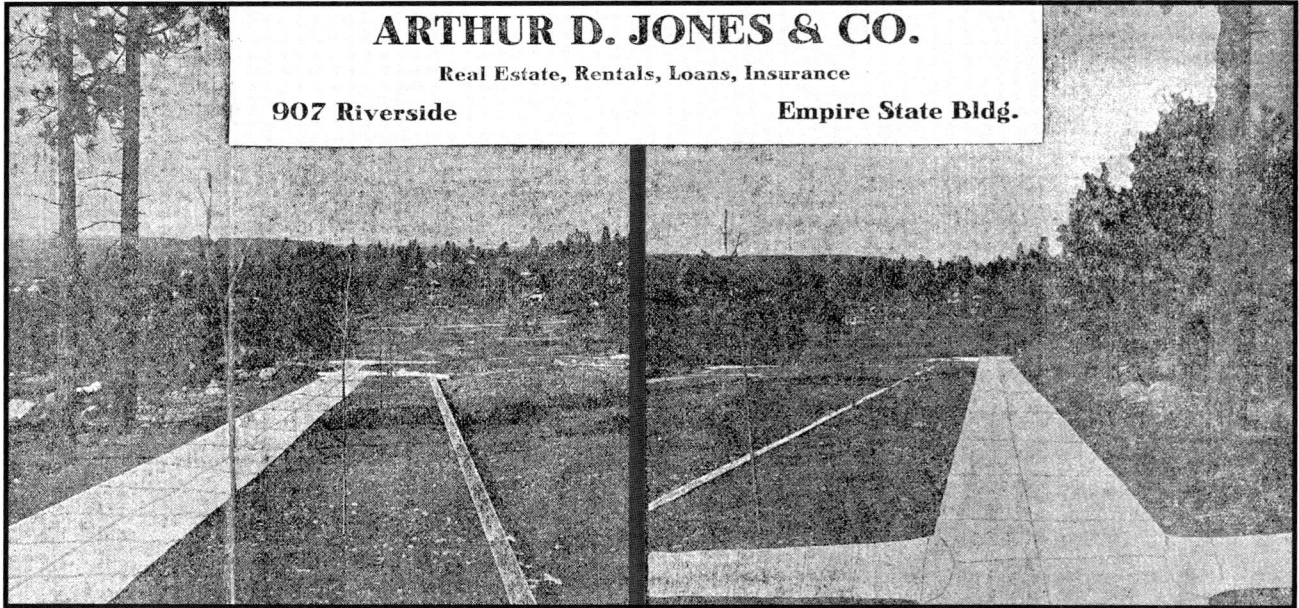

This newspaper photo in the June 10, 1910, *Spokesman-Review*, refers to the above article. It shows two sidewalks that were in place in 1910, next to the pond. This ad took up three-fourths of a page.

Cannon Hill Park, 1922. *(Frank Guilbert, MAC L95-111.454)*

Cannon Hill Park in the 1920s. *(Frank Guilbert, MAC L95-111.454)*

One of the 26 New Homes Built or Building in Cannon Hill Park

--- gas mains are laid now in Cannon Hill Park

For the first time in the history of addition development in Spokane gas mains have been put in as part of the original improvement. No other new addition in Spokane has gas mains. A great many of the old ones have no gas.

But Cannon Hill Park has gas to start with.

Mains are laid now on all the streets that are to be paved so that there will be no tearing up of pavement.

Houses in Cannon Hill Park can have gas at any time. With the coming of the gas and the completion of the new car line the last part of the pioneering will have passed. Cannon Hill Park is now practically a completed residence district on Cannon Hill.

These actions show what the big interests of Spokane think of Cannon Hill Park. First the Washington Power company decided to run a new car line, a special extension of their Cannon Hill line, in order to get the trade of Cannon Hill Park. This line is now building, and will be in operation by September.

Then the gas company ran a supply main and latteral mains on street after street in order to be prepared for the homes that are there now and are coming.

If you haven't seen Cannon Hill Park lately you will be surprised at its appearance now. Twenty-six houses are either built or being built—

A detail of a 1910 *Spokesman-Review* ad announcing that gas mains were laid in Cannon Hill Park. This was the first addition in Spokane to have gas installed.

Six

Building Spokane, Some of the Common House Styles in Spokane

The first homes in Spokane were constructed by Native Americans. Of the six tepees in this photo, three are covered with snow. Those were obviously not occupied and may have been used for storage of wood and food. Sometimes during cold weather, more that one family lived in a tepee. *(MAC photo)*

A Sampling of the First Styles of Homes in Spokane

Native American Tepees

Tepees (also spelled teepees or tipis) are tent-like houses used by the early Native Americans in the Spokane area. Tepees typically are made of a cone-shaped wooden frame with a covering of animal hides. They are designed to erect and dismantle quickly. As a tribe moved from place to place, each family would bring their tepee poles and animal hide tent along with them.

During cold weather, fires would be built in the center of the tepee with a flap at the top for the smoke to exit. The entry way to the tepee was left open to whatever extent was necessary to allow a draft for the fire to burn.

A mid-1880s photo of downtown Spokane Falls structures. These were Folk style houses. The structure on the left appeared to house more than one family. *(Courtesy SPLNWR)*

Early Pioneer and Folk, 1873-1880

The first houses in Spokane were mostly "Early Pioneer" style or as referred to by some "Folk style." These homes were typically built by their occupants or by nonprofessional builders. All were relatively simple houses that provide basic shelter. These types of homes were built by the first settlers into an area and many of them later served as working men's dwellings or were torn down as their owners gained financial status. Presenting a stylish appearance was not important and homes were typically built with logs or rough lumber. They basically were constructed as temporary places to live.

Early pioneer homes were designed to minimize the cost of heating. Since heating and cooking stoves were costly, sometimes a cook stove was all a family could afford.

The difference between heating and cooking stoves was the length of time the stove would burn before the wood had to be replenished. Cook stoves lasted about three hours before the wood had to be replenished. A wood-heating stove would burn all night if loaded with wood and the controls adjusted.

Because of the heating systems being concentrated in one or two rooms, all the rooms needed to open to each other.

Gathering firewood was a necessary chore in preparation for the cold months. *(MAC photo)*

A Folk style home in downtown Spokane Falls, mid-1880s. *(Courtesy SPLNWR)*

The other obvious factors in homes of this decade were a lack of bathrooms, indoor plumbing and no closets, a minimum number of windows, and few interior or exterior details. Spokane's first controlled plumbing systems were gravity. A source of water would be found at a higher elevation and piped downhill to a residence. Sewers operated in a similar manner and generally emptied into the river.

Mortgage money was limited or non-existent, as were building codes. There was also a lack of foundations, exterior paint, and adequate decorative wood trim for the interior walls and ceilings. Early homes were often similar because of the limited number and variety of products that could be transported by horse and wagon.

Another Folk style home with Victorian details in downtown Spokane Falls, mid-1880s. *(Courtesy SPLNWR)*

American Queen Anne, 1880-1910

When mansions began to appear in Spokane from 1880 to 1910, one of the most common styles was the American Queen Anne, which used medieval forms, both with and without the addition of classical detailing.

The main features of the Queen Anne style are a steeply pitched roof with an irregular shape, a dominant front-facing gable, patterned shingles, and cutaway bay windows. Fanciful, elaborate, or intricate designs were also used to avoid a smooth-walled appearance. These homes often have a partial or full-width porch, which is usually one story high and extends along one or both side walls. About half of the houses had delicate turned porch supports and abundant spindle-work ornamentation.

Of all the house styles in Spokane, the American Queen Anne was among the most elaborate. The Queen Anne came to America during the machine age and became an architectural fashion in the 1880s and 1890s.

Widely published pattern books touted spindles and towers and other flourishes associated with Queen Anne architecture. Spokane's wealthy population pulled out all stops as they built lavish "castles" using Queen Anne elements. Factory-made, precut architectural parts for Queen Anne structures were shuttled across the country on the railroads. Many of these decorative elements can be seen in Spokane homes.

Some American Queen Anne houses are loaded with "gingerbread" and turrets. Contrary to a popular belief that turrets alone make a house a Queen Anne many are made of brick or stone in addition to all the other features.

How the name came about

Anne Stuart was the Queen of England, Scotland, and Ireland in the early 1700s. During that time, art and science flourished. One hundred and fifty years later, British architect Richard Norman Shaw and his followers used the term Queen Anne to describe the artwork that originated in Europe. Although their buildings didn't resemble the formal architecture of the Queen Anne period, the name stuck.

In America, as builders added spindle work and other flourishes, Queen Anne houses grew increasingly elaborate. The Queen Anne style in the United States became entirely different from the Queen Anne style in England. Both styles were nothing like the formal, symmetrical architecture found in England during the time of Queen Anne's reign.

The most predominant area in Spokane for the Queen Anne style was Browne's Addition. While many of these homes have been preserved as private homes, others have been converted into apartment houses and a few offices.

The qualities that made Queen Anne architecture so regal also made it fragile. These expansive and expressive buildings proved expensive and difficult to maintain. During the beginning of the new century, Queen Anne houses had begun to lose their popularity.

This home at 2003 West First Avenue is an excellent example of a Queen Anne. It was built for mining investor Thomas J. Edgington in 1889.
(Bamonte)

Tudor Houses

A Tudor house may have a steeply pitched roof, is usually side-gabled, and has a facade dominated by one or more prominent cross gables, typically steeply pitched. A decorative (i.e., not structural) half-timbering present on about half of the examples as well as tall, narrow windows, usually in multiple groups and with multi pane glazing. Massive chimneys, commonly crowned by decorative chimney pots, are also typical.

A relatively small percentage of Tudor houses have stucco walls. These are most common on modest examples built before the widespread adoption of brick-and-stone veneering techniques in the 1920s. In the early decades of the century, wood-frame houses could be most easily disguised as masonry by applying stucco cladding over the wooden studs. Brick wall cladding is the most common Tudor subtype. Walls of solid brick masonry were sometimes used on landmark examples early in this century, but brick became the preferred wall finish for even the most modest Tudor cottages after masonry veneering became widespread in the 1920s. Brick first-story walls are commonly contrasted with stone, stucco, or wooden cladding on principal gables or upper stories. False half-timbering occurs on about half the houses in this style, with in-filling of stucco or brick between the timbers and, quite often, elaborate decorative patterns in the arrangement of timbers or brick.

The majority of Tudor homes in Spokane are classified as Tudoresque in style, as they relate to or resemble the style of the Tudor period.

This non-English Tudor style house, at 729 West Shoshone Avenue overlooking Cannon Hill Park, is the home of the Mounsey family. *(Bamonte)*

This Tudoresque home located on Park Place, fronting Corbin park, was completed in 1908. The McKenzie family has owned this home since 1984. It was constructed following a house plan published by the Ballard Plannery. (See below) *(Courtesy Gina McKenzie)*

This is the house plan from the Ballard Plannery Co., Inc. plan book. The narrative in the book states: "No. 77. We can recommend this beautiful home to anyone wishing something out of the ordinary. The cuts [house plans which are also pictured in this ad] speak for themselves. The cost of the house ranges from $9,000 to $12,000, according to requirements. Two sets of Plans, Specifications, Material List and Blank Contract, $30.00. One set of Plans and Specifications, $25.00."

Craftsman Bungalow Houses

The bungalow is one of Spokane's more common structures. The identifying features are typically low-pitched gabled roofs with widened enclosed eve overhangs. The roof rafters are sometimes exposed, with wood beams or braces commonly added under the gables, porches, or roof. These are supported by tapered square columns, frequently extended to ground level.

The basic feature of the bungalow is the front gabled roof, which the majority of these have. The porches are sometimes full or partial width. Many bungalows are a story and a half tall with center shed or gable dormers. Their porches are generally contained under the main roof, often with a break and slope. The bungalow was the dominant style for smaller houses being built from 1905 into the 1920s

Typically "Craftsman bungalow" referred to houses that were exceptionally well-crafted on both the interiors and exteriors. They were popular from 1905 to 1930, especially in the Manito Park and Cannon Hill Park areas and around Audubon Park.

For a period of almost 30 years, bungalows were the dominant style for smaller to medium-sized houses built throughout the country. As a result, a flood of pattern books appeared, offering plans for Craftsman bungalows; some even offered pre-cut packages of lumber and detailing to be assembled by local labor.

For a time, bungalows became the most popular and fashionable smaller houses in the country. Some were still built after 1930, but that style rapidly faded.

A Hyslop-designed bungalow located at 525 Waverly Place which fronted Corbin Park. This photo was on the Mother's Day Tour sponsored by the MAC in May 2011. *(Courtesy Gina McKenzie)*

Eclectic Houses

The eclectic style of home design is perhaps the most difficult to describe. One definition of the term eclectic is "picking from various possibilities; made up of material from various sources; diverse; heterogeneous." There are other definitions of the word, just as there are many variations in the eclectic house style.

Because the eclectic house style defies a single description, the term can be applied to almost any home that blends a combination of several styles, incorporating a variety of different design elements. Some eclectic homes will borrow a roof from one style, windows from another, and materials from yet a third. An eclectic style house may include architectural touches such as columns, corbels, and arches from Colonial, Italian Renaissance, and Mission styles. The classification of an eclectic house is, to a great extent, subjective. Ask three experts to classify an eclectic house, and you will probably get three different answers.

This American Four-Square at 1226 North Summit Boulevard was built in 1905. The architects were White & Hyslop. *(Courtesy Nancy Compau)*

Cutter & Malmgren were the architects for the home at 2203 South Manito Boulvard, built in 1907. *(Courtesy Nancey Compau)*

Mission Houses

Mission homes have open overhanging eaves and porch roofs supported by large, square piers that are commonly arched. Their wall surfaces are usually smooth stucco. Their roofs are typically red tile.

California was the birthplace of the Mission style and many of its landmark examples are concentrated there. The earliest were built in the late 1890s.

By 1900, under the influence of fashionable architects and national builder's magazines, this style was spreading north and east. Although never common outside of the southwestern states, scattered examples were built in early 20th century suburbs throughout the country. Most date from the years between 1905 and 1920, with a few notable examples in Spokane.

A great variety of shaped dormers and roof parapets mimic those found on some Spanish Colonial Mission buildings. Few are precise copies of the original models. Most examples have prominent one-story porches either at the entry area or covering the full width of the facade; these sometimes have arched roof supports to simulate the arcades of Hispanic buildings.

Mission-like bell towers occur on a few examples. Detailing is generally absent, although patterned tiles, carved stonework, or other surface ornamentation is occasionally used. Elaborate landscaping is common on most examples.

This Mission Revival style home at 1128 West Eighth Avenue was built in 1911 for John and Ellen Rudberg. It originally sold for $17,000. It was designed and built by Aaron L. Lundquist, Builder/Home Designer.
(Courtesy Marianne Guenther Bornhoft, photographer Ryan Lindberg)

The Mission style Opportunity Township Hall, now the Spokane Valley Heritage Museum. At the time of this photo, this was the main street of Opportunity. The architect who designed this building, C. Harvey Smith, began practicing in the Spokane area around 1888. He designed a number of schools in the Inland Northwest, including one in Chewelah, Washington, and one in Mullan, Idaho. He also designed a number of business blocks, such as one for E. H. Stanton at the corner of Hamilton and Mission, and various private residences around the area. *(Courtesy Spokane Valley Heritage Museum)*

The Spokane Valley Heritage Museum was founded in 2005 by Jayne Singleton. It officially opened August 18, 2005, and is located in a Spokane Valley Landmark and historic building, which was originally built as the Opportunity Township Hall.

Built in 1912, the building has been a center of community activity for almost 100 years. Museum volunteers renovated the building and are continuing to preserve it for future generations.

During its short tenure, the museum has achieved many milestones. Extraordinary exhibits have included "Apollo 11, One Small Step," "United We Stand, WWII on the Homefront," and "Under One Sky, Spokane Valley, 1800-1899." The Spokane Valley Heritage Museum was also selected as one of only six museums in the state to host a traveling Smithsonian Exhibit, "Between Fences." During fair weather, the museum's outside exhibits are open.

The museum has hosted group tours, including Boy Scouts, fraternal organizations, senior groups, car clubs, and student field trips for private, parochial and public schools.

Guided by a board of directors, daily operations are accomplished by a director and 22 regular volunteers. The museum is also assisted by students from various schools and colleges.

The museum is funded by the generosity of the citizens and business owners of the community and through fund-raisers, grants, and memberships. It is a non-profit, tax-exempt organization that is open year around.

Colonial Houses

On July 24, 1910, the *Spokesman-Review* published an article from a famous Minnesota architect, Arthur C. Clausen, who recommended the colonial style house and summarized its history:

WHEN IN DOUBT BUILD COLONIAL
So-called American Renaissance Architecture is style
which has proved appropriate
Clausen gives history
Tells prospective builders that wood columns painted
white do not make colonials.
By Arthur C Clausen.

Domestic styles of architecture, come and go very much as the fashions. A few years ago a brown stone front in the Romanesque style, made popular by H. H. Richardson, was considered the proper thing for a practical home. This was soon followed by a reaction to brick construction and in its turn was followed by what has been called the bungalow craze and the building of homes in various forms of cement construction (the designs being somewhat along the craftsman style). Through it all, however, one style always found favor with a few, and every so often, shows us its superiority by becoming again the popular style of American domestic architecture. It is the colonial style.

The American Renaissance.
While not a native of this country it may be justly considered the American Renaissance of the classic orders and may have found its greatest development and greatest favor in this country. While styles of architecture can never be traced directly to certain men, being the product of gradual development on the part of many designers, the original colonial style is credited largely to Sir Christopher Wren and the Adams brothers of England. However, even the great Sir Christopher did not develop it the style to any great extent. It remained for the young architects who came over here from England during the colonial period of our history, carrying with them the impression of what was considered the new and popular style of England, then bearing the name of the Georgian style, and to adapt it to our needs and develop it into what we call today the colonial style of American architecture.

Colonial Period Harmonious.
The colonial period of American architecture is the only time in the history of our country when all the arts

This example accompanied the article by Arthur Clausen (printed above).

and crafts were in harmony. The colonial house contained colonial furniture, bric-a-brac, picture frames, candlesticks, and even its occupants were dressed in harmony with the general brilliant and contrasting color schemes of the colonial style. So exquisite was the design of the furniture and bric-a-brac, and so careful the workmanship that produced them that the originals command the highest price even today, and in our more modern furniture and bric-a-brac that comes the nearest to be as faithful copies of the original command the best price were the originals cannot be obtained. The colonial style, having received its greatest development under the intense patriotism of that period, bids fair to always stand out distinct from other styles of architecture as the best one adapted to American life and ideals.

What Makes the Colonial Type.
During the colonial period, cut stone was less used, all moldings and carved details being made of wood. For this reason it is been nicknamed by some "the carpenter's renaissance." This makes it all the more appropriate as a domestic style, since the average home builder cannot afford the great expense of cut stone cornices, balustrades and columns.

Some people have the impression that having wood porch columns painted white warrants considering their home as being in the colonial style. Such is not the case, however. The columns must not only be distinctly colonial, but the cornices balustrade, windows, roof, materials of which the building is made, etc. Even the arrangements of the grounds – In fact, everything about the home must be in harmony and in colonial design before it can be properly considered as a distinctly colonial home.

When in Doubt.
If you are unable to decide as to what style in which you have your home designed, instruct your architect to make it colonial. You can not miss the mark far if you plan of the home is regular in its proportions and you will have a home always in harmony with American life, it's patriotism and ideals.

This Colonial Revival home showing Neo-classical influence at 2308 West Third Avenue was built in 1900 for James Clark, developer of Anaconda mines and brother of the well-known mining magnate Patrick "Patsy" Clark. Architect Albert Held designed the house. Today, it is the Isabella Club, a residential substance-abuse treatment facility for young girls who are either pregnant or have a child. (Souvenir Spokane, *Shaw & Borden, circa 1905*)

Homes of Some of Spokane's Wealthy, Famous or Infamous

John J. Browne's Mansion

The Brownes' Second Empire/French style mansion, located half a block west of Hemlock on First Avenue. The family lived there from 1888 to 1902, then sold it to railroad magnate Robert E. Strahorn and his wife, Carrie Adell (Green) Strahorn. *(Sketch from the* Northwest Magazine *April 1880)*

On July 15, 1966, excerpts of letters from Mrs. Boyd Hamilton (J. J. Browne's daughter) of Oakland, California, appeared in the *Spokesman-Review*. Mrs. Hamilton recalled her childhood in Browne's Addition as follows:

> I remember in those days we got around with horses, or trains – bicycles came later. And we had quite an assortment of horses, a fairly large team for the carriage, which had a high seat which the coachman, I believe, called the box, a low comfortable seat for the ladies or gentlemen, and a jump seat folded into the floor and pulled up when needed for the children. The team of Hambletonians or other fast trotters were for the Surrey and "old Fred," one of the larger horses, was used for the Phaeton. We also had a road wagon, a light buggy either for the team or a single horse. We also had various riding horses.... "The stable faced Pacific near the back of our grounds. ... I think is still there and has been converted into flats or an apartment. Our grounds went back to the Campbell place, which is now a museum. We had a rose garden and a greenhouse between the two places. At the end of first Avenue was the white colonial home of John Finch and his beautiful wife. Boyd Hamilton and I were married in the home on September 20, 1900. …
>
> My father had for several years owned a farm on Moran Prairie, including the hill, now I believe called Brown Mountain – a considerable acreage on the flat. After Mr. Moran, for whom the place was named, was killed by a bull, father bought that property and built the house, called the White House by the men on the farm – where the family lived until father's death, March 25, 1912. He, for a time, and my sisters, Irma and Hazel, drove into town – Father to the office and the girls to school. A fast team made the trip in 40 minutes or so to town. Because of the climb, up what was now Rockwood Boulevard, the trip home was slower. After father bought the first autos, a National and a Franklin, the horses receded into the background. Until the boys learned to drive we had chauffeurs. That was the story as transportation methods and the city progressed. The 15-room house at Glen Rose, which was surrounded by a 1500-acre estate, was burned to the ground in 1936.

Robert E. Strahorn was born in Center County, Pennsylvania, on May 15, 1852. He spent the first four years of his life in Pennsylvania. At the age of four, his parents moved to northern Illinois, where the family farmed. Although he only attended school for 10 years, he read constantly and studied diligently. From 1870 to 1877, he worked as a reporter, editor, and correspondent. During the Sioux War of 1875 in Wyoming and Montana, he worked for General Crook as special correspondent for the *New York Times*, *Chicago Tribune* and *Denver News*, personally participating in every war that was fought in that area. As a war correspondent, he excelled.

Mr. Strahorn became interested in the railroad business while accompanying several railroad surveying parties. This opened up a complete new field for him. He had a reputation for great executive ability, which brought him into prominence as the promoter and builder of the North Coast Railroad. Throughout almost the entire existence of the company, Mr. Strahorn was its president and active manager. In connection with this, he also organized the Spokane Union Terminal project, which brought five railroads under one grand passenger terminal in Spokane.

He was also the organizer and president of the West Coast Railway. In September of 1877, Mr. Strahorn married Carrie Adell Green. Mrs. Green later authorized *Fifteen Thousand Miles By Stage*, which included testimonials of her travels with her husband by railroad and stagecoach.

Robert E. Strahorn Mansion

The Strahorn Tudor style family home at 2216 West First Avenue was built in 1885 for the John J. Browne family. In 1902, Brownes sold the residence and seven lots to Robert E. Strahorn for $35,000. The photo was taken after Strahorn's $10,000 remodeling project. The grounds originally included six blocks – from Pacific Avenue to Riverside Avenue, and all the blocks east of the house and back to Coeur d' Alene Avenue. Shortly after the turn-of-the-century, Mr. Browne built a house on the slopes of Browne's Mountain and moved his family there. The Strahorn house was eventually broken up into apartments and became so badly deteriorated that it was demolished in 1974 to build a parking lot for the Cheney Cowles Museum (The MAC). *(MAC, L87-189)*

The front of the Strahorn house at 2214 West First in 1914. The auto on the left is a Baker electric car and the other is a Great Arrow. *(Libby MAC L95-12.121)*

William H. Cowles Mansion

The Cutter and Malmgren-designed Victorian/Shingle style residence of William H. Cowles, president of the Review Publishing Company, located at 2602 West Second Avenue. It was demolished in the 1970s to make way for condominiums. Mr. and Mrs. Cowles lived in an apartment in the Review Building when they were first married. *(Public domain)*

William Cowles and party at his home on 2602 West Second Avenue, during a visit by President Taft in 1909. The Cowles family own the *Spokesman-Review*. *(Public domain)*

Austin Corbin

Austin Corbin's Early Classical Revival style home at 815 West Seventh Avenue, built in 1898. Architects – Cutter and Malmgren. (The Western Architect, *October 1908, courtesy Nancy Compau*)

Aubrey White

A sleigh in front of Aubrey White's Colonial Revival house at 2123 West First Avenue. This home was originally built for J. P. Graves in 1899-1900. In 1911, Graves sold it to his friend Aubrey White. It currently contains six apartments. The architects were Cutter and Malmgren. *(Libby photo, MAC L94-40.5)*

Amasa Campbell was one of the foremost mining operators in the Northwest. He was an owner of some of the most valuable mining properties, as well as numerous other businesses, in the Inland Northwest.

Campbell was born in Salem, Ohio, on April 6, 1845, the son of John and Rebecca Campbell. There were 10 children in the family. Amasa was the youngest; his father died just prior to his birth.

In 1867, at the age of 22, Amasa went to Omaha, Nebraska, where he accepted a position with the Union Pacific Railroad, a position he held until the completion of the line. In 1871, he obtained his first mining position in Utah, which gave him exposure and a foundation to mining. He continued in the mining industry in that state until he came to Spokane in 1887, at which time he entered into a partnership with John A. Finch.

On March 26, 1890, in Youngstown, Ohio, Mr. Campbell married Grace M. Fox, the only daughter of George and Mary Fox of Canton, Ohio. They had one daughter – Helen.

Mr. Campbell died on February 16, 1912. He was a heavy cigar smoker and starved to death in his mansion as a result of throat cancer.

On the passing of both Mr. and Mrs. Campbell, their daughter, Helen Campbell (Powell), donated the house and grounds to the Eastern Washington State Historical Society/Northwest Museum of Arts and Culture (The MAC). For many years it served as a museum. In 1960, a new building was completed next to this residence (named for Major Cheney Cowles, who was killed during World War II). In 2001, a large exhibition hall was built next door to the Cheney Cowles Center that houses the library and archives.

Amasa Campbell

The Amasa Campbell English Tudor half-timber style home at 2316 West First Avenue, erected in 1898, was designed by Cutter and Malmgren. It was donated to the Eastern Washington Historical Society for use as a museum. *(Courtesy Spokane Public Library, NWR)*

Francis Cook

Francis and Laura Cook's Folk Victorian home, which they had built in 1892. It was located on the site of the present Cathedral of St. John's parish house. *(Courtesy Adi Song, Cook's great-granddaughter)*

James Monaghan

The James Monaghan house, designed by Preusse & Zittel, at 217 East Boone Avenue. This is an example of a Queen Anne house, built in 1901, at a cost of $13,000. At the time, an average home cost $5,000 to build. It was classified as the finest residence on the north side of the river. Today it houses the Gonzaga University Music Department. *(MAC, L-96246E)*

James N. Glover spent $100,000 to build and furnish his home on Eighth Avenue. Glover's house contained a hall that was two stories high with a wood-carved balcony. Its walls were hung with blue tapestry, and a marble fireplace was ornamented with lions heads. The master bedroom suite overlooked the hall. Throughout, the house was opulent; even the windows in its pantry had leaded glass. The grounds covered two and one-half large city lots in an area intersected by basalt outcroppings and steep inclines. However, in 1888, when he had it built, the location had been remote and one of Glover's few neighbors remarked that his wife had been frightened by passing Indians.

In 1893, Glover mortgaged his house to Dutch lenders then defaulted on his loan. Two other owners occupied it briefly before the Dutch sold the house in 1898 to attorney Frank H. Graves. Graves, his wife Maud, and their two sons lived there six years, and then sold the place in 1904 to Charles and Emeline Sweeny for $50,000 in cash. The Sweenys' home at Pacific and Chestnut served as a $20,000, and the Sweenys assumed a $20,000 mortgage with the Hypotheekbank. On July 30, 1904, the *Spokane Daily Chronicle* reported the sale as "the largest of a private residence in the city's history." Also, in November, 1904, the Sweenys bought a lot and a half adjacent (on the west) to their property, for $11,000, from Graves's brother, Jay P. Graves. The Sweenys erected a large, handsome brick house for their daughter, Mary Gertrude, when she married Francis J. Finucane.

In 1908, Charles Sweeny sold the former Glover home to railroad contractor Patrick Welch, for a reported $80,000.

During the time Charles Sweeny and his family lived in the Glover house, they impressed Spokane's community with elegant and perpetual parties. The Glover and Graves families had scarcely entertained, but the Sweenys staged elaborate and frequent parties that created an air of festivity across the city to the valley below. One gathering arranged by one of Sweeny and Emeline's sons, Charles, was the talk of the town for months. An orchestra played on the mezzanine while dancers swirled in the high room, and a lavish dinner was served at midnight.

James Glover

In 1888, James Glover commissioned young architect Kirtland Cutter to build his Tudor mansion at 321 West Eighth Avenue, shown here in 1891. This was the first Cutter-designed mansion in Spokane and originally occupied a seven-acre lot. *(MAC, L92-91.10)*

Patsy Clark

The Patrick Clark's Richardsonian Romanesque (Eclectic) style home at 2208 West Second Avenue, built in 1897-98. Clark was one of Spokane's most important mining magnates. Cutter & Malmgren, architects. The builder was D. B. Fotheringham. *(From* Vintage Postcards *courtesy Duane Broyles and Howard Ness)*

James Glover

This Tudor Revival/Shingle style home is supposedly the same Glover house that was in the original downtown photo on page 29. There are only small parts, like the entrance gable that may have been reused, after it was moved to 1725 West First Avenue in Browne's Addition and extensively remodeled. In front of this home is the historical marker stating it was the Glover house: however, there doesn't seem to be much comparison to the other structure. *(Bamonte)*

Chapter Seven

John A. Finch

The John A. Finch Neoclassical style home, built in 1897 at 2340 West First Avenue, was designed by Kirtland K. Cutter. *(Courtesy SPLNWR)*

John Finch was the senior partner of the firm of Finch and Campbell. He and Amasa Campbell were among the significant people to develop the mining industry in the Inland Northwest, especially properties in the Coeur d'Alene Mining District.

Finch was born in Cambridgeshire, England, on May 12, 1854, and came to the United States in 1862. The family resided in Cleveland, Ohio, for many years. There, Finch was associated with the manufacture of iron and steel and later was in the same line of business at Youngstown, Ohio. After several other moves, he made his way to Leadville, Colorado, where he worked in mining for a year. In 1887, Finch came to Spokane and began to acquire mining properties in the Coeur d'Alenes in connection with Amasa Campbell. They purchased the Gem Mine and then organized the Milwaukee Milling Company with financial backing from friends in Milwaukee and Youngstown. With Mr. Campbell as president and Mr. Finch as secretary and treasurer, their company operated both mines successfully for 12 years.

In 1891, they began the development of the Standard Mine, which they opened and developed. Later they opened the Hecla Mine, which is still in operation today. In 1893, they extended their operations into British Columbia, where they opened and developed the Enterprise and Standard mines in the Slocan District.

On September 3, 1896, in Chicago, Mr. Finch married Charlotte Swingler, a daughter of M. M. and Sandy Swingler of Spokane. The Swinglers came to Spokane in 1884.

Thomas J. Humbird

Originally built for Dr. James Sutherland, this Colonial Revival home at 2020 West Third Avenue was later the home of Thomas J. and Agnes Humbird, prior to building their mansion on Sumner Avenue. The Humbird Lumber Company had sawmills in Sandpoint, Idaho, and Newport, Washington. The Humbirds later built their home at 612 West Sumner Avenue, which was the most expensive home in that area and overlooked the city. *(Bamonte)*

The Humbird family was prominent in the lumber business beginning in the late nineteenth century. The Sandpoint Lumber Company was combined with lumber holdings of Edward Rutledge in December 1900 to form the core of a new business, the Humbird Lumber Company. Thomas J. Humbird became manager of the company in 1902, and was involved in the operations of several mills, including the Sandpoint mill.

The main Humbird Lumber Company operation was located on Lake Pend Oreille in Sandpoint, Idaho. Humbird's mill was one of the largest sawmills in the area, owning 200,000 acres of timberland, most of which was located in Bonner County, Idaho.

From an article in the *Wisconsin Labor Advocate, Volume 1.* (La Crosse, Wisconsin, Friday, June 10, 1887. Number 43.) "At Hudson, Thomas J. Humbird and Agnes D. Hyslop were married at the residence of the bride's parents. The groom is the son of John A. Humbird, the well known lumberman and railway magnate, and the bride the daughter of ex-Mayor Hyslop."

Thomas J. Humbird's second home in Spokane

The Humbird Tudor style family home at 612 West Sumner Avenue. They moved into this home from Browne's Addition. *(Bamonte)*

Byron R. Lewis

This house at 2319 West Pacific Avenue was originally built 1900 for William Q. O'Brien who sold it to B. R. Lewis in 1908. It is in the Free Classic Queen Anne style. At the time, the B. R. Lewis Lumber Company was the largest lumber company in Idaho. In 1916, Lewis sold it to Arthur L. Hawes, who was the manager of the Spokane Drug Company. *(Bamonte)*

The great B. R. Lewis, a Browne's Addition resident and major player in the timber industry

In the *Spokesman-Review* of August 11, 1907, a story appeared about the B. R. Lewis Company that took up two full pages. The significance of size and importance of the B. R. Lewis Company was lost as the historic plaque in front of the house gives the primary credit to the vice-president and manager of the Spokane Drug Company, Arthur L. Hawes. The plaque does give a secondary credit of the house to the second owner before Hawes and simply refers to him as a lumberman. William Q. O"Brian had this residence built in 1900.

On May 2, 1903, the *Coeur d'Alene Press* notified the public that Byron R. Lewis of Minneapolis, where his B. R. Lewis Lumber Company was in operation, had arrived in town, along with a couple of other men, to open a bank, aptly called the Bank of Coeur d'Alene.

Lewis soon announced that his company planned to build a large sawmill within the year – a fully equipped plant "with planing mill, lathe and shingle mills and all the modern machinery." Apparently, he had already bought up timberland in the area. Lewis was an experienced lumberman, with more than 20 years experience in the industry, and had the financial backing that would soon change the entire face of Coeur d'Alene and its surrounding region. Although Lewis' association with the timber industry in North Idaho only lasted a short time, he is credited with planning and establishing the largest logging and saw milling operation up to that time.

True to his word, Lewis completed his large mill in the fall of 1904. It was, according to the *Spokesman-Review* on September 23, 1904, "one of the most complete to be found in the Northwest." The previous February, Lewis had purchased the sawmill the Kennedy brothers

The B. R. Lewis Lumber Company planing mill, circa 1907, claimed to be the largest in the United States at the time. *(Courtesy SPLNWR)*

The 1907 *Spokesman-Review* article about the B. R. Lewis lumber operation. It was spread across two pages with a total measurement of 34 x 22-1/2 inches. It was rare to give one company this much ink at the time and shows the importance and impact of the company.

were building on what is now known as Blackwell Island, located at the point where Lake Coeur d'Alene becomes the Spokane River. The old Fort Sherman grounds were across the river, a fortunate positioning for Lewis. In June 1905, as the fort grounds were being parceled off, Lewis was able to purchase an additional 100 acres on which to expand his lumberyards.

One of the most striking features of the B. R. Lewis Company's enterprise was their stable of horses, which they used for both the sawmill and logging operations. The company owned more than 200 draft horses, many of which were unusually large and capable of hauling and skidding immense loads of logs. Most of Lewis's logging activities were on the west side of Coeur d'Alene Lake, centered in and around the Mica Creek and Mica Bay areas. However, Lewis was always looking for ways to improve his methods and, by 1907, according to an August 11, 1907, article in the *Spokesman-Review*: "The old method of hauling logs by wagon and loading by chains and horses has been abandoned by the B. R. Lewis Lumber Company. They have their own railroad and run temporary branches into the dense forest, cut down the trees by the thousands, and load them with the latest type of steam-loading machinery that it is possible to secure."

The company was now employing 450 workers in the plant. At that later date, they claimed a plant of this magnitude, which covered an area of 240 acres, would normally employ 1,600 workers if it were not for their automated labor-saving equipment. As it was, the mill crew turned out an entire train load, consisting of 40 to 70 cars, of lumber every day, at a value of about $10,000.

Photos of the B. R. Lewis horse logging operation in 1907 – the largest in Idaho.
(Courtesy SPLNWR)

Chapter Seven

Governor Marion Hay

The late Governor Marion E. Hay's Tudor-style home at 930 East 20th Avenue. *(Bamonte)*

Marian Hay was the seventh governor of Washington State from 1909 to 1913. Hay (1865-1933) came to Davenport, Washington in 1888 and established a mercantile business. In 1899 he moved to Wilbur and opened the M. E. & E. T. Hay Department Store. Hay was mayor of Wilbur and chairman of the Lincoln County Republican Central Committee, 1898-1902. In 1908 he was elected lieutenant governor of Washington, and after Governor Cosgrove's resignation because of ill health, Hay became governor in 1909. As governor, he focused his attention on government corruption, calling a special legislative session to investigate and impeach dishonest state officials. He was a strong backer of the women's suffrage movement, and supporter of amendments to the state's constitution, allowing the public to enter initiatives and referendums to recall public officials from office. Hay, his wife Lizzie, and five children were the first to occupy the governor's mansion on the Olympia Capitol Campus. His wife selected the furnishings for the house, where many still remain to this day, including a large grandfather clock. Governor Hay also presided over the opening of the Alaska-Yukon-Pacific Exposition in Seattle on June 1, 1909.

The following caption under the photo, on the left of this page, appeared in the December 2, 1915, issue of the *Spokane Daily Chronicle*. However, the address is incorrect. It is actually 930 East 20th Avenue.

> The Rockwood residence at West 930 20th Ave., transferred this from H. H. McLane to former M. E. Hay, is shown above. The property was accepted at a valuation of $25,000, the consideration being represented by other realty to the extent of $15,000 and by $10,000 in cash. The deal was negotiated by the realty department of the Pacific Northwest Investment Society, Old National Bank building.

On May 25, 1935, while living at Tacoma, eight-year-old George Weyherhaeuser (the young son of a wealthy timber baron) was walking home from school for lunch when kidnappers abducted him. As part of their plans, the kidnappers had rented the bungalow at 1509 West 11th Avenue in Spokane in anticipation of their crime.

According to a neighbor, four men and two women had occupied the house for a month. The neighbor told police she suspected they were in the business of bootlegging because of the way they tore in and out of the alley in their cars.

The house has five rooms on two floors. Tall hedges surrounded the exterior reaching almost to the top of the first three windows. The owner of the house was Mrs. E. A. Evans, whose husband was a Congregational minister. He had died about five years prior to this incident. She and her husband had lived at the house for many years.

Mrs. Evans said the house was in excellent condition when she turned it over to the F. L. Prescott & Co., at 411 West Sprague Avenue. The ad for this residence was in the *Spokesman-Review* on April 12, 1935. It read: "RM. MOD., Southside, only $28 Prescott company, 411 Sprague, Maine 6067."

The case was solved on June 8, when Margaret Waley purchased a $20 cigarette case in Salt Lake City with a five dollar ransom bill. Her husband, Hammon, and William Diamond had met each other at the Idaho State Penitentiary in 1930. In April 1935, they planned to rob a bank but when they read an article in the Seattle papers that George's grandfather had died and left a fortune, they changed plans deciding kidnapping was more lucrative. Their ransom demand was for $200,000.

This bungalow at 1509 West 11th Avenue is where George Weyherhaeuser was held captive following his kidnapping at Tacoma. *(Bamonte)*

According to Spokane resident Ellen Ferris, who recalls this incident, following George's rescue and return to Tacoma, within minutes being allowed to play with his friends, his parents noticed a small tent erected in a neighbor's front yard, which featured a poster advertising an attraction: "See George Weyerhaeuser – 5 cents."

Chapter Seven

Glover's Last home

This Greek Revival/Shingle style home at 1408 North Summit Boulevard was built in 1909 for James N. Glover. It was his last home. Architects – Cutter and Malmgren. *(Courtesy Nancy Compau)*

Francis Finucane

The residence of Francis Finucane, the vice-president of Holley Mason Hardware. This French Eclectic home, built sometime prior to 1908, was located on 323 West Eighth Avenue. It was demolished in 1960 to make way for the Stevens/Ben Garnett road extension, which was cut through the cliff. Cutter and Malmgren were the architects. *(*The Western Architect, *October 1908 – Courtesy Nancy Compau)*

Homes of Some of Spokane's Wealthy, Famous or Infamous

August Paulsen's home

The Paulsen Tudor style home at 245 East 13th Avenue, circa 1920. *(All Paulsen photos courtesy Joel Moore, Paulsens' grandson)*

The north side of the Paulsen home. The family donated this home to the Cathedral of St. John.

The August Paulsen Family

August Paulsen was born near Copenhagen, Denmark, July 29, 1871. He received some schooling in his native land, but was largely self-educated. In 1888, at the age of 17, he had saved enough money to come to America. He spent his first winter in San Francisco attending business college. For several years, he worked in the woods of northern Michigan and on lumber vessels. In 1892, he came to Spokane where he worked on a dairy farm for $6.00 a month. During that time he saved enough money to fulfill his ambition of moving to the Coeur d'Alene Mining District, which was still in the discovery period. Two years later he bought a bicycle and rode the Mullan Road to Wallace, Idaho, where he again found employment on a dairy farm. He later became a partner in the Hercules mine.

August met Myrtle White in Wallace when her sister Mrs. Anna Conners introduced them. He saw Myrtle again when she visited the Hercules Mine with the sister of Jerome Day's secretary, the day after Paulsen's discovery of the main Hercules vein. On September 15, 1902, August and Myrtle were married.

In the early 1900s, the Paulsens moved to Spokane. They had four children: Clarence, Howard, Pauline, and Frances. During the 12 years August Paulsen worked at the Hercules, he accumulated fatal amounts of rock dust in his lungs, which plagued his health throughout his life. Shortly before Christmas in 1926, August and his wife traveled to California. He hoped that a warmer climate and being attended by a respiratory physician might cure his lung problem. On March 11, 1927, August passed away at the age of 57 from silicosis caused from breathing rock dust.

Myrtle (White) Paulsen by new car.
(All photos this page courtesy Joel Moore)

August Paulsen with son.

Myrtle White Paulsen.

Daniel Twohy

Daniel W. Twohy's Tudor home at 22 West Sumner. Twohy was president of the Old National Bank & Union Trust Co. Architects: Cutter and Malmgren. (The Western Architect, *October 1908, courtesy Nancy Compau*)

Ford D. Markham

1907 Ford D. Markham Shingle style home at 2001 West 8th Avenue. Markham was manager of the National Life Insurance Company. Architect: W. W. Hyslop. (The Western Architect, *October 1908, courtesy Nancy Compau*)

Louis Davenport

This Tudor style residence was built for Louis Davenport and sold to the Richard B. Porter family. It was demolished in 1967 to make way for an expansion of Sacred Heart Hospital. *(MAC L94-10.30)*

Charles F. Clough

Neoclassical style home of C. F. Clough at 1406 West Ninth Avenue, built in 1907. Clough was the president of Clough Real Estate Company. Architect: Loren L. Rand. *(*The Western Architect, *October 1908, courtesy Nancy Compau)*

Henry M. Richards

Shingle style home of Henry M. Richards at 2136 West Riverside, built in 1908. Richards was the first vice-president of Spokane and Eastern Bank, and a president of the Washington Water Power Company. **Architects: Cutter and Malmgren.** *(The Western Architect, October 1908, courtesy Nancy Compau)*

R. B. Paterson

Prairie-style home of R. B. Paterson at 508 West Seventh Avenue. Paterson was the president of the Spokane Dry Goods Company and vice-president of the Dry Goods Realty Company. This was later the home of Senator Clarence Dill. Following that, it contained dentist offices. It was built prior to 1908. **Architect: John K Dow.** *(The Western Architect, October 1908, courtesy Nancy Compau)*

William Gray

William and Clara Gray's Queen Anne home on the southwest corner of Fifth Avenue and Washington Street. It was there from 1892 to 1931, when it was demolished. *(From "A Race for Empire and Other True Tales of the Northwest,"* Spokesman-Review, *1896)*

F. Rockwood Moore

Cutter designed the F. Rockwood Moore Tudor home built on West Seventh Avenue in 1889. Moore, the first president of Washington Water Power, died in 1895. George Turner, who became a U.S. senator in 1897, and his wife, Bertha, then purchased the home. It was demolished in 1940 and today the property is part of the Corbin-Moore-Turner Heritage Gardens. *(MAC, L93-60.15)*

The Motie Family (First Miss Spokane)

Construction of the Moties' new Craftsman home at 614 West Thirteenth Avenue began in 1909. The photo on the right was taken in 1910, the same year it was completed. Frank and Anna Motie were the parents of the first Miss Spokane, Marguerite Motie. Marguerite held that position from 1912 to 1939. At the time, she was considered the ambassador for the city. Her father was a Realtor who was with the firm Barne, Motie & Ready, located in the Jamieson Building. There were eight girls in the Motie family. Frank was a deeply religious Catholic, and Anna was a convert to his faith. As the house was being constructed, they had their parish priest bless it and embed a Catholic medal in the plaster above the front door. *(All photos on this page from the Dorothy Bayne Marchi collection)*

From left: Mayor Hindley, Marguerite Motie, Francis Cook, and Governor Marion Hay.

Marguerite Motie with her mother, father, and a friend during a housecleaning session.

The eight Motie girls, from left: Vivian, Emily, Frances, Miriam, Ruth, Marguerite, Dorothy, and Esther, circa 1905.

Chapter Seven

Henry Kaiser

Henry Kaiser headed companies responsible for the construction of Boulder, Grand Coulee, and Bonneville dams. He also founded Kaiser Aluminum and invented the Kaiser car. When Kaiser had this home built in 1908, on June 14, 1908, the *Spokesman-Review* **took special note and printed a lengthy descriptive article about it, remarking that is was a unique residence with a "roof garden."** *(Courtesy SPLNWR)*

A portion of the article stated:

> HENRY KAISER'S NEW HOME ON GRAND STREET EMBODIES ATTRACTIVE FEATURES CEMENT AND TILE EXTERIOR Charming Color Effects in Yellow, Red and Green - Floors Hardwood -Novel Inglenook.

Something which is wholly unique and original as well as attractive in the effective design of the residence of Henry J. Kaiser has just been completed on the east side of Grand street at the head Sumner Avenue. The house plan is strikingly adapted to the unusual site, which is near to and high above the street, and which commands an exceptionally fine view ...

While conforming to no type of architecture, the house embodies features from the Swiss and from the Spanish mission, which are made to harmonize, attractively It is one of the many exclusive designs which Architect W. W. Hyslop has made. ...

Perhaps the most unique feature of the house, and one which has no counterpart in Spokane, is the roof garden, or open lounging room on the roof, with parapet and port holes and awning stretched above, following the roof.

Effectiveness is added by a cornice of tile extending from the parapet in harmony with the roof design. The exterior walls of the house are cement, in massive effect ... the main rooms have oak floors and the finish is select fir in green stain ... the entire north end is taken up by an inglenook, containing a large fireplace with massive steel hood. ...

Separating the dining room and the living room are swinging doors with small panes of opalescent glass. ... On the south wall is a row of French windows.

Daniel Morgan

This Neoclassical style house at 242 East Manito Place, overlooking Manito Park, was designed in 1907 by the architectural firm of George Keith and Harold Whitehouse. It was built for Daniel Morgan, vice-president of Fred Grinnell's company. Between 1922 and 1924, Morgan served one term in the State House of Representatives and two in the State Senate. During his tenure as a public servant, he was instrumental in securing legislation for the development of the Columbia Basin. *(Bamonte)*

Edward J. Roberts

The Victorian Queen Anne home built in 1889 for Bernhard Loewenberg at 1923 West First Avenue. Loewenberg was a Prussian immigrant who owned a mercantile in Spokane Falls. After the Great Fire of 1889, he went broke and sold it to Edward J. Roberts, who also moved to Spokane in 1889. Roberts was a prominent Northwest civil engineer, specializing in railroad construction. At one point in his career, he built the longest railway extension in the shortest amount of time (550 miles in six months). Mr. Roberts held prominent positions for both D. C. Corbin and Charles Sweeny in the railroad and mining industries. In 1883, he married Mary Tracy from England. They had six children, five boys and a girl. The house is now a popular bed and breakfast. *(Bamonte)*

Chapter Seven

William Pettet

This Folk style house with added wings at 1735 North West Point Drive appears to be the oldest house of record in Spokane. The original log house was built in 1872 by William Maxwell, who later sold it to William Pettet. During its history, the house received several single-story add-ons to the left and the right. *(Valerie Powell collection)*

William Pettet was apparently one of a few survivors of an ill-fated expedition during the great westward migration of the mid-1800s, similar to the infamous Donner Party tragedy.

There is no record of Mr. Pettet being a member of the Donner Party. However, there were a number of wagon trains that suffered similar fates on the overland trail to California. In *Spokane and the Inland Empire* (1912), Nelson W. Durham, managing editor of the *Spokesman-Review*, wrote of an incident that occurred in November of 1846.

> When they passed through Kansas they experienced considerable trouble with the Indians and at different times had to reckon with the hostility of the red men, engaging them in a severe fight on the Truckee river in order to recover stock driven away by them. When near Truckee lake they were overtaken by a snow storm at which time Mr. Pettet joined a party of six and started for the Sacramento valley, leaving behind their wagons and about sixty people who, refusing to proceed, camped at the lake. Mr. Pettet and his companions reached Sutter's Fort in safety, but those who remained all perished save four and these were insane when they finally secured assistance.

William Pettet was 65 when he moved to Spokane in 1883. He became one of Spokane's most prominent citizens. Anticipating the city's rapid growth, Mr. Pettet invested in real estate, amassing considerable wealth as his numerous properties appreciated in value. He was one of the original partners in the formation of Washington Water Power Company.

Designing Spokane: The Architects' Contributions

Spokane architecture

Since Spokane's inception and its early move to build lasting, attractive, and functional houses and buildings, structural engineers and architects have been used on almost every project to ensure reliable construction and assembly. Since the city first created building codes, standards have continuously increased to assure that goals are met and exceeded to insure safety, reliability and durability of projects.

Building materials are far better and safer than those of the past. For instance, all concrete is scientifically tested for durability and strength, wiring is far better, with circuit breakers, and two-by four-walls have been replaced with two-by-six walls and, in many buildings, with metal studs. This is just a short list of improvements that today's architects factor into their designs.

Spokane has become a melting pot for architectural styles. While some localities lean more toward certain styles than others, many early residential streets in Spokane reflect an eclectic mix. There are examples of domestic architecture from nearly every civilized country in the world, together with many hybrid styles, the result of combining elements to meet the owner's desired effect. Consequently, many homes in Spokane do not easily fit into tidy, clearly defined or traditional categories.

There are two major purposes for the design of Spokane's early homes. Many of these people who located here in the late 1800s to early 1900s came from the eastern United States or Europe. When they met with success here, the homes they built reflected their financial status.

It was natural that in building their new homes in Spokane, many chose to embody the characteristics of the best architecture of their places of origin. This explains why early Spokane had homes of Colonial, English, German, Swiss Chalet, and bungalow mixtures. However, in Spokane, any home no matter what its style, which is pleasant to look at, homelike, and convenient, and is in a good location, is typically easily marketable.

Early architects

During Spokane's early building boom, there was a demand for good architects. When the first architects arrived in Spokane, commissions were abundant and it was a lucrative livelihood. Architects typically would be listed by their own name. Today, most architects are employed by or are partners in large architectural firms, and the company name may or may not include the founder's name.

For instance, the 1896 *Spokane City Directory* lists the following 11 architects: Boardman L. M., 312-313 Traders blk; Cutter & Malmgren, 5th floor First Nat'l Bank Bldg; Dow J. K., 621 The Rookery; Finch F. D., 324-325 Fernwell Bldg; Grove T. M., 7 Falls City blk; P. Held Albert, 615 The Rookery; Pennington J. K. S., 511 Howard st; Poetz J. C., 2422 Bridge av; Preusse & Zittell, 50-51 Jamieson Bldg; Rand L. L., 520 The Rookery; Eaton & Haynes, 23 Review Bldg.

At the time, there were no architectural firms listed. Each person stood on the quality of his individual work, or if he had employees, their work was a reflection on him.

Modern architects

Today (2011) there are 64 business listings for architects in Spokane. The majority of these are architectural firms with numerous employees.

A major change in the field of architecture is in the tools of the trade. Rulers, compasses, drawing boards, T-squares, bevels, and pencils were the primary tools used by the architects up to the 1980s. Today, Computer-Aided Design and Drafting (CADD) and Building Information Modeling (BIM) technology has replaced the earlier traditional paper and pencil as the most common method for creating design and construction drawings.

The Historic Landmarks Survey

In 1978, a historic landmarks survey was conducted by Spokane's City Plan Commission. The commission identified buildings, sites, structures, objects, and districts that had historic, architectural, archaeological or cultural importance to the community. It then prepared an extensive report of the considerable number of historical landmarks that been inventoried. The report also included a list of the architects who had played a major role in Spokane's architectural design and their most important commissions. A section of maps show the various neighborhoods and historic districts. The report from this project is without a doubt one of the best resources for information about Spokane's architectural history.

A primary goal of the project was to develop a community awareness of the city's historic and cultural background, and to assist in the preservation or restoration of the valuable properties and objects identified in the survey. It also recorded information that would be required for placement on a historic register.

The survey coordinator and principal of the project was Moritz Kundig, who was a graduate of the Swiss Federal Institute of Technology, in Zürich, Switzerland. His degree was in architecture and urban design, and he was a avid student of architectural history. Kundig was a member of the National Trust for Historic Preservation, and the chairman of the Committee on Historic Preservation of the Washington State Council of Architects. He continued to pursue a long and productive career as a Spokane architect.

Another key member of this project was Nancy Compau, who would become the head of the Spokane Public Library's Northwest Room, a position she held for 20 years. Nancy is considered one of Spokane's most knowledgeable historians, especially in the field of buildings and residences. Furthermore, crucial to gathering data for the survey was the volunteer work of women from the Junior League of Spokane.

An era of great demand

As discussed earlier in the book, Spokane's development was brought about by the Northern Pacific Railroad, the mining activity in the Coeur d'Alenes and in Stevens and Pend Oreille counties, and the timber industry that operated throughout the entire Inland Northwest. As Spokane became the main supply point for the entire Inland Northwest, there was a great demand for every manner of business and service. The rebuilding of Spokane following the Great Fire of 1889 created an even larger demand, which was then intensified by a period of major economic growth and prosperity.

For the architects who came to Spokane around that time, the opportunities were nearly limitless. The remainder of this chapter covers some of the region's most accomplished architects who designed many of the beautiful and artistic commercial buildings and residences in Spokane during this era.

Herman Preusse & Julius Zittel

The upscale areas of early Spokane, especially during the "Age of Elegance," were designed with a strong European influence. Both of Spokane's earliest and most prominent architects came from Germany. Herman Preusse was born in Germany in 1847. When he was three years old, his father died and his mother married one of Germany's leading architects. Under his influence, Preusse received one of the finest architectural educations in Germany. Drawing on the experience and education he received in his stepfather's office, he gained early recognition as one of Germany's upcoming young architects.

Drawn by promising opportunities in America, a young and booming nation, Preusse moved to New York in 1870. Following a number of successful career moves in the United States, he settled in Spokane Falls in 1882. In 1887, Preusse hired Julius Zittel. Zittel was only 18 years of age, but within six years, his talents and skill led to a partnership

Julius Zittel
(Spokane and the Inland Empire, *N. W. Durham*)

with Preusse. The partnership lasted for 18 years. They designed and supervised the construction of some of the finest buildings in Spokane, including Gonzaga College, St. Aloysius Catholic Church, the Carnegie Library, and the Auditorium Theatre. Preusse was the first professional architect in Spokane, and one of four architects listed in the 1888 Spokane Falls Directory.

By 1906, there were over 40 listed, some of them the most prominent houses designed for the newly-developing area.

John C. Poetz

Under Mr. Poetz's personal supervision many of the palatial residences and substantial business blocks had been designed and constructed. Mr. Poetz was Kirtland Cutter's first partner. He was born in St. Paul, Minnesota, June 23, 1859 and received a public school education. At the age of 18 he began study at St. Paul and Minneapolis of

Herman Preusse (pronounced Proy-suh)
(Spokane and the Inland Empire, *N. W. Durham*)

John C. Poetz
(Spokane Falls and Its Exposition 1890)

the practical construction of buildings. At the age of 21, he continued his professional training under the direction of H. Sackville Trehern, a well-known civil engineer.

He began his career as an architect in Minneapolis at age 25 and from there moved to Los Angeles. Mr. Poetz moved to Spokane in 1888.

Chauncey B. Seaton

Chauncey Seaton was born on March 17, 1848, in Cyrus, Crawford County, Ohio. He spent most of his early youth on a farm attending the county schools until the age of 14, when he entered school at Wooster, Ohio. At the age of 19, he took a course in architecture at a technical school in Chicago, Illinois. Following his education he went south to Selma, Alabama, where he practiced his profession for about four years. He then returned to Chicago until the spring of 1887 at which time he relocated to St. Paul, Minnesota.

In August 1889, he came to Spokane Falls and immediately established himself as an architect. During a short residence here, he designed and directed some of the most striking buildings in the city. One of his most notable buildings was the Exposition Building, which was completed in 1890. It later burned.

William J. Ballard

One of Spokane's leading architects, William Ballard, designed some of the most attractive homes in Spokane. Many of the homes he designed are often mistaken today for Cutter homes. Mr. Ballard had a number of other financial interests in the area, including in the Coeur d'Alene Mining District.

Mr. Ballard was born in Plainfield, Illinois, on November 4, 1871. Prior to coming to Spokane,

Chauncey B. Seaton
(Spokane Falls and Its Exposition 1890)

William J. Ballard
(Spokane and the Inland Empire, *N. W. Durham*)

he was married at Los Angeles on September 22, 1905, to Mrs. Alina L. Chamberlain, the daughter of G. L. Chamberlain. The couple had three children – Laura, Gilbert and Earl. He brought his family to Spokane in 1908 and established a business called the Ballard Plannery Company, Incorporated. Sometime around 1910, he published a book containing 92 house plans. These plans could be purchased for $10 to $30 from The Plannery.

While in Spokane, Mr. Ballard designed and supervised the architecture for the Empire Hotel and for a large number of other buildings, ranging in price from $30,000-$40,000. His specialties were cottage homes and apartment houses.

According to U.S. censuses, he left Spokane for Los Angeles sometime between 1920 and 1930. According to Durham in his book *Spokane and the Inland Empire*, which was published in 1912, Ballard is responsible for designing over 600 homes inthe Northwest. His firm consistently employed three to four men who entered his employ as students and remained.

Note the similarity of this Kirtland Cutter-designed home at 1718 W. Ninth Avenue to the Ballard Plannery house on the following page. *(Courtesy Linda Yeomans)*

A Ballard plan which appeared in a 1910 *Spokesman-Review* ad. This style is common in the Spokane area. *(Ballard Plannery book courtesy NWRSPL)*

BALLARD PLAN BOOK IN GREAT DEMAND; BOUGHT IN CHINA AND AUSTRALIA

The Ballard Plannery company, issuing the Porter-Ballard plan book system in connection with the activities of the Western Retail Lumbermen's association of Spokane, has sold over 3000 set of plans for homes throughout the United States and other countries this year, it is stated by W. J. Ballard. Since the inauguration of the system two years ago, 4162 sets of plans have been sent out.

"We believe that our office sends out more sets of plans than any other architect's office in the United States," Mr. Ballard says. "This year we have sold plans in every state of the union, in Australia, Denmark and China. An inquiry has just been received from Douglas, Alaska. At present the orders run from 10 to 25 daily."

No. 49.

Scores of people admire this beautiful residence. It is strictly California in design, with a large porch across the front. The living room occupies one end of the building; it has a fine mantel and book-cases, occupying one entire end, and seats along the wall, as shown in the cuts. The dining room is of good size, with a fine built-in buffet. This house is designed for a heating system. The cost ranges from $7,000 to $10,000.

Two sets of Plans, Specifications, Material List and Blank Contract, $30.00.

One set of Plans and Specifications, $25.00.

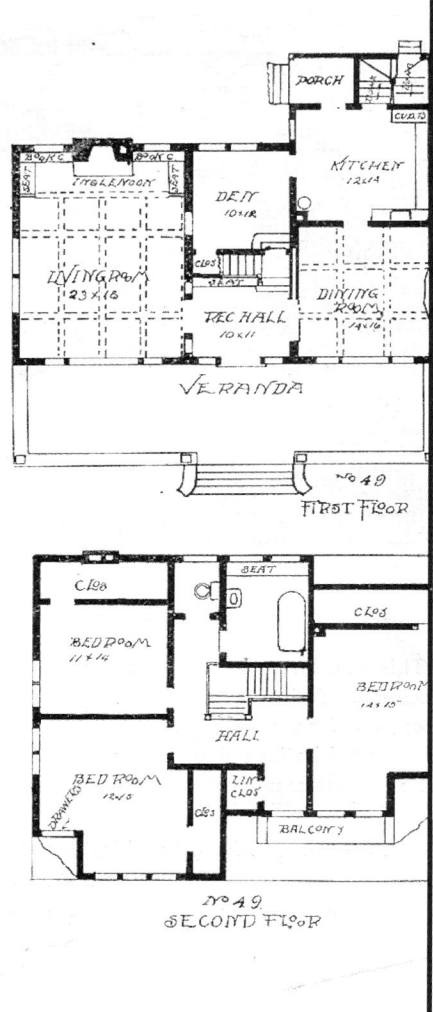

An article that appeared in the *Spokesman-Review* in 1907, about the Ballard Plannery Company plan. The plan (No 49) is a common one in the Spokane area – often mistaken for a Cutter design.

Kirtland K. Cutter, and how he became a renowned Spokane Architect

Kirtland K. Cutter, Spokane's most famous architect, was born in Cleveland, Ohio, in 1860. His father, a banker with the Merchant's National Bank of Cleveland, provided young Cutter with a comfortable lifestyle. However, he was greatly influenced by his great-grandfather, Professor Jared Kirtland, while living at Kirtland's country estate. A well-connected and respected naturalist, Kirtland socialized with many of the nation's notable people. This period of Cutter's life appears to have given him a high degree of sophistication and confidence. Cutter studied painting and sculpture at the Art Students League in New York.

He then spent several years traveling and studying in Europe. Upon Kirtland's return to the United States, his uncle Horace Cutter, a banker in Spokane Falls, convinced the younger Cutter to join him there. Cutter was an artist and it does not appear that his training included any formal education in the field of architecture, but he had an ability to visualize beautiful designs and transfer them to paper. He was a talented illustrator and, through his travels, He had been exposed to a wide variety of architectural designs, from which he developed his own unique eclectic style. His enthusiasm, charming sophistication, and connections to wealthy and influential individuals (early contacts acquired primarily through his Uncle Horace) would become contributing factors to his eventual international fame. After Cutter had already acquired a reputation as an outstanding architect, an article in the *Northwest Tribune* on July 27, 1894, announced under "General News–Items of Interest to the Reader" that Horace L. Cutter, uncle of famed architect Kirtland Cutter and "the fugitive cashier of the First National Bank of Spokane, has escaped to Central America." This was following the depression of 1893 and Cutter was well-established by this time.

Horace Cutter
(Spokane Falls and Its Exposition 1890)

The Great Fire of 1889 and Cutter's start

Spokane's fire on August 4, 1889, decimated most of the downtown business district, consuming 25 city blocks and destroying 60 brick and stone buildings (about half of these buildings were large commercial structures referred to at the time as "blocks"). The fire created an opportunity for Cutter's architecture practice to flourish (along with everyone else's involved in the reconstruction of Spokane).

Rebuilding the city began immediately and, by the end of the year, there were an estimated 500 buildings under construction. Naturally, architects and builders were in great demand. Herman Preusse, who had arrived in Spokane Falls in 1882, was already well established as an accomplished and talented architect, the city's first professional in that field. Having designed many of the commercial buildings lost in the fire, Preusse was quickly overwhelmed with new reconstruction projects, which created a need for more architects. As a result, the timing was perfect for

Kirtland Kelsey Cutter
(Spokane Falls and Its Exposition 1890)

Cutter's business to flourish. His name is now associated with many of Spokane's greatest historical mansions and commercial buildings and is one of the most recognizable names in Northwest architecture.

After moving to Spokane Falls about 1886, he had gone to work for his Uncle Horace as a bank clerk. He also was employed for a time by Preusse. Cutter's first architectural commission was designing a home for his uncle in 1887. The next year he formed a partnership with a young draftsman by the name of John C. Poetz. Soon after the fire, Karl G. Malmgren began working for them as a draftsman and, in 1894, replaced Poetz as Cutter's partner. Cutter relied heavily on Malmgren to turn his architectural designs into technical drawing. The Cutter-Malmgren partnership lasted 23 years. To a great extent, Cutter produced the ideas and Malmgren engineered the plans. Although the firm often employed other draftsmen, Malmgren was its key engineer.

Some of Cutter & Malmgren's best commissions came from respected Spokane businessman Louis M. Davenport, who played a significant role in bringing attention to Spokane during this same era. After the fire, he opened a small restaurant called the Waffle Foundry. Within a few months, he moved his business into a permanent location, naming it Davenport's Restaurant. The restaurant quickly reached great acclaim, and Davenport commissioned Cutter to assist as he expanded and remodeled the restaurant. Because of his success, Davenport was later backed by a group of local capitalists interested in building a first-class hotel. That hotel was designed by Cutter & Malmgren.

Cutter's marriage in 1892 to the daughter of one of Spokane's richest and most influential entrepreneurs also helped boost his career. At the age of 32, on October 5, 1892, Kirtland Cutter married 20-year-old Mary Edwine Corbin, the daughter of Spokane's prominent businessman Daniel C. Corbin. She was one of Corbin's three children: Austin, Mary and Louise, with Mary being the middle child. On November 8, 1893, Kirtland and Mary had a son, Kirtland Corbin Cutter.

Karl Malmgren
(Spokane Falls and Its Exposition 1890)

Following a four-year marriage, while in Europe, the Cutters divorced on June 30, 1896. As a condition of the divorce, the child's grandfather, Daniel C. Corbin, had Kirtland Cutter agree to a stipulation that the child would not carry the Cutter name and instead would be called Corbin Corbin. Cutter also agreed to a limited relationship with his son. In return D. C. would provide for the child's financial needs for the rest of his life. In the divorce decree, Kirtland alleged his wife refused to return to the United States with him; Mary alleged she was sick and unable to travel, and that he left her in France with no means of support.

Corbin was instrumental in keeping Cutter's son from him. In one of the provisions of Kirtland Cutter's will, he states, "I make no provision in this my last Will and Testament for my son, Corbin Corbin, for the reason that his Grandfather, the late D. C. Corbin of Spokane, Washington, in his will, made suitable provision for him on the stipulated condition that his surname be changed to 'Corbin'.

Cutter's good fortune changes

Cutter experienced some difficult times following his divorce from Mary Corbin. Because of his high profile, on September 4, 1907, The *Spokesman-Review* gave the following detailed account of a humiliating incident that took place about a year and a half after he married his second wife, society woman Katharine Phillips Williams:

KICKS ARCHITECT OFF STREET CAR
Jack Williams Applies Boot to Kirtland K. Cutter.

Kirtland K. Cutter, society man and architect, whose reputation is national, was kicked from a Manito park car last Thursday evening by "Jack" Williams, society man and former secretary of the Sullivan Mining company, who now has offices with former Judge George Turner in the Fernwell building. Mr. Cutter received the kick as he was descending the steps of the car at Sixth avenue and Washington street, but he landed on his feet when he struck the ground, and after picking up his hat, which fell in the mud, due to his hurried flight, he hastened on his way to his home without glancing back or making any remarks to his assailant. On account of the social prominence of the two men the occurrence has caused much talk among the members of the Spokane club and the Country club.

Mr Cutter is married to Mr. Williams' divorced wife, the wedding taking place soon after the divorce was granted ... According to the chronicle of those who saw the melee, it occurred on a Manito park-bound car at 5:40 o'clock last Thursday afternoon. The car was crowded with home-going residents of the hillside and Manito park neighborhoods. Because of the crowded condition of the car and the fact that Mr. Cutter kept going after the kick had been administered most of those on the car were not aware of what had happened. "The first that I knew that trouble had broken out between the erstwhile friends, Cutter and Williams, was when I heard Mr. Williams say, "You get off the car " said a wealthy resident of the hill, who was just in the rear of Mr Williams.

"Then, " said the spectator, "Mr. Cutter's hat shot into the air. He followed the hat from the car, never said a word, and ignored the little mishap ... The affair occurred at Sixth avenue and Washington street. It was raining cats and dogs. Cutter thumped his umbrella into position first and then gathered his hat from the mud. He went up Sixth avenue in the direction of his home. "The affair occurred so quickly that I did not comprehend at the time that a kick had been delivered. Mr. Williams was standing in a crowd on the rear platform of the car and Mr. Cutter had been inside the car... Another friend of Mr. Williams said: "...Jack told me that he had been waiting for a chance to plug Cutter for some time, and this was the first opportunity he had to deliver the chastisement.

This incident was a great embarrassment to Cutter, especially since it was published in the *Spokesman-Review*. Although he was well established in Spokane and could have easily made a living, he was now uncomfortable. He was already familiar with the need for architects in California as he had made a number of trips there designing significant homes.

Cutter's most prosperous years began around 1897 and lasted into the early 1900s. During those years, he was the architect of choice for many of the wealthy Spokane families. He designed the majority of the mansions directly below the rim of the Manito plateau, "The Hill," which were some of his first major commissions. Among them were the homes he designed for both Daniel and Austin Corbin on Seventh Avenue in 1889. Also, around the same time, Cutter began receiving commissions in Seattle, sometimes in partnership with Malmgren and other

A "Young Sport" K. Cutter with his captain's hat.
(Cutter collection, courtesy Jean Oton)

architects. In 1898-1900, Cutter and Malmgren designed a large home on First Hill in Seattle for lumber baron C. D. Stimson.

By 1902, Cutter's West Coast business had grown to the point that he sent an assistant, Edwin Wager, to Seattle to establish a branch office. Two others, architect Andrew Willatzen and draftsman Carl Nuese, soon joined the firm. Whether in combination with others or alone, Cutter did a great deal of work in Seattle. In 1903, he designed the Rainier Club, and between 1908 and 1909 with Malmgren, the Swiss chalet-style Seattle Golf and Country Club. Also, in Seattle, he designed the Crary Building, the Washington Securities Company Building, and residences for L. B. Peebles, C. J. Smith, T. J. Heffernan, Samuel Hill, and another house for C. D. Stimson, this time in The Highlands overlooking Puget Sound. His work also spread to the Tacoma area. In 1913, Cutter received a commission in Santa Barbara, California, to build a winter vacation mansion in the Eclectic/Mission style for William H. Cowles, for whom he had built a much smaller Browne's addition dwelling in 1903.

Kirtland and his wife, Katharine, aboard a cruise ship to Europe. *(Cutter collection, courtesy Jean Oton)*

The W. H. Cowles's winter mansion at Santa Barbara, California, designed by Cutter in 1913. This structure was located on 156 acres of one of the choicest locations in the United States, commanding a view of the Pacific Ocean on three sides and the dramatic spine of the Santa Inez Mountains on the fourth. *(MAC L 84-297.4. 209.)*

Cutter continued to practice architecture in Spokane until 1923 when he moved to Long Beach, California. In the year of Cutter's departure, there were 19 architects listed in the Spokane directory – many of these had been successfully practicing in Spokane for the past 20 years.

The housing market was rebounding, and Spokane ranked among the top 20 Pacific Coast cities in granting building permits according to a Federal Reserve Bank report that appeared in appeared in the *Spokane Press* on March 18th.

During his tenure in Spokane, although Cutter's practice extended into other states, most of his work was accomplished in Spokane. When the big money poured into the city in the late 1800s and the wealthy built their elegant mansions, Cutter was able to command a substantial commission for his services. As the demand for these mansions slowed, Cutter found himself in an extremely competitive position. The bottom was falling out of the upscale market to which he catered. Consequently, his competition was meeting the demand for more affordable house plans. By the time he left Spokane, the market for upscale homes had greatly declined. He went in search of a market compatible with his price and talents, which he found in California. Prior to moving, he sold his existing practice to a longtime Spokane assistant, Henry C. Bertelsen, to whom he owed several months' salary. Cutter settled the debt by selling the contents of his office to Bertelsen and his secretary, Dana Agergaard, for the sum of one dollar "and other valuable considerations." Thanks to this transaction and the diligent collecting of archivist Edward Nolan, the bulk of Cutter's architectural drawings and records, to that time, are preserved at the Northwest Museum of Arts and Culture in Spokane.

The "Chalet Hohenstein" Swiss Chalet style home of Kirtland Cutter at 628 West Seventh Avenue was the only style of this kind by Cutter. This home was built in 1887 and demolished in 1928. *(MAC, L87-1.36501.28)*

Kirtland Cutter and his second wife, the former Mrs. Williams, on their patio in Spokane at his Chalet at 628 West Seventh Ave. *(Cutter collection, courtesy Jean Oton)*

Kirtland and Katharine during their later years.

Cutter's final years

When Kirtland and his wife, Katharine, made the move to Long Beach, he was 63 years old. By that time most of his traveling and socializing days were over. They lived quietly in a small apartment off East Ocean Boulevard and for 16 years he continued his profession in California, but at a slower pace.

Kirtland and Katharine had a close relationship with her daughter, Kathryn, from her previous marriage to Jack Williams. Kathryn and her husband lived in Honolulu and both families made frequent visits to see each other. Also, during this time, Kirtland reestablished a quiet relationship with his son, Corbin Corbin, whom he saw on numerous occasions.

Kirtland Cutter's son and daughter-in-law: Corbin Corbin Jr. and Genevieve Corbin

Kirtland learned his son had graduated from the Naval Academy at Annapolis. As a young naval officer, he had fallen in love and married a movie actress and *Vogue* model, Genevieve Wilment. They had a son, named Corbin Corbin Jr., who used the nickname of "Joe." On Joe Corbin's birth certificate, dated July 21, 1926, his father is listed as "hotel manager" and his mother as "housewife." At the time Corbin Corbin Jr. (Joe) was born, Corbin Corbin Sr. was 32 years old and Genevieve was 26.

From all indications and evidence, it appears Corbin and Genevieve had a close and loving relationship. Part of this evidence is contained in a photo album given to Jean Oton by their son Joe. Obviously Corbin was given a substantial trust account by his grandfather, as they traveled extensively and lived a good life.

On December 6, 1972, Corbin Corbin died at Midway Hospital at Los Angeles as a result of complications from diabetes.

Kirtland Cutter's son, Corbin Corbin, and his daughter-in-law, Genevieve Corbin. *(Cutter collection, courtesy Jean Oton)*

Chapter Eight

The final resting place of Kirtland and Katharine Cutter is not as described in *Kirtland Cutter: Architect in the land of Promise,* by Henry C. Matthews.

Although Matthews's 1998 book is the premier source about the life and work of Kirtland Cutter, there is one small section that needs correcting. Cutter's ashes were not, in fact, scattered in the Pacific Ocean.

The last paragraph on page 379, chapter 15, titled "Long Beach: The Last Years (1925-1939)," states:

> Jess Jones, now an architect in his own right,[40] carried out his partner's final request. Although state law prohibited the sprinkling of the ashes of the dead on land or sea, he walked out to the end of a pier, accompanied by his young son Richard, and released the mortal remains of Kirtland Cutter over the waters of the Pacific Ocean.[41]

Under footnote #41 it is stated: "Richard Jones Interview. He recalls carrying the box that contained Cutter's ashes." This statement is incorrect, for the ashes of both Kirtland Cutter, his wife Katharine P. Cutter, and her daughter (Kathryn W. Walker) are all interred in Kona, Hawaii, under a common gravestone. Mr. Cutter was too significant to the architecture of this area to ignore what appears to be such a major mistake.

In 1994, Jean Oton, a local historian, began doing research on Kirtland Cutter to give local programs and talks she presented around Spokane. As part of her research, she made telephone contact with Corbin "Joe" Corbin Jr. Following this contact, they developed a friendship that lasted up until Joe's death on October, 13, 1998, at the age of 73.

During those four years, Jean would contact Joe Corbin on a regular basis and long conversations would ensue. As a result, Jean learned that until she informed him about his grandfather, he had no idea he was related to a famous architect. He stated he met them on a small number of occasions when he was with his mother and father and had always wondered "who the two nice old people were," but he was never told of the connection. With Joe's help, they both learned where the remains of his grandparents were interred. This came about in several ways, which Joe initiated.

Joe died at Studio City Convalescent Hospital at the age of 73, from end-stage skin cancer of the face. Prior to that time, with Jean's help, he made a concerted effort to find out as much as he could about his grandparents, Kirtland and Katharine Cutter. At the time of his death he lived at 11429 Ventura Boulevard in Studio City, California.

During the last years of Joe's life, he gave his friend Charles Daniels power of attorney. It was agreed that Joe would leave his family memorabilia to Jean Oton when he died. After his death, Jean received a package from Mr. Daniels containing numerous photos, a photo album, and miscellaneous documents and memorabilia.

In this package was a contact with Mrs. Kenneth (Joan) F. Brown at 3715 Diamond Head Rd., Honolulu, Hawaii. Mrs. Brown was Kathryn Walker's daughter. The exact date of the letter is unknown. However, it was initiated by Joe Corbin and ended up in his possession sometime during his last year of life. It, in part, stated:

> Dear Mrs. Wentz
>
> I know how hard it is to get a family straight especially when you don't really know them. I think it is better to have it written down — here it is:
>
> Katherine P. Carter (1868 to 1933) Maiden name was Katherine Phillips and she married a Jack Williams and lived in Spokane. They had a daughter Kathryn Williams and she married a Frederick Schaefer and lived in Hawaii. They had two children Joan Schaefer Brown (me) and Frederick Schaefer — both of us live in Hawaii.
>
> Katharine Phillips Williams divorced her husband and married Kirtland Cutter and they moved to Long

Beach, California where she died and he died later on. A few years later my mother and Katharine Cutter's daughter brought the ashes to Honolulu to a solarium.

... When Kathryn Walker, my mother, died we decided to have all three buried together in Kona which she (my mother) loved. She also had a first cousin (Marjorie Capps) who lived here in Kona and was very close to all of us. Do not hesitate to call or write if you have need of further information. If anything interesting comes from all this I will love to know.
Aloha, Joan Brown

Another letter of major significance also appeared in this package. It was written by Stephanie Ackerman, the cemetery chair of Christ Church Episcopal in Hawaii. It read as follows:

Dear Mr. Corbin,

I apologize for the delay in getting back to you in regards to an inquiry via your caretaker, Jean Oton. You are requesting information/confirmation on the remains of your grandfather, Kirkland [sic] Cutter.

I was not able to find any family still around that was old enough to remember his death, except for one who remembered that he died in Los Angeles back in the 1930s. The Rev. Carol Arnie and I found an entry in the register that two urns for Katharine Phillips Cutter and Kirkland Cutter were re-interred and brought here from the Nuuanu Columbarium on Oahu. Their remains were buried here at Christ Church Episcopal in the Capp's plot on March 1, 1965 by the late Rev. Norman R. Alter.

I was sorry to hear that you're not well and hope this information puts your mind at ease and clears up any misinformation that has been printed. Take care and may God be with you.

Sincerely,
Stephanie Ackerman, Cemetery Chair
Christ Church Episcopal, Kealakekua, Kona. Hawaii

Kirtland and Katharine remained together until her death in 1933. Prior to that time, they made a decision that upon their deaths they wished to be cremated. At the time, there were still a number of relatives on his wife's side of the family, including Katharine's daughter, Kathryn Walker. When Kirtland died in 1939, she had their remains interred at Nuuanu Columbarium on Oahu. In 1963 Kathryn died and two years later on March 1, 1965, they were reinterred, with Kathryn's remains being placed with her mother and stepfather. Their remains are now at Christ Church Episcopal Cemetery in Kona, Hawaii.

The authors felt this was an important correction for those who wish to pay their respect to Spokane's most famous architect.

Kirtland Cutter's headstone (see arrow) at the Christ Church Episcopal cemetery. The Cutters' cremated remains were buried in the Capps' plot on March 1, 1965. Cutter, his wife Katharine and stepdaughter Kathryn all lie under the same headstone. *(Courtesy Father Dick Tardiff, Rector, Christ Church Episcopal, Kealakekua, Hawaii)*

Left: Genevieve Wilment in "She's a Good Fellow."
(All photos on this page, Cutter collection, courtesy Jean Oton)

Genevieve Wilment and Corbin Corbin, in his Navy ensign uniform, while they were dating.

Genevieve and Corbin Corbin on their honeymoon. *(Cutter collection, courtesy Jean Oton)*

Harold C. Whitehouse

Whitehouse came to Spokane in 1907 and quickly rose to the top of his field. During his career, he designed 80 churches in the Northwest, one of which was the Cathedral of St. John the Evangelist in Spokane.

Prior to moving to Spokane in 1907, he had worked as a draftsman in Boston, but had no formal architectural training. Whitehouse soon established himself in Spokane, becoming active in the All Saints Episcopal Church. In 1908, he married Katherine Cox Weston.

Also, in 1908, he formed an architectural firm with architect George Keith. In 1915 he acquired a new partner, Ernest V. Price. Whitehouse and Price designed over 2,400 projects throughout the Northwest. In addition to the churches, they designed schools, government buildings, homes and businesses including buildings on the campuses of the University of Idaho, the University of Washington, Washington State University, and Whitworth College. Among Whitehouse's most beloved local buildings are those he designed for Levi Hutton's orphanage, the Hutton Settlement.

In 1923, Whitehouse took an extensive trip through Europe and visited and studied churches and cathedrals, all of which helped him when he began design work for The Cathedral of St. John the Evangelist. When he returned, the church purchased the present property where the cathedral now stands and they dedicated the site in 1925. The first portion of the cathedral was completed in four years and additional work was done until 1957. He worked closely with sculptors, masons and woodworkers from throughout the Northwest to produce meticulously detailed work. The University of Oregon holds a number of his architectural drawings. The plans for the Hutton Settlement and the Cathedral of St. John are at the Northwest Museum of Arts and Culture in Spokane.

The firm continued until Price's retirement in 1964. Whitehouse was a registered architect in Idaho, Montana, Oregon, and Washington, and his projects are many and varied.

Keith & Whitehouse's first major project

In the July 10, 1910, issue of the *Spokesman-Review*, a photo of a Keith & Whitehouse project was placed at the top of the real estate section of the newspaper. Below that were the blueprints for the first three floors. That project was the Spokane Country Clubhouse on the Little Spokane River. It read, in part, as follows:

> "Country Life" Type of Architecture Is Shown in Design and Plans for New $50,000 Country Club House on Little Spokane
>
> WORK IS RUSHED ON NEW COUNTRY CLUB
>
> Elaborate $50,000 Structure on Banks of Little Spokane to Be Complete in September.
>
> MODEL TYPE: FEATURES
>
> Spacious Verandas, Private Dining Rooms and Shower Baths Included in the Plans
>
> In one of the choicest spots along the banks of the Little

Harold C. Whitehouse
(Courtesy SPLNWR)

The Spokane Country Club drawing designed by Keith & Whitehouse. This structure was completed in 1910 and was completely destroyed by fire on May 1, 1946.

Spokane River, about 8 miles north of the city, and just West of the Graves Waikiki Ranch, construction work is forging ahead on the $50,000 home of the Spokane country club. Already the foundation is in, an[d] actual construction work on the first floor is under way. The building committee and the architects Keith & Whitehouse, have settled all details in the plans and early in the fall, the city rendezvous's will be thrown open with the formalities.

The Spokane country club had acquired almost 65 acres on which to establish its new home. The landscape architects are busy planning the grounds, golf links and courts and P. L. Peterson, the contractor in charge of the building promised all in readiness sometime in September.

"Country Life" in Architecture

Architectural beauty of the real country life is embodied in the plans for the $50,000 building. The clubhouse is divided into two separate buildings, a main club house and a "men's annex." Both buildings will be of frame construction largely, with the sides covered with a special shingle. There are three floors in each building, including the basement which is at a level with the ground. Each floor has its distinctive features and every modern touch has been added to the plans to give the country club a model building in all details.

The ground floor of basement of the Main building was constructed largely to accommodate women club members.. Here toilet rooms, showers, baths, restrooms, club boudoirs, lockers and the feminine conveniences have been arranged. Each room was well furnished and attractive. The spacious rest room resembles the large living room of the urban homes, and here a massive fireplace has been built. The ceilings are heavily beamed and the walls are wainscoted several feet from the floor. Window seats and cozy corners all add to the attractiveness of the entire lower floor of the Main building..

On the ground floor of the men's annex, separated from the main building by a drive, a similar arrangement has been planned. Locker rooms, shower bathrooms, drying room, toilets and a professionals work shop make up the arrangements. These rooms are finished handsomely with hard wood floors, wainscoting, paneling and beamed ceilings. ...

Another Whitehouse and Price project, the Cathedral of St. John the Evangelist, one of Spokane's most beautiful churches. Construction began in 1927. *(MAC, L87-1.7699d-54)*

Spokane's Mid-Century Modernist Architects

After the period of classical architectural design which dominated Spokane's development in the century's first half and is the subject of this book, the second half of the century was characterized by modernist architecture.

Following World War II, with Whitehouse and Price, Henry Bertelsen, and Bill DeNeff still practicing, the movement began in Spokane. Its leaders prior in the late 1940s were Ken Brooks who was first associated with Carroll Martell and Tom Adkison who was first associated with Royal McClure. By 1955, they were joined by Harvard graduates Bruce Walker and Bill Trogdon, UW graduate John McGough, and Swiss-educated Moritz Kundig. Brooks has often been referred to as the "father of modernist architecture in Spokane" because of his national award winning Washington Water Power Headquarters building for which he also employed the architects above who were only a few years younger than Brooks. Other names appearing about this time in association with Brooks were Russ Smith and Henry Swoboda.

Other well known names of the period include Walt Foltz, Bill James Sr., Gordon Ruehl, John Culler, Fulton Gale, Don Erickson, Ron Tan, Dale Brookie, Bob Grossman, Ben Nielsen, Bruce Blackmer, Steve McNutt, Fred King, John Aylor, Ed Musgrove, Bruce Mauser, Bill Marshall, Fred Creager, Joe Hensley, John Leigh, Ron Sims, Bob Cuppage, Ed Deeble, Arne Barton, Don Murray, Ed James, Ernie Hicks, Don Neraas, Kim Barnard, Dayton Holloway, and Warren Heylman.

The custom of individual names like Walker-McGough was replaced with initials WMFL and today is Integrus. McClure and Adkison became today's ALSC. Trogdon-Smith became TSG and Tan-Brooks-Kundig became TBK, and they merged into Northwest Architectural Company which today is NACI Architecture. With the advent of initialized and generic firm names, along with team design, it is today more difficult to identify a firm or a building with the name of an individual as was common in the first half of the century.

However, among the modernists were many preservationists of historic buildings and one revivalist who was Glen Cloninger.

Kenneth W. Brooks
The Father of a Classic Breed of Modern Architects in Spokane

The first of Spokane's more modern architects was Kenneth Brooks. Brooks was born in Cedarvale, Kansas, on June 9, 1917. He attended high school in Independence, Kansas. In 1940, he received his bachelor's degree in architectural engineering from the University of Illinois. Following his education he was awarded the prestigious Francis J. Plym Fellowship, which would pay him to travel in Europe for six months. However, due to the war in Europe, he postponed the fellowship.

Kenneth W. Brooks.
(Courtesy Edna Brooks)

During World War II, Brooks joined the U.S. Engineers Department and served in various capacities from 1940 to 1946. Upon being discharged from the Army, he spent over a year working for the New York office of Skidmore Owings & Merrill. While there, Brooks passed the National Council of Architectural Board examination and became licensed in New York. His next move, upon leaving that firm, was to Spokane, going to work for George M. Rasque, a longtime Spokane architect who specialized in school construction.

In 1948, After a few months working for Rasque, Brooks went to Europe on the Plym Fellowship. In Sweden, he volunteered to work in the Town Planning Office in Stockholm and Goteborg.

Following his travels in Europe, he returned to Spokane and went to work for the architectural firm of Carroll Martell Architects. This was short-lived as he decided to pursue a Master of Architecture degree from the University of Illinois. He received that degree in 1949 and returned to Spokane to make it his home. In 1950, he married Edna Harrington who grew up in Spokane. They had four children: William (Bill) Brooks, Barbara Brooks-Pratt, Ann (Brooks) Harper, and Joy Moorhead.

By 1951, the age of 34, he was ready to open his own practice with an emphasis in high architectural design and urban planning. His clients included individuals, corporations, educational institutions, hospitals, the U.S. government, and the governments of Australia and the Republic of China.

While in Spokane, Brooks became involved in a variety of community activities. He lectured about a variety of topics to hundreds of different community organizations.

Brooks designed several structures at the Spokane Expo '74 and was also one of the primary planners of the event. By the 1970s, he was in partnership with Joseph Hensley and Fred Creager. Over the next fifteen plus years, Brooks, Hensley, & Creager received high architectural acclaim at the local, regional, national, and international levels. Over a thirty-year period the firm designed twelve award-winning projects. His two most distinguished are the 1959 Washington Water Power Company in Spokane, and his 1977 Art-Drama-Music Complex at Columbia Basin Community College in Pasco. Both of these buildings received National American Institute of Architects Honor Awards.

Brooks became a Fellow of the American Institute of Architects in 1967. He retired in 1991, and passed away on August 8, 1996.

In 1959, Brooks designed the headquarters for the Washington Water Power Company, now Avista Utilities. This important commission won the National American Institute of Architects award. *(Bamonte photo)*

Glen Cloninger
Spokane's Late Century Neo-eclectic Architect

As Spokane Falls grew and rapidly became the center of the Inland Northwest, those with wealth recognized the natural beauty and potential of the city's location and aimed to enhance that beauty through its architecture. The adage "a man is recognized and judged by his wealth" was soon to make an impact on Spokane Falls. What better way to show your wealth than through your home?

The future of Spokane Falls also appeared to be on solid ground. Capitalists in the early 1900s recognized that Spokane Falls was situated in the heart of an empire of 150,000 square miles. Its draw of wealth came from mining, lumbering, water power, and agricultural resources throughout eastern Washington, eastern Oregon, northern Idaho, western Montana, and southeastern British Columbia. The wealth and potential for business from those resources was seemingly unlimited.

The first architects to locate in Spokane Falls recognized the extent of the newly acquired wealth in the city and the potential opportunity. For many, cost simply wasn't an issue – they were anxious to design artistic, as well as comfortable, homes and commercial buildings. Spokane's first generation of architects succeeded in meeting those aspirations, making it clearly apparent that their architectural art would endure over the centuries as evidence of their belief in its future greatness.

Although there are many beautiful homes being built today that are designed by great architects, there is still a market for the magnificent old buildings that were designed during this early period of European style. With that thought in mind, we introduce the work of the late Glen Cloninger.

Glen Cloninger was a unique person and the first architect in Spokane to revive the early styles of the century, who chose to build his practice around these styles on a regular basis.

Cloninger was born on July 28, 1944, in Spokane. He graduated in 1968 from Montana State University with a Masters of Architecture. He later served on MSU's board of directors from 1996 to 1999. Cloninger was an architect in Spokane beginning in 1968. In 1973 he opened his firm, Glen A. Cloninger & Associates, which employed from one to seven people (most of the time he had just one other architect). His first major project begun in 1976 was the Tapio Office Center located just off the Freya/Thor freeway ramp.

In 1966, Glen married Pamela Marie Briggs. Three children came from that marriage: Blake, Brooke, and Brittney. That union lasted over 43 years, until Glen's death in 2010. He was a devoted family man – family came first, career second.

As with Cutter, he was well-traveled. During his lifetime, Cloninger visited 50 states and 46 countries, each time gaining new insights into architectural styles. He also made his travels a family experience. Various members of his family accompanied him on these trips – creating a lasting and educational experience along the way.

During a trip to Helsinki, Finland, Cloninger discovered the quaking aspen tree and its many uses for decoration. From that time on the quaking aspen always was featured in the landscaping of his architecture. On another trip he learned the meaning of the word Tapio (God of the Forest). His next design was the aspen-surrounded, Tapio Office Center.

He was among Spokane's colorful and talented architects, designing some of the area's most prestigious residences and buildings. Some people consider him the Kirtland Cutter of this era. As with Cutter, his designs were European influenced. The main difference in today's construction from earlier Cutter era homes is the improved quality of concrete, wiring, and the general building codes. Up until the 1960s, the main structure of a house was framed with two-by-fours. Today two-by-sixes are used, homes now have fiberglass insulation, and the electrical systems are much safer. Besides the artistic character of his architecture, Cloninger was insistent on using the best quality materials.

Cloninger's signature designs were built with brick-and-stone masonry fashioned after the Gothic Revival Tudor style found in the 16th century chateaus of France. His style was rare and was used primarily for unique architecturally-designed houses. The identifying features of Cloninger homes are steeply pitched hip roofs; busy roof lines with many vertical elements (spirals, pinnacles, turrets, gables, and shaped chimneys and numerous dormers).

Cloninger was a man of his word. He would stand for what he believed, at one time going to the Supreme Court of Washington to fight the neighborhood for a development he planned to build the Grapetree Village on East 29th Avenue. At the time, specific community members argued that his plans did not fit with the area, claiming they were too grandiose for Spokane. Cloninger believed he could better his community and the court agreed. He won this case and completed the project in 2007. His first large architectural project for his fledgling firm was to design and build H.U.D. housing for the Colville Confederated Indian Tribes at Nespelem. During the course of his contacts with the Chief Harvey Moses, their friendship grew out of mutual respect for one another. Following the completion of the project, Chief Moses passed away. Glen was the only white man invited to attend the Indian funeral and burial. The amount of respect Glen had shown for the tribe and they, in return, for him was an indication of who he was and what he stood for. Chief Moses was laid to rest in a plain pine wood coffin lined with a red Indian blanket with the chief holding an eagle feather.

That image struck Glen with its plain and simple elegance and its ties to nature and the environment. At that moment, he decided and instructed his wife, Pam, to make certain that when it came his time to be laid to rest, she would do for him exactly what had been done for Chief Harvey Moses. Glen's body was laid to rest in a plain pinewood coffin, lined with a red Indian blanket.

The Cloninger family among quaking aspen trees near his home: From left: Brooke, Karen, Coulter, Blake, Bridger, Pam, Glen, and Brittney. *(All photos in this section courtesy Cloninger family)*

Chapter Eight

An architectural rendering of the East Pinecrest Road Addition.

During Cloninger's career his work appeared on the Travel Channel, on HDTV's Dream Builders, and in numerous magazines. He has been the architect of hundreds of homes and buildings, winning numerous awards throughout the Inland Northwest. He was exceptionally proud of the design of his Rose Circle Columbarium and Campanile, located just inside the entrance to Riverside Cemetery. He was laid to rest at the foot of this magnificent and award-winning monument. This is also significant as it was an addition to a Kirtland Cutter design.

The impact of Cloninger's mind and hands can be see throughout the Inland Northwest. His dreams were magnificent and he made them happen.

Cloninger was chosen to renovate and add the Columbarium and Campanile at the Riverside Mausoleum located at the Riverside Cemetery.

260

Magazines featuring Cloninger's architectural work.

Riverside Memorial Park's original arched entrance, a Cutter design. It was an honor for Cloninger to design the similar Columbarium and Campanile.

Chapter Eight

Grapetree Village on East 29th Avenue.

Glen and Pam Cloninger's home.

INDEX of SPOKANE'S FIRST ARCHITECTS

This list of architects is from the 1978 Survey of Historic Landmarks, Spokane's City Plan Commission. Most practiced primarily during the first 25 years of the century for projects completed not later than the mid-century. Moritz Kundig was the survey coordinator and principal of the project.

BALLARD PLANNERY
   429 E. Baldwin - Johnson Residence
   2612 W. Dean - Haas Residence
   2206 S. Manito Blvd. - Renshaw Residence

BAUME, EDWARD
   Practiced in Spokane c 1910-1923. Baume worked with K. K. Cutter in Southern California after 1923.

BOARDMAN, LORENZO
   Practiced in Spokane 1889 - 1896.
   1 N. Post - Whitten Block

BURNHAM, DANIEL H. AND COMPANY, CHICAGO
   Old National Bank Building

CARPENTER, WILLIAM J.
   b. England. Practiced in Spokane 1889 - 1890. (Possibly later in St. Petersburg, Florida)
   1923 W. 1st - Loewenberg/Roberts Mansion
   908 W. Frederick - Forrest/Currie Home

COWLEY, ARTHUR
   425 W. 2nd - Spokane Safe & Lock - altered by Cowley
   1102 W. 2nd - Albert Apartments
   804 S. Monroe - Fire Station
   608 S. Stevens - Altadena Apartments

COWLEY & RIGG
   1101-1109 W. 1st
   1220 S. Division - Dr. Cunningham Residence

CREUTZER, J.A.
Practiced in Spokane c 1905. d. Seattle 1929 c.
   1211 W. 6th - Rhodehamel Residence
   1627 W. 9th - Lundquist Residence
   817 S. Adams - Lundquist Residence

CUTTER & POETZ
   705 W. 7th - Marycliff Gatehouse/Chapel 323 W. 8th - Glover Mansion
   209 - 13 W. Riverside - Pedicord Hotel

CUTTER & MALMGREN
   2123 W. 1st - White Apartments
   2316 W. 1st - Cheney Cowles Museum
   Grace Campbell Memorial House
   2328 W. 1st - Wakefield House
   2340 W. 1st - Finch Mansion
   2208 W. 2nd - Patrick Clark Mansion
   1300 E. 4th
   727 W. 6th - Post Mansion
   701 W. 7th - Undercliff/Gordon Hall/F. Lewis Clark Mansion
   820 W. 7th - Corbett Residence/Aspray
   1718 W. 9th - Grande Manor Home
   919 S. Adams - Jasper House
   719 W. Main - The Crescent
   1725 W. Pacific - Rutter House
   2236 W. Pacific - Dr. Luhn Cottage 3
   33 N. Post - W.W.P. Substation
   151 - 65 S. Post - Joel's
   152 S. Post - Steam Plant
   305 W. Riverside - Arcade/Sons of Norway
   510 W. Riverside - Sherwood Building
   1002 W. Riverside - The Spokane Club
   825 W. Spokane Falls Boulevard - Old W.W.P. Building
   1214 W. Sprague - Myrtle Apartments
   1212 N. Summit Boulevard - Thomas Residence/Grotto Home 502 W. Sumner
   612/622 W. Sumner - Humbird/Gaiser Mansion
   1408 Summit Boulevard
   2203 South Manito Road

CUTTER & PEHRSON
   926 W. Sprague - Chronicle Building

CUTTER & PLUMMER
   928 W. 7th - Reinhardt Residence (interior)

DONCHOE, PATRICK T.
   Practiced in Spokane 1889 - 1891; also constructed buildings in Ellensburg.
   1114 - 1216 N. Superior - Old Holy Names

DOW, JOHN K.
   b. 1862, d. 1961, Kent, Washington. Practiced in Spokane 1889 - 1937. (See L. L. Rand, an occasional partner throughout their careers)
   1332 W. 8th - The Castle/Gordon Residence
   1405 W. 9th - Coolidge/Rising home
   245 E. 13th - Paulsen Residence
   1527 W. Mallon - Grace Baptist Church
   301 - 14 W. Riverside - M. M. Seller/Jensen-Byrd
   517 W. Riverside - Mohawk Building
   905 W. Riverside - Great Western/Empire State Building
   108 N. Washington - American Legion Building
   9 S. Washington - Hutton Building
   407 S. Washington Westminster Congregational

DOW & HUBBELL
   417 W. Riverside - A. Paulsen Building
   Metals American Legion building

GALBRAITH, I. J.
b. 1859 Monongehela, PA. Practiced in Pittsburgh, PA and Montana prior to arrival in Spokane in 1903.
1111-19 W. 1st - The Commercial
628 N. Monroe - Old Hill Apartments
706 N. Monroe - Vinter & Nelson

GROVE, MARTIN T.
Practiced in Spokane 1889 - 1905. Few of Grove's structures are known to be standing but he designed the J. J. Browne house, later remodeled by K. K. Cutter.
1332 S. Division

GUENTHER, COUNT EMIL
One of Spokane's most important architects, as chief designer of the early school buildings, he has had a long-lasting effect on the city. Practiced in Spokane 1890 - 1895, later in California.
152 S. Monroe - Old Spaghetti Factory

HELD, ALBERT
b. 1866, Minnesota; d. 1924. Practiced in Spokane from 1890 until his death in 1924. His range of standing buildings is exceeded only by Cutter. First Spokane architect to join the A.I.A.
1015 W. 1st - I OOF
2404 W. 2nd - Weil Residence
2308 W. 3rd - James Clark Mansion/Isabella Club
1305 W. 5th - Casa Loma Apartments
2001 W. 9th - Gordon Residence (remodeling)
729 S. Bernard - Breslin Apartments
1420 E. Celeste - Spokane & Inland RR
157 S. Howard - Old Holley Mason Building
165 S. Howard - Old Home Telephone Building
507 S. Howard - Knickerbocker Apartments
623 S. Howard - Alexandria Apartments
720 W. Main - Palace/Nordstrom
506 W. Mission - Judge Blake's Residence
728 N. Monroe - Ricardo
802 N. Monroe - Jenkins Building/Sea-First Branch
242 W. Riverside - Realty Building
526 W. Sumner Matthews Residence
1226 W. Riverside - San Marco Apartments

HELD & ZITTEL
1910 W. 1st - Kilner House

HELD & PERMAIN
2425 W. Pacific - C.P. Robbins

HELMLE, CHARLES F.
Practiced in Spokane 1890 - 1895, designer of original Spokane High School (South Central).

HUBBELL, CLARENCE Z.
1725 W. 9th - Phair House
9. S. Washington - Hutton Building

HYSLOP, W. W. (See also Westcott)
Innovative designs by Hyslop are comparable to K. K. Cutter, particularly in style, quality and durability. His buildings are often assumed to be much more recent than they are. Practiced in Spokane c. 1910 - 1918.
1821 N. Monroe - Monroe Apartments
2009 w. Pacific - The Avenida
1905 w. 2nd - The Elm Apartments
928 W 7th - Reinhardt Residence - (exterior)
34 E. 8th - Martin Residence
2001 W. 8th - Markham Residence
1319 N. A Street - Mack Residence
180 S. Cannon - Marlboro Apartments
1115 S. Grand - Kaiser Residence
525 W. Waverly Place
615 W. Waverly Place
2913 N. West Oval
1515 E. 19th

JABELONSKY, CARL HUGO
b. 1879 Sweden, trained as a Civil Engineer and architect. Practiced in Spokane c. 1908 - 1917. Moved to NY in 1919.
152 S. Browne - Goofy's/Wilton Hotel
2319 N. Monroe - Hogan

JONES, ALFRED
Practiced 1899 - 1909. Joined firm of Jones & Levesque. Practice in Spokane around 1912
608 W. 2nd - Plechner
238 E. 13th
212 S. Lincoln - First Baptist Church (w/Whitehouse and Price)
414 W. Main - Kemp and Hebert/Liberty Furniture
155 S. Oak - Espanola Apartments
1120 W. Riverside - Smith Funeral Home/Rochester Apartments
523 S. Washington - Kempis Apts.

KEITH, GEORGE (See also H. C. Whitehouse)
b. 1878, Minneapolis, d. ?.Partners c. 1908 - 1914. Practiced in Spokane and Inland Empire 1908 - c. 1920.
2206 E. 17th - Hutton Mansion
2715 S. Grand - Manito Masonic Temple

KEITH & WHITEHOUSE
108 S. Jefferson - Parsons s Hotel
711 W. Shoshone - Clark House
2414 W. 2nd Waird Residence
Spokane Country Club

MALMGREN, KARL G.
Practiced in Spokane 1895 -1914 in firm of Cuttler & Malmgren. From 1915 - c. 1920 alone.

MORRISON

1628 W. 9th.- Johnson Residence

MORRISON & STIMSON
1305 E. Overbluff - Dr. Hopkins Residence

NIVER, WORTHY (See J. K. Dow)
Practiced in Spokane 1890 - 1892.
614 W. Sprague - Title Building
115 N. Washington - Lang Building
407 S. Washington - Westminster Congregational

PEHRSON, G.A.
Practiced in Spokane c. 1920 - c. 1968. Began as a draftsman with K. K. Cutter. One of the most influential architects of 20th century Spokane.
524 W. 7th - Roosevelt Apartments
1424 W. 9th - Womans Club Cottage 411 E. 14th
508 E. 14th
1420 E. Overbluff - J.J. Marischell Residence
407 W. Riverside - Paulsen Medical and Dental Building
601 W. Riverside - Spokane and Eastern Building
1023 W. Riverside - Roman Catholic Chancery
703 W. Shoshone - Munsel Residence
538 W. Sumner - Herbert Residence
1703 N. Washington - Greek Orthodox

POETZ, JOHN C.
Practiced in Spokane 1888 - c. 1910. Original partner of K. K. Cutter and H. Sackville Treherne. d. 1929.

PREUSSE, HERMANN (Also see Julius Zittel)
Practiced in Spokane 1882 - 1901. Spokane's first architect. b. 1847 Germany, Practiced in Germany, New York and Chicago. Many architects including Cutter were draftsmen for him. Firm of Preusse and Zittel. 2 N. Howard - Hazel Block/Merton
117 N. Howard - Woodward Building
1830 W. Pacific - Baum Residence
501 W. Riverside - Fernwell Building
705 W. Riverside - Jamieson/Zukor
715 W. Riverside - Kuhn Building
920 W. Sprague -
124 N. Stevens - Bodie/1889 Building

PREUSSE & ZITTEL
618 W. 1st - Victoria Hotel
202 W. 2nd - The Armory
801 W. 2nd - Bump Block/Carlyle Hotel
1404 W. 8th - Allenburg House
1827 W. 9th - G. D. Brown Residence
1903 W. 9th - Ray Residence
217 E. Boone - Monaghan Mansion
320 E. Boone - St. Aloysius R. C. Church
502 E. Boone - Gonzaga Administration Building
10 S. Cedar - Carnegie Library
101 S. Howard - Columbia Building
5021 N. Nelson - St. Patricks R. C. Church

1103 W. Riverside - Our Lady of Lourdes R.C. Cathedral
1115 W. Riverside - Our Lady of Lourdes Rectory
E. 1624 S. Riverton - Nash Residence
1114 - 1216 N. Superior - Holy Names

PRICE, ERNEST V. (See H. C. Whitehouse) Partner, 1915 - 1966.
315 W. Sumner - Price Home
319 W. Sumner
405 W. Sumner

RALSTON/McCARTHY/KENNEDY/GRIEVE/CUTTER
300 - 400 N. Monroe - Designed the handrails and four small pavilions placed over the main structural piers of the Monroe Street Bridge. The plans for the Monroe Street Bridge were stolen from Cuyahoga County in Ohio by Spokane's engineers and used almost as they were drawn, with the exception of extending it a foot to make it longer than the Rocky River Bridge. This was revealed in an article that appeared in the January 27, 1912, *Spokesman-Review* and was corroborated when Tony Bamonte contacted Bill Dobish, director of the Cuyahoga County Engineers Office. Mr. Dobish provided Bamonte with a complete set (16 pages) of plans for their bridge. The similarity of these plans corroborated the 1912 allegations. When the Monroe Street Bridge was remodeled in 2008, an engineer for the project contacted Bamonte. He requested the use of the plans obtained from Cuyahoga County as there are no Cutter plans for bridge.

RAND, LOREN L. (See also Dow)
Practiced in Spokane 1888 - 1930+.
515 W. 4th - Lewis & Clark High School
1406 W. 9th - Clough Residence
2315 E. Bridgeport - Bemis School
318 S. Cedar - First Presbyterian Church
415 S. Freya - Sheridan School
2502 W. Gardner -
815 E. Kiernan - Longfellow School
152-164 S. Lincoln - Spokane Dry Goods

RAND & DOW
801 W. 2nd - Bump Block/Carlyle Hotel
739 S. Chandler - Sargent House
1819 N. Normandie - France Residence
1108 W. Riverside - Masonic Temple

RAND - HUBBELL
1415 S. Bernard - Roosevelt School

RAND - ROONEY
2904 E. 37th - Adams School (addition)

REID BROTHERS OF SAN FRANCISCO

830 W. Sprague - Germond Building

RIGG, ARCHIBALD
b. 1878. Practiced in Spokane 1912 (Rigg and Zittel). (Rigg and Van Tyne c. 1959.)
714 W Sprague Avenue Peyton Annex #2 (Brady's Gym)

RIGG & VAN TYNE
15 S. Howard - Symons Building
1108 W. Riverside - Masonic Temple
315 W. Sprague

RITCHIE, WILLIS A.
b. 1864, Ohio; d. 1931. Practiced in Spokane 1893 - 1920; his structures were designed throughout the state including the State Capitol; King, Whatcom, Jefferson, Clark and Thurston County Courthouses.
1116 W. Broadway - Spokane County Courthouse
1015 S. Grand - Cunningham Residence/Alta Vista Apartments

SAUNDERS, A.C.
b. 1860, England. Practiced in Spokane 1898 - 1901.
309 S. Wall - Wilson Apartments

SEATON, CHAUNCEY B.
Practiced in Spokane 1890 - 1896.
929 W. Riverside - Review Building

STONE
801 W. 2nd - Bump Block/Carlyle Hotel

SWEATT, ROBERT C.
b. 1846, Mississippi. Practiced in Chicago for 20 years. Structures designed include the Union Depot. Practiced in Spokane 1904 - 1915. Firms included Stritesky & Sweatt, Sweatt & Diamond.
3128 N. Hemlock - Old Spokane Children's Home
815 N. Jefferson - Hinkle Apartments/Old Company Health Building
10 N. Post - Peyton/Great Western buildings
1203 W. Riverside - Knights of Pythias
300 N. Wall - Frances Willard School
Wallace, Idaho - Episcopal Church
Otis Orchards - Bungalow
Cashmere, WA 1st Baptist Church

SWEATT & STRITEKY
2301 W. Pacific - Westminister Apartments

SWEATT & WENTZELL
716 W. Sprague - Peyton Building

TAYLOR, JAMES K.
904 W. Riverside - Federal Building/Post Office

WESTCOTT
335 W. Sprague - Avis/Old Garden Dance Hall
529 W Sumner Cliff Airie

WHITE, C. FERRIS, F.A.I.A.
b. Chicago 1867; d. 1932 Everett, Washington. Practiced in Spokane 1890 - 1915 and continued to practice in Everett. His designs are occassionally mistaken locally for Frank Lloyd Wright. He designed virtually all of Potlatch, Idaho.

WHITE & HYSLOP
829 W. Mansfield - Zuimby Residence
2509 W. Mission - Paine House

WHITE & PERMAIN
416 S. Coeur d'Alene - Stroback Residence

WHITEHOUSE, HAROLD C.
See George Keith, partner 1908 - 1914 and E. V. Price, partner 1915 - 1968. b. 1884, Massachusetts; d. 1974.

WHITEHOUSE & PRICE
127 E. 12th - Catherdral of St. John Episcopal
2315 E. Bridgeport - Bemis School (Alteration)
318 S. Cedar - First Presbyterian church (Alteration)
2503 S. Grand - (Old) St. James Episcopal Church
212 S. Lincoln - First Baptist Church (w/Jones)
2028 S. Oneida Place
1020 W. Riverside - Civic Building/Chamber of Commerce 525 W. Sprague - Ramp Garage

ZITTEL, JULIUS (See also Herman Preusse)
b. 1869, Germany, studied architecture in Chicago. Practiced in Spokane 1887. Preusse and Zittel, Zittel and Rigg and others. Note: Zittel was State Architect of Washington during the building boom of the early 1900s.
403 E,. Mission
525 E. Mission - Heath Branch Library
221 N. Wall - City Hall

Nine

How Real Estate Was Sold: Ads From the Early Real Estate Companies

This ad was placed in the *Spokane Daily Chronicle*, Wednesday, October 14, 1925. *(Courtesy Rob Higgins)*

A Seehorn's moving van, in the late to early 1800s, transporting a family's belongings to their new home. *(MAC L85-1502)*

Sometimes when families were having a home built they lived in tent-houses similar to the one pictured here at 2913 East Fifteenth Avenue. *(MAC L85-2638)*

Ad from Sunday morning August 25, 1907, *Spokesman-Review*.

Ad from Sunday morning July 28, 1907, *Spokesman-Review*.

Browne Park Addition

The Home of the Business Man

Browne Park Addition comprises three hundred and twenty acres of the best land to be found in eastern Washington. Five hundred of the most beautiful sites in or near the city.

Browne Park Addition is located on Moran Prairie, one and one-half miles southeast of the city limits, on the Spokane & Inland Electric road. Twenty minutes' ride to and from the city. This new addition is a portion of J. J. Browne's beautiful home place, and lies at an elevation of four hundred feet above the center of the city.

Browne Park Addition offers more for your money than any other addition lying at the same distance from the center of the city. It is just far enough away from the noise, dirt and heat of the city to make the addition ideal.

Browne Park Addition offers a home for profit, a home for health, quiet and ease. All the advantages of enjoying a home with all the comforts and conveniences of inside additions.

Let us show you these tracts. A liberal discount to those who will build immediately.

J. J. BROWNE, 409 Traders Block

Ad from Tuesday morning July 30, 1907, *Spokesman-Review*.

1402 Lots Sold in Manito Park

Three Years' Time

Certainly an enviable record and one which can not be duplicated in Spokane, and in but few cities in the country.

There's a Reason

The "Manito kind" of homesites are not found elsewhere. $400 in very small amounts will secure a beauty.

The Fred B. Grinnell Company

TERMINAL BUILDING.   MAIN AND LINCOLN.
Manito office, 29th and Grand.

Only 118 Colborn & Morgan Acre Tracts Left

Never before in the history of irrigated lands in the state of Washington have so many tracts been sold in so short a time. Now there are only 118 of them left and your chance to secure one of these acre home sites close to your daily work will soon be gone.

Water in Abundance

Yesterday morning the electric current was turned into the motor which is to run the mammoth pump which has been installed in the Colborn & Morgan water system. All expectations were realized; the pump worked beautifully; the water was turned into the mains and those who have already built homes and planted orchards and gardens turned the water through their hydrants and found, as had been told them, there was water in abundance.

Come Out Today

Take a Hillyard car today to the end of the line, where we have a branch office. It will be a pleasure to you to see these tracts of fine loam soil and it will be a pleasure to us to show them to you. We will have carriages waiting for you and you will have no walking to do.

$350 Each
NAME YOUR OWN TERMS

Acre home sites which furnish the living and close to your work.

The Fred B. Grinnell Company

TERMINAL BUILDING.   MAIN AND LINCOLN.

The ad on the left was advertised on Sunday July 1, 1907 and the one on the right was July 7. Both were printed in the *Spokesman-Review*.

Valleyford

Has All These Four

First—The rich, black loam of Moran prairie. You can see the richness of the product on the ground right now.

Second—Located on the Spokane & Inland just 16 miles from the terminal depot, the entire city will bid for the fruits of Valleyford.

Third—In the valley, with the rising pine hills, on three sides, and with schools, and churches, and stores, and electric lights, and water in the house, and all the comforts of a city, a more ideal country home could not be imagined.

Fourth—Valleyford is a good place and is going to grow and its lands increase in value. Founded by Spokane & Inland railway interests to make traffic for the road, it would fail of its purpose if it did not grow and become a great shipping point. The man who buys now will share in that growth and in the increase in value.

Come out with us to Valleyford today and see the land and its richness for yourself. Trains at 8:10 a. m. and 1:05 p. m.

Prices $100 to $250 an Acre
Sold on Easy Instalments

Arthur D. Jones & Co.

907 Riverside Ave.   Empire State Building

Read What Vice President Fairbanks Said Yesterday About Spokane and Then Buy Realty

The Northwest Boulevard Addition
Is the Best Property in Spokane at the Price

You can take your own time in paying for this property. We require only a small payment down and the rest will come in such small monthly instalments that you can pay for a lot and hardly miss the money.

The city water mains are laid, which gives Northwest Boulevard all the water you will care to use.

The entire tract is surrounded by improved property, so there will be no waiting for city conveniences. Three car lines serve the addition and through service is established down Northwest Boulevard, the thoroughfare that divides the property, so it is not necessary to change cars in order to reach the addition.

Northwest Boulevard has electric lights, good schools and churches, quick delivery to all stores and is within practical and possible walking distance of Howard and Riverside. It is only one mile northwest of the court house.

Call for free car tickets and go out and see this tract.

Finch Investment Company

Telephone 537   507 Empire State Building

Spokesman-Review July 2, 1907.   *Spokesman-Review* July 12, 1907.

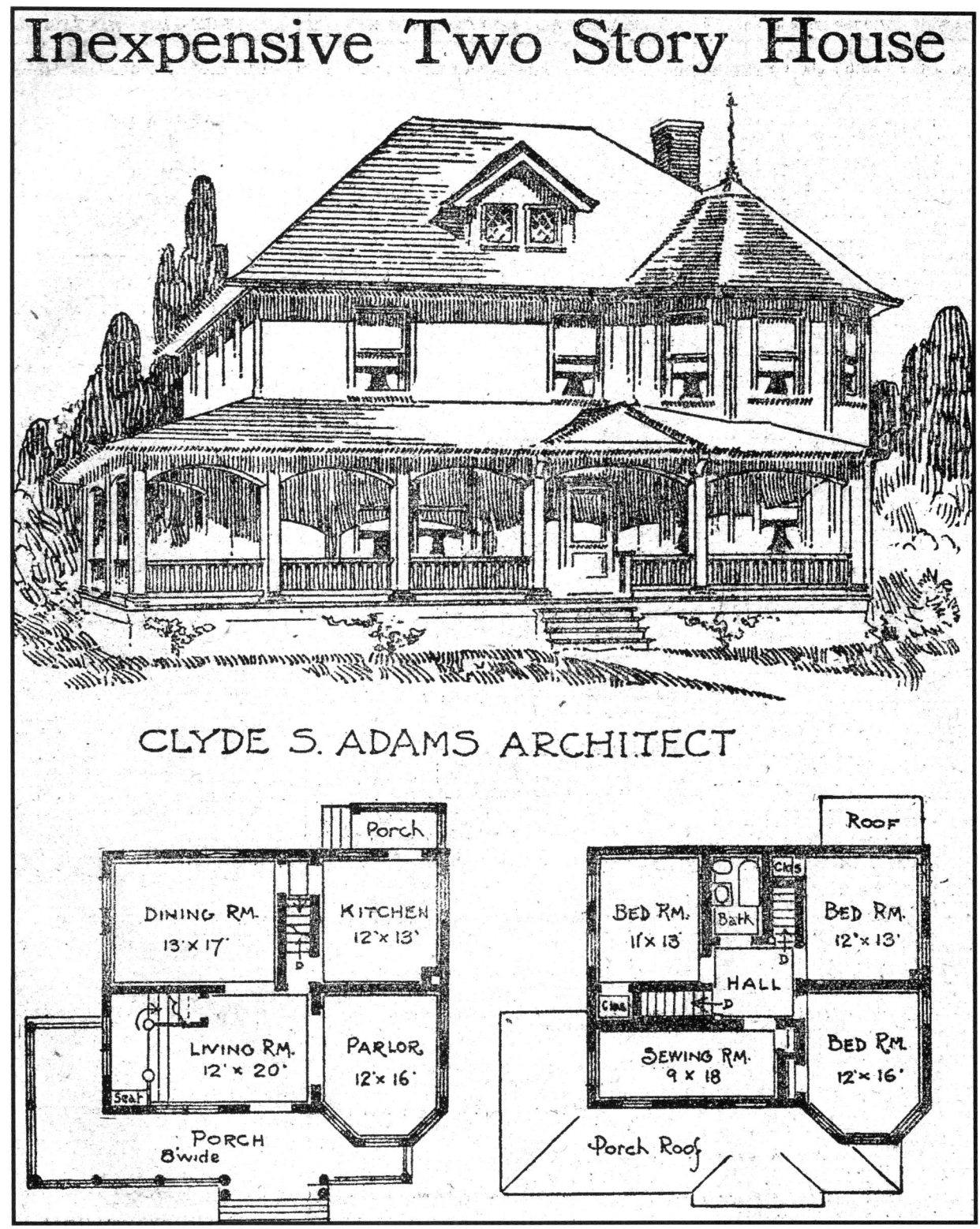

This architectural drawing by Clyde S. Adams, appeared, in the *Spokesman-Review* Sunday morning edition, July 28, 1907. An estimate of the cost of the house was made by a local architect. The estimate of excavation is based on soil, a site free from rock requiring no blasting. The following estimate shows cost on the house itemized in Spokane. Excavating $175; Stonework $225; Lumber $500; Plumbing $275; Millwork $600; Carpentry $500; Painting and Glazing $300; Stairs $150; Hardware $150; Hot Air Heating $150. This makes a total of $3,025 for the construction of this home.

Residence of Charles Patullo, southeast corner of Twelfth avenue & Adams street.

An ad in the July 7, 1907, *Spokesman-Review* featured the above house, taking up over half a page. The story started out as follows:

OWNS ATTRACTIVE ENGLISH BUNGALOW
CHARLES PATULLO'S RESIDENCE AT 12TH
AND ADAMS IS DISTINCTIVE
LARGE, TASTEFUL LIVING ROOM
HARDWOOD FLOORS THROUGHOUT FIRST
STORY – WOULD LIVE IN COOLER UNIQUE
FEATURES

Charles Patullo's residence, which he recently bought from the Chamberlin Real Estate Improvement Company, at the southeast corner of 12th Avenue and Adams Street, has a number of distinct eastern features. Built in the style of an English cottage with dark stain siding to the belt course and half timber above, the exterior of the house is unusually attractive.

Across the front is a spacious veranda, 10 feet wide and covered with an extension of the main roof, supported by square columns, resting on the rustic basalt rock buttress. These rocks, which are also used in the foundation, are moss covered and were carefully selected. The roof is painted dark red, the wide cornice being supported by 8 x 10 lookout beams, a latch opens into the hallway in the middle of the house, the hall is 12 x 12, finished in red Oak in a range with a built-in seat, having panel back. The stairs to the second floor ascend from the hall, having tapering Post and turned pilasters. At the first landing is a door which opens into the kitchen.

Attractive living room.

On the left of the hall is a living room, with which it is connected by a single sliding door. The living room was 18 x 23, finished in red Oak, with cross beam ceiling. The walls are treated in delicate brown. At one end of the room is a clinker brick fireplace 8 feet wide, with mantle extending to the ceiling, built with recesses and shelves for vases.

The heavy metal shelf extends beyond the fireplace, forming the top of the bookcases on each side and the cap the paneled back the built in seats adjoining the bookcases. The bookcases have leaded glass doors, and are just beneath sash windows, which also have small leaded panes.

The house was built by the Chamberlain Real Estate and Improvement Company and sold to Mr. Patullo, without the lot, for $7,500.

The Yardley ad

There are two things that are significant about this ad in February 18, 1912, *Spokesman-Review.* The first was the real estate company, Elmendorf & Elmendorf at South 5 Howard Street. Frederic Elmendorf was the first president of the Spokane Association of Realtors.

The second significant item was that the ad was for Yardley in Hillyard. There was a picture of the general contractor M. C. Murphy, the man who had a contract for building the Northern Pacific's $300,000 yard and railroad shop at Yardley. The ad read:

> This is the man who will start the values of Yardley lots on their upward march. YARDLEY IS THE PLACE. It's the man who gets it NOW who'll get ALL the benefits of ALL the increase in value. There were a lot of people who KNEW what Yardley MUST become IF the yards went in. But they wanted to be SURE about the yards. One question is settled, and Yardley lots are going fast. Yardley, as the mechanical focus of transportation, that would be the headquarters for the Northern Pacific's gigantic $4,000,000 improvement project.... This is your last chance. Call for a free folder and learn what $25 will do for you. Elmendorf & Elmendorf.

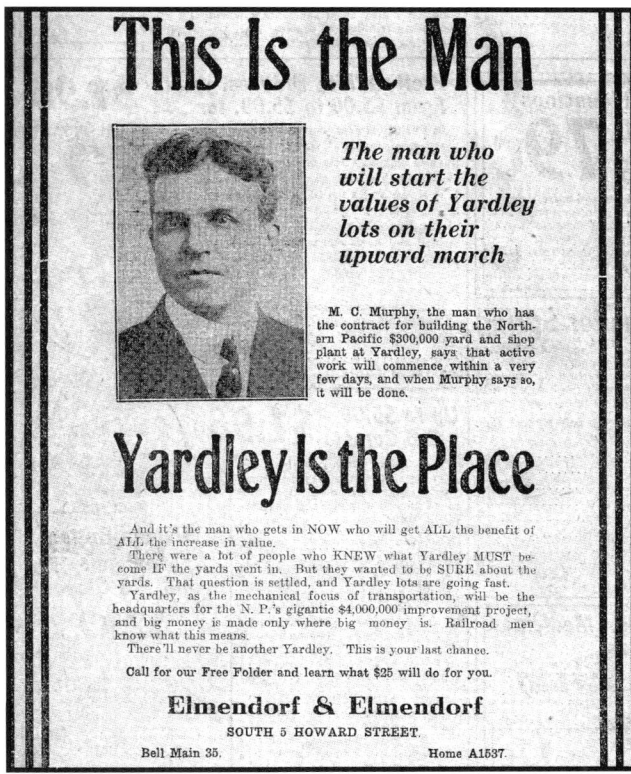

The Feltis ad

The above photo appeared in the Sunday morning February 18, 1912, *Spokesman-Review.* It read:

> C. E. Feltis of the Thompson-Gillis Investment Company will erect the residence shown above on the south side of 13th Avenue, west of Ferris Court, just a short distance east of Grand Boulvard. The house will cost $15,000. The site, which is just west of August Paulsen's $75,000 mansion was purchased a short time ago for $3,000.
>
> The house will be a rustic clinker brick and stone structure. It will have 11 rooms. On the first floor there will be a large living room 19 x 32, a dining room and kitchen. The living room and dining room will be paneled and hope and trimmed in old copper. In the basement there will be a large ballroom and den. South American mahogany and ivory enamel will be used for finishing the ballroom and the second floor, where there will be four bedrooms and a bath. The den will be finished in hewn oak with all rustic affects.
>
> The site has frontage of 70 feet and is 200 feet in depth. It overlooks the city from a convenient angle, as well as the surrounding territory. It is in a district recently improved with about $200,000 worth of fine residences, including the homes of E. J. Cannon, J. P. McGoldrick, George W. O'Dell, August Paulsen and several others.
>
> Mr. Feltis has started work already and expects to have the house completed in the latter part of June. Mr. Feltis has spent about $50,000 in houses on the Hill which were all sold before completed.

Substantial Homes in Whitings and Forest Park Additions on North Side

The Sunday February 18, 1912, *Spokesman-Review* touted the new homes for sale in Whitings and Forest Park Additions on Spokane's north side.

At the bottom of the ad, the following identifications were made: Upper left: New residences at 808, 810 and 814 Dalton (formally Effie), built by Andrew Pearson). Lower left: Eight room modern home at 706 Euclid Avenue, owned by J. F. Strong. This is located on the northeast corner of Mill Street [now called Wall street] and Euclid Avenue. It has hardwood floors and built-in features. Upper right – Residence of E. T. Cushman. 712 Dalton Avenue. It has six rooms with all built-in features. It cost about $4,000. Lower right – House built and owned by J. F. Strong at 1014 Dalton Ave. It has seven rooms and a sleeping balcony. It was built at a cost of $2,500.

The Growth in Spokane's Business District in 1912

This same issue of the newspaper also had an article concerning plate glass store windows. It read as follows:

NEW DEVELOPMENT ON SPRAGUE NOTED
Plate glass fronts replace old granite and brick walls and retail trade grows.
PEDESTRIANS ARE LURED.
Avenue rapidly is becoming attractive and active business thoroughfare.

The progress of a growing city is best shown in the gradual transitions which take place in the business sections – proving these transitions are indicative a growing and spreading business.

Years ago the change became apparent when the retail district moved up from Main and Front avenues, where business was transacted in Spokane when the city was a village. Riverside avenue, a mixed street of business, banks and lodging houses, became the retail thoroughfare. It still is, but the retail district spread rapidly. Sprague avenue was annexed and became a semi-retail avenue, and the wholesale houses took place along the Northern Pacific Railroad tracks. The jump to Second avenue and all along the side streets, from the river to Third avenue, came gradually.

A new change, something of a second transition, is taking place on Sprague avenue today. In the last six months "dead" storerooms, by which term is implied stores or offices which do not attract a large daily buying traffic, have been converted into business establishments which draw trade in large volume from day to day.

Plate Glass Replaces Solid Walls

A few years ago the corners were largely large granite boulders or brick walls, with small doorways, and no display window space. In fact, nothing attractive, as the stores were built on old lines. One of the first recent changes was made when the railroad ticket offices moved out from the high rent rooms on Riverside avenue to the block south, where, with large plate glass windows, neatly decorated, gave a semblance of new life. This was evidenced in the improvements wrought by the O. W. R. & N., the Idaho & Washington Northern and the Northern Pacific ticket offices going to Sprague avenue, replacing unattractive establishments which drew only a nominal volume of trade.

This avenue was quite as good for all general purposes for those ticket offices, as the purchasers of transportation are not to any great extent "drop in" business, such as stores on Riverside avenue value highly.

Change on Post Street

The erection of the Eiler piano house, jointly occupied by the Inland Club, brought about a great change on the Post street corner. From a dingy, almost desolate-looking corner this building has changed the corner into one not only attractive, but because of the club advantages brings hundreds more of passersby than formally went that way. Farther west, on Lincoln street, small but attractive retail stores have taken the place of the unattractive stores. At Monroe street, changes have been wrought, that while not materially improvements in one sense have directed and drawn a large daily traffic. And from the traffic past a given point values are largely calculated.

Important change at Stevens Street

The change being affected on Stevens street and Sprague avenue by the Hays & Wooley Company, retail clothiers, is important. The old granite walls once acting as a barrier to retail trade on Stevens street are being replaced by plate glass fronts and wide entrances. The stores that were willing to occupy these closed corners have moved along on the same street to brighter and more attractive storerooms, with the result that in a few weeks a new stream of traffic will be following up and down Sprague avenue. The removal of the Spokane Valley Irrigated Land company office on Washington and Sprague to the upper floors of the Hutton building has made a change there. A neat and attractive confectionery store has replaced it. Here hundreds in a day wait for the cars bound for the south side. The change wrought in the southeast corner of the same junction point, where Ham, Yearsley & Ryrie were established for several years, is important in as much as the Spokane Trunk company has opened up an attractive retail store there. It is not to be doubted that experience has shown that business offices thrive as well or better in the office buildings above ground. Such offices do not bid for "drop-in" trade so much as the retail store does. Retail stores, where buyers can see merchandise displayed, undoubtably give a scene of life and activity which an office cannot hope to give, and the pedestrians are not slow to notice this fact.

Spread of Business General

Among the changes being made or which have been made are the remodeling work on the Groff Tailor shop, the Y. W. C. A. cafeteria, the Arlington hotel on Bernard, the Lyric theater, near Sprague, on Washington; the Stowell drugstore and several smaller but just as important ones.

The entire change is making out of Sprague avenue a more active retail thoroughfare on which practically every commodity can be purchased.

In this connection also it is interesting to note the spread in other directions, such as the enlarging of stores on Riverside avenue, the encroachment of the retail traffic upon Main avenue, as is noticed in the new Martindale store on Post and Main, the new Crescent store on Wall and Main, and among others, Joyners drugstore enlargement on Howard and Main. It is a fact to be reckoned that 1912 is seeing more real enlargement of the retail business district than in any recent year.

Many Attractive Homes Are Being Built in Roosevelt Addition

These homes appeared in the February 4, 1912, *Spokesman-Review* with the following captions: Upper left: Group of homes on 18th Avenue, near Conklin Street. These homes average about $3,000 and are not only well built, but the grounds are well maintained. Upper right: Residence of J. E. Schooley at E. 1007 Seventeenth Avenue. This is a five-room modern residence, built at a cost of about $4,200. Lower left: Home of A. B. Crouch at E. 933 Seventeenth Avenue, being a six-room modern residence, with built-in features, and costing $2,600. Lower right: Home of Mrs. Maud Balder at E. 1206 Sixteenth Avenue, built at a cost of 3,400. J. H. Hariff was the contractor.

This ad, which appeared in the same edition of the *Spokesman-Review,* stated the following:

Have you ever compared an acre tract with a city lot? Here's a little food for thought. A 50 foot city lot is neither productive nor income bearing until you improve it. You pay $200 and upwards for a lot. There are five lots to the acre. That figure is up $1000 or more per acre. These lots may be 25 to 30 miles from Howard and Riverside by streetcar. Now you can buy an acre tract at Meadow Lake the same distance in minutes as the $200 lot above referred to, for $100 an acre and upward. That's $20 or more a lot.

A Meadow Lake tract is income bearing. Each acre can be made to pay you $200 or more each year. You can make your first payment, the land will pay for itself thereafter; that is, if properly cultivated. If you don't, it will still pay for itself in a few years but the enhancement in value, or 10 acre tract at Meadow Lake will eventually become too valuable for garden purposes, and will be cut up into quarter and a half acre tracts. ... You owe it to yourself to take advantage of the opportunity offered, so buy a tract at Meadow Lake right now, before the electric trains are running, and before the prices advance. Tracts hundred dollars an acre up is still the price. Name your own terms.

Seven-room modern house on Fifteenth avenue, near Bernard, bought by G. M. Ferris from Amos Carl for $7000. The deal was made by the Northwest Loan and Trust company.

Residence of L. P. Mailhot at E1707 Mission avenue. It was built at a cost of about $3000.

The following article appeared in the Sunday morning February 11, 1912, *Spokesman-Review*:

Attorney Ferris buys a home, pays $7000 for property on 15th Ave. Attorney G. M. Ferris of Cannon, Swan and Ferris, has purchased from Amos H. Carl, contractor, a seven room modern home on Fifteenth Avenue between Bernard and Butte streets for $7,000. The sale was negotiated by the real estate department of the Northwest Moment Trust Company.

The house occupies lot 20, block 3, South Side Cable Addition. The interior is finished in select curly fir with hardwood floors and has all the modern built-in features. The lower floor has five rooms, including large living room, den, dining room, kitchen and bedroom besides lavatory. The living room has a large Grub [a popular hand-made brand of tile at the time] tile fireplace. The basement of the house is complete being cemented and partitioned. A fruit room, laundry, cold storage and fuel room are provided.

There are two bedrooms and a tile bathroom on the second floor, besides a sleeping balcony. Each bedroom has two large closets.

Attorney G. M. Ferris will make it his new future home.

In the right column is part of an ad covering two full pages in the Wednesday October 14, 1925, *Spokesman-Review* for the "SPOKANE HOME EXPOSITION" Oct. 15 to 21 inclusive. Also, on the top masthead it stated: THE REALTORS WELCOME YOU!

Part of this celebration was a prize of a new house that was to be part of a drawing. It was advertised in the following manner: "This modern four room bungalow, complete in every detail and ready to move into." This was a first-of-a-kind ad which promoted realtors in general, but specifically centered on Spokane's larger real estate companies.

Ad in the June 5, 1910, *Spokesman-Review*.

How Real Estate Was Sold: Ads From Early Real Estate Companies

Scenes in Rockwood, Where Rough Wilderness Is Rapidly Becoming Realm for Costly Homes

The top picture shows the beautiful scenic effect on Highland boulevard and Rockwood boulevard, where the two come to a junction. The upper drive shown in the picture is Highland boulevard, separated from Rockwood boulevard by an attractive parking strip set with trees and shrubs and to be sodded. From this point the scenic view is one perhaps unexcelled anywhere on the South Side. The picture in the center is from a scene on Overbluff road just east of the intersection at Highland. The lower picture shows the terrace separating Rockwood and Highland boulevards. This terrace is planted with various forms of attractive plants. The steps shown in the picture lead from Rockwood boulevard up to Highland boulevard.

Ad in the Sunday morning July 3, 1910, *Spokesman-Review*.

Chapter Nine

LIBERTY LAKE
"Spokane's New Summer Colony"

We have platted a beautiful summer town on the shores of this lake—far famed for its natural beauties and ideal in every respect for a summer resort. Many lots have been spoken for—spoken for by men who will build summer cottages and make their home here during the summer months, a hot weather refuge for Spokane. Liberty Lake has everything that goes to make a lake ideal for such a refuge. Best bathing facilities in the northwest—gently sloping sand beach, warm water, bath houses, bathing suits, springboards and rafts; fine boating and lots of good boats; fishing is good. Car service to the shore of the lake and excellent time schedule. Supplies, ice, etc., easily at hand. We intended placing these lots on the market a month ago, but have met with unavoidable delay. It has been exasperating alike to us and to those anxious to build their summer homes this year, who have besieged us with inquiries. It is with a genuine pleasure, therefore, that we announce

100 Choice, Sightly Lots
Will Be Placed on the Market
Thursday, August First

Please notice—Only 100 lots will be put on the market. That's all that are ready. We have over that many inquiries already, and there will be a decided rush. These lots, as we said, are choice and sightly. All afford a beautiful view of the lake and mountains. Every lot will have spring water and sewer. A look at the plat will satisfy you that this will be one of the most beautiful summer towns in America in a few years. Laid out like a park and will be beautified like a park. The hotel, newly furnished, will be opened to the public August 1, furnishing first-class accommodations to all who come. A new dancing pavilion will be erected in the very near future. Another year thousands of dollars will be spent in further improvements, the plans for which are already made. Take a run out today; ask our campers how the lake suits them. Pick out a location that suits you and drop in and see us Monday. We will be glad to talk it over with you. We regret that this opening sale is so limited, but it's unavoidable. However, if you don't get one of them it will not be our fault, as we've given you fair warning.

Newly Furnished Hotel Will Open August 1

Palouse Land Company
222-5 Lindelle Block, Spokane

This Sunday morning full-page ad in the *Spokesman-Review* introduces the development on Liberty Lake and mentions a new hotel and "summer town."

The Liberty Lake train depot, circa 1912. Inset is Steve Liberty *(Public domain)*

Roderick MacKenzie's hotel, which was advertised in the Liberty Lake ad. MacKenzie came to this area in June of 1890. He purchased 806 acres of land surrounding Liberty Lake where he farmed, built a hotel, and kept a fleet of boats on the lake. By 1912, it was considered one of the most popular resorts in the county. Inset is MacKenzie. *(Public domain)*

Ad in the Sunday morning August 25, 1907, *Spokesman-Review*.

Spokane Association of Realtors®, 1911 to 2011: An Answer to a Calling

On September 2, 1911, the following appeared in the *Spokesman-Review*:

Real Estate Men Elect F. E. Elmendorf President of New Spokane Association

F. E. Elmendorf was elected president of the Spokane Realty association at the luncheon held in the Hall of the Doges, at Davenport's, yesterday; Theodore Genisch secretary and Gordon C. Corbaley vice president. The meeting was attended by about 50 prominent real estate dealers, who enthusiastically endorsed the movement. S. E. Hege and Wilbur S. Yearsley were named to the executive board to serve with the three officers.

The association is primarily a booster organization, which will be maintained in its present semi-business and social form until the first annual meeting, which will be held the last Friday in December this year. At that time new officers will be elected.

At the meeting of the executive board after the luncheon yesterday W. S. Yearsley was requested to prepare a comprehensive review of the progress in the farming communities around Spokane and read it before the meeting two weeks hence.

Other matters of vital importance to the city, such as the apple show, street carnival, crops, interstate fair, railroad rate decisions and new railroad construction, and all issues bearing directly or indirectly upon Spokane's progress will be discussed from time to time.

It was brought out yesterday that there are 497 real estate dealers in Spokane and that on conservative estimate more than 60% of the new capital which has been brought into Spokane from time to time has been through the influence of the real estate men.

Frederic E. Elmendorf

Frederic E. Elmendorf was born in New York state on November 10, 1870. He came to Spokane from Brooklyn in 1891. His first job in Spokane was as a cashier for the street car department of the Washington Water Power Company. On March 25, 1892, he founded the real estate firm and insurance business of Elmendorf & Elmendorf, taking his brother, J. D. Elmendorf, as a partner. His first

Frederic Elmendorf
He became the first president of the Spokane Association of Realtors when it formed in 1911.
(Courtesy Spokane Association of Realtors)

office was located on the second floor of the Jamieson Building, which occupied two rooms. His business later occupied suites in the Traders Bank, which is now the Spokane and Eastern Building, and later in the Rookery Building.

In 1890, F. E. Pope purchased a half interest in the firm, which then became Elmendorf & Pope. In 1920, H. L. Anthony, with others, bought out Pope's interests. He was president of his company up to his retirement, at which time he became chairman of the board. At the time, his firm employed 30 people and was among the larger real estate companies in Spokane.

Mr. Elmendorf served as the first president of the Spokane Board of Realtors from 1911 to 1912, which was at the time a one-year commitment. In addition to real estate, his company also specialized in real estate loans and the insurance business. He was one of the earliest boosters for the Columbia Basin Reclamation and the construction of the Grand Coulee Dam.

Mr. Elmendorf passed away on March 26, 1941. He was survived by his widow, Margaret H. Elmendorf, who lived at the family home at 241 East Ninth; a daughter in Seattle, Mrs. Ron Johnson; and a son, E. A. Elmendorf, in Cleveland, Ohio.

Origin of the word REALTOR®

In 1916, Charles N. Chadbourn, a past president of the Minneapolis Real Estate Board, saw a news headline that read: "Real Estate Man Swindles a Poor Widow." He learned the man, August H. Frederick, was not associated with either a local or national real estate association.

Without some definitive way of conveying to the general public whether or not a "real estate man" was legitimate or was bound by a given code of ethics, this type of case would be allowed to persist. Consequently, Chadbourn coined the word "realtor," and proposed it be used to signify membership in a professional real estate organization.

After Chadbourn's proposal, a resolution was passed on March 27, 1916, making the term REALTOR® official. The term was a formal means of conveying that a real estate agent or broker was a member of the National Association of Real Estate Boards (NAREB).

The national association was founded in Chicago on May 13, 1908, under the name National Association of Real Estate Exchanges. There were 120 founding members, 19 boards, and one state association. The name was changed to National Association of Real Estate Boards in 1916, the same year the term Realtor became official. In 1974, the official name "National Association of Realtors" was adopted. It is now the largest trade association in North America.

When the association formed, its primary objective was "to unite the real estate men of America for the purpose of effectively exerting a combined influence upon matters affecting real estate interests." In 1913, they adopted a Code of Ethics with the Golden Rule as its theme ("do unto others as you would have them do unto you"). The term Realtor® conveyed that the person using the term subscribed to that code of ethics. As such, the term quickly gained acceptance.

On May 18, 1917, the association filed paperwork with the Secretary of State of Illinois to secure a copyright of the word. The collective marks REALTORS® and REALTOR® were then registered with the United States Patent and Trademark Office on September 13, 1949, and January 10, 1950, respectively, under registration numbers 515,200 and 519,789.

The Spokane Association of Realtors

When the Spokane Association of Realtors (SAR) was formed in 1911, it was specifically for the best interest of the public and the individuals in that field. Its purpose was to determine fair market value for both buyers and sellers, and set high industry standards. Its founding took place three years after the National Association of Real Estate Exchanges was formed.

The Spokane Association of Realtors does not have original documentation regarding its founding. However, as nearly as can be ascertained by word of mouth, charter members included the following: Fred E. Baldwin, Fred K. Jones, F. S. Barrett, L. G. McCormick, Phil T. Becher, T. J. Meenach, D. W. Bruins, W. G. Merryweather, W. R. Cooley, W. E. North, Frederick E. Elmendorf, Z. A. Pfile, Jay W. Fancy, C. H. Rogers, Fred B. Grinnell, Carl Shuff, S. E. Hege, George B. Thompson, Arthur D. Jones, and J. E. Watkins.

A rigid test to determine competency in the field is required to become a licensed realtor in the state of Washington. To reflect the outcome of various and ongoing court decisions regarding real estate liability and practices, the paperwork to complete real estate transactions also constantly changes. Every possible loophole is covered to protect both buyer and seller, the goal being total fairness to both parties.

The Spokane Association of Realtors membership is composed of residential and commercial real estate brokers, real estate salespeople, and others engaged in all aspects of the real estate industry, where a state license to practice is required. They are pledged to a code of ethics and standards of practice, which includes duties to clients and customers, the public, and other realtors.

They are required to enforce the code of ethics through a Professional Standards Council or Committee. Trained members of the association form hearing panels charged with the responsibility of hearing testimony and evaluating evidence from complaints filed by the public or other members against association members for alleged violations of the code of ethics.

If the panel finds the member in violation, disciplines recommended may be one or more of the following: a letter of warning or reprimand, educational courses, suspension or expulsion of membership, fines and probation. All recommended disciplines by professional standards hearing panels are subject to the ratification by the Association's board of directors before the discipline takes effect.

According to the records available, the first "Constitution and By-Laws" of the Spokane Realty Board was published on March 19, 1915. The 3.5-by-6-inch publication was 16 pages long and titled *Constitution and By-Laws of the Spokane Realty Board*. Article I of that publication states:

> The name of this Association shall be "Spokane Realty Board." Article II, under objects it states: The objects of this Board shall be to bring the real estate men of Spokane and vicinity together for the advancement of the interest of the real estate business; to secure for the broker the exclusive agency of all property listed or offered for sale by him; to effect uniform rates of commission to be charged in real estate transactions; to create and maintain among members, a high standard of business ability and integrity, and a spirit of fair and honorable competition, assuring to both buyer and seller the services of responsible and trustworthy agents, upon a definite and uniform standard of contracts and charges, to the end that the interests of buyer, seller and broker may be alike protected; to discourage and prevent unfair divisions of brokers' commissions with those not engaged in the real estate business; to encourage and foster all movements in the interest of civic betterment and municipal improvement; to maintain and operate a listing exchange where members may offer exclusive listings to each other, and thereby enable them to better serve owners of property listed for sale by co-operation.

The Spokane Association of Realtors office at 1924 North Ash. Phone number 326-9222. *(Courtesy Tom McArthur)*

Chapter Ten

Joe Mann
2011 President of the
Spokane Association of Realtors

Joe Mann,
2011 President during the
Spokane Board of Realtors centennial

As the president of the Spokane Association of Realtors, Joe Mann wanted to do something to celebrate the Association's centennial and also something that would be of benefit to Spokane. Mostly, he wanted to do something the public would like and that would be educational. What could be a better gift for the realtors in his association to give their customers than a history book of early Spokane?

With that in mind, he contacted Rob Higgins, Association Executive Officer. Together they put their plan into action. They decided this book would be about the city's earliest history and how its homes and buildings played a major part in what Spokane is today.

Joe Mann's background

Joe was born in Albany, Georgia, in September 1946. Following his military service in 1978, he operated a franchise for Success Motivation Institute. His job there was teaching people how to set and achieve goals. In 1980, he went to work as a salesman for Caterpillar Tractor where he worked for a year. In 1981, he was the sales director for a "start-up" computer company, Quality Micro Systems, where he worked until 1988. When he began working for that company, he was the 80th employee; by 1988, he helped build the company up to 1,300 employees.

In 1988, Joe was recruited by another technology company, which was located in Seattle, as vice president of sales and marketing where he worked until 1989. From there he was again recruited to Output Technology (OTC) of Spokane to head the European Operations Divisions from 1989 to 1991. During that job he lived in the Netherlands. In 1991 Joe moved to Spokane. In 1993 he became a realtor.

Joe and his wife, Joyce, live in the Spokane Valley. They will celebrate 22 years of marriage on November 18, 2011. They were married in 1989 in Upland, California, and have three children, two boys and a girl.

Joe was a member of the U.S. Air Force from 1969 to 1978 with the rank of captain at a radar site outside of Da Nang, Viet Nam. His last military assignment was on the faculty of Air University teaching leadership to captains and lieutenants. His education includes a BS in chemistry from Auburn University in 1968 and MS in Systems Management, University of Southern California in 1975. He was also a graduate of the Dale Carnegie School in 2008.

Joe has served as a Washington State Certified Real Estate Instructor since 1995 to the present. In 2004 he was voted "Most Inspirational" by his peers at Windermere Valley. In 2011 he was voted to be Spokane Association of Realtors' President.

Prior to that he was chosen to be Director of the Spokane Association of Realtors, 2009-2010. He is also a Football Referee/Official and has been an American Legion Baseball Commissioner. In 2000 he joined the Spokane County Board of Equalization (currently Chair) and has served as the City of Spokane Valley Planning Commissioner since 2008. He also works with a number of charities.

Robert M. Higgins, Executive Vice President Association of Realtors

Rob Higgins was hired to serve as the Executive Vice President of the Spokane Board of Realtors in June of 1985.

Rob was born in Wallace, Idaho, in June 1948. His parents were both born in Spokane and prior to Rob's first birthday they had moved the family back to Spokane.

**Robert M. Higgins,
Executive Vice President
Spokane Association of Realtors**

He attended grade school and high school in Spokane. He attended Gonzaga University for two years and graduated from Eastern Washington University in 1971. He served as an officer in the U.S. Army from 1971-1974. After his military service, Higgins earned a masters degree from Texas A & M University.

He and his wife Barbara were married in Texas in 1974. They moved back to Spokane after graduate school in 1976. They have three children and four grandchildren.

Upon moving back to Spokane, Higgins was hired as the Executive Director of the Spokane Taxpayers Association. He left the Taxpayers Association in 1979 and began his real estate career as a real estate salesperson with Wolff & Walker, Inc. in the Spokane Valley. He worked in commercial real estate until he became the EVP of the Spokane Board of Realtors in 1985.

Rob has served four different terms on the Spokane City Council. He was fist elected to the Spokane City Council in 1981 and again in 1985. He served as mayor pro-tem for the city from 1982 through 1989. He again served on the Spokane City Council from 1998 through 2003. He was elected Spokane's first City Council president in 2000, serving in that position from 2001 through 2003.

Higgins received a gubernatorial appointment to the Washington State Transportation Commission in 1990, serving on the Commission for two years. He also served on the Governor's Blue Ribbon Committee on Transportation in the mid-nineties.

Rob was recognized by the Spokane Association of Realtors with a special recognition of appreciation and was recognized by the Washington Association of Realtors as the 2003 Association Executive of the Year.

He is proud to be serving as the EVP of the Spokane Association of Realtors and feels privileged to be working with President Joe Mann and all the many volunteers as we celebrate our Centennial year in 2011.

Chapter Ten

Presidents of the Spokane Board of Realtors
1911 to 2011

1911	F. E. Elmendorf	1962	V. A. Widmer
1912	Carl Shuff	1963	George C. Nichols
1913	W. E. North	1964	Clark C. Hege
1914	S. E. Hege	1965	James S. Black
1915	George B. Thompson	1966	Charles A. Sullivan
1916	Fred K. Jones	1967	Carl Guenzel
1917	L. G. McCormick	1968	Thomas G. Brown
1918	F. E. Pope	1969	C. Fritz Nelson
1919	J. E. Watkins	1970	Lloyd Roach
1920	Arthur D. Jones	1971	H. A. Everest
1921	F. S. Barrett	1972	Charles Stolz
1922	F. W. Anderson	1973	Chet G. Arnold
1923	Robert Grinnell	1974	Leroy Johnson
1924	Phil T. Becher	1975	Jack Maselli
1925	Paul A. Schedler	1976	Howard B. Ness
1926	C. M. Cryor	1977	Robert Viall
1927	Charles Freese	1978	David L. Chantry
1928	L. W. Merager	1979	C. Pat Haskins
1929	Walter Merryweather	1980	Ed Kiemle, Jr.
1930	Ralph W. Watson	1981	Lynda Maselli
1931	W. R. Orndorff	1982	Bill Hunt
1932	W. R. Orndorff	1983	Jim Cory
1933	T. J. Meenach	1984	Bill Feldman
1934	T. J. Meenach	1985	Don Walker
1935	R. R. Rogers	1986	Beverly Numbers
1936	R. R. Rogers	1987	Doreen Underwood
1937	Ford S. Barrett Jr.	1988	Gerald Hagood
1938	Ford S. Barrett Jr.	1989	Jim Carollo
1939	Arthur D. Jones, Jr.	1990	Terence Sullivan
1940	Charles W. Eggert	1991	Gerald E. Boyd
1941	Lowell M. Baker	1992	Claudia Kehoe
1942	C. A. Hines	1993	Ron Criscione
1943	J. L. Siegmund	1994	David R. Black
1944	Clarence M. Livingston	1995	Beverly Gates
1945	R. J. Burns	1996	Thomas A. Crowley
1946	H. Y. Moser	1997	Greg Benner
1947	Carl Hege	1998	Mitch Swenson
1948	Clyde H. Jones	1999	Bob Robideaux
1949	G. E. Brede	2000	Sabrina Jones
1950	A. J. Zerbach	2001	Steve Flinn
1951	C. Emery Bear	2002	Jack Morse
1952	Ray T. Bigelow	2003	Jim Dashiell
1953	Ray Orth	2004	Sandy Alderman
1954	Wayne T. Tefft	2005	Dave Crosby
1955	R. C. Goodrich	2006	Vic Plese
1956	Dean H. Burns	2007	James Young
1957	Wm. O. Marshall	2008	Patti McKerricher-Boyd
1958	Alvin J. Wolff	2009	Jeannette Karis
1959	Alvin J. Wolff	2010	Linda Miller
1960	Wm. C. Spedden	2011	Joe Mann
1961	Joseph P. Wieber		

Spokane's Oldest Real Estate Companies

Arthur Delos Jones, 1859-1934

By 1912, Arthur Jones had acquired the reputation as the owner of the oldest and largest real estate firm in the city of Spokane.

Born in 1859 on a farm in Cass County, Michigan, Jones spent the first 18 years of his life living and working on his parents' farm. He received his higher education in Iowa. He then worked for a short time as a school teacher and in the advertisement industry.

In 1887 Jones moved to Spokane to be near his sweetheart, Ada Stinson. He married her on Christmas Day that same year. Following their marriage, he spent the rest of his life in Spokane becoming involved in the real estate and insurance businesses. He soon rose to the highest level of accomplishment in his industry. His businesses included real estate, rental, loan and bond departments. He was also the manager for numerous land companies and a stockholder in four Spokane banks. During much of his life in the Spokane area, he owned a 2,000-acre wheat farm at Liberty Lake.

As a real estate developer, Jones was a major force in the development of numerous "additions" within the city and a number of town sites. Some of the additions he platted include Hillyard (plus Hillyard's Second and Third Additions), Richland Park, The Hill, and Cannon Hill Park. Some of the town sites he platted were Valleyford, Steptoe, Parkwater, Freeman, Mount Hope, Waverly Heights, Spring Valley, Geary Fairbanks, Oroville Acres, Sprague Avenue Addition and Hayford.

Among the major highlights of Jones's career was being one of the original promoters of the Grand Coulee Dam project. Other major real estate ventures he was involved in included the procurement and selling of the original post office site at Riverside and Lincoln to the government and securing the property for the Davenport Hotel for Louis Davenport and his investors.

Many of the landmark buildings in Spokane today are products of Jones' efforts. His firm received the contracts, financed by F. Lewis Clark, to build the Empire State Building at Riverside and Lincoln and the old Spokane Club at Washington and Riverside (later known as the Chamber of Commerce Building, the Metals Building and the American Legion). They also built the following buildings: Pedicord Hotel, Riverside Court Building, the Somerset, the Rombeck, the Wolverton, the Galena, the Chamberland Garage, the Chronicle, and the annex to the Temple Court. The Arthur Jones Company was also the agent for the Review and Chronicle buildings.

Mr. Jones was a member of the Spokane City Council from 1891 to 1893 and one of the six founders of the Spokane Chamber of Commerce, which was founded in 1897. He was also a member of the "Good Roads Association," a 32nd degree Mason and Shriner, and a member of the Spokane City and Country Clubs.

Arthur and Ada Jones had three children. Of the three, W, Scott Stinson Jones was the only one who remained in Spokane to continue the family business. Scott married Edith M. Kemp in 1915. He met her in a Sunday school class in the balcony of the First Baptist Church in Spokane. It was love at first sight, and their marriage lasted until her death in 1945. Seven years later, Scott married LaVina H. Green.

During the later years of Scott's career, much of the family business was sold to James S. Black, whose son Dave Black carries on the business in partnership with Bob Tomlinson. Because of Tomlinson-Black's roots in the Arthur Jones Company, it is technically the oldest real estate company in the Inland Northwest. It is also the largest.

Arthur D. Jones, who died in 1934 at the age of 74, was truly one of the Inland Northwest's major pioneer builders, contributing substantially to the development of the area. Even today, generations of his descendants and their families remain in Spokane in successful business pursuits.

Arthur D. Jones and friends exiting the driveway of his home at 1718 West Riverside Avenue, circa 1910. Inset: This 1910 *Spokane Chronicle* ad states that Arthur D. Jones & Co., established in 1887, is the oldest real estate firm in Spokane. *(Courtesy Jim & Milaine McGoldrick)*

The Arthur D. Jones Company was located in the Wolverton Block for several of its earlier years. The photo of this building states on the front and flag "Arthur Jones Real Estate." This photo appeared on page 18 of the 1889 *Spokane Falls Illustrated*. A photo of the same building also appeared in that publication on page 21, entitled "Spokane Hardware," and again on page 22 as Clough & Graves Real Estate. During most of Jones's business career, his office was at 125 South Lincoln. For a number of years, he also maintained an office in the Hillyard area.

An Article appeared in the January 8, 1911, *Spokesman-Review* that describes the Arthur D. Jones business and new building:

BIG REALTY FIRM IN NEW HOME
FROM DESK ROOM IN 1887, ARTHUR D
JONES AND COMPANY GROWS RAPIDLY
HAS BUILDING OF ITS OWN
FIRM IS REORGANIZED SOME OF THE OLD
EMPLOYEES BY STOCK IN CONCERN –
MODEL OFFICES FITTED UP.

From the desk room in judge Mickle's office in the old Wolverton building to elaborate offices in a new building built by the company, Arthur D. Jones and Company has made a study advance in 23 years which is interesting, not only to the Spokane pioneer, but to the younger generation who watched the perseverance of local concerns and their faith in Spokane.

Arthur D Jones and Company, one of the largest real estate firms in the city, has just moved to its new home in the Arthur G Jones building on the southwest corner of Main Avenue and Lincoln Street. The building was erected at a cost of $78,000 and the office fitted up at an expense of about $16,000. It is designed as a permanent home of the company, which until recently consisted of Mr. Jones himself. A few months ago, however, some of the older employees of the firm bought stock in the organization and the company was formed, although the firm has been incorporated for some years.

Firm organized in 1887.

The history of the firm dates back to 1887, when Mr. Jones opened up the real estate business in judge Mickles office, who was then city Attorney. It was a full year before he made a single deal. Today his company does $1,500,000 worth of real estate business alone, besides a heavy insurance, mortgage and rental business.

During the big fire of 1889, Mr. Jones was burned out, as were many others, and among the striving real estate men of that day now prominent in city affairs were C. F. Clough and J. P. Graves. After the fire Mr. Jones opened up in the Crescent building on Riverside, near Monroe, renting an office for $75, which a few hours before, went begging for $15. From there to the old green block on Riverside, then to an office on the site now occupied by the Old National Bank Building, then to First Avenue, near Stevens Street, the Temple court and the Exchange Bank Annex, and eventually to the Empire State building was that itinerary of Mr. Jones, known as Arthur D. Jones and Company. It was 10 years ago that the office was moved to the third floor of the Empire State, and a short time later to the ground floor office, occupied until the new building on Lincoln was completed a few weeks ago.

Started on nothing

Starting on nothing Mr. Jones has worked up a big business, not only in real estate but also in the insurance, bonds and mortgage business, not to mention the rental business, now a large factor. The company was incorporated about 17 years ago for $20,000. Later it was increased to 50,000 and at present is 100,000. The new home of the company is perhaps one of the finest offices in the city. It has been planned as a model real estate office. The building is 110 x 60', with plate glass front on four sides. It has two stories and basement. The second floor is elaborately finished in marble, with terrazzo floor in the hall and hard maple in the offices, which are unusually large, averaging about 20 ft. square. The finish is quarter sawed oak and a large vault is provided for the tenants. The basement is equally well-finished. C. Z. Hubble was the architect.

The Arthur D. Jones office building at 125 South Lincoln. It was demolished in 1940 to make way for an addition to the downtown Post office.
(Public domain)

Anthony, Baker & Burns

Anthony, Baker & Burns, founded in 1892 and originally called Elmendorf & Pope, is the second oldest real estate company in Spokane (they closed their doors in 2010). The history of Anthony, Baker & Burns was written in 1960 and was included in their *Office Policies and Procedures* manual. It contains their general history up to that time:

> The firm was organized in 1892 and has been in continuous operation since that time under five different names. The employees are all proud of the fact that they work for a firm that has been in business over 66 years and enjoys a good reputation. The firm was organized by F. E, Elmendorf. For a short time, his brother joined him, and the firm became known as Elmendorf and Elmendorf. In 1916, Mr. Pope bought an interest and the name was changed to Elmendorf and Pope. In 1921, H. T. Anthony joined the firm and soon thereafter purchased the interest of Mr. Pope, and in 1927 the firm name was changed to Elmendorf-Anthony Company. In the year 1927 Lowell Baker joined the Mortgage Department, and in 1932 Ron Burns became connected with the firm. In 1944 the Elmendorf-Anthony Company, a Corporation, sold its business to a partnership composed of H. T. Anthony, Lowell M. Baker and Ron J. Burns.
>
> In 1946 the firm name was changed to Anthony, Baker & Burns, a partnership. At the same time the separate corporation name was changed to Anthony, Baker & Burns, Inc., which corporation is required by FHA to handle mortgage business. The partnership, however, controls the mortgage business. In 1958 the interest of H. T. Anthony was purchased by R. J. Burns and Lowell Baker, who in turn sold part of Mr. Anthony's interest to R. C. Hunner, Wallace Baker and Dean Burns. H. T. Anthony is still connected with the company and is the president and owner of Anthony, Baker & Burns, Inc. The managing partners of the partnership are Lowell Baker and Ron J. Burns.

F. S. Barrett & Company

F. S. Barrett & Company Realtors was founded in 1894. F. S. Barrett is the oldest real estate company in Spokane to always go by the same name. They ceased doing business in 2009.

The Future of Real Estate
by Joe Mann, President, Spokane Association of Realtors

Is home ownership continuing as an "American Dream"? Will buyers and sellers still use Realtors? Will there be single family homes 100 years from now? How will the laws governing real estate change? What will happen to the real estate buying and selling process? Will the "Green" movement actually become a market? Will home and property values continue to increase at the annual pace of the last 100 years? These questions and more bounce around in the heads of economists, financial planners, politicians and even the average person on the street.

There are some things about the future that one can readily see, but there are many more that are dim and fuzzy. There are sure to be events that will occur and circumstances to affect real estate that no one now sees or even suspects. What are those things that the future will bring? This chapter predicts a few.

Technology

In the U.S., we are all becoming more technology-savvy and involved with it from necessity. Our homes are "climate controlled". Lights turn on when we clap our the hands or enter a room. We sleep on light-weight adjustable air mattresses or "memory foam" beds. New materials that are lighter, softer, warmer or cooler, better insulated, lower cost, longer lasting or simply easier to clean are being introduced into home construction.

Prepare for homes to begin to change even more as energy efficiencies determine how we live. Homes will be smaller, use more sustainable technology (meaning "green"), and will have more built-in technology for cleaning and maintenance. Some will use recycled materials and even more will have easily replaced components.

Expect home "life spans" to get longer and longer. Yet, Americans will still want differentiation and uniqueness in their homes. Some will still want that custom home on a hill that is expensive and a status symbol.

Homes

As our population increases worldwide, the basic needs for food, clothing and shelter will increase. In addition, as we become accustomed to more information availability, we will want more and better comforts. Our homes will have more creature comforts and be easier to live in. Today, there is a trend toward more urban living. Look for more ways for people to own single family dwellings, but in more densely populated areas. "Zero lot line" or "shared wall" homes will proliferate. Since transportation will continue to be more expensive, expect people to have less need for private transport and demand more public conveyances. We will find ways to move more people more conveniently than ever before. These changes will dictate more "clustered" living. Also, we will need highly efficient delivery systems that provide homes with the necessities.

Lifestyle

We will see the corner grocery store go away. Instead the mega stores will deliver to housing complexes that will have a central receiving location for homeowners to pick up their food orders. More naturally-grown food will be available, but it will be grown on ever-smaller tracts of land. New efficiencies in growing crops will see year-round production of previously seasonal crops. In America we will import more and more food since the costs of producing within the United States will begin to prohibit farming as we know it today.

Many more people will "telecommute" and otherwise work from home. Therefore, their housing needs will require very high speed communications and systems built into the home. In addition, they will have needs for exercise, recreation and entertainment in the home or very close by.

Many families are having children much later in life, so they may postpone buying a home until they are ready to have children. However, as the population grows so will housing needs. Because couples will postpone having children, they will also postpone buying a home. Most will rent close to their work. More rental units will be built, and more investors who own those units will enter the market.

The Industry

Real Estate as a career will continue in its climb to more professionalism and technical expertise. More people are entering the profession with advanced educations, universities are offering degrees in Real Estate, and the requirements for licensing are becoming more stringent.

The expenses and continuing educational requirements are trending upward. More and more in the future, realtors will have to work full time. Realtors will have to be career-minded in order to keep up with the requirements.

In addition, realtors are becoming more mobile. "Mobility" or having all real estate data at your fingertips is becoming the norm. Whether in a cellular telephone or some other lightweight mobile electronic device, all data pertaining to any property is readily available. Look for this trend to continue into the next century. Easy access to information is a demand from children to the elderly. Real estate will be no exception.

As legal requirements of home ownership become increasingly intricate, more home owners will require the services of realtors. The realtor will be required to become more legally competent than ever before and be able to explain difficult legal issues without giving legal advice. The function of providing legal advice will continue to be exclusively limited to lawyers.

Realtors' services will change. The industry will have to change to serve a public with more requirements for new kinds of information than ever. Realtors will be more disciplined, more professional, and more competent simply because the public will demand it. Look for more distinctive brands offering more beneficial services. The expense of providing that information will increase. Look for fewer small firms except in very small markets.

The National Association of Realtors will become more powerful as a professional organization with strong influence in the political area at all levels. More licensees will become Realtors than ever before because of the expanding benefits of membership including legal representation, political clout and defense of property rights and the profession of Realtor.

Home Buying and Selling

The Statute of Frauds in all states which requires real estate transactions to be in writing will be modified to allow for electronic contracts that are legal and binding. This will include texting via cell phone and messages via other media not yet invented. The documents necessary will become less complex in order to accommodate the efficiencies of electronic media.

However, home buyers will still need to "experience" a home. No amount of electronics will replace the buyer's need to touch, feel, smell and taste the atmosphere of a home. New technologies will be developed to allow the buyer to virtually "see" a neighborhood and the siting of individual homes, but nothing will be able to replace the sensory experience of walking through a home to feel how a breeze flows through, or the texture of a hardwood floor or a stone countertop.

Only a Realtor-conducted tour will help a potential buyer to talk through and experience a home before making a purchasing decision. In addition, the Realtor will continue to serve as a trusted advisor for things the buyer wouldn't know before buying, such as was the home subject to liens, or was the neighborhood built with private street or public street requirements.

Going Green

This "movement" will become a mainstream market in real estate. Regardless of the political and ideological debate on this subject, we have limited resources for building structures. Many however, are renewable. Look for more construction materials to be renewable. You will see more regulation to govern how we use scarcer materials. And, other regulations will require "recycling" of home building materials.

The electrical grid in the United States will have to be upgraded, expanded and improved to allow more efficient power transmission. In addition, the utilities will have to allow for more homeowners to produce their own energy and sell the surplus to them. The energy system will have to have the capacity for surges in availability and storage of energy. Once cost-efficient electrical storage is developed, look for more wind farms and other technologies to generate electricity to appear on the market.

Electric cars will lose their attraction as owners discover the enormous cost of removing, destroying and replacing batteries. More "hybrid" technologies will come about especially in the area of transportation, home heating and communications. Energy creation and use will become to driving economic engine in the United States.

In short, the future for real estate in general, and home ownership in particular looks bright. Our history clearly has indicated "under all is the land…" That won't change.

Appendix
Historic Downtown Buildings
Compiled by Rob Higgins and Doris Woodward
Sources used: Historical Preservation Study (City-County of Spokane) and
Spokane Building Blocks by W. W. Hyslop (1983)

ALGER-BRISTOL HOTEL, 1904
  (same name today)
  210 S. Sprague Avenue
  Architect/Builder: Unknown

AMERICAN LEGION, 1901
  (same name today)
  108 N. Washington Street
  Architect/Builder: John K. Dow

ARMSTRONG HOTEL BUILDING, 1903
  (Home of Jacoy's)
  N.W. Corner Sprague & Washington
  Architect/Builder: Unknown

AVENIDA APARTMENTS, 1909
  (same name today)
  2009 W. Pacific Avenue
  Architect/Builder: W. W. Hyslop

BALKAN HOTEL, 1908
  (Community Building)
  31 W. Main Avenue
  Architect/Builder: C. E. Wentzel

BENNETT BLOCK, 1890
  N.E. Corner Main & Howard
  Architect/Builder: Unknown

BRESLIN APARTMENTS, 1910
  (same name today)
  729 S. Bernard Street
  Architect/Builder: Albert Held

BROADVIEW DAIRY, 1910
  (same name today)
  411 W. Cataldo Avenue
  Architect/Builder: R. Edward Vincent

BROADWAY PHARMACY, 1910
  (Bryant Apartments)
  1704 W. Broadway Avenue
  Architect/Builder: Unknown

BUCHANAN BUILDING, 1911
  (same name today)
  28 W. Third Avenue
  Architect/Builder: F. P. Rooney
     & L. R. Stritesky

CAMBERN DUTCH SHOP WINDMILL, 1929
  (Lorien Herbs & Natural Foods)
  1102 S. Perry Street
  Architect/Builder: Charles R. Wood

CARNEGIE LIBRARY, East Side Branch, 1914
  (same name today)
  25 S. Altamont Street
  Architect/Builder: Albert Held

CARNEGIE LIBRARY, Heath Branch, 1914
  (same name today)
  525 E. Mission Avenue
  Architect/Builder: Julius Zittel

CARNEGIE LIBRARY, Main Branch, 1904
  (same name today)
  10 S. Cedar Street
  Architect/Builder: Preusse & Zittel

CARNEGIE LIBRARY, North Monroe Branch, 1914
  (same name today)
  925 W. Montgomery Avenue
  Architect/Builder: Albert Held

CASCADE LAUNDRY COMPANY, 1913
  (same name today)
  1007 W. Spokane Falls Blvd.
  Architect/Builder: Loren L. Rand

CEDARS APARTMENTS, 1911
  (same name today)
  508 S. Cedar Street
  Architect/Builder: Edward J. Baum

CHAMBER OF COMMERCE BUILDING, 1931
  N Side Riverside, W of Monroe
  Architect/Builder: Unknown

CLEMMER THEATER, 1915
  (Bing Crosby Theater, formerly The Met)
  901 W. Sprague Avenue
  Architect/Builder: E. W. Houghton

COLTON-REILLY AUTO COMPANY AND FISK
RUBBER COMPANY BUILDINGS, 1911
  (same name today)
  914-930 W. Second Avenue
  Architect/Builder: Unknown

COLUMBIA BUILDING, 1907
  S.E. Corner First & Howard
  Architect/Builder: Unknown

COMMERCIAL BLOCK, 1906
  (same name today)
  1111-1119 W. First Avenue
  Architect/Builder: Isaac J. Galbraith

COMMISSION BUILDING, 1906
  (same name today)
  216 W. Pacific Avenue
  Architect/Builder: James M. Geraghty

CRESCENT BUILDING, 1917
  (The Crescent)
  701 W. Main Avenue
  Architect/Builder: Loren L. Rand

CROWE & COMPANY, 1909
    (Luminaria)
    154 S. Madison Street
    Architect/Builder: Unknown

DAVENPORT HOTEL, 1914
    (same name today)
    10 S. Post Street
    Architect: Kirtland K. Cutter & G. A. Pehrson

DOWLING & CATTLE WAREHOUSE, 1911
    (same name today)
    117 W. Pacific Avenue
    Architect/Builder: Unknown

ELDRIDGE BUILDING, 1925
    (Rocket Bakery)
    1319-1325 W. First Avenue
    Architect/Builder: Gustav Pehrson

ELEKTRO-COLD, 1900
    (Joel's, now Churchill's)
    E. Side Post, S. of Railroad
    Architect/Builder: Unknown

ELKS CLUB, 1919
    (North Coast Life)
    1114 W. Riverside Avenue
    Architect/Builder: Edward J. Baume & K. K. Cutter

EMPIRE STATE BUILDING, 1900
    (Great Western Building)
    901 W. Riverside Avenue
    Architect/Builder: John K. Dow

FERNWELL BUILDING, 1890
    (same name today)
    505 W. Riverside Avenue
    Architect/Builder: Herman Preusse

FINCH MEMORIAL NURSES HOME, 1929
    (same name today)
    852 N. Summit Boulevard
    Architect/Builder: Whitehouse & Price

FIRE STATION NO. 1, 1890
    N. Side First E. of Stevens
    Architect/Builder Unknown

FIRE STATION NO. 3, 1912
    (same name today)
    1229 N. Monroe Street
    Architect/Builder: Unknown

FIRE STATION NO. 9, 1930
    (same name today)
    804 S. Monroe Street
    Architect/Builder: Arthur Cowley

FIRST CONGREGATIONAL CHURCH of Spokane, 1890
    (same name today)
    411 S. Washington Street
    Architect/Builder: John K. Dow & Worthy Niver

FOX THEATER, 1930
    (Martin Woldson Theater at the Fox)
    1001 W. Sprague Avenue
    Architect/Builder: Robert Reamer
    and Whitehouse & Price

FREQUENCY CHANGING STATION, 1908
    (same name today)
    1421 E. Celesta Avenue
    Architect/Builder: Albert Held

FULLER COMPANY WAREHOUSE, 1919
    (W. P. Fuller & Company Warehouse)
    111-115 E. Desmet Avenue
    Architect/Builder: Unknown

GERMOND BLOCK, 1890
    (same name today)
    816-830 W. Sprague Avenue
    Architect/Builder: Reid Brothers
    of San Diego

GLOBE HOTEL, 1908
    (same name today)
    204 N. Division Street
    Architect/Builder: Albert Held

GREEN-HUGHES Printing Company Building, 1911
    (same name today)
    19 W. Pacific Avenue
    Architect/Builder: Unknown

HALE BLOC, 1905
    (same name today)
    231 W. Riverside Avenue
    Architect/Builder: Unknown

HILLYARD HIGH SCHOOL, 1912
    (same name today)
    5313 N. Regal Street
    Architect/Builder: Westcott & Gifford

HOLLEY-MASON Hardware Building, 1905
    (same name today)
    157 W. Howard Street
    Architect/Builder: Albert Held

HOME TELEPHONE & TELEGRAPH Building, 1907
    (same name today)
    165 S. Howard Street
    Architect/Builder: Albert Held

HOTEL UPTON, 1910
    (Grand Coulee Building)
    106 S. Cedar Street
    Architect/Builder: Loren L. Rand

HOXSEY BLOCK, 1910
    (same name today)
    1002-1014 S. Perry Street
    Architect/Builder: Art Bengel

HUGHES & CO. PLUMBERS, 1912
    (Kershaw's)
    E. Side Howard N. of tracks
    Architect/Builder: Unknown

HUTTON BUILDING, 1907
    (same name today)
    9 S. Washington Street
    Architect/Builder: John K. Dow & Clarence Hubbell

INLAND CASKET COMPANY FACTORY, 1910
    (same name today)
    2320 N. Atlantic Street
    Architect/Builder: Ballard Plannery
    and G. A. Pehrson

KEMP & HEBERT BUILDING, 1908
    (Auntie's Bookstore, formerly Liberty Furniture)
    402 W. Main Avenue
    Architect/Builder: Alfred Jones

KNIGHTS OF PYTHIAS, 1912
    (N.A.C.)
    S.W. Corner Riverside & Jefferson
    Architect/Builder: Unknown

LANG BUILDING, 1890
    (Grand Army Hall/Grand Armory Hall)
    115 N. Washington Street
    Architect/Builder: Worthy Niver

LEVY BLOCK, 1892
    (same name today)
    118 N. Stevens Street
    Architect/Builder: Uknown

LOEWENBERG BUILDING, 1890
    S.E. Corner Spokane Falls Blvd.
    & Howard Street
    Architect/Builder: Unknown

LORRAINE HOTEL, 1909
    (same name today)
    308 W. First Avenue
    Architect/Builder: Loren L. Rand

MADISON HOTEL, 1907
    (unoccupied)
    S.E. Corner First & Madison
    Architect/Builder: Unknown

MASONIC CENTER, 1905
    (same name today)
    1108 W. Riverside Avenue
    Architect/Builder: Rand & Dow
    and Rigg & Van Tyne

MEAROW BLOCK, 1905
    (Richmond Hotel)
    225 W. Riverside Avenue
    Architect/Builder: Unknown

METROPOLE APARTMENTS, 1901
    (same name today)
    178½ S. Howard Street
    Architect/Builder: Charles F. White

MILLER BUILDING, 1890
    (Hotel Lusso)
    808 W. Sprague Avenue
    Architect/Builder: William J. Carpenter

MONTGOMERY WARD BUILDING, 1929
    (Spokane City Hall)
    808 W. Spokane Falls Boulevard
    Architect/Builder: Unknown

MONTVALE BLOCK, 1899
    (Montvale Hotel)
    1001 W. First Avenue
    Architect/Builder: Unknown

MORGAN BLOCK, 1909
    (Fairmont Hotel)
    315 W. Riverside Avenue
    Architect/Builder: Alfred Jones

NATIONAL HOTEL, 1905
    (same name today)
    201 W. Riverside Avenue
    Architect/Builder: Unknown

NEW MADISON HOTEL, 1906
    (same name today)
    1020-1029 W. First Avenue
    Architect/Builder: Unknown

NORTHERN PACIFIC DEPOT, 1890
    First Avenue and Bernard

ODD FELLOWS 100F LODGE, 1909
    (IOOF Lodge, Odd Fellows Building)
    1015-1017 W. First Avenue
    Architect/Builder: Albert Held &
    P. L. Peterson

OLD SPOKANE CITY HALL, 1912
    (same name today)
    221 N. Wall Street
    Architect/Builder: Julius Zittel

OLD NATIONAL BANK BUILDING, 1910
    N.E. Corner Riverside & Stevens
    Architect/Builder: Unknown

OUR LADY OF LOURDES CATHEDRAL, 1904
    Riverside & Madison
    Architect/Builder: Unknown

PARSONS HOTEL, 1910
    S.W. Corner First & Jefferson
    Architect/Builder: Unknown

PAULSEN BUILDING, 1908
    (The Paulsen Center)
    415-427 W. Riverside Avenue
    Architect/Builder: Dow & Hubbell

PAULSEN DENTAL AND MEDICAL BUILDING, 1927
    (same name today)
    407 West Riverside Avenue
    Architec Gustav Pehrson

PEDICORD HOTEL, 1893, 1902
    (same name today)
    S. Side Riverside, W. of Browne
    Architect/Builder: Unknown

PEYTON BUILDING & ANNEX, 1898
    (same name today)
    722 W. Sprague Avenue
    Architect/Builder: Herman Preusse, Kirtland
    K. Cutter & Karl Malmgren and
    Robert Sweatt & Archibald Rigg

POLYNESIA, 1965
(Black Angus, now Anthony's)
N.E. Corner Bridge & Lincoln
Architect/Builder: Unknown

REALTY BUILDING, 1910
(The Delaney Apartments)
N. Side of Riverside, E. of Bernard
Architect/Builder: Albert Held
& H. J. Farney

REVIEW BUILDING, 1890
(same name today)
999 W. Riverside Avenue
Architect/Builder: Chauncey B. Seaton

ROBERTSON BUILDING, 1913
(Glen Dow Academy)
307-309 W. Riverside Avenue
Architect/Builder: Kirtland K. Cutter
& Karl Malmgren

ROUNDUP GROCERY WAREHOUSE, 1948
(Thomas Hammer Coffee)
210 W. Pacific Avenue
Architect/Builder: Unknown

SAFE DEPOSIT BUILDING, 1895
(later called Barrett Building,
F. S. Barrett Realty Co.)
N. Side Sprague, E. of Stevens
Architect/Builder: Unknown

SALVATION ARMY BUILDING, 1921
(Luigi's Italian Restaurant)
248 W. Main Avenue
Architect/Builder: Archibald C. Rigg

SAN MARCO APARTMENTS, 1904
(same name today)
1229 W. Riverside Avenue
Architect/Builder: Albert Held

SARANAC HOTEL, 1909
(same name today)
25-29 W. Main Avenue
Architect/Builder: H. M. Keeny

SCHADE BREWERY, 1903
(now Schade Towers)
East Side of Sheridan between
Spokane Falls Blvd. & Olive
Architect/Builder: Unknown

SEARS & ROEBUCK BUILDIING
(Spokane Public Library, demolished)
906 W. Main Avenue
Architect/Builder: Sears & Roebuck

SEEHORN STORAGE & TRANSFER CO., 1898
(Seehorn-Lang Building)
165 S. Lincoln Street
Architect/Builder: Unknown

SMITH FUNERAL, 1912
(North Coast Life Insurance Co.)
1124 W. Riverside Avenue
Architect/Builder: Jones & Levesque

SPOKANE CLUB, 1911
(same name today)
1002 W. Riverside Avenue
Architect/Builder: Kirtland K. Cutter

SPOKANE COUNTY COURTHOUSE, 1894
(same name today)
1116 W. Broadway Avenue
Architect/Builder: Willis A. Ritchie
& David Fotheringham

SPOKANE FLOUR MILL, 1895
(same name today)
621 W. Mallon Avenue
Architect/Builder: E. P. Allis

STEAM PLANT SQUARE, 1916
(same name today)
850 W. Steam Plant Alley
Architect/Builder: Cutter & Malmgren

SYMONS BLOCK, 1917
(same name today)
525 W. Sprague Avenue
Architect/Builder: Rigg & Van Tyne

TRANSIENT HOTEL, 1904
(Minnesota Building)
423 W. First Avenue
Architect/Builder: C. Ferris White

WASHINGTON CRACKER COMPANY, 1904
(same name today)
304 W. Pacific Avenue
Architect/Builder: Unknown

WASHINGTON FURNITURE BUILDING, 1909
(Community Building)
35 W. Main Avenue
Architect/Builder: Unknown

WASHINGTON POST BUILDING, 1902
(same name today)
223 W. Second Avenue
Architect/Builder: Unknown

WASHINGTON WATER POWER SUBSTATION, 1909
On the river at Post street
Architect : Cutter and Malmgren

WHITTEN BLOCK, 1889
(Post Street Ale House)
1 N. Post Street
Architect/Builder: Lorenzo Boardman

WILLARD HOTEL, 1911
(Otis Hotel)
1101-1109 W. First Avenue
Architect/Builder: Arthur Cowley
and Archibald Rigg

WOODWARD BUILDING, 1890
(Soulful Soups)
117 N. Howard Street
Architect/Builder: Herman Preusse

Selected Bibliography

A History The Washington Water Power Company, 75 Years: 1889-1964. Spokane, The Washington Water Power Company, 1989

Anderson, Fred O. "How the Present Spokane County Developed." Manuscript, 1965.

Andrews, Ralph W. *Historic Fires of the West*. New York: Bonanza Books, 1966.

Articles of Incoporation. Spokane Falls, Washington Territory.

Askman, Allegra. "A New Story About an Old Fire." *The Falls*, a weekly journal. Spokane, WA, v. 2, no. 25 (June 24, 1976).

Atlases: Ogle, 1912. Metzger, 1941.

Bamonte, Tony and Suzanne Schaeffer Bamonte. *Life Behind the Badge: The Spokane Police Department's Founding Years, 1881-1903*. Spokane: Tornado Creek Publications, 2008.

———. *Manito Park, A Reflection of Spokane's Past*. Spokane: Tornado Creek Publications, 2004.

———. *Miss Spokane, Elegant Ambassadors and Their City*. Spokane: Tornado Creek Publications, 2000.

———. *Spokane and the Inland Northwest: Historical Images*. Spokane: Tornado Creek Publications, 2004.

———. *Spokane's Legendary Davenport Hotel*. Spokane: Tornado Creek Publications, 2001.

Becher, Edmund T. *History, Government and Resources of the Spokane Area*. Spokane: Spokane Public Schools, 1965.

———. *Spokane Corona, Eras and Empires*. Spokane: C. W. Hill Printers, 1974.

Bond, Roland. *Early Birds in the Northwest*. Nine Mile Falls, WA: Spokane House Enterprises, 1971-1972.

Cochran, Barbara F. *Seven Frontier Women and the Founding of Spokane Falls*. Spokane: Tornado Creek Publications, 2011.

Code of Washington Territory. Sec. 3050, chapter 238, 1883.

Commemorating a Half Century of Continuous Electric Service, 1889-1939. Washington Water Power Co.

Cook, Francis H. *The Territory of Washington, 1879*. Reprint. Edited by J. Orin Oliphant. Cheney, WA: State Normal School, 1925.

Drury, Clifford M. *A Tepee In His Front Yard*. Portland, Oregon: Binfords & Mort, Publishers, 1949.

Durham, Nelson Wayne. *Spokane and the Inland Empire* (also *History of the City of Spokane and Spokane Country*). Vols. 1, 2, and 3. Spokane-Chicago-Philadelpha: S. J. Publishing Co., 1912.

Dyar, Ralph E. *News For An Empire*. Caldwell, Idaho: Caxton Printers, Ltd., 1952.

Edwards, Jonathan. *An Illustrated History of Spokane County, State of Washington*. Spokane: W. H. Lever, 1900.

Fahey, John. *The Days of the Hercules*, University Press of Idaho, 1978.

———. *D. C. Corbin and Spokane*. Seattle: University of Washington Press, 1965.

———. *Shaping Spokane: Jay P. Graves and His Times*. Seattle: University of Washington Press, 1994.

Fargo, Lucile. *Spokane Story*. New York: Columbia University Press, 1950

First Fifty Years. Westminster Congregational Church, 1879-1929. Spokane, WA: Empire Printing Co., 1929.

Fuller, George W. *A History of the Pacific Northwest*. New York: Alfred A. Knopf, 1960.

Glover, James N. *Reminiscences of James N. Glover*. Fairfield, Washington: Ye Galleon Press, 1985.

Gulick, Bill. *Manhunt: The Pursuit of Harry Tracy*. Caldwell, Idaho: Caxton Press, 1999.

History of the Electrical Industry in Spokane and the Inland Empire." Washington Water Power, 1959. Manuscript.

Hook, Harry H. and Francis J. McGuire. *Spokane Falls Illustrated*. Minneapolis: Frank L. Thresher, 1889.

Hyslop, Robert B. *Spokane's Building Blocks*. Spokane, WA: Privately printed, 1983.

Kingston, Ceylon S. *The Inland Empire in the Pacific Northwest*. Fairfield, Washington: Ye Galleon Press, 1981

Laws of Washington Territory. Chap. 51. Olympia, W. T., 1888.

Magnusen, Richard G. *Coeur d'Alene Diary*. Portland, OR: Metropolitan Press, 1968.

Mann, Larry, *Birth of a City: Spokane, 1871-1915*. Master's thesis, Eastern Washington University, 1980.

Matthews, Henry C. *Kirtland Cutter, Architect in the Land of Promise*, Seattle, University of Washington Press, 1998.

McGoldrick, James P. *The McGoldrick Lumber Company Story, 1900-1952*. Spokane: Tornado Creek Publications, 2004.

———. *The Spokane Aviation Story, 1910-1941*. Spokane: Tornado Creek Publications, 2007.

Morgan, Murray. *Skid Road: An Informal Portrait of Seattle*. New York: The Viking Press, 1951.

Spokane City Directories, Spokane: R. L. Polk & Company, all available years.

Spokane County Auditor's Records, various. Spokane Auditor's Office, Spokane County Courthouse, Spokane.

Spokane Falls and Its Exposition. Buffalo and New York: Matthews-Northrop & Co., 1890.

Spokane City Council Minutes, 1880-1903. Eastern Washington Archives, Cheney, Washington.

Spokane Illustrated: The Western Architect. Minneapolis, American Institute of Architects, 1908.

Mutschler, Chas. V., Clyde L. Parent and Wilmer H. Siegert. *Spokane's Street Railways, An Illustrated History*. Spokane: Inland Empire Railway Society, 1987.

Nelson, Judy. *The Chinese in Spokane 1860-1915*. Master's thesis, Eastern Washington University, 1994.

Pratt, Orville C. *The Story of Spokane*. Privately printed, 1948.

Ryker, Lois Valliant. *With History Around Me: Spokane Nostalgia*. Fairfield, Washington: Ye Galleon Press, 1979.

U.S. Federal Censuses. <http:www.ancestry.com>.

Washington State Digital Archives. Eastern Washington University, Cheney, Washington. <http://www.digitalarchives.wa.gov/>

Woodward, Doris J. *The Indomitable Francis H. Cook of Spokane: A Man of Vision*. Spokane: Tornado Creek Publications, Spokane: 2010

Newspapers

Morning Review. Various issues.

Northwest Tribune (Cheney), Various editions

Spokane Daily Chronicle, Various editions.

Spokane Press, Various editions.

Spokan Times, Various issues.

Spokane Falls Review, Various issues.

Spokesman-Review, Various issues.

Spokesman-Review Supplement.

Index

Abbott, Emma, 76
Adams, Charles F., 190, 191
Adams, Clyde S.; See under Architects
Adams and Co.; See under Real estate firms
Additions/neighborhoods, 165-196 passim
    Browne Park (Moran Prairie), 271
    Browne's, 25, 44, 46, 53-56, 59, 73, 84,
    111, 120, 173-176, 200, 217,
    218, 235
    Cable, 279
    Dennis and Bradley's, 57, 59
    Cannon Hill Park, 191-196
    Cannondale's, 48
    Cannon's, 25, 42, 44, 53, 54, 84, 173
    Corbin Park, 180, 181
    East Pinecrest Road, 260
    Forest Park, 276
    Havermale, 21
    Hillyard, 102-103, 275
    Keystone, 21
    Manito (formerly Montrose), 182-184, 270, 272
    Northwest Boulevard, 272
    Peaceful Valley, 2, 35, 122, 123, 160
    Riverfront, 21
    Rockwood, 280, 281
    Roosevelt, 278
    South Hill, 55, 60, 63, 72, 111, 120, 131, 182-184
    Spokane Heights, 55, 58
    Twickenham, 79, 115
    Whitings, 276
    Yardley, 275
African Americans, 39
Age of Elegance, 115, 239
Agricultural land, 272, 278, 284
Aiken, Frank, 88
Allen, Hiram, 68
Anthony, H. T.; See Anthony, Baker & Burns under real estate firms…
Anthony, Baker & Burns; See under Real estate firms…
Anti-Saloon League, 124
Apple production, 108, 152
Architects, 237-238 (List from Survey of Historic Landmarks, 263-266)
    Adams, Clyde S., 273
    Ballard, William J., 202, 240-242
    Bertelsen, Henry, 247
    Boardman, L. M., 237
    Brooks, Kenneth W., 256-257
    Clausen, Arthur C., 208
    Cloninger, Glen, 258-262 (Residence, 262)
    Creager, Fred, 257
    Cutter, Kirtland, 38, 94, 109, 131, 135, 145, 174, 176, 184, 211, 213, 214, 216, 217, 229, 231, 232, 237, 243-253, (Residence, 248)
    Dow, John K., 120, 135, 136, 231, 237
    Finch, F. D., 237
    Held, Albert, 130, 143, 147, 207, 237
    Hensley, Joseph, 257
    Hubbell, Clarence Z., 136
    Hyslop, W. S., 181, 203, 204, 229, 234
    Keith, George, 235, 253, 254
    Kundig, Moritz, 238
    Malmgren, Karl G., 94, 131, 135, 211, 213, 214, 217, 229, 231, 237, 244, 245
    Martell, Carroll, 257
    Pehrson, Gustav A., 136
    Pennington, J. K. S., 237
    Poetz, J. C., 237, 239-240, 244
    Preusse, Herman, 31, 34, 45, 48, 49, 64, 81, 87, 93, 215, 237, 239, 243
    Price, Ernest V., 253, 255
    Rand, Loren L., 237
    Rasque, George M., 257
    Ritchie, Willis A., 104, 105, 106
    Seaton, Chauncey B., 98, 99, 100, 240
    Smith, C. Harvey, 206
    White and Hyslop, 204
    Whitehouse, Harold, 141, 235, 253-255
    Zittel, Julius, 65, 215, 237, 239
    See also Modernist architects/architecture
Architectural styles, 197-208
Arlington Block; See under Buildings…
Arlington Hotel; See under Hotels
Arlington Stables, 101
Arthur H. Jones Company; See Jones under Real estate firms…
Auditorium Building/theater; See under Buildings…; Theaters…
Automobiles, 116-117, 123, 125, 130, 133, 211, 212, 228, 252, 292, 164
Aviation/air shows, 158-160

Baer, Harry, 75, 81, 96
Bailey, Mary J., "Babe", See Downing, Babe
Baker, Wallace; See Anthony, Baker & Burns under Real estate firms…
Balzer, Charles, 184-185, 162
Ballard, William J.; See under Architects
Ballard Plannery, 202, 241-242
Black, James S., 291
Bancroft School; See under Schools
Bank failures, 103
Banks, 84
    Bank of Spokane Falls, 25, 44, 103
    Browne National Bank, 103
    First National Bank, 34, 42, 74, 86, 87
    Marble Bank, 44, 49
    Old National Bank, 211, 136
    Providence Trust Company, 55
    Spokane and Eastern, 231
    Spokane National Bank, 84
Barrett, F. S., Co.; See under Real estate firms…
Bartoo, George, 116
Baseball, 78, 79, 115
Bassett, George W., 6, 8, 9
Bassett, Minnie Maria, 11
Bassett, Wilbur Fiske, 9, 10
Bean, Walker L., 73
Belt, Horatio, 55
Benham, I. T., 30, 86
Benjamin, Caroline Abygail, See Costello, Caroline…
Benjamin, Richard Manning, 9, 11, 12, 17
Benjamin family, 14, 17
Bennett, B. H., 70
Bennett Block; See under Buildings…
Berg, F. O., 116; See also F. O. Berg Company
Bertelsen, Henry; See under Architects
Betts, Catherine, 163, 164
Bickford, Monte, 86

Bicycles, 113, 214
Bing Crosby Theater; See under Theaters
Black, James S. 291
Blackwell Frederick A., 120, 130, 131
Blalock, John, 31
Blalock, Martha "Mattie" Hyde, 31
Blalock Block; See under Buildings…
Bloomsday, 77
Board of Park Commissioners; See Spokane Park Board
Bohemian Girl, 76
Bolster, Herbert, 79
Bond, Rowland, 9, 11, 12
Boulter, Roy L., 116
Bower and Sawyer; See under Real estate firms
Boyd, L. Frank, 146
Brants, George, 42
Bravinder, Ben, 42
Breweries, 125
Brick industry, 82, 83, 86-87, 190
Brickell, E. J., 83, 103
Bridges, 26, 30, 53-54, 57, 68, 82, 91
    Division Street, 60, 61
    Howard Street, 30, 91
    Monroe Street, 57, 60, 98, 110, 119, 122
    Post Street, 30, 54, 82
Briley, Bob, 123
Brook, Henry, 86, 87, 190
Brooks, Edna Harrington, 257
Brooks, Kenneth W.; See under Architects
Browne, Anna W. (Stratton), 46
Browne, John J., 23, 25, 29, 30, 38, 39, 46, 70, 175
    Banking interests, 44, 103
    Civic involvement, 45, 168
    Financial reversal, 45, 103
    Real estate/buildings, 44, 45, 46, 47, 53, 54, 76, 87, 103
    Residences, 209, 210, 271
    Spokane Falls Chronicle, 30, 44
    Street railways, 54, 55
Browne Block; See under Buildings…
Browne's Addition; See under Additions…
Browne's Mountain, 47
Brownlee, Archibald, 80
Bryant School; See under Schools
Buehner, Philip, 51
Buffalo Bill's Wild West Show, 115
Building trades, 123, 125; See also Brick industry
Buildings/business blocks, (Downtown buildings still existing, 297-300)
    Arlington Block, 90
    Auditorium Building, 45, 64, 97, 109, 119
    Bellevue Block, 109, 145
    Bennett Block, 70, 127
    Blalock Block, 31
    Browne Block, 47, 87
    Cannon Block, 85
    Central Block, 64, 85
    Chronicle Building, 291
    Concordia Hall, 92
    Crescent Block, 71, 93, 94
    Crescent store, 49, 71, 94
    Eagle Block, 81
    Empire State/Great Western Building, 71, 120, 135, 291
    Falls City Block, 76
    Fernwell Block, 31
    Frankfurt Block, 80, 81
    French Block, 87
    Glover Block, 34
    Great Eastern Block, 112
    Holley Mason, 143
    Hutton Building, 140
    Hyde Block, 71, 85, 87
    Jamieson Block, 80, 85, 87
    Keats Block, 84, 87
    Kemp and Hebert, 143
    Lamona Block, 97
    Lindelle Block, 97, 140
    Mearow Block, 143
    Metals Building, 132
    Northern Pacific Depot, 104
    Paulsen Building, 122, 129, 136, 138, 139
    Paulsen Dental and Medical Building, 136, 139
    Peyton Building/Annex, 112
    Pfister Block, 144
    Review Building, 68, 69, 98, 122
    Riverside Court, 291
    Sears Building, 65
    Somerset Building, 291
    Tapio Office Center, 258
    Temple Court, 128
    Union Block, 66, 73, 87
    Vandorn & Bentley Block, 85
    Van Valkenburg Block, 85, 87
    Wolverton Block, 85, 86, 291, 292, 293
    Ziegler Block, 85, 129
    See also non-commercial buildings by name, e.g. Spokane Club; Masonic Temple, etc.
Buildings, Public
    Carnegie Library, 65, 239
    Spokane City Hall, 26, 65
    Spokane County Courthouse, 104, 106, 110
    Spokane Public Safety Building, 104-105
Burns, Martin, 156
Burns, R. J.; See Anthony, Baker & Burns under Real estate firms…

C and C Flour Mill; See under Flour mills
Cable Addition; See under Additions…
California House; See under Hotels
Campbell, Dr. A. S., 51
Campbell, Amasa B., 65, 120, 214, 218
    Residence, 214
Campbell, Grace M. Fox, 214
Campbell, Helen, 214
Canada Island, 32, 50
Cannon, Aniel R., 48
Cannon, Anthony M., 23, 29, 39, 42, 48, 70, 191
    Banking interests, 25, 44, 49, 103
    Civic involvement, 31, 45, 168
    Financial reversal, 45, 103
    Railroad/Street Railway interests, 45, 54, 55
    Real estate/buildings, 44, 45, 48, 53, 54, 76, 85, 103
    Residence, 48, 49
    Spokane Falls Chronicle, 30, 44
Cannon, Jennie F. (Pease), 48
Cannon Block; See under Buildings…
Cannon Hill Park; See under Parks
Cannon Island, 32
Cannondale's Addition; See under Additions…
Cannon's Addition; See under Additions…
Cannon's sawmill; See under Sawmills

Carl, Amos H.; See under Contractors...
Carlisle, C. B., 68
Carnegie, Andrew, 65
Carnegie Library; See under Buildings, Public
Carson's restaurant, 50
Cataldo, Fr. Joseph, 62, 63
Cemeteries
    First in Spokane, 175
    Greenwood..., 45, 67, 84, 101
    Fairmount Memorial Park/Association, 38, 84, 101, 116, 142
    Mountain View, 84
    Pioneer cemetery in Browne's Addition, 84
    Riverside, 260, 261
Centennial Flour Mill; See under Flour mills
Central Block; See under Buildings...
Central School; See under Schools
Chadbourn, Charles N., 286
Chamberlin Real Estate Improvement Co.; See under Real estate firms...
Charities, 62, 64, 128, 139, 141
Cheney, 29-30
Chinese, 29, 39, 82, 85
Chinn, S. O., 155-156
Chronicle Building; See under Buildings...
Churches, 27, 62, 84, 98
    Cathedral of St. John the Evangelist, 253, 255
    First Congregational (Westminster), 98
    First Presbyterian, 71, 87
    Grace Baptist, 124
    Our Lady of Lourdes Cathedral, 63, 122, 143
    Pilgrim Congregational, 124
    St. Aloysius, 239
    St. Joseph's, 62
    St. Michael's Mission, 63
    Vincent Methodist, 119, 130
City Beautiful Club, 162, 166, 167
City Charities Commission, 128
City Park Transit Company; See under Street railways
Clark, F. Lewis, 54, 99, 113, 120, 128, 133, 135, 168, 176, 291
    Residences, 135, 184
Clark, James, Residence, 207
Clark, Patrick, 120, 217 (Residence)
Clark, Winifred Wyard, 135
Clemmer, Howard S., 138
Clemmer...; See under Theaters...
Cloninger, Glen; See under Architects
Cloninger, Pamela Briggs, 258
Cloninger family, 259
Clough, Charles F., 32, 99, 293, 230 (Residence)
Clough & Graves Real Estate; See under Real estate firms...
Clubs, 64, 97, 135, 147, 152, 153, 162-163, 166, 167, 238; See also Spokane Club
Coeur d'Alene Park; See under Parks
Colborn & Morgan; See under Real estate firms...
Colleges, 40, 62-63, 82; See also Gonzaga
Compau, Nancy, 238
Commercial Hotel; See under Hotels
Comstock, James M., 93, 113, 114
Concordia Hall; See under Buildings...
Consumers' Light and Power Company, 109
Contractors/builders
    Benham, I. T., 30, 86
    Brook, Henry, 86, 87
    Carl, Amos H., 279
    Feltis, C. E., 275

    Fotheringham, David B., 106
    Johnson, Frank, 87
    Lindquist, Aaron L., 205
    Murphy, M. C., 275
    Pearson, Andrew, 276
    Peterson, P. L., 254
    Phair, Frederick, 136
    Rounds-Clist Company, 136
Cook, Francis, 35, 72, 78, 182, 233
    Residence, 215
    Spokan Times, 27, 35, 44, 68, 70, 72
    Street railway, 55, 56, 58, 60, 72, 130, 182
Cook, Laura (McCarty), 72
Coolidge, Calvin, 5
Corbaley, Gordon C., 285
Corbin Anna Louise Larson, 38
Corbin, Austin, 38, 111, 184
    Residence, 213, 245
Corbin, Corbin, 244, 249, 252, 253
Corbin, Daniel C., 38, 73, 82, 111, 113, 120, 180, 244, 252
    Residence, 184, 245
    Wealth, 121
Corbin, Genevieve Wilment, 249, 252, 253
Corbin, Louisa, 38
Corbin Art Center, 38, 111
Corbin Ditch, 38
Corbin-Moore-Turner Heritage Gardens, 146, 232
Corbin Park; See under Parks
Costello, Caroline Abygail Benjamin, 9, 11, 14, 15
Cowles, Cheney, 214
Cowles, William H., 69, 71, 168, 169
    Residences, 176, 211, 212, 246, 247
Cowley, Henry Thomas, 14, 33, 39, 42, 43, 68, 69, 86, 98
    Real estate investments, 19, 20
Cowley, Lucy Abigail (Peet), 19
Cowley family, 19
Crescent Block; See under Buildings...
Crescent store; See under Buildings...
Crosby, Bing, 164
Crystal Island, 32, 50
Crystal Laundry, 32
Curtis, Frank, 54
Custer, General George A., 41
Cutter, Horace L., 88, 243
Cutter, Katharine Phillips Williams, 245, 248-251
Cutter, Kirtland; See under Architects
Cutter, Kirtland Corbin; See Corbin, Corbin
Cutter, Mary Edwine Corbin, 244

Daggett, Floyd, 170
Dallam, Frank M., 69, 88
Davenport, Elijah, 71, 93, 144
Davenport, Louis M., 93, 94, 109, 145, 168, 244
    Residence, 230
Davenport Hotel; See under Hotels
Davenport's Restaurant, 109, 144, 145, 244
Davie, John T., 86-87, 190
Davis, George A., 20, 21, 31, 50
David, George I., 90
Dawson, James Frederick, 170, 172, 173
Day Eugene, 137
Day, Harry L., 137, 138, 140
Day, Jerome, 137
Dennis, G. B., 57
Dennis and Bradley's Addition; See under Additions...

304

Deuber, Peter, 92
Diamond Match, 10
Dill, Clarence, Residence, 231
Dillman, L. C., 99
Division Street Bridge; See under Bridges
Dixon, Cromwell, Jr., 160
Dodd, Sonora Smart, 161, including Residence
Dodson, George, 83
Dodson's Jewelers, 83
Dooley, T. J., 55
Douglas, Harlan, 176
Douglas, Stephen, 4
Dow, John K., See under Architects
Downing, Babe, 6, 8, 11, 13, 14, 15, 16, 17
Downing, James J., 6, 9, 11, 12, 13, 15, 17, 18
Downing, Marcia, 8, 13, 17
Doyle, Leonard W., 112
Drumheller, Daniel M., 32, 87
Duncan, John W., 185-186
Durham, Nelson W., 69, 71
Durkin, Jimmie, 124
Dutch investment, 45, 92-93, 103, 108, 109, 182, 216
Dutch Jake; See Goetz, Jacob
Dwight, Daniel, 76

Eagle Block; See under Buildings...
Echo Roller Mills; See under Flour mills
Edgington, Thomas, Residence, 200
Edison Electric Illuminating Company, 44, 51, 53, 54
Electric lighting, 44, 51, 53, 54 125, 135
Electricity, See Electric lighting; Interurban railways; Waterpower/electricity
Elevators, 134
Elmendorf, Frederic, 275, 285
Elmendorf, J. D., 285
Elmendorf, Margaret H., 286
Elmendorf & Elmendorf; See under Real estate firms...
Elmendorf & Pope; See under Real estate firms...
Elsom, Thomas H., 71, 73, 74
Empire State Building; See under Buildings...
Erickson, P., 87
Expo '74; See under Fairs...
Exposition Building; See under Fairs...

F. O. Berg Company, 93
F. R. Moore & Co., 50
Fairmount Memorial Park/Association; See under Cemeteries
Fairs/expositions, 78, 97, 108, 182
  Expo '74; 100, 105, 257
  Exposition Building, 96, 99-100, 240
  Fruit Fair, 108
  National Apple Show, 152
  Northwestern Industrial Exposition, 96, 97, 99-100
  Spokane Interstate Fair/Fairgrounds, 108, 159, 160
  Washington & Idaho Fair Association, 78, 180, 181
Falls City Block; See under Buildings...
Falls View Hotel; See under Hotels
Farmers' market, 126
Fassett, Charles M., 32
Father's Day, 161
Fellowes, Eugene J., store, 64
Feltis, C. E.; See under Contractors...
Felts Field, 160
Fernwell Block; See under Buildings...
Ferries, 53

Ferris, Ellen, 225
Ferris, G. M., Residence, 279
Ferris, Joel E., 168
Finch, Charlotte Swinger, 218
Finch, John A., 120, 168, 175, 214, 218
  Residence, 218
Finch Investment Company, 272
Finnish, 122, 123
Finucane, Francis and Mary G., Residence, 216, 226
Fire of 1889; 84, 86, 90-94
  Aftermath/rebuilding, 74, 75, 82, 87, 91-93, 95-97, 103, 104
  Tent city, 93, 95, 96
Fires, Post-1889; 112
First National Bank; See under Banks
First Presbyterian Church; See under Churches
Fitch, George A., 51
Fleming, Charles A., 32, 163
Florence Crittenton Home, 141
Flour mills, 20-22, 30, 110
  C and C, 51, 53, 54, 108
  Centennial, 51
  Echo Roller Mills, 20, 21, 34, 36, 50, 51, 82
  Northwest Milling and Power Company, 107, 108, 109
  Spokane Flour Mills, 108, 109, 110
Flynn, Elizabeth Gurley, 154-155
Forest Park Addition; See under Additions...
Forrest, Robert W., 31, 32, 53, 66, 103
Fort George Wright, 66, 106-107
Fort Spokane (military), 29
Fotheringham, David B., 32, 106
France, Walter, 15
Frankfurt Block; See under Buildings...
Free speech movement, 154-155
French, Henry, 87
French Block; See under Buildings...
Fruit Fair; See under Fairs...
Funk, Leonard, 186
Furth, Fred, 93

Galland-Burke Brewery, 125
Gandy, Dr. Joseph, 66
Gandy, Lloyd, 90
Gardens, 146, 169, 186, 232
Gas lighting/mains, 53, 135
Genish, Theodore, 285
Geraghty, James M., 52
Gillespie, William, 92
Gilliam, Lane C., 36
Glover, James, 3, 6, 9, 12, 14, 15, 16, 19, 20, 22, 29, 39, 44, 66, 70, 109, 175
  Banking interests, 34, 86, 103
  Civic involvement, 31, 32
  Platting of town, 23, 24
  Property transactions, 11, 13, 17, 18, 21, 25
  Residences, 29, 216, 217, 226
  Spokane Falls Chronicle, 30, 44
  Wealth fluctuations, 103, 121
Glover, Susan, 12, 18, 19
Glover and Gilliam's Livery Stable, 36, 89
Glover Athletic Field, 160
Glover Block; See under Buildings...
Glover Island, 32, 50
Goetz, Jacob "Dutch Jake", 14, 75, 81, 96
Gonzaga College/University, 40, 62, 82, 86, 87, 118, 146, 215, 239
Grand Hotel; See under Hotels

305

Grant, Ulysees S., 36, 37
Grapetree Village, 259, 262
Graves, Frank H., 80, 216 (Residence)
Graves, Jay P., 60, 120, 130, 131, 168, 169, 182, 183, 187, 213, 216, 293
    Residence, 131
Graves, Will, 182
Gray, Clara Smiley, 26
Gray, William C., 25, 26, 31, 232 (Residence)
Great Eastern Block; See under Buildings…
Great Northern Railroad; See under Railroads
Green movement, 296
Greenwood Cemetery/Memorial Park; See under Cemeteries
Grimmer, J. M., 78
Grinnell, Fred; See under Real estate firms……
Grocery stores, 125, 126

Hall of the Doges, 145
Ham, David, 113
Hamilton, Charles Keeney, 158-160
Hanauer-Graves Company; See under Real estate firms…
Harrison, S. K., 88
Havermale, Elizabeth, 20
Havermale, Samuel G., 19, 20, 21, 31, 39, 50, 66
Havermale Island, 32, 50, 102
Hawkins, H. G., 117
Hay, Gov. Marion E., 224 (Residence), 233
Hayward, Harry C., 75, 76, 92
Hazelwood Dairy, 109
Hege, S. E., 285
Held, Albert; See under Architects
Hercules Mine, 120, 121, 137
Higgins, Barbara, 289
Higgins, Robert M., 289
Hill, James J., 102
Hillyard, 102-103, 275
Hindley, William J., 32, 124, 128, 233
Hogan, Frank, 182
Holmes, Mary J., 97
Holy Names Academy; See under Schools
Homeless, 127, 128, 151, 152
Homestead acts, 7
Hopkins, Charles B., 68, 71, 73, 74
Horse racing, 77-78, 180, 181
Hospitals, 66-67
    Deaconess, 127-128
    Sacred Heart, 66-67, 128, 230
    St. Luke's, 127
Hotel Spokane; See under Hotels
Hotels
    Arlington, 70, 90
    California House, 25, 26, 27, 36, 68, 82
    Commercial, 71
    Davenport, 93, 94, 122, 291
    Empire, 241
    Falls View, 84
    Grand, 70
    Hotel Spokane, 53, 97
    Keystone House, 84
    Merchants, 144
    Pedicord, 219
    Pennington, 109, 145
    Richmond, 143
    Savoy, 127
    Sprague House, 34
    Western House, 26, 27
    Windsor, 26
Houghton, Alice (Ide); See under Real estate firms
Houghton, Horace E., 80
House prices, 111, 202, 205, 216, 273, 276, 278, 279
Housing trends, future, 295
Howard, Oliver O., 22, 24
Howard, Richard, 117
Howard Street Bridge; See under Bridges
Hughes, Lilam, Lillian and Lucy, 167
Humbird, Agnes Hyslop, 219
Humbird, John A., 219
Humbird, Thomas J., Residences, 219, 220
Hunner, R. C., 294
Hutton, Levi, 120, 121, 137, 138, 139, 140-142
    Residences, 140
Hutton, May Arkwright, 120, 121, 128, 137, 139, 140-141
Hutton Settlement, 141-142, 253
Hyde, Eugene B., 31, 66, 88, 146
Hyde, Rollin, 31
Hyde Block; See under Buildings…
Hypothekbank, See Northwestern and Pacific Hypotheekbank
Hyslop, W. W., See under Architects
Hyslop, Robert B., 181 (Includes Residence)

Ide, Chester D., 80
Ide, Clarence W., 80
Immigrants, 101, 120, 122, 138; See also Chinese; Japanese; Finnish
Industrial Workers of the World, 154-155
Ingersoll, Audley, 115
Inland Telephone and Telegraph Co., 74
Interurban/electric railroads, 121, 130, 131, 283
    Coeur d'Alene & Spokane, 130, 131, 169
    Interurban Terminal Building, 122, 130
    Spokane and Inland Empire, 130, 131, 271
Irrigation, 38

Jail, 104, 105, 141, 155-156
Jamieson Block; See under Buildings…
Japanese, 82
Jenkins, Col. David P., 63, 106
Jenkins University, 63, 82
John W. Graham Co, 112
Johnson, Frank, 87
Jones, Ada Stinson, 291
Jones, Arthur D., Residence, 292
    Real estate; See under Real estate firms…
Jones, May C., 62
Jones, Rolla A., 90
Joseph (Nez Perce chief), 22
Joy's Opera House; See under Theaters…
Junior League of Spokane, 238

Kaiser, Henry, Residence, 234
Keats Block; See under Buildings…
Keith, George; See under Architects
Keystone House; See under Hotels
King, Chuck, 110
King, Clement B., 29
Knights of Labor, 83
Kuhn, Aaron, 113
Kundig, Moritz; See under Architects

Labor unions, 83, 99, 154-155

Ladies Benevolent Society, 62
Ladies Library and Aid Society, 64
Lake property; See vacation property
Lamona Block; See under Buildings…
Land entitlements, 4, 5, 7
Land offices, 39
Landscape architecture; See Olmsted Brothers
Latham, Dr. Edward, 67
Latham, Dr. Mary, 65, 67, 81, 128
Latham, Warren, 128
Lawlessness, 105, 114, 124
Lewis, Byron R., 220-223 (Residence, 220)
Lewis, William S., 9
Lewis and Clark High School; See under Schools
Libby, Isaac C., 63
Liberty, Stephen E., 15, 47, 283
Liberty Lake, 15, 47, 130, 282, 283
Liberty Park; See under Parks
Lidgerwood Cable Company; See under Street Railways
Lincoln, Abraham, 3, 4, 5
Lincoln School; See under Schools
Lindelle Block; See under Buildings…
Livery Stables, 36, 89, 101
Lockhart, J. T., 39
Loewenberg, Bernhard, Residence, 235
Logan School; See under Schools
Long Lake Lumber; See under Lumber business
Lumber business, 5, 111, 113, 115
    A. M. Fox, 148
    B. R. Lewis, 220-223
    Boise Cascade, 5
    Diamond Match, 10
    Eastern Washington & Idaho Lumbermens' Association, 148
    Humbird, 219
    Long Lake, 9
    McGoldrick, 10, 59, 148-151
    Ohio Match, 10
    Spokane Falls Lumber & Mfs. Co., 51
    Spokane Lumber Association, 111
    See also Match production; Sawmills
Lundquist Aaron L., See under Contractors/builders

MacKenzie, Roderick, 283
Maguire, John, 75
Manito Grocery, 126
Manito Park; See under Parks
Mann, Joe, 288-289
    Future of real estate, 294-296
Mann, Joyce, 288
Marble Bank; See under Banks
Markham, Ford D., Residence, 229
Marshall, Henry C., 55
Mason, F. H., 134
Masonic Temple, 144
Masterson, Dr. James H., 27
Match production, 10
Matheny, Jasper M., 12, 15, 17, 18, 21
Maxwell, William, Residence 236
McClure, John R., 13
McClure, Marcia, See Downing, Marcia
McGoldrick, James Patrick, 148-149
McGoldrick, Milton, 149
McGoldrick Lumber; See under Lumber business
McKenzie family, Residence, 202
McLane, H. H., Residence, 224

McLeod, Alexander, 53
McPherson, James, 100
Meadow Lake, 278, 284
Medicine/physicians, 51, 65-67
Merriam, Dr. Cyrus K., 66
Miller, Victor C., 156-157
Millionaires, 45, 103, 111, 120, 121
Mining war in the Coeur d'Alenes, 115
Mining wealth, 37-39, 41, 81, 99, 103, 111, 115, 120, 131, 137-140,
    207,
214, 217, 218
Miss Spokane, 123, 233, 163, 164
Modernist architects/architecture, 256-257
Monaghan, James, 29, 113, 215 (Residence)
Monaghan, John Robert, 118, 146, 147
Monroe Street Bridge; See under Bridges
Montrose Park: See under Parks, 55
Moore, Frank Rockwood, 31, 103, 184
    Residence, 232
Moore, Herbert C., 32, 124
Moran, Joseph, 15, 47
Moran Prairie, 47, 108, 271, 272
Morgan, Daniel, Residence, 235
Morse, George E., 109
Moses (Nez Perce chief), 13, 259
Mother Joseph, 66
Motie, Marguerite, 123, 233
Motie family, 233 (includes residence)
Mounsey family, Residence, 201
Mount Spokane State Park, 72
Murphy, M. C.; See under Contractors…
Murray, Idaho, 37

Natatorium Park; See under Parks
Nation, Carrie A., 124
National Association of Realtors, 286, 296
National Register of Historic Places, Spokane buildings on
    Corbin Park Historic District, 181
    Dodd residence, 161
    Empire State/Great Western, 120
    First (Westminster) Congregational Church, 98
    Peyton Building/Annex, 112
    Spokane Flour Mill, 110
Nelson, Carl, 123
Newbery, Arthur A., 106, 133
Newell, William A., 31
Newspapers, 27, 30, 35, 44, 68-71, 84
    Spokan Times, 27, 35, 68, 70
    Spokane Falls/Spokane Chronicle, 14, 20, 30, 68, 69, 70, 155
    Spokane Falls Review, 69
    Spokane Press, 71, 155
    Spokesman-Review, 68, 69, 71, 155
Nine Mile Falls power plant, 131
Nolan, Edward, 247
Norman, William S. "Billy," 53, 73, 74
Northern Pacific Railway, 1, 18, 19, 23, 24, 38, 104, 131, 139
    Completion/arrival in Spokane, 25, 30, 34, 36, 37, 85
    Fatal accidents, 100-101
    Land grants/sales, 3, 4, 5, 6, 20, 40, 42, 43, 72, 113, 148
    Promotion of settlement, 40-41, 113
Northwest Milling and Power Company; See under Flour mills
Northwest Museum of Arts and Culture, 24, 181, 214, 247, 253
Northwestern and Pacific Hypotheekbank, 45, 92-93, 96, 103, 108,
    113, 182, 216
Northwestern Industrial Exposition; See under Fairs…

307

Odell, Hal, 77
Ohio Match, 10
Olmsted, Clara Hyde, 31
Olmsted, Elmer D., 114
Olmsted Brothers, 131, 167, 170-172, 178, 180, 181, 186, 191
One Hundred and fifty Thousand Club (150,000 Club), 167, 162-163
Oppenheimer, Simon, 107-110
Oregon Railway and Navigation Company; See under Railroads
Oton, Jean, 250
Our Lady of Lourdes Cathedral; See under Churches

Pacific Railway Acts, 4-5
Palouse Land Company; See under Real estate firms…
Panic of 1893; 45, 103-104, 111, 113
Park board; See Spokane Park Board
Parker, Samuel, 35
Parks, 54, 55, 57, 59, 115, 163, 165-196 passim
    Cannon Hill, 87, 190-196
    Cliff, 192
    Coeur d'Alene, 44, 54, 55, 146, 147, 165, 168, 173-174
    Corbin, 78, 180-181
    Liberty, 87, 176-179
    Manito/Montrose, 55, 59, 182-189, 192, 162
    Natatorium, 57, 79, 115
    Twickenham, 57, 115
Paterson, Robert B., 93, 113
Pattern books, 200, 202, 203, 241-242
Patullo, Charles, Residence, 274
Paulsen, August, 120, 121, 137-139, 140, 228
    Residence, 139, 227, 275
Paulsen, Myrtle White, 121, 137, 138, 139, 228
Paulsen family, 228
Payne, Joseph, 53
Peaceful Valley; See under Additions…
Pearson, Andrew; See under Contractors…
Pedicord Hotel; See under Hotels
Pennington Hotel; See under Hotels
Peone, Baptiste, 15
Perkins, James A., 14
Pershal, M. L., Residence, 193
Pettet, William 53, 236, Residence, 236
Peyton, Col. Isaac N., 112
Peyton Building; See under Buildings…
Pfister Block; See under Buildings…
Phoenix Sawmill; See under Sawmills
Pioneer Educational Society, 63
Plate glass windows, 276, 277
Playfair Race Track, 78, 159
Poetz, J. C.; See under Architects
Poole family 19
Pope, F. E., 286
Porter, Richard B., Residence, 230
Post, Frederick, 15, 21, 22, 24, 46, 84
Post Falls dam and powerhouse, 130
Post Street Bridge, 30, 54, 82
Potter, Dr. W. W., 175
Pratt, Nelson S., 156
Preusse, Herman; See under Architects
Price, Ernest V.; See under Architects
Pride of Spokane (restaurant), 93
Prostitution, 105, 114, 155
Providence Trust Company; See under Banks

Race tracks; See Horse racing
Races, Foot, 77

Railroads, 4-5, 102, 105, 120, 125
    Great Northern, 102-103, 105, 122
    Oregon Railway and Navigation Company, 63, 82
    Seattle, Lake Shore and Eastern, 82
    Spokane and Palouse Railway, 45
    Spokane Falls and Northern Railroad, 38, 82, 111
    Spokane International Railroad, 38
    West Coast Railway, 210
    See also Interurban/electric railroads; Northern Pacific; Union Station
Rambo, George B. M., 87
Rand, Loren L.; See under Architects
Real estate board; See Spokane Association of Realtors
Real estate/firms/developers/agents, 55, 267-284
    Adams and Co., 94
    Anthony, Baker & Burns, 294
    Barnes, Motie & Ready, 233
    Barrett, F. S., & Co., 294
    Bower and Sawyer, 94
    Chamberlin Real Estate Improvement Co., 274
    Clough and Graves, 97, 230, 292
    Colborn & Morgan, 272
    Dillman, L. C., 99
    Dry Goods, 231
    Elmendorf & Elmendorf, 275, 285
    Elmendorf & Pope, 286
    Grinnell, Fred B., 187, 188, 235, 270, 272, 280
    Hanauer-Graves Co., 278, 284
    Houghton, Alice (Ide) 80, 81
    Jones, Arthur D., 94, 120, 133, 134, 192, 194, 272, 279, 291-293
    McCrea & Merryweather, 189
    Palouse Land Company, 282
    SDS, 132
    Stocker, George K., 55
    Thompson-Gillis Investment Company, 275
    Tomlinson-Black, 291
    Tilton and Stocker (and Fry), 55
    Williams, H. M., and Houghton, 80, 81
    See also Real estate investment …
Real estate investment/investors in early Spokane, 103, 113, 120, 164, 182-184; See also Brickell; Browne; Cannon; Clark, F. Lewis; Cook; Corbin; Finch; Forrest; Glover; Graves; Hogan; Jones; Moore; Pettet, etc.
Real estate profession, future of, 294-296
Real estate promotion/advertising, 192-194, 267-284; See also Agricultural Land
Realtor
    Ethics and standards, 286
    Origin and meaning of word, 286
    Role and training today, 295-296
Reavis, John T., 97
Reddy, William, 87
Reugh, Wendell, 176
Review Building; See under Buildings…
Revivals, 151-153
Rhea, Joseph, 100
Rice, Ren, 151
Richards, Henry J., Residence, 231
Ridge Condominiums, 176
Rima, Lorenzo W., 23, 24, 31
Rima's jewelry store, 50
Ritchie, Willis A.; See under Architects
Roberts, Edward J., Residence, 235
Robertson, Calvin, 87
Rockwood residence, 224

308

Rockwood Addition; See under Additions…
Roller rinks, 36, 75, 76
Roosevelt, Theodore, 146-147
Roosevelt Addition; See under Additions…
Ross, Andrew J., 55
Ross Park Railway; See under Street railways
Rothrock, Frank M., 138
Routhe, E. A., 55
Rudberg, John, Residence, 205
Rutter, Robert L., 168

Sacred Heart Hospital, 66-67, 82, 90
Saint, See St.
Saloons and taverns, 30, 75, 81, 96, 105, 114, 124
Sandburg, Carl, 153
Sandifer, Paul, Jr., 138
Sanitation, 51, 52
Sawmills, 9, 10, 11, 30, 83, 91, 107, 108, 109
    B. R. Lewis, 221
    Cannon's sawmill, 48
    McGoldrick, 148; See also under Lumber business
    Phoenix Sawmill, 9, 10, 108
    Spokane Mill Company, 83, 91, 107
Schmautz, Steve, 132
Schools, 63, 64, 103
    Bancroft, 64
    Bryant, 64
    Central, 64
    Franklin, 154
    Holy Names Academy, 63
    Lewis and Clark, 63, 64, 147
    Lincoln, 64
    Logan, 64
    Marycliff, 135
    Spokane High School, 63, 64, 119
    St. Michael's Mission Scholasticate, 63
Scranton, Babe, See Downing, Babe
Scranton, Seth B., 6, 8, 9, 11, 12, 13, 15, 17, 18, 19, 35
Sears Building; See under buildings…
Seaton, Chauncey; See under Architects
Seattle, Lake Shore and Eastern; See under Railroads
Sewage/industrial waste in Spokane River, 51, 52, 102, 199
Sewer system, 125
Shannon, Bill, 56
Shantytowns, 43, 122
Sheehan, Dennis, 88
Sherman, William T., 22
Sigg, William, 123
Simonson, John, 56
Smart, William Jackson, 161
Smith, C. Harvey; See under Architects
Sorosis Club, 64
South Hill; See under Additions…
Spear, Joseph H., 87, 190
Spokan Garry (Spokane chief), 20
Spokan Times; See under Newspapers
Spokane
    City charter (new), 102
    City limits, 31, 33, 102
    County seat, 27, 29-30
    Incorporation, 31, 33
    Mayors, 32, 93, 99, 106, 114, 124, 128, 146, 170, 186, 233, 156, 163
    Name, 3, 35, 102
    Plat, 23, 24
    Population, 29, 30, 36, 39, 66, 84, 89, 96, 97, 111, 118, 122, 166, 162, 163
    Presidential visits, 146-147, 212
    Promotion, 162-164
    Town site/settlement, 3, 6, 8, 11
    Wealth; See Lumber business; Millionaires; Mining; Real estate
Spokane Advertising Club, 152, 153, 162-163
Spokane Amateur Athletic Club, 97, 147
Spokane and Montrose Motor Railroad; See under Street railways
Spokane and Palouse Railway; See under Railroads
Spokane Association of Realtors, 164, 181, 287
    Founding officers and charter members, 285-286, 287
    Constitution and bylaws, 287
    Presidents, 1911-2011; 290
    See also Elmendorf; Higgins; Mann
Spokane Brewing and Malting Company, 125
Spokane Cable Railway; See under Street railways
Spokane Chamber of Commerce, 97, 104, 140, 162, 163, 291
Spokane Children's Home, 141
Spokane Chronicle; See under Newspapers
Spokane City Council, 31
Spokane City Hall; See under Buildings, Public
Spokane City Water Works; See Waterworks
Spokane Club, 128, 132-135, 140, 291
Spokane College, 63, 82
Spokane Country Club, 254-255
Spokane County Courthouse; See under Buildings, Public
Spokane Dry Goods Company, 231
Spokane Electric Light and Water Power Company, 50, 51
Spokane Falls and Northern Railroad; See under Railroads
Spokane Falls Chronicle; See under Newspapers
Spokane Falls Gas Light Company, 53
Spokane Falls Lumber & Mfs. Co.; See under Lumber business
Spokane Falls Review; See under Newspapers
Spokane Fire Department, 88-89, 104, 105, 112
Spokane Flour Mills; See under Flour mills
Spokane Hardware, 95
Spokane Heights; See under Additions…
Spokane High School; See under Schools
Spokane Hotel; See Hotels – Hotel Spokane, 53, 97
Spokane Humane Society, 67
Spokane Indians, 1, 2, 15, 20, 33, 35, 42, 63
    Teepees, 197-198
Spokane International Railroad; See under Railroads
Spokane Intermodal Facility, 104
Spokane Interstate Fair; See under Fairs
Spokane Medical Society, 66
Spokane Methodist Episcopal College, 40
Spokane Mill Company; See under Sawmills
Spokane National Bank; See under Banks
Spokane Park board, 163, 167-173, 177, 178, 185, 186
Spokane Police Department, 31, 85, 91, 92, 101, 104, 105, 114, 116, 123, 124, 146, 147, 151
    Brutality and corruption, 154-156
Spokane Press; See under Newspapers
Spokane Public Library, 64-65, 67, 104
Spokane Public Safety Building; See under Buildings, Public
Spokane Street Railway Company; See under Street railways
Spokane River, See Bridges; Ferries; Sewage… in; Waterpower
Spokane River vacation property, 269
Spokane Traction Company; See under Street railways
Spokane Valley Heritage Museum, 206
Spokane-Washington Improvement Company, 182, 187
Spokane Water Power, 108-109

Spokesman-Review; See under Newspapers
Sprague, John Wilson, 24
Sprague House; See under Hotels
Squire, J. N., 30
St. Joseph's Children's Home, 63
St. Joseph's Church; See under Churches
St. Michael's Mission Church; See under Churches
St. Michael's Mission Scholasticate; See under Schools
Stevens, Isaac J., 3
Stevenson, Adlai, 97
Stocker, George K.; See under Real estate firms...
Strahorn, Carrie Adell Green, 209, 210
Strahorn, Robert E., 210
    Residence, 209, 210, 211
Street railways, 45, 54-61, 98, 111, 114, 115, 119, 133, 174, 191, 194
    City Park Transit Company, 98
    Lidgerwood Cable, 98
    Ross Park, 57, 59, 98, 102
    Spokane and Montrose, 55, 56, 58, 60, 130, 182
    Spokane Cable, 57, 79, 98
    Spokane Street Railway, 45, 55, 56, 60, 98
    Spokane Traction Company, 60, 130, 131, 169
    Washington Water Power, 98, 99
Streets - Construction/paving, 61, 111, 118, 123, 133, 173, 182, 191
Strikes, 99; See also Free speech movement; Labor unions; Mining war...
Stroback, Paul J., 100
Suburban Rapid Transit Company, 61
Sullivan, John T., 154-157
Sunday, Billy, 124, 151-152, 154
Sweeny, Charles, 113, 120, 216 (Residence)
Swift, L. M., 14, 15, 17
Swift, Mrs. L. M., 14, 15, 20

Taber, Edward G., 46
Tabernacle, for Billy Sunday revival, 151, 152
Taft, William H., 147, 212
Telephone, 71, 73-74, 135
Temperance movements, 85, 124, 151, 152, 153
Theaters and productions, 75, 76, 127
    Auditorium, 76, 97, 107, 119
    Bohemian Girl, 76
    Clemmer/Audian/State/Met/Crosby, 138
    Concordia Hall, 75, 76
    Falls City Opera House, 75, 76
    Goetz and Baer, 81, 96
    Joy's Opera House, 34, 75
    Nanon, 97
Tilton and Stocker (and Fry); See under Real estate firms...
Timber; See Lumber business
Tomlinson-Black Company; See under Real estate firms...
Triplet, N., 87
Turner, George, Residence, 146, 184, 232
Turner, Wesley, 156
Twickenham Addition; See under Additions...
Twickenham Park; See under Parks
Twohy, Daniel W., Residence, 229
Typhoid fever, 51

Union Block; See under Buildings...
Union Station, 105, 210
University Club, 97, 135
Upriver Dam, 50, 51
Utilities, 50-53; 194; See also Waterpower/electricity
Vacation property, 269, 282, 283

Valleyford, 272, 291
Van Dorn, J. N., 76
Vandorn & Bentley Block; See under Buildings...
Van Valkenburg, Mary J., See Downing, Babe
Van Valkenburg Block; See under Buildings...
Villard, Henry, 25, 36, 37

Wadham & Bartlett grocery, 125
Waffle Foundry, 93
Wakefield, J. C., 175
Wallace, Henry C., 5
Warner, Alexander "Jack," 44, 48
Warren, Joel, 61, 91, 114
Washington & Idaho Fair Association; See under Fairs...
Washington Brick and Lime Company, 87, 190
Washington Water Power, 44, 53, 57, 60, 79, 98, 107; 115, 125, 131, 231, 232, 236
    Headquarters building, 256, 257
    Substation at Post Street, 131
    WWP Street and interurban railways, 98, 99, 130, 285
Water system, city, 194
Waterpower/electricity, 11, 44, 50, 51, 53, 54, 104, 108-109; See also Electric lighting; Interurban railways; Washington Water Power
Waters, Major Sidney D., 92
Waterworks, 20, 50, 51, 103
Watson, Charles, 77
Welch, Patrick, 113, 216
Western House; See under Hotels
Wetzel, Daniel, 83
Weyerhaeuser, George, 225
Wheaton, Frank, 22
White, Aubrey, 166-170, 186
    Residences, 169, 213
White family, 166, 168
Whitehouse, Catherine Cox Weston, 253
Whitehouse, Harold C.; See under Architects
Whitehouse, L. H., 31
Whitelaw, James,   Residence, 193
Whitings Addition; See under Additions...
Whitworth College/University, 131, 253
Williams, H. M., and Houghton; See under Real estate firms
Williams, Jack, 245
Windsor Hotel; See under Hotels
Witherop, J. W., 175
Witherspoon, William W., 88, 116, 117
Wobblies; See Industrial Workers of the World
Wolfe's Lunch Counter, 90
Wolverton, W. M., 86
Wolverton Block; See under Buildings...
Woman's Christian Temperance Union, 85, 124
Women's suffrage, 141
Woodbury, Arthur K., 68
Woydt, Edward, 147

Yardley, 275
Yearsley, Wilbur S., 285
Yeaton, Cyrus F., 12, 17, 18, 19, 21
YMCA, 62-63, 163

Ziegler Block; See under Buildings...
Zittel, Julius; See under Architects